ANTHONY HAYWOOD
CAROLINE SIEG

VIENNA
CITY GUIDE

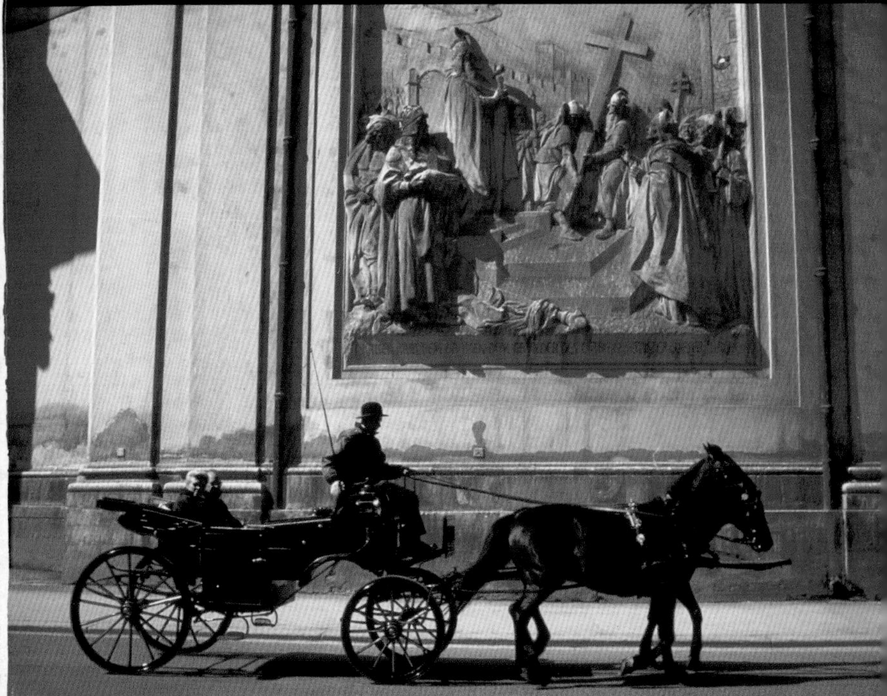

INTRODUCING VIENNA

Karlskirche (St Charles' Church; p80)

JON DAVISON

'Vienna remains Vienna, and that's the worst anyone could ever say about it', quipped the Austrian writer Alfred Polgar. It also ranks among the world's most liveable cities.

The humorist Karl Farkas has a different angle on this. He said, 'We Viennese look with confidence into the past'. And what about the future? Well, it can probably look with confidence into that too. Few cities in the world match Vienna for its remarkably high quality of life. Throw in some excellent programs for sustainable development and we're talking about a city with a future.

We often see Vienna in terms of its grand past: angelic choirboys, monumental palaces, *Fiaker* (horse-drawn carriages) and flamboyance. The tones of Mozart, Beethoven and Brahms and the filigree paintings or sketches of Klimt, Schiele and Kokoschka. But this is to ignore its dynamic present. Vienna has an astoundingly colourful contemporary culture and arts scene; a burgeoning culinary culture; bustling and lively pubs, bars, coffee shops and beer houses; picturesque vineyards on its edges; an idiosyncratic rock and club scene; and extraordinarily innovative performance arts.

Throw in lakeside excursions to Burgenland or trips to the Danube Valley, Znojmo in the Czech Republic or Bratislava in Slovakia and Vienna becomes not just the city we think we know but also one we still need to discover.

VIENNA LIFE

'Vienna has an astoundingly colourful contemporary culture and arts scene, a burgeoning culinary culture...'

With almost 1.7 million inhabitants, Vienna is large, it's flamboyant and at the same time it retains some of the features of a Habsburg-ruled province – close-knit and with a love for escalating even the most trivial into the absurdly grandiose.

The year 2010 will go down as an important one for the Viennese, as they voted in a referendum on five issues that have been on their minds for some time. They rejected a toll for vehicles entering the city. It was uncharacteristically 'ungreen' for this environmentally conscious capital. Oddly, voters favoured making the introduction of caretakers in housing blocks compulsory. Now this sounds like the Viennese village coming to the fore. Perhaps it is. Once federal laws are amended, it may even be implemented.

Educational reforms to make available all-day schools have long been sought by Viennese. At present, most are half-day, making it hard for poorer families in which both parents work. The fourth reform accepted by voters – if only narrowly – is the most interesting for visitors: the round-the-clock operation of the metro train system on weekends (taking in the early hours of Saturday and Sunday). Although this one was a close call, Vienna's transport authority soon got to work on it, and as a result the capital's nocturnal scene might get a boost on weekends. This will cost €5 million each year but it's music to the ears of everyone, especially the large number of visitors to Austria's capital.

Meanwhile, a spate of building is taking place, most importantly the construction of Vienna's first and only central train station, which is due to open from 2012.

And politics? Well, here it's business as usual, with Vienna living up to its tradition of being 'Red' – all its mayors since 1945 have come from the left-of-centre Social Democratic Party of Austria (SPÖ), even if its hold is not as strong today as in past years.

KRZYSZTOF DYDYNSKI

Café Leopold (p180): cafe by day, trendy meeting place by night

HIGHLIGHTS

1

GREG ELMS

❶ Stephansdom
The 14th-century Gothic heart and soul of Vienna (p54)

❷ Fernwärme
Detail of Hundertwasser's Fernwärmewerk Spittelau (p98)

❸ Belvedere
Johann Lukas von Hildebrandt's magnificent baroque palace and gardens (p102)

❹ Riesenrad
Enjoy great views from inside a Viennese icon (p111)

❺ MuseumsQuartier
Vienna's bustling cultural ensemble, where time fuses cleverly with space (p86)

❻ Kirche am Steinhof
Otto Wagner's art-nouveau church built inside a psychiatric hospital (p126)

ARCHITECTURAL ICONS

Baroque splendour, neoclassical behemoths, inspired art-nouveau masterpieces, the razor-sharp edges of postmodernism and the organic, architectural eccentricity of Friedensreich Hundertwasser – Vienna's architectural icons work boldly on the senses and take the traveller on a journey forward and back in time.

2

RICHARD NEBESKY

3

RICHARD NEBES

KRZYSZTOF DYDYNSKI

GREG ELMS

GREG ELMS

LOCAVORE

Enjoy it all! Vienna's lively Naschmarkt farmers market complete with food stalls; traditional Beisln *and neo-*Beisln*, where the top chefs put local and seasonal offerings through their paces; the beloved sausage stand; formal restaurant dining; hip eateries; and places for picnic lunches.*

STEPHEN SAK

1 Atmospheric Beisln
Vienna's beer houses offer a colourful, traditional eating experience (p153)

2 Naschmarkt
Of the many farmers markets, Naschmarkt is the culinary capital (p80)

3 Picnic Paradise
Urbanek – a miniature emporium of delicious hams and wine (p162)

4 Bitzinger Würstelstand am Albertinaplatz
Vienna has sausage stands galore! Opera-goers prefer this one after a show (p158)

5 Stylised Eateries
Kunsthalle in the MuseumsQuartier – convivial style in former imperial stables (p88)

2

GREG ELMS

3

ANTHONY HAYWOOD

5

YADID LEVY/ALAMY

4

RICHARD NEBESKY

DACS/THE BRIDGEMAN ART LIBRARY

STEPHEN SA

ART FOR ART'S SAKE

Take Dürer, Rembrandt and Caravaggio, throw in Biedermeier, expressionism and Jugendstil *(art nouveau), then reel at the bizarre installations and 'happenings' of Vienna Actionism – the capital showcases the beauty of the truly historic and the shock of the new.*

PETER BARRITT/ALA

THE ART ARCHIVE/ALAMY

HEATH COX/ALAMY

RICHARD NEBESKY

❶ Oskar Kokoschka
Discover Austria's expressionist in the Leopold Museum (p86) and Albertina (p70)

❷ Hermann Nitsch
Modern shocks inside the MUMOK in the MuseumsQuartier (p88)

❸ Gustav Klimt
Vienna's art-nouveau guru, housed in the Secession (p62), Leopold Museum (p86), Kunsthistorisches Museum (p69) and Oberes Belvedere (p102)

❹ Ferdinand Georg Waldmüller
Austria's early 19th-century painter features in the Wien Museum (p80) and Oberes Belvedere (p102)

❺ Grand Masters
A treasure trove of art in the Kunsthistorisches Museum (p69)

❻ Egon Schiele
Sketches, portraits and breathtaking paintings, showcased in the Leopold Museum (p86)

KRZYSZTOF DYDYNSKI

GREG ELM

VIENNA BY THE GLASS

Vienna offers fascinating perspectives of life over a glass – whether in a fine Viennese cafe, behind the newspaper in a coffee house, out among the vineyards or inside a minimalist bar designed by Adolf Loos.

KRZYSZTOF DYDYNSKI

KFS/IMAGEBROKER

ELVELE IMAGES LTD/ALAMY

RICHARD NEBESKY

❶ Café Drechsler
Vienna's traditional coffee house reinterpreted for the 21st century (p179)

❷ Café Sacher
Touristy, unashamedly! The baroque *Sacher Torte* is *de rigueur* (p176)

❸ Palmenhaus
Elegant drinking in a *Jugendstil* glasshouse (p174)

❹ Wines of the Wachau
First-rate wines among spectacular Danube Valley scenery (p220)

❺ Loos American Bar
Adolf Loos' 1908 masterpiece of mirrors, sparkling brass and onyx (p175)

❻ Café Gloriette
Where sweeping views of Schönbrunn unfold beyond the glass (p184)

MUSICAL VIENNA

Vienna is famous for its boys' choir and white Lipizzaner horses dancing to classical music. But don't forget its vibrant contemporary music scene and a very hot tip for aficionados of the Schrammelgittare *– the Viennese contra guitar.*

RUSSELL MOUNTFORD

G-PHOTO/ALAMY

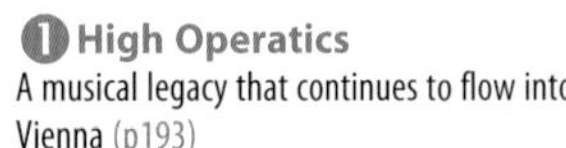

❶ High Operatics
A musical legacy that continues to flow into Vienna (p193)

❷ Vienna Boys' Choir
These guys have struck the right note since the 15th century (p194)

❸ Equine Ballet
White Lipizzaner stallions have pranced through history (p68)

JAMES DAVIS PHOTOGRAPHY/ALAMY

CONTENTS

THE AUTHORS

Anthony Haywood

Born in the port city of Fremantle, Western Australia, Anthony first pulled anchor in the late 1970s to travel to Europe, North Africa and the US. He later studied comparative literature and Russian language. While travelling to Moscow in the very early 1990s he detoured to Vienna – the start of a fascination with the capital, which he loves for its unusual contrasts of high and low culture, and of course for the Viennese themselves and their humour, the famous *Wiener Schmäh*. Anthony works as a freelance journalist and writer. His publications include numerous Lonely Planet guidebooks, a cultural guide to Siberia, travel articles, short stories and translations. He coordinated this book and wrote the Introducing Vienna, Highlights, Getting Started, Neighbourhoods, Eating and Excursions chapters.

Caroline Sieg

Caroline's relationship with Vienna began after high school, when her best friend relocated to the city. Subsequent trips to the capital yielded countless hikes in the Wienerwald, *Heurigen*-filled afternoons and a profound obsession with *Würstchen mit Kren* (sausages with freshly grated horseradish) and *Mohr im Hemd* (steamed chocolate-hazelnut pudding). These days, this half-Swiss, half-American travel writer hangs her hat in Berlin.

LONELY PLANET AUTHORS

Why is our travel information the best in the world? It's simple: our authors are passionate, dedicated travellers. They don't take freebies in exchange for positive coverage so you can be sure the advice you're given is impartial. They travel widely to all the popular spots, and off the beaten track. They don't research using just the internet or phone. They discover new places not included in any other guidebook. They personally visit thousands of hotels, restaurants, palaces, trails, galleries, temples and more. They speak with dozens of locals every day to make sure you get the kind of insider knowledge only a local could tell you. They take pride in getting all the details right, and in telling it how it is. Think you can do it? Find out how at **lonelyplanet.com**.

GETTING STARTED

With cultural attractions that are the envy of many European capitals, and only 1.7 million occupants, Vienna is the kind of place you might explore over a few days or over a lifetime. Its compact size means that much of your exploration can be done on foot, complemented by public transport to get around the suburbs. Even first-time travellers are likely to land running in the metropolis. With a few exceptions, it's also a place where you can wake up and plan your day according to whim.

WHEN TO GO

Vienna's character changes with the seasons. The city looks just as glorious – some would say even more so – under a layer of snow; it glows in a warm spring or colourful autumn, and swelters and bends in the heat of a midsummer sun. In terms of climate, it is in a relatively mild continental zone. During a cold winter the thermometer can plunge to chilly depths and may limit the time you spend outdoors to a few hours; the advantage of winter, however, is that sights and the city at large are comfortably free of crowds. A warm spring is an ideal time to visit – there are few crowds, the parks and gardens are coming to life and the temperatures are high enough for you to enjoy outdoor as well as indoor pursuits. Come Christmas the good burghers of Vienna roll out the welcome mat with *Christkindlmärkte,* Christmas markets full of charm and grace, and the all-important *Glühwein* (mulled wine).

In summer you will find an enormous range of musical events. The granddaddy of them all is the Donauinselfest, a free concert attracting more than three million screaming revellers! One drawback worth keeping in mind: some of the city's world-famous institutions, such as the Vienna Boys' Choir, the Lipizzaner stallions and the Staatsoper, all take breaks.

FESTIVALS & EVENTS

Vienna's calendar of events is a ceaseless cascade of classical concerts, jazz and rock festivals, balls, gay parades, communist gatherings and art happenings. The following is by no means a complete listing of annual events; check the Tourist Info Wien website (www.wien.info) for a more comprehensive list, or read the weekly *Falter* paper. For a full list of public holidays, see p234.

January & February

FASCHING

The Fasching season, a carnival time of costumes and parties, actually runs from November to Ash Wednesday, but February is traditionally the time when most of the action takes place. Look for street parties and drunken Viennese in silly get-ups.

OPERNBALL

www.wiener-staatsoper.at; 01, Staatsoper

Of the 300 or so balls held in January and February, the Opernball (Opera Ball) is number one. Held in the Staatsoper, it's a supremely lavish affair, with the men in tails and women in shining white gowns.

March & April

INTERNATIONAL AKKORDEON FESTIVAL

☎ 0676-512 91 04; www.akkordeonfestival.at, in German

Running from the end of February through to the end of March, the International Accordion Festival features exceptional players from as close as the Balkans and as far away as New Zealand.

FRÜHLINGSFESTIVAL

Alternating each year between the Musikverein and the Konzerthaus, this spring festival of classical concerts generally runs from the end of March to the beginning of April.

ARGUS BIKE FESTIVAL

www.bikefestival.at, in German

Kicking off the cycling season in early or mid-April, this two-day free festival held on Rathausplatz is a cross between a trade fair and a celebration of the bicycle, with a dirt bike contest, test courses, electric bicycles and high-performance bikes on show and going through their paces.

OSTERKLANG FESTIVAL

www.theater-wien.at

Orchestral and chamber music recitals fill some of Vienna's best music halls during this 'Sound of Easter' festival. The highlight is the opening concert, which features the Vienna Philharmonic.

May & June

VIENNA MARATHON

☎ 606 95 10; www.vienna-marathon.com

The city's top road race is held in April or May.

LIFE BALL

www.lifeball.org

This AIDS charity event is one of the highlights of the ball-season calendar and is often graced by international celebrities. It's normally held in the Rathaus around the middle of May (though it can be as late as July) and attracts some colourful and flamboyant outfits. Mottos for 2011 and 2012, respectively, are 'Spread the Wings of Tolerance!' and 'Fight the Flames of Ignorance!'

SOHO IN OTTAKRING

www.sohoinottakring.at, in German

The multicultural streets bordering the Gürtel in Ottakring come to life in May and June with Soho in Ottakring. Hairdressing salons, disused offices and fishmongers are transformed into art galleries, bars, band venues and art shops, all of which attract an arty crowd.

IDENTITIES – QUEER FILM FESTIVAL

www.identities.at, in German

Identities is easily Vienna's second largest film festival, showcasing queer movies from around the world. It normally takes place at the beginning of June every second year (2011 is an on-year).

DONAUINSELFEST

www.donauinselfest.at, in German

For the younger generation, the Donauinselfest on the Donauinsel (Danube Island) occupies the top spot on the year's events calendar. Held over three days on a weekend in late June, it features a feast of rock, pop, folk and country performers, and attracts almost three million onlookers. Best of all, it's free!

REGENBOGEN PARADE

www.hosiwien.at, in German

In late June Vienna is taken over by the Regenbogen Parade (Rainbow Parade), a predominantly gay and lesbian festival attracting some 150,000 people. Expect loads of fun, frolicking and bare skin.

WIENER FESTWOCHEN

☎ 589 22 22; www.festwochen.or.at

Considered to be one of the highlights of the year, the Vienna Festival hosts a wide-ranging program of the arts, based in various venues around town, from May to mid-June. Expect quality performance groups from around the world.

VIENNA INDEPENDENT SHORTS

http://viennashorts.com

Vienna's premiere short film festival attracts entries mostly from German-speaking countries; it's usually held at one cinema over seven days.

July & August

JAZZ FEST WIEN

☎ 712 42 24; www.viennajazz.org

From the end of June to mid-July, Vienna relaxes to the smooth sound of jazz, blues and soul flowing from the Staatsoper and a number of clubs across town.

IMPULSTANZ

☎ 523 55 58; www.impulstanz.com

Vienna's premiere avant-garde dance festival attracts an array of internationally renowned troupes and newcomers between mid-July and mid-August. Performances are held in the MuseumsQuartier, Volkstheater and a number of small venues.

KLANGBOGEN FESTIVAL

☎ 588 85; www.theater-wien.at

The KlangBogen Festival ensures things don't flag during the summer holidays. Running from July to August, it features operas, operettas and orchestral music in the Theater an der Wien plus a few other locations around town.

MUSIKFILM FESTIVAL

01, Rathausplatz

Once the sun sets in July and August, the Rathausplatz is home to screenings of operas, operettas and concerts. They're all free, so turn up early for a good seat. Food stands and bars are close at hand and are swamped by hordes of people, creating a carnival-like atmosphere.

GÜRTEL NIGHTWALK

07, 08, 09, the Gürtel

Usually on the last Saturday night in August, a handful of open stages are set up near locations on the Gürtel U-Bahn viaduct, featuring local independent music acts.

VOLKSSTIMMEFEST

www.volksstimmefest.at, in German

For a weekend in late August or early September, the Communist Party fills the Prater with music and art. The festival, which has been running since 1945, features some 30 live acts and attracts a bizarre mix of hippies, world music fans and party supporters.

September & October

LANGE NACHT DER MUSEEN

http://langenacht.orf.at; adult/child €12/10

On the first Saturday of October, around 500 museums nationwide open their doors to visitors between 6pm and 1am. One ticket (available at museums) allows entry to all of them, and includes public transport around town. You'll be hard pushed to visit all 80-plus museums in Vienna though.

VIENNALE FILM FESTIVAL

☎ 526 59 47; www.viennale.at

The country's best film festival features fringe and independent films from around the world. It is held every year in October, with screenings at numerous locations around the city. See p198 for more details.

November & December

WIEN MODERN FESTIVAL

☎ 242 00; www.wienmodern.at

This festival takes an opposing view to many of the city's music festivals by featuring modern classical and avant-garde music. The festival runs throughout November, with many performances in the Konzerthaus.

CHRISTKINDLMÄRKTE

Vienna's much-loved Christmas market season runs from mid-November to Christmas Day. See p147 for more details.

SILVESTER

The city council transforms the Innere Stadt into one huge party venue for Silvester (New Year's Eve). It's an uproarious affair, with more than enough alcohol consumed and far too many fireworks let off in crowded streets.

COSTS & MONEY

By European standards, Vienna isn't an expensive city. It's cheaper than Paris, London or Rome, but more expensive than Prague or Budapest. Shopping splurges or special items aside, accommodation and eating out will be the most expensive items in your budget.

Bearing in mind financial and other regular crises, there are numerous ways of getting best value out of a trip. Some involve advance planning and booking ahead (see p20). At the 'hard class' end of the budget the obvious way to reduce costs is to stay in hostels and grab your food from market stalls or supermarkets. See the boxed texts in each neighbourhood of the eating section of this book for selected market locations (eg p158).

For those on a midrange budget or business travellers, booking well ahead at the lower end of the scale of midrange hotels, especially using the internet, will keep the purse in reasonable shape and the eyebrows straight in the accounts department. See the Sleeping chapter (p207) for more on price ranges.

If you're in town for an all-out splurge on an upmarket hotel and fine dining and cultural experiences, the sky will be your limit – in Vienna there is no shortage of very, very fine places where you can enjoy this kind of experience.

For most travellers eating out well is part of the experience of a city, and Vienna is one place where fine food is available for all budgets. One trick is to order the set lunch menus or lunch dishes, which are invariably cheaper but no less worthy than their evening counterparts.

The cost of visiting museums and enjoying performing arts can be kept in check by buying combined tickets for museums and theatre 'rush' tickets a couple of hours before performances. Also see the 'It's Free' boxes in each neighbourhood section (eg p71) for some ideas. Some museums also have one day each month with free admission.

On average, staying at a two- to four-star hotel (double room per person), eating out twice a day, taking in a show and a couple of museums and downing a few cups of coffee will set you back around €170 to €250 per day. Anyone staying in dorms in hostels and eating low-cost can expect to survive on about €45 to €50 per day.

HOW MUCH?

72-hour transport ticket (from machine) €13.60

Bratwurst from a stand €2.80

Glass of beer in Beisl (0.5L) €3.40

An Achterl of wine (0.125L) €2.90

Nightclub entry €5-15

Copy of Vienna's newspaper, Falter €2.40

20-minute Fiaker (horse & carriage) ride €40

Box of 23 Mozart Kügeln (marzipan chocolates) €9.90

120mm Perzys Wiener Schneekugel (Perzy Vienna Snowball) €24

INTERNET RESOURCES

Checking out a few things on good websites before you leave can save you a lot of time and help you quickly find your feet when you arrive. As well as the excellent official websites, there are a few informal ones that offer good insights.

Austria Press and Information Service (www.austria.org) Run by the Austrian embassy in Washington DC, this gives a good introduction to the country and the capital, including a recipe for Wiener Schnitzel.

Falter (www.falter.at, in German) This is Vienna's listings newspaper – a wealth of information for what's on.

Hauptstadt (www.hauptstadt.at, in German) Film programs, clubbing dates, music and other events, arranged in a useful calendar format.

Lonely Planet (www.lonelyplanet.com) A first stop for Vienna highlights at a glance, blogs, and for hot topics and tips on the Thorn Tree from fellow travellers.

MuseumsQuartier (www.mqw.at) All about the MQ and its venues. By clicking on 'Links' (at the bottom) you reach a great list of hotlinks to cultural institutions.

Tourist-Info Wien (www.wien.info) The main official Vienna city tourist information website. As well as having the usual offerings it has sections such as www.viennahype.at, with a more happening angle.

Vienna Metblogs (http://vienna.metblogs.com) This multilingual blog site ranges from the banal to the inspiring and insightful – it's as unpredictable and insightful as the Metblogs get.

Vienna Webservice (www.wien.gv.at) The official Vienna city council website, with everything from the current weather through to interactive maps for address searches, information on sights, and services for Viennese residents. Not all of it is in full length in English, but a lot is.

Virtual Vienna Net (www.virtualvienna.net) Informative nonofficial website with a forum and some good articles, such as on the Jewish Vienna pages. Interesting for short-term visitors as well as expats.

Wieninternational (www.wieninternational.at) Weekly bilingual (German and English) online magazine with short and feature articles on all aspects of culture, economy and society, often with a focus on European integration.

Wien-Konkret (www.wien-konkret.at, in German) Politics, sport, nightlife and much more – a good source of information.

Wikipedia Districts of Vienna (http://en.wikipedia.org/wiki/Districts_of_Vienna) Detailed overview of Vienna's districts.

SUSTAINABLE VIENNA

Part of Vienna's high quality of life is its leading role in Europe that sees it right near the top of the list of that continent's 'green' cities. This is a key aspect of its status as one of the world's most liveable cities. The city council, for instance, has its own climate protection program with goals to reduce greenhouse gases by 21% on the 1990 level. A good way to reduce your own impact from the outset is to use rail transport as much as possible if travelling from within Europe.

Vienna is very easy to get around, either by foot or by using the city's cheap and excellent public transport. Spend a few minutes sniffing the fumes of the Gürtel – a six-lane, fume-packed highway to hell – and you will probably appreciate the benefits of Vienna's trams and subway as an alternative to cars. Night buses are available, which are a more climate-friendly choice than taxis and, in a 2010 referendum, a majority of Viennese who voted were in favour of the subways running

ADVANCE PLANNING

If you are in town between June and early September, advance planning is especially useful to avoid long queues. Book admission tickets online when possible (or go early to buy your ticket) and visit early or late in the day. To avoid bottlenecks, plan your itinerary with a sprinkling of outdoor landmarks – cemeteries, parks, the Danube River and the canal – or with less usual sights such as Vienna's Justizpalast (p74) or the main university building (p73).

Well ahead: Before you book your train or plane to Vienna browse the accommodation options online (p207) or use the official city tourist website www.wien.info.at for bookings – it could save you a lot of time later. For a top restaurant with limited tables such as Restaurant Bauer (p155) or one that is immensely popular such as Kim Kocht (p164), reserve well ahead. If you've got your heart set on a show at the Spanish Riding School (p67), check out the performance dates on the website and book as early as possible. The same applies in summer to other classical arts and theatre if you want good seats for a specific performance.

One week ahead: If you're travelling in summer, now is the time to go online and book your ticket for Schloss Schönbrunn (p118), Schloss Belvedere (p102) and the Kaiserappartements (p66). This is also the time to book a table in one of the upmarket restaurants if you want to be sure of a place on a Friday or Saturday.

One or two days ahead: Check *Falter* (p19), websites of venues in the Drinking & Nightlife chapter of this book, the official city website (p19), and start reading blogs such as Vienna Metblogs (p19) to plan your day or night.

all night. If implemented, this will make getting around in the small hours even easier.

Another great transport option is the inexpensive Citybike (see p228) – a network of more than 60 bicycle hire stations across the city (two at the Prater). You register your Visa or MasterCard for security, a token €1 is deducted, and after the first hour (which is free) the fee of €1 per hour is charged. If you're spending a month or so in Vienna, consider buying an inexpensive second-hand bike and enjoying the pleasures of Vienna's cycling paths.

Much has changed in recent years in Vienna when it comes to restaurants and minimising the impact on the environment. Austria has an *Umweltzewichen* (Environmental Badge) that offers orientation as to whether a restaurant or hotel has adopted environmentally friendly practices. While its list of places is not enormous (about 90 in Vienna), there are many other establishments that fill some but not all of the criteria. For instance, the capital is experiencing a boom in the use of regional produce. This is all about chefs going 'locavore' and using quality local produce to create fresh flavours. It's also sound environmental practice. A great deal of this fresh produce comes from the nearby Waldviertel. Meats are often organic and sourced from farms where the animals are not simply the product of *Fleischfabriken* (meat factories). A place like Die Burgermacher (p164) offers a green alternative to the typical global franchise hamburger joint. See the GreenDex on p259 for a list of places with good environmental credentials.

Accommodations with green credentials are less plentiful but some do exist; you will find the ones we liked in the GreenDex too.

Finally, Vienna's green spaces are great for relaxing – and there's no shortage of them. Visit the Lobau (p115), the Donauinsel (p115) and the Donau-Auen National Park, or any one of the parks in town – just remember to sort your rubbish whenever possible or carry out what you take in.

BACKGROUND

HISTORY

FROM THE BEGINNING

The 25,000-year-old statuette the *Venus of Willendorf* is evidence of inhabitation of the Danube Valley since the Palaeolithic age. Vienna, situated at a natural crossing of the Danube (Donau) River, was probably an important trading post for the Celts when the Romans arrived around 15 BC. The Romans established Carnuntum as a provincial capital of Pannonia in AD 8, and around the same time created a second military camp some 40km to the west. Vindobona, derived from the Vinid tribe of Celts, was situated in what today is Vienna's Innere Stadt, with the Hoher Markt at its centre and borders at Tiefer Graben to the northwest, Salzgries to the northeast, Rotenturmstrasse to the southeast, and Naglergasse to the southwest. A section of the southwestern border had no natural defence, so a long ditch, the Graben, was dug. A civil town sprang up outside the camp that flourished in the 3rd and 4th centuries; around this time a visiting Roman emperor, Probus, introduced vineyards to the hills of the Wienerwald (Vienna Woods).

In the 5th century the Roman Empire collapsed and the Romans were beaten back by invading Goth and Vandal tribes. During the Dark Ages, the importance of the Danube Valley as an east–west crossing meant that successive waves of tribes and armies attempted to wrest control of the region, and as a result Vindobona foundered.

BEST BOOKS ON VIENNA'S HISTORY

- *A Nervous Splendour: Vienna 1888–1889* (1979) and *Thunder at Twilight: Vienna 1913–14* (1989), by Frederic Morto, are highly enthralling accounts of seminal dates at the end of the Habsburg rule. The first deals with the Mayerling affair (the murder-suicide of Franz Josef I's son and the son's lover), and the second with the assassination of Franz Ferdinand in Sarajevo.
- *Fin-de-Siècle Vienna: Politics and Culture* (1980), by Carl E Schorske, is a seminal work on the intellectual history of Vienna in seven interlinking essays.
- *Guilty Victim: Austria from the Holocaust to Haider* (2000), by Hella Pick, is an excellent analysis of Austria during this period.
- *Last Waltz in Vienna* (1981), by George Clare, provides a moving account of a Jewish upbringing in the interwar years leading up to the Anschluss (the annexation of Austria by Germany in 1938).
- *The Austrians: A Thousand Year Odyssey* (1997), by Gordon Brook-Shepherd, is one of the few books to tackle the history of Austria from the Babenbergs through to the country's entry into the EU, and is great for a general overview.
- *Vienna and the Jews, 1867–1938: A Cultural History* (1989), by Steven Beller, gives an insightful look into the cultural contributions that Vienna's Jewish community made to the city.

TIMELINE

AD 8

Vindobona, the forerunner of Vienna's Innere Stadt, becomes part of the Roman province of Pannonia.

1137

Vienna is first documented as a city in the Treaty of Mautern between the Babenburgs and the Bishops of Passau.

1155–56

Vienna becomes a residence of the Babenbergs; a new fortress is built on Am Hof and Babenberg's Margavate is elevated to Duchy.

The rise of Charlemagne, the king of the Franks, marked the end of the Dark Ages. In 803 he established a territory in the Danube Valley west of Vienna, known as the Ostmark (Eastern March). The Ostmark was constantly overrun by Magyars, a nomadic band of peoples from the Far East who had settled the Hungarian plain, until King Otto the Great crushed the Magyar army in a decisive battle in 955. However, the region received no mention in imperial documents until 996, when it was first referred to as 'Ostarrichi'. The forerunner of the city's modern name – 'Wenia' – first appeared in the annals of the archbishopric of Salzburg in 881.

THE BABENBERG DYNASTY

Some 21 years after Otto's victory, the Ostmark was handed over to Leopold von Babenberg, a descendant of a noble Bavarian family. The Babenberg dynasty was to rule for the next 270 years.

The Babenbergs were a skilful lot and it wasn't long before their sphere of influence expanded: in the 11th century most of modern-day Lower Austria (including Vienna) was in their hands; a century later (1192) Styria and much of Upper Austria were safely garnered. Heinrich II 'Jasomirgott' (so called because of his favourite exclamation, 'Yes, so help me God') was the most successful Babenberg of them all, convincing the Holy Roman Emperor to elevate the territory to a dukedom; Heinrich II moved his court to Vienna in 1156.

Vienna was already an important and prosperous city by this stage, welcoming clerics, artisans, merchants and minstrels to its population. Its citizens enjoyed peace and economic success; the Viennese were awarded staple rights in 1221, which forced foreign tradesmen on the Danube to sell their goods within two months of landing, allowing locals to act as middlemen for commerce downstream. In 1147 Stephansdom (St Stephen's Cathedral; p54), then a Romanesque church, was consecrated and a city wall was built. A king's ransom flowed into the city in 1192: Richard the Lionheart, on his return home from the Crusades, was captured by the then ruler, Leopold V. Richard had purportedly insulted the Babenberg ruler at the Siege of Acre (1189–91), and an astronomical figure was demanded in exchange for his release. Leopold used the money paid to found Wiener Neustadt. Under Leopold VI, Vienna was granted a city charter in 1221, ensuring further prosperity.

In 1246 Duke Friedrich II died in battle, leaving no heirs. This allowed the ambitious Bohemian king, Ottokar II, to move in and take control. He bolstered his claim to Austria by marrying Friedrich II's widow. Ottokar gained support from Vienna's burghers by founding a hospital for the poor and rebuilding Stephansdom after a destructive fire in 1258. However, he refused to swear allegiance to the new Holy Roman Emperor, Rudolf von Habsburg, and his pride proved costly – Ottokar died in a battle against his powerful adversary at Marchfeld in 1278. Rudolf's success on the battlefield began the rule of one of the most powerful dynasties in history, a dynasty that would retain power right up to the 20th century.

THE HABSBURGS' REIGN BEGINS

Rudolf left the government of Vienna to his son Albrecht, who proved an unpopular ruler – he removed the staple right and began taxing the clergy. His successor, Albrecht II, was far more competent, and while he gained the nickname 'the Lame' due to his polyarthritis, he was also known as 'the Wise'. The city, however, struggled under a string of natural

1273–76

Ottokar II hands the throne to a little-known count from Habichtsburg (Habsburg); Rudolf I of Habsburg occupies Vienna and the Habsburg dynasty commences, running until 1919.

1420–21

Under Duke Albrecht V, the first large-scale persecution of Jews in Vienna (known as the Wiener Geserah) takes place.

1529

The first Turkish siege of Vienna occurs but the Turks mysteriously retreat, leaving the city – Vienna survives and construction of the city walls begins.

THE JEWS OF VIENNA

Vienna's love/hate relationship with its Jewish population is a tale of extreme measures and one that began almost 1000 years ago.

Shlom, a mint master appointed by Duke Leopold V in 1194, is the first documented Jew to have lived in Vienna. For the next few hundred years the Jewish community lived in relative peace inside the city, even building a synagogue on what is now Judenplatz. In 1420 the Habsburg ruler Albrecht V issued a pogrom against the Jews for reasons unclear in historical annals, although it is speculated that the motive amounted to acquiring Jewish money and property to finance the fight against the Hussites. Poor Jews were expelled while the richer class were tortured until they revealed their hidden wealth, and then burned to death. Over the ensuing centuries Jews slowly drifted back to the city and prospered under Habsburg rule. Both parties were happy with the arrangement – the Jews had a safe haven, and the Habsburgs could rely on Jewish financial backing. However, it all turned sour with the arrival of bigoted Leopold I and his even more bigoted wife, Margarita Teresa, who blamed her miscarriages on Jews. In 1670, Jews were once again expelled from the city and their synagogue destroyed, but the act weakened the financial strength of Vienna, and the Jewish community had to be invited back.

The following centuries saw Jews thrive under quite benign conditions (compared with those of other Jewish communities in Europe at the time); in the 19th century Jews were given equal civil rights and prospered in the fields of art and music. It was in Vienna that Theodor Herzl published his seminal *Der Judenstaat* (The Jewish State) in 1896, which laid the political foundations for Zionism and ultimately the creation of Israel. But the darkest chapter in Vienna's Jewish history was still to come. On 12 March 1938 the Nazis occupied Austria, and with them came persecution and curtailment of Jewish civil rights. Businesses were confiscated (including some of Vienna's better-known coffee houses) and Jews were banned from public places, obliged to sport a Star of David and go by the names of 'Sara' and 'Israel'. Violence exploded on the night of 9 November 1938 with the November Pogrom, known as the Reichskristallnacht. Synagogues and prayer houses were burned and 6500 Jews were arrested. Of the 180,000 Jews living in Vienna before the Anschluss (the annexation of Austria by Germany), more than 100,000 managed to emigrate before the borders were closed in May 1939. Another 65,000 died in ghettos or concentration camps and only 6000 survived to see liberation by Allied troops. For more about Vienna's Jewish heritage, see p110.

disasters; first a plague of locusts in 1338, then the Black Death in 1349, followed by a devastating fire.

In his short 26 years, Rudolf IV, Albrecht's successor, founded the University of Vienna in 1365, built a new Gothic Stephansdom in 1359 and set about reforming the city's social and monetary environment. He is better known for his famous forgery of the *Privilegium maius,* a document supposedly tracing the Habsburg lineage back to early Roman emperors. Albrecht V, the next in line, ruled in a time of upheaval when Hussites ravaged parts of Lower Austria and bad harvests befell farmers. The foul air may have led to Vienna's first pogrom (see the boxed text, above).

In 1453 Friedrich III was elected Holy Roman Emperor, the status Rudolf IV had attempted to fake. Furthermore, he persuaded the pope to raise Vienna to a bishopric in 1469. Friedrich's ambition knew few bounds – his motto, '*Austria est imperator orbi universo*' (AEIOU), expressed the view that the whole world was Austria's empire. To prove this he waged war against King Matthias Corvinus of Hungary and initially lost; Corvinus occupied Vienna from 1485 to 1490.

What Friedrich could not achieve through his endeavours on the battlefield, his son, Maximilian I, was able to acquire through marriage. Maximilian's own marriage gained him

1683

The Turks are repulsed at the gates of Vienna for the second time; Europe is free of the Ottoman threat and Vienna begins to re-establish itself as the Habsburgs' permanent residence.

1670

The second expulsion of Jews ordered by Leopold I; the financial strength of Vienna is severely weakened and Jews are soon invited back to the city.

1740–90

Under the guidance of Empress Maria Theresia and her son Joseph II, the age of reform, influenced by the ideas of the Enlightenment, kicks into gear.

Burgundy, while his son Philip's gained Spain (and its overseas territories). The marriages of Maximilian's grandchildren attained the crowns of Bohemia and Hungary. This prompted the proverb, adapted from the *Ovid:* 'Let others make war; you, fortunate Austria, marry!' Maximilian, a ruler on the cusp of the Middle Ages and the Renaissance, encouraged the teaching of humanism in Vienna's university and also founded the Vienna Boys' Choir (see p194).

With the acquisition of so much land in such a short time, control of the Habsburg empire soon became too unwieldy for one ruler. In 1521 the Austrian territories were passed from Karl V to his younger brother, Ferdinand, who soon faced problems of insurrection and religious diversity in Vienna. He promptly lopped off the head of the mayor and his councillors and placed the city under direct sovereign rule.

TURKS, COUNTER-REFORMATION & BAROQUE

Rebellion and religion were not the only problems facing Ferdinand. The Turks, having overrun the Balkans and Hungary, were on the doorstep of Vienna by 1529. The city managed to defend itself under the leadership of Count Salm, but the 18-day siege highlighted glaring holes in Vienna's defences. With the Turks remaining a powerful force, Ferdinand moved his court to Vienna in 1533 and beefed up the city's walls with star-shaped bastions.

Soon after the siege, Ferdinand went about purging Vienna of Protestantism, a hard task considering that four out of every five burghers were practising Protestants. He invited the Jesuits to the city, one step in the Europe-wide Counter-Reformation that ultimately led to the Thirty

THE TURKS & VIENNA

The Ottoman Empire viewed Vienna as 'the city of the golden apple', though it wasn't the *Apfelstrudel* (apple strudel) they were after in their two great sieges. The first, in 1529, was undertaken by Suleiman the Magnificent, but the 18-day endeavour was not sufficient to break the resolve of the city. The Turkish sultan subsequently died at the Battle of Szigetvár in 1566, but his death was kept secret for several days in an attempt to preserve the morale of the army. This subterfuge worked – for a while. Messengers were led into the presence of the embalmed body, which was placed in a seated position on the throne, and unknowingly relayed their news to the corpse. The lack of the slightest acknowledgement of his minions by the sultan was interpreted as regal impassiveness.

At the head of the Turkish siege of 1683 was the general Kara Mustapha. Amid the 25,000 tents of the Ottoman army that surrounded Vienna he installed his 1500 concubines. These were guarded by 700 black eunuchs. Their luxurious quarters may have been set up in haste, but were still overtly opulent, with gushing fountains and regal baths.

Again, it was all to no avail – perhaps the concubines proved too much of a distraction. Whatever the reason, Mustapha failed to put garrisons on the Kahlenberg and was surprised by a quick attack from a German/Polish army rounded up by Leopold I, who had fled the city on news of the approaching Ottomans. Mustapha was pursued from the battlefield and defeated once again, at Gran. At Belgrade he was met by the emissary of the sultan. The price of failure was death, and Mustapha meekly accepted his fate. When the Austrian imperial army conquered Belgrade in 1718 the grand vizier's head was dug up and brought back to Vienna in triumph, where it gathers dust in the vaults of the Wien Museum (p80).

1805 & 1809

Napoleon occupies Vienna (twice) and removes the Holy Roman Emperor crown from the head of Franz II, who reinvents himself as Kaiser Franz I.

1850

The city limits of Vienna are expanded, mostly to include the area within the *Linienwall*. The *Vortstädte* become the 2nd to 9th districts and the old city becomes the 1st.

1857

City walls are demolished to make way for the creation of the monumental architecture of the Ringstrasse.

Years War (1618–48). Maximilian II eased the imperial stranglehold on religious practice, but this was reversed in 1576 by the new emperor, Rudolf II, who embraced the Counter-Reformation. Rudolf ruled from Prague and left the dirty work in Vienna to Archduke Ernst, who was highly successful at cracking down on anti-Catholic activity.

In 1645 a Protestant Swedish army marched within sight of Vienna, but did not attack – by this time Vienna was once more in the hands of the Catholics. Leopold I, whose reign began in 1657, emptied much of the royal coffers on buildings and histrionic operas, prompting the baroque era through the construction of the Leopold wing of the Hofburg (p64). Encouraged by his wife and Viennese Christians, he instigated the city's second pogrom (see the boxed text, p23).

Vienna suffered terribly towards the end of the 17th century. The expulsion of the Jews left the imperial and city finances in a sorry state and a severe epidemic of bubonic plague killed between 75,000 and 150,000 in 1679. Four years later, the city was once again under siege from the Turks. However, Vienna rebuffed the attack, and the removal of the Turkish threat helped bring the city to the edge of a new golden age.

THE REFORM YEARS

The beginning of the 18th century heralded further baroque projects, including Schloss Belvedere (p102), Karlskirche (p80) and Peterskirche (p64). At the helm of the empire was Karl VI, a ruler more concerned with hunting than the plight of Vienna's citizens, who enjoyed few social and economic privileges (the staple right had long been abolished). Close to 25% of the population was either employed by the court or closely linked to it, and the court payed poorly. Coupled with a severe housing shortage, a lack of shops (most were used for accommodation), and pedlars crowding the city streets, the average citizen struggled. Having produced no male heirs, the emperor's biggest headache was ensuring that his daughter, Maria Theresia, would succeed him. To this end he drew up the Pragmatic Sanction, co-signed by the main European powers – most of whom had no intention of honouring such an agreement. After ascending the Habsburg throne in 1740, Maria Theresia had to fight off would-be rulers in the War of the Austrian Succession (1740–48). She had hardly caught her breath before the onset of the Seven Years' War (1756–63). The Habsburgs retained most of their lands, but Silesia was lost to Prussia.

Maria Theresia is widely regarded as the greatest of the Habsburg rulers, ushering in a golden era in which Austria developed as a modern state. In her 40 years as empress, she (and her wise advisers) centralised control, reformed the army and the economy, introduced public schools, improved civil rights and numbered houses (initially for conscription purposes). Her son, Joseph II, who ruled from 1780 until 1790 (he was jointly in charge from 1765), was even more of a zealous reformer. He issued the Edict of Tolerance (1781) for all faiths, secularised religious properties and abolished serfdom. Yet Joseph moved too fast for the staid Viennese and was ultimately forced to rescind some of his measures.

The latter half of the 18th century (and beginning of the 19th) witnessed a blossoming musical scene never before, and never again, seen in Vienna or Europe. During this time, Christoph Willibald Gluck, Josef Haydn, Wolfgang Amadeus Mozart, Ludwig van Beethoven and Franz Schubert all lived and worked in Vienna, producing some of the most memorable music ever composed.

1900

Vienna becomes the centre of the *Jugendstil* (art nouveau) movement through its association with Otto Wagner and related artists, called Vienna's Secession.

1910–14

Vienna's population breaks the two million barrier, the greatest it has ever been. The rise is mainly due to exceptionally high immigration numbers – the majority of the immigrants are Czechs.

1914–18

WWI rumbles through Europe and Vienna experiences a shortage of food and clothes. War-induced inflation destroys the savings of many middle-class Viennese.

A CRUMBLING EMPIRE

Napoleon's rise in the early 19th century spelled hard times for Vienna. He inflicted embarrassing defeats on the Austrians and occupied Vienna twice, in 1805 and 1809. Due to the Frenchman's success, Franz II, the Habsburg ruler of the time, was forced into a bit of crown swapping; he took the title of Franz I of Austria in 1804 but had to relinquish the Holy Roman Emperor badge in 1806. The cost of the war caused the economy to spiral into bankruptcy, from which Vienna took years to recover.

The European powers celebrated Napoleon's defeat in 1814 with the Congress of Vienna, and the capital regained some measure of pride. The proceedings were dominated by the skilful Austrian foreign minister, Klemens von Metternich.

The Congress heralded the beginning of the Biedermeier period (see p36 for a rundown of the arts during this time), named after a satirised figure in a Munich magazine. It was lauded as a prelapsarian period, with the middle class enjoying a lifestyle of domestic bliss and pursuing culture, the arts and comfort 'in a quiet corner'. In reality, censorship and a lack of political voice were taking their toll, pushing Vienna's bourgeois population to the brink. The lower classes suffered immensely: a population explosion (40% increase between 1800 and 1835) caused massive overcrowding; unemployment and prices were high while wages were poor; the Industrial Revolution created substandard working conditions; disease sometimes reached epidemic levels; and the water supply was highly inadequate. On top of all this, while the ideals of the French Revolution were taking hold throughout Europe, Metternich established a police state and removed civil rights: the empire was ready for revolution.

In March 1848 it broke out: the war minister was hanged from a lamppost, Metternich fled to Britain and Emperor Ferdinand I abdicated. The subsequent liberal interlude was brief, only lasting until the army reimposed an absolute monarchy. The new emperor, Franz Josef I, was just 18 years old.

Franz Josef promptly quashed the last specks of opposition, executing many former revolutionaries. He soon abated his harsh reproaches and in 1857 ordered the commencement of the massive Ringstrasse developments around the Innere Stadt. His popularity only began to improve upon his marriage in 1854 to Elisabeth of Bavaria; nicknamed Sisi by her subjects, she became the It girl of the 19th century.

The years 1866–67 were telling on the empire's powers: not only did it suffer defeat at the hands of Prussia, but it was forced to create the dual Austro-Hungarian monarchy, known as the Ausgleich (compromise). Vienna, however, flourished through the later half of the 19th century and into the 20th. Massive improvements were made to infrastructure – trams were electrified, gasworks built and fledgling health and social policies were instigated. Universal male suffrage was introduced in Austro-Hungarian lands in 1906. The city hosted the World Fair in 1873, which coincided with the major glitch of the era – a huge stock-market crash. Culture boomed; the fin-de-siècle years produced Sigmund Freud, Gustav Klimt, Gustav Mahler, Johannes Brahms, Egon Schiele, Johann Strauss and Otto Wagner.

The assassination of Franz Ferdinand, nephew of Franz Josef, in Sarajevo on 28 June 1914 put an end to the city's progress. A month later Austria-Hungary declared war on Serbia and WWI began.

1918

The Austrian Republic is declared on the steps of Vienna's Parliament; red, white and red are chosen as the colours of the nation's flag.

1919

The Treaty of St Germain is signed; the Social Democrats take control of the Vienna City Council, marking the beginning of a period known as Rotes Wien (Red Vienna).

1938

Hitler annexes Austria with Germany in a process called Anschluss; he is greeted by 200,000 Viennese at Heldenplatz. Austria is officially wiped off the map of Europe.

RED VIENNA

With Austria's fascist, Nazi and, more recently, far-right political history, it's surprising to learn that Vienna was a model of social democratic municipal government in the 1920s, the most successful Europe has ever witnessed. The period is known as Rotes Wien, or Red Vienna.

The fall of the Habsburg empire left a huge gap in the governing of Vienna. By popular demand the Social Democratic Workers' Party (SDAP) soon filled it, winning a resounding victory in the municipal elections in 1919. Over the next 14 years they embarked on an impressive series of social policies and municipal programs, particularly covering communal housing and health, aimed at improving the plight of the working class. Their greatest achievement was to tackle the severe housing problem Vienna faced after the war by creating massive housing complexes across the city. The plan was simple: provide apartments with running water, toilets and natural daylight, and housing estates with parkland and recreational areas. This policy not only gained admiration from within Austria but also won praise throughout Europe. Many of these colossal estates can still be seen in the city; the most celebrated, the Karl-Marx-Hof (p127), was designed by Karl Ehn and originally contained an astounding 1600 apartments. Even so, Karl-Marx-Hof is by no means the biggest – Sandleitenhof in Ottakring and Friedrich-Engels-Hof in Brigittenau are both larger.

For the interested, the Architekturzentrum Wien (p88) organises guided tours of the main Red Vienna housing complexes.

THE REPUBLIC OF AUSTRIA

Halfway through WWI Franz Josef died, and his successor, Karl I, abdicated at the conclusion of the war in 1918. The Republic of Austria was created on 12 November 1918, and although the majority of citizens pushed for union with Germany, the victorious allies prohibited such an act. The loss of vast swaths of land caused severe economic difficulties – the new states declined to supply vital raw materials to their old ruler and whole industries collapsed. Unemployment soared, not only due to the influx of refugees and ex-soldiers but also because a huge number of bureaucrats, once employed by the monarchy, simply had no job to go back to. Vienna's population of around one million was soon on the verge of famine.

By 1919 women were also enfranchised; now all Viennese adults could vote by secret ballot for the city government. The socialists (Social Democrats) gained an absolute majority and retained it in all free elections up until 1996. Their reign from 1919 to 1933, known as Red Vienna (see above), was by far the most industrious and turned the fortunes of many working-class citizens around.

The rest of the country was firmly under sway of the conservatives (Christian Socialists), causing great tensions between city and state. On 15 July 1927, in a dubious judgment, right-wing extremists were acquitted of an assassination charge. Demonstrators gathered outside the Palace of Justice in Vienna (the seat of the Supreme Court) and set fire to the building. The police responded by opening fire on the crowd, killing 86 people (including five of their own number). The rift between Vienna's Social Democrats and the federal Christian Socialists grew.

FASCISM RISING

Political and social tensions, coupled with a worldwide economic crisis, weakened the Social Democrats, giving federal chancellor Engelbert Dollfuss the opportunity he was looking for: in 1933 he dissolved parliament on a technicality. In February 1934 civil war erupted, with

1945

WWII ends and a provisional government is established in Austria; Vienna is divided into four occupied quarters: American, British, Soviet Union and French.

1948

Graham Greene flies to Vienna and roams through postwar rubble for inspiration for a new film script. The script he pens is *The Third Man,* Vienna's most legendary and iconic film, starring Orson Welles.

1955

Austria regains its sovereignty – the Austrian State Treaty is signed at the Schloss Belvedere; over half a million Austrians take to the streets of the capital in celebration.

the Schutzbund, the Social Democrat's militias, up against the conservatives' Heimwehr. The Schutzbund were soundly beaten, and the Social Democratic party outlawed. However, Dollfuss' reign was short-lived – in July of the same year he was assassinated in an attempted Nazi coup. His successor, Schuschnigg, buckled under increasing threats from Germany and included National Socialists in his government in 1938.

On 12 March 1938, German troops marched across the border into Austria, just one day before an Austrian referendum on integration with Germany was to be held. Hitler, who had departed Vienna many years before as a failed and disgruntled artist, returned to the city in triumph, and held a huge rally at Heldenplatz on 15 March in front of 200,000 ecstatic Viennese. Austria was soon incorporated into the German Reich under the Anschluss.

The arrival of the Nazis was to have a devastating effect on Vienna's Jews in particular, though many non-Jewish liberals and intellectuals were also targeted. After May 1938, Germany's Nuremberg racial laws were also applicable in Austria, and thousands of Jews and their property fell prey to the Nazis. Austria joined Germany's WWII machine from 1939 to 1945. In WWI Vienna felt little direct effect from the war; this time the city suffered a heavy toll from Allied bombing towards the end of the conflict. Most major public buildings, including the Staatsoper and Stephansdom, received damage, around 86,000 homes were rendered unusable or ruined and around 3000 bomb craters dotted the cityscape. Almost 9000 Viennese died in air raids (many buried in cellars under collapsed apartment blocks) and over 2000 lost their lives in the defence of the city. On 11 April 1945 advancing Russian troops 'liberated' Vienna; raping and pillaging by the Red Army further scarred an already shattered populace.

POST-WWII

Soon after liberation Austria declared its independence from Germany. A provisional federal government was established under Socialist Karl Renner, and the country was occupied by the victorious Allies – the Americans, Russians, British and French. Vienna was itself divided into four zones; this was a time of 'four men in a jeep', so aptly depicted in Graham Greene's *The Third Man*.

Delays caused by frosting relations between the superpowers ensured that the Allied occupation dragged on for 10 years. It was a tough time for the Viennese – the rebuilding of national monuments was slow and expensive and the black market dominated the flow of goods. On 15 May 1955 the Austrian State Treaty was ratified, with Austria proclaiming its permanent neutrality. The Allied forces withdrew, and in December 1955 Austria joined the UN. The economy took a turn for the better through the assistance granted under the Marshall Plan, and the cessation of the removal of industrial property by the Soviets. As the capital of a neutral country on the edge of the Cold War front line, Vienna attracted spies and diplomats: Kennedy and Khrushchev met here in 1961, Carter and Brezhnev in 1979; the UN set up shop in 1983.

1986 TO THE PRESENT

Austria's international image suffered following the election in 1986 of President Kurt Waldheim, who, it was revealed, had served in a German *Wehrmacht* (armed forces) unit implicated in WWII war crimes. But a belated recognition of Austria's less-than-spotless WWII record was a long time coming. In 1993 Chancellor Franz Vranitzky finally admitted

1973–79

The VIC, otherwise known as UNO City, is designed and built by Austrian architect Johann Staber – it is built north of the Danube River. Vienna becomes the third international seat of the United Nations.

1986

Vienna ceases to be the capital of surrounding Bundesland of Niederösterreich (Lower Austria). It is replaced by Sankt Pölten.

1995

After resounding support from its populace and a referendum where 60% voted 'Yes' to joining, Austria enters the European Union (EU).

that Austrians were 'willing servants of Nazism'. Since then, however, Austria has attempted to make amends for its part in atrocities against the Jews. In 1998 the Austrian Historical Commission, set up to investigate and report on expropriations during the Nazi era, came into being, and in 2001 Vienna's Mayor, Dr Michael Häupl, had this to say: 'Having portrayed itself as the first victim of National Socialism for many years, Austria now has to admit to its own, active participation in the regime's crimes and recognize its responsibility to act instantly and quickly.'

With its entry into the EU in 1995, Austria entered a new age of politics. This move was endorsed by the populace, who voted a resounding 66.4% in favour of EU membership in the June 1994 referendum. Support soon waned, however, as prices increased with the introduction of the euro, but most Austrians have resigned themselves to the fact that the EU is here to stay.

After the 1999 national elections, Austria suffered strong international criticism when the far-right Freedom Party (FPÖ) formed a new federal coalition government with the Austrian People's Party (ÖVP) under the leadership of Chancellor Schlüssel. The new administration, despite having been democratically elected, was condemned before it even had the opportunity to put a foot wrong. The EU acted immediately and imposed sanctions against Austria by freezing all high-level diplomatic contacts, while Israel withdrew its ambassador.

The problem arose from the then leader of the FPÖ, Jörg Haider, and his flippant and insensitive remarks towards foreign members of state, and his xenophobic rabble-rousing. Many Austrians, irrespective of their views towards the FPÖ, were upset at the EU's preemptive move, believing that Austria would not have been targeted had it been a more important player in European affairs. In any event, sanctions proved not only futile but counterproductive, and they were withdrawn by the EU in September 2000.

In the 2002 elections the FPÖ's popularity took a nosedive, dropping to a mere 10.1% (from 26.9% in 1999). The ÖVP, with 42% of the vote, secured another term in government; Haider instantly offered his resignation, and soon after a second term of the ÖVP-FPÖ coalition began in earnest.

The October 2006 national elections proved quite a shock. Most believed that, despite a close race, the ÖVP would once again lead the country. However, they were pipped at the post by Alfred Gusenbauer's Social Democratic Party (SPÖ), which received 35.34% of the national vote (ÖVP gained 34.33%, the Greens 11.05% and the FPÖ, under new leader HC Strache, won 11.04%).

In 2008 the grand coalition headed by Gusenbauer collapsed over disagreements about the country's EU policy. Early elections held in September of that year resulted in extensive losses for the two ruling parties and corresponding gains for HC Strache's FPÖ and Haider's BZÖ (Future Alliance of Austria); the Green Party (Die Grünen) was demoted to 5th position. Still, SPÖ and ÖVP renewed their coalition under the leadership of the new SPÖ party chairman, Werner Faymann. Then Jörg Haider died in a car accident in October that year and was succeeded by Herbert Scheibner as BZÖ party chairman and by Gerhard Dörfler as governor of Carinthia.

The global financial crisis impacted Vienna with dips in tourism and increases in unemployment, but overall it has weathered the storm fairly well. Clearly, the amount of construction around the new train station development (see p31) demonstrates that the city is looking to the future.

2000

ÖVP-FPÖ coalition, and the FPÖ's campaign on a platform with posters declaring 'Stop the foreign tide. Put Austria First' leads to EU sanctions against Vienna.

2002

Along with 12 other members of the EU, Austria drops its schilling and adopts the euro; the FPÖ vote collapses during the elections.

2008

Austria cohosts the UEFA European Football Championship (Euro 2008) with Switzerland – the final match is played at Vienna's Ernst-Happel stadium.

ENVIRONMENT & PLANNING

THE LAND

Vienna (elevation 156m) occupies an area of 415 sq km in the Danube Valley, the most fertile land in Austria. More than 700 hectares are under vineyard cultivation in the Vienna region, and nearly 90% of the wine produced is white. The largest wine-growing area is Stammersdorf in the northeast of the city.

To the west and north of the city are the rolling hills of the Wienerwald (p126), the much-loved Vienna Woods. These are the only hill ranges to speak of and the rest of the city is relatively flat. The Danube divides the city into two unequal parts, with the old city and nearly all the tourist sights to the west of the river. The Danube Canal branches off from the main river and winds a sinewy course south, forming one of the borders of the historic centre, the 1st district (Innere Stadt; p53). The long, thin Donauinsel (Danube Island; p115), which splits the Danube in two as it courses through Vienna, is a recreation area populated with beaches, playgrounds and pathways. Just to the east of the island is a loop of water called the Alte Donau (Old Danube), known for its beaches and water sports in summer and its ice skating in winter.

Almost half the city is given over to green spaces, more than any other European capital. Major parks include the Prater (p110), a massive belt of green just to the southeast of the Innere Stadt, and Lainzer Tiergarten (p126), a forested area home to wild animals and enthusiastic walkers in the far western reaches of the city.

GREEN VIENNA

Recycling is well established in Vienna – 295,000 tonnes of waste are recycled annually. This isn't only dictated by conscience – Viennese are compelled to do so by law. Vienna's widespread use of environmentally friendly trams and buses powered by gas has helped keep the city's air reasonably clean, and the Wienerwald does its part as an efficient 'air filter'. The city's water supply, which flows directly from the Alps, is one of the cleanest in the world, although many of the older houses still have lead pipes. This has resulted in one in every 10 houses recording lead in the water supply, but levels are generally too low to cause harm.

The Fernwärme incinerator (p98) has one of the lowest emission levels of any incinerator in the world. This plant processes waste matter, burning 260,000 tonnes of it annually to supply heating for more than 40,000 homes in Vienna.

In 2009 and 2010 the Mercer Quality of Living survey chose Vienna as the world's number-one most liveable city – the survey was partially based on green spaces: the metropolitan area boasts 280 imperial parks and gardens. In spring, 400 species of rose bloom in the Volksgarten. The recreation areas of Prater, the Wienerwald and the surrounding hills encircling Vienna invite visitors to go on walks, day trips, hikes and bicycle tours. Covered in more than 100 kilometres of bicycle paths and trails, the city is also extremely bike-friendly, and has a bike scheme with more than 60 bike stations scattered around town – this scheme alone accounts for 8% of the city's transport traffic. Roughly 20% of the city's population commutes to work by bike – that figure is expected to rise by at least 3% in each coming year.

WIEN IST EIN HUNDEKLO

English academic John Sparrow could easily have had Vienna in mind when he penned 'that indefatigable and unsavoury engine of pollution, the dog' in a 1975 letter to *The Times* newspaper. The streets of the capital are strewn with dog poo; approximately 8.3% of households own a dog, which, at a conservative calculation, equates to 65,000 dogs, and while the Viennese love their dogs, the majority are loath to clean up their mess.

The city caters well for dog owners – 870,000 sq metres of parkland in Vienna are designated dog-only zones. Yet poo is everywhere: on footpaths, between parked cars, on grass verges, in parks and even in doorways. In 2006, a campaign under the slogan *'Wien ist ein Hundeklo'* (Vienna is a dog's toilet) collected 157,000 votes in a matter of months in support of its demands for a council cleanup program and penalties for owners who neglect to clean up after their pets. Unfortunately the ongoing campaign has had little effect to date, but the groundswell of support may change the councillors' minds. In the meantime, a cautionary glance groundwards before stepping out is advisable.

URBAN PLANNING & DEVELOPMENT

'Constant Improvement' seems to be the motto of the city council. It has financed seminal architectural projects, such as the Gasometer (p107), Bücherei Wien (p89) and MuseumsQuartier (p86), creating superb public spaces while managing to retain the buildings' original ambience. 'Urbion', an EU incentive to modernise the West Gürtel area, is another such project. Since 1995 the Gürtel's *Bogen* (disused arched spaces below the tracks of the U6 U-Bahn) have been, and continue to be, skilfully transformed into bars, restaurants and art spaces. The U2 U-Bahn was extended in 2008 and the banks of the Danube Canal and Vienna River continue to be upgraded.

At press time, the biggest construction project is on the site of Vienna's former South Railway Station. The gargantuan project will create a modern, new main railway station with trans-European rail links to the west, east, north and south and an entirely new urban district named Bahnhof City (Train Station City). Plans for the 109-hectare Bahnhof City include office space, around 5000 new apartments, an eight-hectare park, a school, 10 new skyscrapers and 9km of cycle paths. The train station is slated for completion in late 2012/early 2013; the rest is due to be finished by 2015. Vienna's Westbahnhof train station is also undergoing a massive renewal project. When the renovated station is unveiled in late 2011, it will be reborn as a revamped centre with shops, restaurants and state-of-the-art transport facilities.

GOVERNMENT & POLITICS

As well as being the capital city of Austria, Vienna is (and has been since 1922) one of nine federal provinces (*Bundesländer*). Every Austrian federal province has its own head of government (*Landeshauptmann*) and provincial assembly (*Landtag*); therefore the mayor of the city is also the governor of a federal province and Vienna's City Council is a provincial assembly.

The Viennese are the country's staunchest supporters of socialism and are generally a rather cynical, expressive and questioning bunch when it comes to politics. It's not uncommon to hear a heated conversation over the affairs of the state or city at restaurants and bars. People are rarely shocked, or even bothered, with the private lives of their politicians and couldn't care less who is having an affair with whom – their concern is how policy-making will affect their day-to-day lives and the future of their city.

At the time of research, Vienna's mayor was Michael Häupl of the SPÖ. Häupl was elected during the 2005 elections, when the SPÖ increased its number of seats to 55 (the ÖVP came in second with 18 seats, the Greens – Die Grünen –moved up to third with 14 seats, and the FPÖ dropped to last with 13 seats). Elections are held every five years – in fact, the October 2010 mayoral elections corresponded with this guide going to print. However, at the time of writing most polls predicted that the ruling SPÖ would lose seats (and possibly its majority rule) and the FPÖ would gain seats. Additionally, FPÖ head HP Strache was seen as the potential frontrunner for the mayoral seat amid whispers that Häupl may step down if things go south for the SPÖ during the election.

On a national level, the SPÖ has historically held power, but the parliamentary race has often been a closely fought battle. The 1996 election ushered in the first postwar coalition between SPÖ and ÖVP, the country's conservative political machine, and in 2000 SPÖ lost its hold on parliament completely when the ÖVP, in collaboration with the FPÖ, had enough votes to form a government. FPÖ gained international notoriety under its former leader the late Jörg Haider, who expressed admiration for Adolf Hitler's labour policies and made several trips to see Iraq's former dictator Saddam Hussein while he was still in power. Haider, the governor of Carinthia province, resigned as head of the FPÖ in early 2000, following the international outcry generated by the FPÖ's inclusion in the federal coalition government; he died in 2008.

The 2006 elections turned up more than one surprise. To all and sundry, it looked like a shoe-in for the ÖVP; Alfred Gusenbauer's SPÖ trailed the conservatives in opinion polls right up to voting day, and the increasing popularity of the Greens looked set to steal support from the socialists. The SPÖ went on to win the election with 35.34% of the national vote, 1% more than their biggest rival. Haider had split with the FPÖ in 2002 to form another right-wing party, the BZÖ, which looked out of the running next to his old party and its buoyant new leader,

HC Strache. However, he and his party won 4.11% of the national vote and a place in parliament (4% is the minimum to obtain seats).

Four years later, the 2010 national elections produced a landslide victory for the SPÖ – it captured a whopping 78.94% of the national vote. This was a huge blow to the FPÖ, which despite high hopes to catapult the party only secured 15.62% of the vote. The Christian party (CPÖ) trailed with 5.43%, and the BZÖ and ÖVP did not capture any seats: both chose to refrain from fielding a national candidate.

MEDIA

The *Wiener Zeitung* (www.wienerzeitung.at), first published in 1703, is the longest-running newspaper in the world. With such a long and solid journalistic background, it's no surprise that Vienna receives a wide and varied view on political and social matters from its media.

Founded in 1957, Österreichischer Rundfunk (ÖRF; Austrian Broadcasting Corporation; www.orf.at, in German), the country's independent public broadcaster and the dominant force in Austrian media for decades, has faced stiff competition since the privatisation of airwaves in 2002. It owns 13 radio stations (Österreich1, Ö3, FM4, RÖI and nine regional radio stations) and the country's only two non-cable and satellite TV channels, ÖRF1 and ÖRF2.

Austria produces 16 national and regional daily papers, many of which are based in Vienna. Most are owned by their publishing houses and stick to quality over quantity, which results in fierce competition and generally good investigative journalism. Unusually, papers receive state grants, but this has been under review for a number of years and may change in the future.

Neue Kronen Zeitung, a thoroughly tabloid spread, is easily Austria's most-read newspaper. Together with the *Kurier*, its more bourgeois brother, the two papers reach around half the paper-reading population of Austria daily. *News*, owned by German publisher Gruner und Jahr, has the highest per-household readership in Europe for a weekly news magazine. The Newspapers & Magazines section in the Directory chapter, p235, provides a short but succinct list of papers available in Vienna.

ARTS & ARCHITECTURE

In many ways, Vienna's art has waltzed arm in arm with its architecture through the ballrooms of history. From its early Roman beginnings to its 21st-century contemporary constructions, the city's good burghers have played with brick and mortar, often mastering, sometimes excelling, in their attempts. Aside from its Renaissance examples, the city is embellished with a healthy array of architectural styles, many of which are within easy reach of the Innere Stadt. Highlights abound, but the peak periods of baroque and *Jugendstil* (art nouveau) that emblazoned the city with a plethora of masterpieces are in a class of their own; for some, their collective brilliance outshines all other attractions in Vienna.

Like its architecture, the city's art peaked in its *fin de siècle* years, spawning *Jugendstil,* the Secession *(Sezession),* the *Wiener Werkstätte* (WW; Vienna Workshop), and greats including Gustav Klimt, Otto Wagner, and Egon Schiele. WWII and Austria's voluntary embrace of Nazism created another artistic generation altogether, one attempting to come to grips with its at times unsettling heritage. Perhaps the most vivid expressionists to rise from the group are those of the Actionism art movement, whose work revolves around violent self-hatred.

While the Viennese love their contemporary visual arts and cinema – regularly taking a look at both – visitors are more likely to encounter Viennese music. Contemporary pickings are slim (legendary DJ-duo Kruder & Dorfmeister are definitely the cream of the crop, while nobody can forget Falco's 'Rock Me, Amadeus'), but Vienna's musical history is rich, glorious and immensely accessible. Beethoven, Mozart, Haydn and the Strauss family all did their stints in this city, and Vienna isn't about to let you forget it. Visit the Vienna Philharmonic and you certainly won't want to.

Guilt, self-loathing, a pathological distaste for being Austrian and a fondness for dogs: these are the themes you'll see again and again in Viennese cinema, literature or painting. The legacy of WWII has left an indelible mark on Vienna's modern artists, and is particularly prevalent in the sadomasochistic obsessions of film director Michael Haneke and the general hatred of humanity in Elfriede Jelinek's novels.

MUSIC

Above all else, Vienna is known for music. It is a sign of the perhaps disproportionate importance of music to this city that after both world wars, when resources were so low that people were starving, money was still put aside to keep up performances at the Staatsoper. Today, it's impossible to avoid music in Vienna; buskers fill the Innere Stadt's main thoroughfares and Mozart lookalikes peddle tickets to concerts at busy tourist spots.

An unmissable Viennese musical experience is a visit to the Vienna Philharmonic. Rated as one of the best orchestras in the world, it plays to packed houses wherever it tours. Started as an experiment in 1842, it grew in popularity in Vienna but did not venture on its first foreign tour until 1898, under the baton of Gustav Mahler. The Philharmonic has the privilege of choosing its conductors, whose ranks have included not only Mahler but also Richard Strauss and Felix Weingartner. The instruments used by the Philharmonic generally follow pre-19th-century design and more accurately reflect the music Mozart and Beethoven wrote. Most of its members have been born and bred in Vienna, making it a truly Viennese affair.

The Habsburgs began patronising court musicians as far back as the 13th century, and by the 18th and 19th centuries the investment was paying off. Composers were drawn to Vienna from all over Europe and music had become a very fashionable hobby. Mozart, Haydn, Schubert and Beethoven all came in search of the Habsburg's ready money; between 1781 and 1828 they produced some of the world's greatest classical music. The Johann Strausses, father and son, kept the ball rolling when they introduced the waltz to Vienna.

Vienna's *Heurigen* (wine taverns; see p173) have a musical tradition all their own – *Schrammelmusik*. Musicians wielding a combination of violin, accordion, guitar and clarinet produce maudlin tunes which form a perfect accompaniment to drunkenness.

Vienna's impact on international jazz, rock or pop music is minimal. Falco (1957–98), a household name for 1980s teenagers, reached the world stage with his hit 'Rock Me

Amadeus', inspired by the film *Amadeus*. A popular name in Vienna's rock circles is Ostbahn Kurti (or Kurt Ostbahn, depending on how he feels at the time), who sings in a thick Viennese dialect. The mainstream Austrian pop of Wolfgang Ambros, Georg Danzer, Reinhard Fendrich and pop/rock singer Christina Stürmer draws large crowds. Viennese singer Mika Vember is also one to watch – she debuted her first solo album, *Now or Now*, in 2007 to much local success and shows promise to make it onto the international radar. Vember also plays the drums and various other instruments, and performs regularly in the capital.

From the late 1980s to the mid 1990s, Vienna played an important role in techno and the electronic scene. The city's connection to Detroit and New York led to the development of downtempo and avant-garde techno, and the resulting tunes played in clubs around the world. Artists on G-Stone Records and Cheap Records (Kruder & Dorfmeister, Patrick Pulsinger, Erdem Tunakan) proved a powerful source for new electronic music, but by the end of the 1990s Vienna's electronic heart had suffered a minor stroke due to over-commercialisation. In the last decade the city's scene has experienced a revival, with old and new artists once again creating waves in the electronic genre. Tosca, a side project of Richard Dorfmeister, is well regarded; DJ Glow is known for his electro beats; the Vienna Scientists produce tidy house compilations; the Sofa Surfers' dub-hop tracks are often dark but well received; Radian spins hard-core electronic for the intellectual crowd; and the likes of Megablast, Makossa and Stereotype continue to go from strength to strength.

top picks

DOWNLOADS

- *The 'Blue Danube' Waltz* – Strauss the Younger
- *Fifth Symphony in C Minor* – Beethoven
- *Cradle Song, Op 49, No 4* – Brahms
- *Der Kommisar* – Falco
- *Die Vorstellung des Chaos'* (The Representation of Chaos), *Part 1, The Creation* – Haydn
- *Shakatakadoodub* (on DJ-Kicks 2: Unofficial Release of True K&D Rarities) – Kruder & Dorfmeister
- *Die Zauberflöte* (The Magic Flute; EMI Classics version conducted by Otto Klemperer) – Mozart
- *'The Trout', Piano Quintet In A Major* – Schubert

VISUAL ARTS & ARCHITECTURE

MEDIEVAL & BEFORE

Vienna's architectural heritage begins with the Romans; in the 1st century the powerful empire built Vindobona, a small military camp, on the site of the Innere Stadt. Romanesque, a style noted for its thick walls, semicircular arches and simple geometry, was predominant in Europe from the 7th to 12th centuries. Only a handful of buildings in the city retain hints of Romanesque – most were replaced with the medieval Gothic style upon the accession of the Habsburgs in the 13th century. Gothic architecture features pointed arches, heavy stonework, lacelike patterns and a dynamic structure.

Vienna's meagre medieval art collection is typified by two-dimensional religious pieces and is bolstered by Europe's earliest portrait, a 14th-century depiction of Duke Rudolph IV. In the Renaissance period, the Viennese shifted their focus from biblical to natural; the Danube school, an active group of painters in Bavaria and Austria from 1500 to 1530, combined landscapes and religious motifs.

What to See

Due to the Habsburg's unquestioned desire to clad everything in baroque, little remains of Vienna's pre-17th century art and architectural legacy. Roman ruins are visible at **Michaelerplatz** (p65) and **Hoher Markt** (p76). The 12th-century Romanesque **Ruprechtskirche** (p76), the city's oldest church, graces the Innere Stadt's old Jewish quarter. The crowning glory of the Gothic era is **Stephansdom** (p54), but further examples of this era exist; **Maria am Gestade** (p76) still retains an elegant Gothic tower, and traces of medieval architecture can be seen in **Michaelerkirche** (p65) and the **Minoritenkirche** (p72). A rarity for Vienna, the remains of a medieval synagogue, are the focus of **Museum Judenplatz** (p75).

The Orangery at the Unteres Belvedere (p103) contains a collection of Gothic religious art, and the Dom- & Diözesanmuseum (p55) is blessed with the earliest European portrait, dating from 1360. The oldest secular murals in the capital, from 1398, are the Neidhart-Fresken (p77).

BAROQUE & ROCOCO

Unwittingly, the Ottomans helped form much of Vienna's architectural make-up seen today. After the first Turkish siege in 1529, the Habsburgs moved their seat of power to the city and set about defending it; strong city walls were built, which stood until 1857 before making way for the Ringstrasse. However the second Turkish siege was the major catalyst for architectural change; with the defeat of the old enemy (achieved with extensive help from German and Polish armies), the Habsburgs were freed from the constant threat of war from the east. Money

VIENNESE COMPOSERS AT A GLANCE

Christoph Willibald Gluck Knowing about Gluck will really get you in good with the intelligentsia, because even though next to no-one has heard of him, this composer paved the way for all the big names by reconstructing opera: he replaced recitatives (which broke up the story and placed the emphasis on the singer) with orchestral accompaniments that kept the story moving along. His major works include *Orfeo* (1762) and *Alceste* (1767).

Josef Haydn People in the know think Haydn (1732–1809) is one of the three greatest classical composers; he wrote 108 symphonies, 68 string quartets, 47 piano sonatas and about 20 operas. His greatest works include *Symphony No 102 in B-flat Major*, the oratorios *The Creation* (1798) and *The Seasons* (1801), and six Masses written for Miklós II.

Wolfgang Amadeus Mozart Iconic Mozart (1756–91) wrote some 626 pieces; among the greatest are *The Marriage of Figaro* (1786), *Don Giovanni* (1787), *Così fan Tutte* (1790) and *The Magic Flute* (1791). The *Requiem Mass*, apocryphally written for his own death, remains one of the most powerful works of classical music. Have a listen to *Piano Concerto Nos 20 and 21*, which comprise some of the best elements of Mozart: drama, comedy, intimacy and a whole heap of ingenuity in one easy-to-appreciate package.

Franz Schubert Born and bred in the city, Schubert (1797–1828) really knew how to churn out a tune: he composed nine symphonies, 11 overtures, seven Masses, more than 80 smaller choral works, more than 30 chamber music works, 450 piano works and more than 600 songs – that's more than 960 works in total – before dying of exhaustion at 31. His best-known works are his last symphony (the *Great C Major Symphony*), his Mass in E-flat and the *Unfinished Symphony*.

Ludwig van Beethoven Beethoven (1770–1827) studied briefly with Mozart in Vienna in 1787; he returned in late 1792. Beethoven produced a lot of chamber music up to the age of 32, when he became almost totally deaf and – ironically – began writing some of his best works, including the *Symphony No 9 in D Minor*, *Symphony No 5* and his late string quartets.

The Strausses and the waltz The waltz first went down a storm at the Congress of Vienna (1814–15). The early masters of the genre were Johann Strauss the Elder (1804–49) and Joseph Lanner (1801–43). Johann Strauss the Younger (1825–99) composed more than 400 waltzes, including Vienna's unofficial anthem, 'The Blue Danube' (1867), and 'Tales from the Vienna Woods' (1868). Strauss also excelled at operettas, especially the eternally popular *Die Fledermaus* (The Bat; 1874) and *The Gypsy Baron* (1885).

Anton Bruckner A very religious man, Bruckner (1824–96) was known for lengthy, dramatically intense symphonies (nine in all) and church music. Works include *Symphony No 9*, *Symphony No 8 in C Minor* and *Mass in D Minor*.

Johannes Brahms At the age of 29, Brahms (1833–97) moved to Vienna, where many of his works were performed by the Vienna Philharmonic. Best works include *Ein Deutsches Requiem*, his *Violin Concerto* and *Symphony Nos 1 to 4*.

Gustav Mahler Known mainly for his nine symphonies, Mahler (1860–1911) – though German-born – was director of the Vienna State Opera from 1897 to 1907. His best works include *Das Lied von der Erde* (The Song of the Earth) and *Symphony Nos 1, 5 and 9*.

Second Vienna School Arnold Schönberg (1874–1951) founded the Second Vienna School of Music and developed theories on the 12-tone technique. His *Pieces for the Piano Op 11* (1909) goes completely beyond the bounds of tonality. Viennese-born Alban Berg (1885–1935) and Anton Webern (1883–1945) also explored the 12-tone technique. At the first public performance of Berg's composition *Altenberg-Lieder*, the concert had to be cut short due to the audience's outraged reaction.

and energy previously spent on defence were poured into urban redevelopment, resulting in a building frenzy. Learning from the Italian model, Johann Bernhard Fischer von Erlach (1656–1723) developed a national style called Austrian baroque. This mirrored the exuberant ornamentation of Italian baroque with a few local quirks, such as coupling dynamic combinations of colour with groovy undulating silhouettes. Johann Lukas von Hildebrandt (1668–1745), another prominent baroque architect, was responsible for a number of buildings in the city centre.

Rococo, an elegant style incorporating pale colours and an exuberance of gold and silver, was all the rage in the 18th century. It was a great favourite with Maria Theresia, and Austrian rococo is sometimes referred to as late-baroque Theresien style.

While Austria didn't produce the same calibre of baroque artists as other central European countries, some striking church frescos were painted by Johann Michael Rottmayr and Daniel Gran. Franz Anton Maulbertsch, working on canvas, was well known for his mastery of colour and light and his intensity of expression.

What to See

It's hard to turn a corner in the Innere Stadt without running into a baroque wall. Much of the Hofburg (p65) is a baroque showpiece; In der Burg square is surrounded on all sides by baroque wings, but its triumph is Nationalbibliothek (p71), by Fischer von Erlach, whose *Prunksaal* (grand hall) is arguably one of the finest baroque interiors in Austria. Herrengasse, running north from the Hofburg's Michaelertor, is lined with baroque splendour, including Palais Kinsky at No 4 and Palais Mollard at No 9. Peterskirche (p64), off the Graben, is the handiwork of Hildebrandt, but its dark interior and oval nave is topped by Karlskirche (p80), another of Erlach's designs, this time with Byzantine touches. The highly esteemed Schloss Belvedere (p102) is also a Hildebrandt creation.

Nicolas Pacassi is responsible for the masterful rococo styling at Schloss Schönbrunn (p119), but the former royal residence is upstaged by its graceful baroque gardens.

The Habsburgs were generous patrons of the arts, and their unrivalled collection of baroque paintings from across Europe is displayed at the Kunsthistorisches Museum (p69). Palais Liechtenstein, the former residence of the Liechtenstein family, now houses the Liechtenstein Museum (p96), which contains one of the largest private collections of baroque paintings and sculptures in the world, and is in itself a gorgeous example of baroque architecture. Not to be outdone, the Albertina (p70) houses a vast number of paintings by Albrecht Dürer, Raphael and Rembrandt.

Sculpture's greatest period in Vienna was during the baroque years – the Providentia Fountain, by George Raphael Donner, and Balthasar Permoser's statue *Apotheosis of Prince Eugene* in the Unteres Belvedere (p103) are striking examples.

NEOCLASSICAL, BIEDERMEIER & THE RINGSTRASSE

From the 18th century (but culminating in the 19th), Viennese architects – like those all over Europe – turned to a host of neoclassical architectural styles. In the mid-18th century, archaeological finds, such as the city of Troy in Turkey, inspired a revival of classical (Greek and Roman) aesthetics in many forms of art. In architecture, this meant cleaner lines, squarer, bulkier buildings and a preponderance of columns (particularly popular in the late 18th century, when romantic classicism relied heavily on Doric and Ionic Greek-style columns).

Meanwhile, the Industrial Revolution was marshalling the forces of technological development across Europe to house its factories and workers. As mechanisation upped the pace of production in the manufacturing industry, the new capitalists demanded more and more factories to produce their goods. In Austria, people flooded into Vienna from the countryside, drawn by the promise of jobs. Demand for housing skyrocketed, and cheap, mass-produced homes swelled the city's newly formed suburbs. Innovations in the manufacture of iron and glass allowed for taller, stronger buildings, and architects took full advantage.

The end of the Napoleonic wars and the ensuing celebration at the Congress of Vienna in 1815 ushered in the Biedermeier period (named after a satirical middle-class figure in a Munich paper). Growing industrialisation and urbanisation had created a cash-rich middle-class eager to show their wealth, and coupled with severe political oppression (a backlash from the revolutionary wars), their expression turned inwards to the domestic arena. Viennese artists produced some extraordinary furniture during this period; deep, well-padded armchairs were particularly popular, but the governing doctrines were clean lines and minimal fuss. Ferdinand Georg Waldmüller (1793–1865), whose evocative, idealised peasant scenes are captivating, is the period's best-known artist.

Revolution in 1848 rocked the empire and set in motion a building boom. Franz Josef I, the newly crowned emperor, was at the peak of his power: when he took it into his head to overhaul the city, the city was overhauled. His ambition to one-up Napoleon's makeover of Paris led him to plan what would become one of Europe's most homogeneous inner-city designs. In the mid-19th century, Vienna was still essentially a medieval city in layout, with an inner area surrounded by fortifications. Franz Josef's plan called for the fortifications to be demolished and replaced with a ring road lined with magnificent imperial buildings. A competition was held to design the new Ringstrasse; once the winner, Ludwig Förster, was chosen, demolition of the old city walls began in 1857.

Although Förster was the overall designer, the buildings were created by a company of successful architects. Heinrich von Ferstel, Theophil von Hansen, Gottfried Semper, Karl von Hasenauer, Friedrich von Schmidt and Eduard van der Nüll all had a hand in the creation of Vienna's architectural wonder. Some of the earlier buildings are Rundbogenstil (round-arched style, similar to neo-Roman) in style, but the typical design for the Ringstrasse is High Renaissance. This features rusticated lower stories and columns and pilasters on the upper floors. Some of the more interesting buildings on the Ring stray from this standard: Greek Revival, neo-Gothic, neobaroque and neorococo all play a part in the boulevard's architectural make-up.

Work on the Ringstrasse and associated buildings comprised one of the biggest building booms in the history of Europe. Thanks to the sheer volume of architecture created during this period, Vienna – despite massive destruction wrought in two world wars, including heavy bombing raids by the Allies towards the end of WWII which damaged almost every public building in the city and destroyed 86,000 houses – is still a showcase of European neoclassicism.

What to See

The **Hofmobiliendepot** (p89) has an extensive collection of Biedermeier furniture – some you can actually try – and more examples can be seen in the **Museum für angewandte Kunst** (MAK; p60). Ferdinand Georg Waldmüller's Biedermeier paintings hang in the **Wien Museum** (p80) and **Oberes Belvedere** (p102), and one of the few uniformly Biedermeier houses is the **Geymüllerschlössel** (p128).

Taking a tram ride around the Ringstrasse (see p134 for the self-guided tram tour) provides a quick lesson in neoclassicism. Neo-Renaissance can be seen in Heinrich von Ferstel's Herrengasse Bank, and High Renaissance in Theophil von Hansen's **Palais Epstein** (p73), Gottfried Semper's **Naturhistorisches Museum** (p70) and Karl von Hasenauer's **Kunsthistorisches Museum** (p69).

Von Hansen also designed the Ring's **Parlament** (p72), one of the last major Greek Revival works built in Europe (take a close look at the statuary out front – perhaps horse-punching was part of the traditional Greek Olympiad). Von Ferstel's **Votivkirche** (p99) is a classic example of neo-Gothic, but the showiest building on the Ring, with its dripping spires and spun-sugar facades, is Friedrich von Schmidt's unmissable **Rathaus** (p73) in Flemish-Gothic. The most notable neobaroque example is Eduard van der Nüll's **Staatsoper** (p195), though it's also worth having a look at Gottfried Semper's **Burgtheater** (p196).

While Franz Josef was Emperor he had a new wing added to the **Hofburg** (p65). The architect, Karl von Hasenauer, stuck very closely to a traditional baroque look, though there are some 19th-century touches – a certain heavy bulkiness to the wing – that reveal it is actually neobaroque. The Technical University and Luigi Pichl's Diet of Lower Austria at 13 Herrengasse are also examples of the neoclassical style. Paul Sprenger's Landeshauptmannshaft next door at 11 Herrengasse is neo-Renaissance.

JUGENDSTIL & THE SECESSION

While the neoclassical style continued into the late 19th century, by the 1880s art nouveau was beginning to bubble up. The clean lines and elegant sturdiness of neoclassicism still held appeal for architects who appreciated history and tradition, but some designers were tired of the style's restrictions. At the same time, the Industrial Revolution had spawned a trend towards cheaply made mass-produced architecture and design, and towards a philosophy of utilitarianism above aestheticism. While it rejected the tradition of neoclassicism, art nouveau was in some ways a very nostalgic, elitist movement, longing for the old days of individual craft and for style above utility.

Vienna's branch of the Europe-wide art-nouveau movement, known as *Jugendstil* (Young Style), had its genesis within the Akademie der bildenden Künste (Academy of Fine Arts). The academy was a strong supporter of neoclassicism and wasn't interested in supporting any artists who wanted to branch out, so in 1897 a group of rebels, including Klimt (1862–1918), seceded. Architects, including Otto Wagner, Joseph Maria Olbrich and Josef Hoffman, followed. At first, *Jugendstil* focused more on interior and exterior ornamentation than on the actual structure of buildings. Its motifs were organic – flowing hair, tendrils of plants, flames, waves – and signature materials included iron, stucco, and plain and stained glass.

By the second decade of the 20th century, Wagner and others were moving towards a uniquely Viennese style, called Secession. Many artists felt *Jugendstil* had become too elitist; others thought it had been debased by commercialism, as more and more '*Jugendstil*-look' artefacts were produced. Secessionism stripped some of the more decorative aspects of *Jugendstil* and concentrated more on functionalism, clarity and geometry.

Olbrich (1867–1908) and Hoffman (1870–1956) had both been pupils of Wagner, but as the 20th century developed so did their confidence and initiative, and they eventually ended up educating Wagner in the Secession style. Olbrich designed the Secession Hall, the showpiece of the Secession (p62), which was used to display other graphic and design works produced by the movement. The building is a physical representation of the movement's ideals, functionality and modernism, though it retains some striking decorative touches, such as the giant 'golden cabbage' on the roof. Interestingly, many scholars believe that Klimt drew the conceptual sketches for the building, and that Olbrich took Klimt's ideas and turned them into architectural reality.

Hoffman was inspired by the British Arts and Crafts movement, led by William Morris, and also by the stunning art-nouveau work of Glaswegian designer Charles Rennie Mackintosh. But by 1901 Hoffman had abandoned the flowing forms and bright colours of *Jugendstil* to concentrate on black and white and the square, becoming one of the earliest exponents of the Secession style. He is best known for setting up the Wiener Werkstätte design studio, but he was also an architect of note. His major work is in Brussels, but some of his lesser structures can be seen on the outskirts of Vienna. Hoffman's folkloric, anti-urban-sophisticate outlook on design later led to the founding of the *Hohe Warte* periodical and was picked up by the Austrian National Socialist Party – apparently Hoffman had no objection to his work being used to endorse Nazi principles.

The Wiener Werkstätte claimed a core membership of greats, including Klimt and Kolo Moser (1868–1918), who set out to change the face of domestic design. They wanted *Jugendstil* to appear not only in galleries and public buildings but in homes (albeit only well-off homes) all over the city. Determined that art wasn't just for walls, they made curtains, furniture, wallpaper, tiles, vases, trays, cutlery and bowls into objects of beauty, declaring, 'We recognise no difference between high art and low art. All art is good'.

Highly ideological, the WW (as they came to be known) joined a Europe-wide anticapitalist, anti-industrial movement espoused by designers such as English Arts and Crafts guru Morris. They promised equality of designers and craftspeople and paid their workers reasonably for their output. The WW thought they could improve the taste of the middle and lower classes – rapidly becoming accustomed to mass-produced, slightly shoddy homewares – by promoting individual design and quality craft for everyday objects. Hang the cost; they held that style was paramount.

The result was works of sublimely simple beauty – pure, abstract, geometric pieces. At the same time, artists such as Oskar Kokoschka were working for the WW, producing postcards and graphic books influenced by Japanese woodcuts and Austrian folk art. Bickering over how to price these gorgeous items (the WW was constantly running at a loss) tore the workshop apart, and in 1907 Moser left. After 1915 the workshop popularised and became, in essence, simply an interior-design company. In 1932 the WW closed, unable to compete with the cheap, mass-produced items being churned out by other companies.

OTTO WAGNER

Otto Wagner (1841–1918) was one of the most influential Viennese architects at the end of the 19th century (the era known as the *fin de siècle*). He was trained in the classical tradition and became a professor at the Akademie der bildenden Künste. His early work was in keeping with his education – he was responsible for some neo-Renaissance buildings along the Ringstrasse. But as the 20th century dawned he developed an art-nouveau style, with flowing lines and decorative motifs, and left the Academy to join the looser, more creative Secession movement in 1899. In the process he attracted public criticism – one of the reasons why his creative designs for Vienna's Historical Museum were never adopted. In the 20th century, Wagner began to strip away the more decorative aspects of his designs, concentrating instead on presenting the functional features of buildings in a creative way.

The most accessible of Wagner's works are his metro stations, scattered along the network. The metro project, which lasted from 1894 to 1901, included 35 stations as well as bridges and viaducts. Wagner's stations were to blend in with the surrounding architecture, wherever they were built, but all of them feature green-painted iron, some neoclassical touches (such as columns), and curvy, all-capitals *fin-de-siècle* fonts. The earlier stations, such as Hüttledorf-Hacking, show the cleaner lines of neoclassicism, while Karlsplatz, built in 1898, is a curvy, exuberant work of Secessionist gilding and luminous glass.

Wagner's Majolikahaus (1898–99) was one of his first Secessionist works. The facade of this apartment block, at Linke Wienzeile 40, is covered in a pink floral motif painted on majolica tiles. Inside, stair railings and elevator grilles are extraordinarily decorative, flowing like vines. Next door, the Linke Wienzeile Building at 38 was created by Wagner and Kolo Moser and is covered in gilded leaves and flowers – inside and out. Ten years later, Wagner designed another residence, this time at Neustiftgasse 40 – where the Linke Wienzeile blocks were designed for the elite, Neustiftgasse was built for workers. The contrast between the two, due both to the clientele and Wagner's shift in architectural focus, is striking. By 1910 Wagner was committed to a futuristic style, and Neustiftgasse is all flat planes and straight lines, with very little ornamentation. The well-lit interior is decorated with marble and metal in greys, blues and white, studded with metal rivets and floored with parquetry.

Perhaps Wagner's most impressive work is the Postsparkasse (p61) at Georg-Coch-Platz 2. Built between 1903 and 1912, this bank looms over the plaza, its exterior of thin panels of marble studded with aluminium rivets topped by statues of protective goddesses. Inside, a reinforced concrete and aluminium courtyard is roofed in glass, and all the building's doors, balustrades and radiators are also aluminium.

No-one embraced the sensualism of *Jugendstil* and Secessionism more than Klimt. Perhaps Vienna's most famous artist, Klimt was traditionally trained at the Akademie der bildenden Künste but soon left to pursue his own colourful and distinctive style. His works, which are a rejection of earlier naturalistic styles, are full of naked female figures, flowing patterns and symbolism and are decorated with gold finishing and strong colours. Even today, sales of his paintings cause a sizable stir in both art and media circles (p103).

A contemporary of Klimt's, Schiele (1890–1918) is classed as one of the most notable early existentialists and expressionists. His gritty, confrontational paintings and works on paper created a huge stir in the early 20th century. Schiele worked largely with the human figure, and many of his works are brilliantly executed minimalist line drawings splashed with patches of bright colour and usually featuring women in pornographic poses. Alongside his sketches, he also produced many self-portraits and a few large, breathtaking painted canvases. The other major exponent of Viennese expressionism was playwright, poet and painter Kokoschka (1886–1980), whose sometimes turbulent works show his interest in psychoanalytic imagery and baroque-era religious symbolism.

The last notable Secessionist – and the one most violently opposed to ornamentation – was Czech-born, Vienna-based designer Adolf Loos. In 1908 Loos wrote a polemic against the rest of the Secessionists, *Ornament and Crime,* slamming the movement's dedication to decorative detail. He was of the opinion that ornament was a waste of labour and material, and that high-quality materials were far more beautiful than any kind of decoration. Loos' work features minimal, linear decoration and geometric shapes. He preferred to work in high-quality materials including marble, glass, metal and wood. Up until 1909, Loos mainly designed interiors, but in the ensuing years he developed a passion for reinforced concrete and began designing houses with no external ornamentation. The result was a collection of incredibly flat, planar buildings with square windows that offended the royal elite no end. They are, however, key works in the history of modern architecture.

What to See

Aside from the Otto Wagner designs mentioned in the boxed text (p39), his beautiful flourishes can be seen in the Kirche am Steinhof (p126) and the Stadtbahn Pavillons (p81). Vienna's public transport system is partly the handiwork of Olbrich, who also designed the Westbahnhof. Hoffman spent many years on the Hohe Warte urban planning project, and in 1903 he designed the Purkersdorf Sanatorium (now restored), a health spa built from largely undecorated reinforced concrete, with an emphasis on planes and lines and using only sparse ornamentation of black-and-white tile and delicate geometric fenestration.

A prolific painter, Klimt's works hang in many galleries around Vienna. His earlier, classical mural work can be viewed in the Kunsthistorisches Museum (p69) and at the Universität Wien (p73), while his later murals, in his own distinctive style, grace the walls of Secession (p62) and MAK p60). An impressive number of his earlier sketches are housed in the Albertina (p70) and Leopold Museum (p86), and his fully fledged paintings are in the Leopold Museum, Wien Museum (p80), and Oberes Belvedere (p102).

The largest collection of Schiele works in the world belongs to the Leopold Museum. More of his exceptional talent is on display at the Wien Museum, Albertina and Oberes Belvedere; Kokoschka can also be seen at the Oberes Belvedere and Leopold.

One of the most accessible designs of Loos is the dim but glowing Loos American Bar (p175), a place of heavy ceilings and boxy booths just off Kärntner Strasse. Also worth a look are his public toilets (p64) on the Graben near the Pestsäule. The Loos Haus (p66), built between 1909 and 1911, is his most celebrated example, and a stark contrast to the spectacle of the Hofburg opposite. Loos's *Raumplan,* or 'plan of volumes', was a system he developed for internally organising houses; using this plan he later built the split-level Rufer and Moller houses. The Wien Museum provides a look into the personal world of Loos, with a reconstruction of a room from the architect's own house.

Pieces by the Wiener Werkstätte are on display at the MAK and can be bought from Woka (p142) and Altmann & Kühne (p131).

MODERN ARCHITECTURE

WWII not only brought an end to the Habsburg empire, but also the heady *fin-de-siècle* years. Vienna was struck by great poverty and serious social problems, and the Social Democrats stepped in to right the situation. The new leaders set about instituting a program of radical social reforms, earning the city the moniker 'Red Vienna'; one of their central themes was housing for the working class.

Between 50,000 and 60,000 apartments were built during the 1920s and early 1930s, many in gigantic apartment blocks. Designed as a city within a city, these superblocks featured central courtyards and community areas, and successfully solved the city's housing problem. Not everyone was pleased with the results; the right wing saw these mammoth structures as 'voter blocks' and potential socialist barracks, and some of Vienna's leading architects, Loos included, criticised the regime for failing to produce a unified aesthetic vision. Nevertheless, they are a lasting testament to the most successful socialist government Europe has yet seen.

Although Vienna experienced a mass of construction between WWII and the early 1970s (to replace war-torn damage), creatively they were lean years; most buildings were cheaply built and lacked any style to speak of. A rare few sport colourful tiled motifs; the working-class district of Meidling is particularly rich in these socially accepted graffiti pieces.

In the early 1970s Viennese architecture felt a new burst of life as architects took on the challenge of building mass housing that was both functional and beautiful, and creating shops and bars with individual flair. The likes of Hans Hollein, Robert Krier and Hermann Czech all expended their considerable energy and talent on such projects.

top picks

THE FIN-DE-SIÈCLE YEARS

- Klimt – *Beethoven Frieze* (p63); *The Kiss* (p103)
- Loos – Loos Haus (p66)
- Schiele – Anything in the Leopold Museum (p86)
- Wagner – Kirche am Steinhof (p126); Postsparkasse (p61)

Since the late 1980s a handful of multicoloured, haphazard-looking structures have appeared in Vienna; these buildings have been given a unique design treatment by maverick artist Friedensreich Hundertwasser. Hundertwasser felt that 'the straight line is Godless' and faithfully adhered to this principle in all his building projects, proclaiming that his uneven floors 'become a symphony, a melody for the feet, and bring back natural vibrations to man'. Although he complained that his more radical building projects were quashed by the authorities, he still transformed a number of council buildings with his unique style.

top picks

NOTABLE BUILDINGS

- **Schloss Belvedere** (p102)
- **Fernwärme** (p98)
- **Hofburg** (p65)
- **Karl-Marx-Hof** (p127)
- **Rathaus** (p73)
- **Schloss Schönbrunn** (p119)
- **Stephansdom** (p54)

With the arrival of the 21st century, Vienna is once again enjoying a building boom. While the Innere Stadt remains largely untouched by the brush of modernism (as a Unesco World Heritage site, it is obliged to retain its architectural uniformity), the outlying districts are experiencing an upsurge in contemporary architecture – some as entirely new edifices, others incorporating existing historical buildings. This new wave of clean, glass-and-steel creations juxtaposes the city's historical core, and to date is successfully dragging Vienna into a new architectural millennium.

What to See

The municipality buildings of Red Vienna are scattered throughout the city. The most famous is **Karl-Marx-Hof** (p127), by Wagner's pupil Karl Ehn, but the largest is Sandleiten Hof, which is at Matteottiplatz in Ottakring – it contains a staggering 1587 apartments.

Among the earliest works of Hollein is the Retti Candleshop at 01, Kohlmarkt 8; its facade features sheet aluminium and a doorway of two Rs back-to-back. The two jewellery stores Hollein designed for Schullin on the corner of Graben and Kohlmarkt have been described as 'architectural Fabergés': their smooth, granite facades appear riven and melting. The architect's best-known work is the **Haas Haus** (p54), whose facade seems to be peeling back to reveal the curtain wall of glass below. Hollein's message here is powerful and correct – modern architecture has a rightful place in the Innere Stadt – but its delivery is suspect.

Krier's low-line housing estates at Hirschstettnerstrasse in Donaustadt, built in 1982 and featuring inward-looking courtyards, are a striking example of Vienna's more recent housing projects. Czech's most celebrated work is the tiny yet immensely popular **Kleines Café** (p177).

Hundertwasser Haus (p106) attracts tourists by the busload, as does the nearby **KunstHausWien** (p106), but Hundertwasser's coup d'état is the **Fernwärme** incinerator (p98); opened in 1992, it's the most nonindustrial-looking heating plant you'll ever see.

Of the 21st-century architectural pieces, the **MuseumsQuartier** (p86) impresses the most. The **Gasometer** (p107) complex is another modern construction to adapt and incorporate historical buildings, while nearby at 03, Rennweg 97, Günter Domenig's T-Center, a long slither of glass and steel lacking any soft edges, is classed as one of the city's top modern conceptions.

CONTEMPORARY ARTS

Vienna has a thriving contemporary arts scene with a strong emphasis on confrontation, pushing boundaries and exploring new media – incorporating the artist into the art has a rich history in this city. Standing in stark contrast to the more self-consciously daring movements such as Actionism, Vienna's extensive Neue Wilde group emphasises traditional techniques and media.

Artist Eva Schlegel has become a strong force in both the local and international art scene – so powerful, in fact, that she was named curator of Austria's contribution to the 2011 Venice Biennale. Schlegel works in a number of media, exploring how associations are triggered by images. Some of her most powerful work has been photos of natural phenomena or candid street shots printed onto a chalky canvas then overlaid with layers and layers of oil paint and lacquer; they manage to be enjoyable on both a sensual and intellectual level.

One of Vienna's best-known contemporary artists, Arnulf Rainer, worked during the 1950s with automatic painting (letting his hand draw without trying to control it). He later delved into Actionism, foot painting, painting with chimpanzees, the creation of death masks, and photographing and reworking classic pieces by Schiele, van Gogh and Rembrandt. Rainer's work expands on the important Viennese existentialist tradition, started by the likes of Schiele. In 2009 an entire museum dedicated to the artist (Arnold Rainer Museum, in Baden, Lower Austria) opened. One exhibition incorporated his art into the architecture of the museum, which is housed in a former bathhouse – a series of crosses were strategically placed around the museum; for example, a colourful cross painting was mounted above a bathing basin, symbolising life/baptistry by pairing the cross with water.

Another prominent artist of note is Elke Krystufek, whose work is influenced by Schiele and Actionism. Krystufek is most well known for exposing herself to the viewer, primarily through her self-portraits utilising mirrors and automatic shutter release, and combinations/collages of herself with sex icons including Marilyn Monroe and Vivienne Westwood. She performed a famous public masturbation in the mid-1990s, and her most recent work comprises a series of paintings exploring the ongoing struggle between art, sex and money. Fans say her art is a contemporary take on the 19th-century notion of the artist as narcissist, and critics find her work disturbing and excessive, but nobody doubts her role in the contemporary Viennese art scene.

Two emerging artists to watch are Daniel Domig and Ingrid Pröller. Austrian-American Domig, whose contemplative paintings often exude an otherworldly dreamy quality, has recently presented a series of drawings done on paper in oil, pencil and ink. The work explores society's feelings of displacement and estrangement as humankind is torn between primitive and civilised needs. Pröller's paintings focus on youth – and often urban – culture. Her early works were dominated by small portraits of young regional sports heroes on canvas, but lately she has moved to large, multiple panels of fiery, deep swathes of colour, which depict young men and women against landscapes.

Actionism has been an important movement in Viennese art since the late 1950s. Once an important member of the group, Günter Brus now uses the more traditional media of painting and drawing for his message. Much of Brus's work is *Bilddichtungen* (image poems), combining shocking images (for example, a string attached to a penis being pulled by a woman's leg) with strong, graphic text that is an integral part of the picture. Some viewers may see Brus's work as abrasive self-hating pornography; others comment on the brilliant tension he creates between desire and repulsion. Hermann Nitsch, another founder of Actionism, conceived the Orgien Mysterien Theater (Orgies and Mysteries Theatre), a pseudopagan performance involving

VIENNESE ACTIONISM

Viennese Actionism spanned the period from 1957 to 1968 and was one of the most extreme of all modern art movements. It was linked to the Vienna Group, formed in the 1950s by HC Artmann, whose members experimented with surrealism and Dadaism in their sound compositions and textual montages. Actionism sought access to the unconscious through the frenzy of an extreme and very direct art; the actionists quickly moved from pouring paint over the canvas and slashing it with knives, to using bodies (live people, dead animals) as 'brushes', and using blood, excrement, eggs, mud and whatever came to hand as 'paint'. The traditional canvas was soon dispensed with altogether and the artist's body instead became the canvas. This turned the site of art into a deliberated event (a scripted 'action', staged both privately and publicly) and even merged art with reality.

It was a short step from self-painting to inflicting wounds upon the body, and engaging in physical and psychological endurance tests. For 10 years the Actionists scandalised the press and public, inciting violence and panic – but they got plenty of publicity. Often poetic, humorous and aggressive, the actions became increasingly politicised, addressing the sexual and social repression that pervaded the Austrian state. The press release for *Art in Revolution* (1968) gives the lowdown on what could be expected at a typical action: '[Günter] Brus undressed, cut himself with a razor, urinated in a glass and drank his urine, smeared his body with faeces and sang the Austrian national anthem while masturbating (for which he was arrested for degrading state symbols and sentenced to six months detention)'. This was, not entirely surprisingly, the last action staged in Vienna.

crucifixions, animal slaughter, buckets of blood and guts, and music and dance. Like Brus's work, many find Nitsch's art incomprehensible, but since 1962 he has held around 100 such events.

While the Viennese have an unmistakable penchant for the avant-garde, there is still space in the city's contemporary art world for more-traditional works. In the 1980s, when painting was supposedly dead as an art form (replaced, apparently, by conceptual art, multimedia and installation art), the Neue Wilde group performed CPR on its still-warm corpse, creating a style of painting that was more about the paint on the canvas than the concept behind it. The Neue Wilde – which includes painters such as Siegfried Anzinger, Herbert Brandl, Maria Lassnig and Otto Zitko – is committed to maintaining the Austrian painting tradition, whether figurative or abstract, and their work crosses a variety of subject matter and styles. Brandl, for example, paints large-scale landscapes where literal representations of mountains and forests dissolve into abstract metaphors and symbols.

LITERATURE

Lacking the variety of German literature or the vein of 'isn't tragedy hysterical?' running through Czech literature, Viennese writing seems to be bowed by the weight of its authors' history. Living under and dealing with the end of an autocratic empire, the guilt of Anschluss, the horror of Nazism, the emotional damage dealt by WWII, neo-Nazism and the general nastiness of human beings and bleakness of life are all very, very popular themes in Viennese literature. Not content to deal with difficult subject matter, Viennese authors have regularly embraced obscure and experimental styles of writing. Overall, the Viennese oeuvre is earnest, difficult and disturbing, but quite frequently it is intensely rewarding.

The *Nibelungenlied* (Song of the Nibelungs) was one of Vienna's earliest works, written around 1200 by an unknown hand and telling a tale of passion, faithfulness and revenge in the Burgundian court at Worms. But Austria's literary tradition really took off around the end of the 19th century, the same time as the Secessionists (p37) and Sigmund Freud were creating their own waves. Karl Kraus (1874–1936) was one of the period's major figures; his apocalyptic drama *Die Letzten Tage der Menschheit* (The Last Days of Mankind) employed a combination of reports, interviews and press extracts to tell its tale – a very innovative style for its time. Peter Altenberg (1859–1919) was a drug addict, an alcoholic, a fan of young girls and a poet who depicted the bohemian lifestyle of Vienna. Hermann Broch (1886–1951) was very much a part of Viennese cafe society. A scientist at heart, Broch believed literature had the metaphysical answers to complement new scientific discoveries. His masterwork was *Der Tod des Virgil* (The Death of Virgil), begun in a Nazi concentration camp in 1938 and finished in 1945, after his emigration to the USA.

Robert Musil (1880–1942) was one of the most important 20th-century writers, but he only achieved international recognition after his death. His major literary achievement, *Der Mann ohne Eigenschaften* (The Man without Qualities), remained – at seven volumes – unfinished. Heimito von Doderer (1896–1966) grew up in Vienna; his magnum opus was *Die Dämonen* (The Demons), an epic fictional depiction of the end of the monarchy and the first years of the Austrian Republic. A friend of Freud, a librettist for Strauss and a victim of Nazi book burnings, Stefan Zweig (1881–1942) had a rich social pedigree. A poet, playwright, translator, paranoiac and pacifist, Zweig believed Nazism had been conceived specifically with him in mind and when he became convinced in 1942 that Hitler would take over the world, he killed himself in exile in Brazil. Arthur Schnitzler (1862–1931), another friend of Freud, was a prominent Jewish writer in Vienna's *fin de siècle* years. His play *Reigen* (Hands Around), set in 1900, was described by Hitler as 'Jewish filth'; it gained considerable fame in the English-speaking world as Max Ophul's film *La Ronde*. Joseph Roth (1894–1939), primarily a journalist, wrote about the concerns of Jews in exile and of Austrians uncertain of their identity at the end of the empire. His recently rereleased *What I Saw: Reports from Berlin* is part of an upsurge of interest in this fascinating writer; his most famous works, *Radetzky March* and *The Emperor's Tomb*, are both gripping tales set in the declining Austro-Hungarian empire.

Perhaps it's something in the water, but the majority of contemporary Viennese authors (at least, those translated into English) are grim, guilt-ridden, angry and sometimes incomprehensibly avant-garde. Thomas Bernhard (1931–89) was born in Holland but grew up and lived in Austria. He was obsessed with disintegration and death, and in later works such as *Holzfällen:*

TOP BOOKS

- *Dicta and Contradicta,* Karl Kraus (1909) – Fans of Dorothy Parker and Oscar Wilde will want to get their hands on this book of aphorisms by the 1920s satirist and social critic. Selections suitable for toilet-wall scribbling include 'Art serves to rinse out our eyes'.
- *The Play of the Eyes,* Elias Canetti (1985) – The third in this Nobel Prize winner's autobiographical trilogy, *Eyes* is set in Vienna just before the Anschluss. Many believe it is a work of genius; it covers the span of human experiences.
- *The Death of Virgil,* Hermann Broch (1945) – Not just a novel, but a complete overhaul of what a novel can be, *The Death of Virgil* is one of German-language literature's stylistic ground-breakers (though it has some similarities to James Joyce's *Ulysses*). Covering the last day of a poet's life, this book is hard, hard work.
- *Bambi,* Felix Salten (1923) – Banned by the Nazis but beloved by alleged Nazi-sympathiser Walt Disney, this is the book that launched the movie that launched a million crying sprees. Nonpurists should look out for the scratch-and-sniff version, *Bambi's Fragrant Forest*.
- *The Radetzky March,* Joseph Roth (1932) – A study of one family affected by the end of an empire, the themes of *The Radetzky March* are applicable to any society emerging from a long-hated, but at least understood, regime. In some ways, it is about life after God.
- *The Third Man,* Graham Greene (1950) – Put some time aside to read the book Greene designed as a screenplay: there is a lot of intriguing and easily missed detail in this complex story of death, morality and the black market in the rubble of postwar Vienna.
- *Beware of Pity,* Stefan Zweig (1938) – Almost Russian in its melancholic psychological complication, *Beware of Pity* weighs logic against emotion in this tale of a hedonistic soldier who lacks direction until he becomes accidentally entangled with a lame girl.
- *Across,* Peter Handke (1986) – Another cheery Viennese novel, *Across* follows an observer of life drawn into 'real being' after he whimsically murders someone. Pretty darn postmodern.
- *The Devil in Vienna,* Doris Orgel (1978) – A book for older kids, *The Devil in Vienna* is the story of two blood-sisters in 1938 Vienna, one Jewish, the other from a Nazi family, and their attempts to maintain their friendship. May get kids all riled up, in a 'why is the world so unjust?' way.
- *Greed,* Elfriede Jelinek (2006) – She's a witty and clever writer, but Jelinek hates all her characters and has a long-standing love/hate relationship with Austria. *Greed* tells the story of a debt-ridden country police officer, his relationships with the townspeople and the lonely local women he manipulates – the novel resounds with the general theme that greed corrupts.

Eine Erregung (Cutting Timber: An Irritation) turned to controversial attacks against social conventions and institutions. His novels are seamless (no chapters or paragraphs, few full stops) and seemingly repetitive, but surprisingly readable once you get into them.

The best-known contemporary writer is Peter Handke (born 1942). His postmodern, abstract output encompasses innovative and introspective prose works and stylistic plays. The provocative novelist Elfriede Jelinek (born 1946), winner of the Nobel Prize for Literature in 2004, dispenses with direct speech, indulges in strange flights of fancy and takes a very dim view of humanity. Her works are highly controversial, often disturbingly pornographic, and either loved or hated by critics. Elisabeth Reichart (born 1953) is considered an important – if obscure and ferocious – writer, producing novels and essays concerned with criticism of the patriarchy and investigations of Nazi-related Austrian guilt, both during WWII and more recently. Edith Kneifl is also firmly on the map as one of Austria's most well-known crime writers. As a trained psychoanalyst, she has published crime stories since the late 1980s, many based in Vienna. See p82 for an interview with Austria's queen of crime.

Many Viennese authors are also playwrights – perhaps the Viennese fondness for the avant-garde encourages the crossing of artistic boundaries. Schnitzler, Bernhard, Jelinek and Handke have all had their plays performed at the premier playhouse in Austria, Vienna's own Burgtheater.

The first great figure in the modern era of theatre was the playwright Franz Grillparzer (1791–1872), who anticipated Freudian themes in his plays, which are still performed. Other influential playwrights who still regularly get an airing are Johann Nestroy, known for his satirical farces, and Ferdinand Raimund, whose works include *Der Alpenkönig* (King of the Alps) and *Der Menchenfiend* (The Misanthrope).

Vienna has a huge range of federal, municipal and private theatres supporting the work of playwrights and librettists; in fact, the Burgtheater (p196) is the premier performance venue in the German-speaking world. The Akademietheater, under the same management, is a more intimate venue that generally stages contemporary plays. The Theater in der Josefstadt (p197) is known for the modern style of acting evolved by Max Reinhardt while Theater an der Wien (p196) favours musicals.

top picks

MUSEUMS & GALLERIES

- Albertina (p70)
- Österreichische Galerie (p102) at Schloss Belvedere
- Kunsthistorisches Museum (p69)
- Leopold Museum (p86)
- Secession (p62)

CINEMA

Modern Viennese cinema is a bleak landscape of corrupt and venal characters beating their children and dogs while struggling with a legacy of hatred and guilt. That's a slight exaggeration, but contemporary film does seem to favour naturalism over escapism, violent sex over flowery romance, ambivalence and dislocation over happy endings where all the ends are tied.

The film industry is lively and productive, turning out Cannes-sweepers such as Michael Haneke, of *The Piano Teacher* fame, and festival darlings such as Jessica Hausner, director of the confronting *Lovely Rita*. A healthy serving of government arts funding certainly helps, as does the Viennese passion for a trip to the *Kino* (cinema), where local, independent films are as well attended as blockbusters by Graz-boy-made-good Arnie Schwarzenegger. A yearly festival, Viennale (p198), draws experimental and fringe films from all over Europe, keeping the creative juices flowing, while art-house cinemas such as the gorgeous *Jugendstil* Breitenseer Lichtspiele (p198) keep the Viennese proud of their rich cinematic history.

That history has turned out several big names ('big' in that they've moved to America and been accepted by Hollywood). Director Fritz Lang made the legendary *Metropolis* (1926), the

TOP FILMS

- *Indien* (1993) – Two of Vienna's greatest comedy artists, Hader and Dorfer, are government workers on the road around Vienna and the surrounding countryside checking kitchen hygiene standards. Very funny but quietly tragic. Directed by Paul Harather.
- *Lovely Rita* (2001) – Director Jessica Hausner shot her first feature film on digital with a cast of nonactor novices and an improvised script. *Lovely Rita* tells the story of a young Viennese woman struggling to escape her bourgeois life through love, but who ends up murdering her parents.
- *Foreigners Out!* (2002) – Documentary about a protest event staged in Vienna in 2000 on the election of Jorg Haider. A concentration camp for asylum seekers was installed near the Opera; immigrants – in a parody of *Big Brother* – could be voted out of the country. Worth seeking out. Directed by Paul Poet.
- *Twinni* (2003) – A period piece set in 1980, *Twinni* is the story of a Viennese teenager who moves to the country in the midst of her parents' divorce. Achingly awkward Jana suffers the attentions of a boy and the scorn of the Catholic church in this sweet film. Directed by Ulrike Schweiger.
- *The White Ribbon* (2009) – Winning scads of awards, including the 2009 Palme d'Or at Cannes and the 2010 Golden Globe for best foreign language film, director Michael Haneke continues his preference for groundbreaking, eye-opening, discomfiting projects with this film, which explores the extensive layers of terrorism. *The White Ribbon* recounts an elderly tailor's memories of strange and disturbing events that occurred shortly before the outbreak of WWI during a year he spent as a teacher in a small German village.
- *Dog Days* (2001) – On Vienna's hottest day in years, the suburbs combust. Six intertwined stories of bondage, sexual abuse, private investigators, car theft and marital breakdown make up a surprisingly humorous film. Directed by Ulrich Seidl.
- *Siegfried* (1924) – Austrian director Fritz Lang turns his hand to the legendary *Nibelungenlied*. It may be silent, black-and-white and not have any special effects, but this remains one of the best action films ever made.
- *Funny Games* (1997) – In another gritty Haneke film, a sadistic duo move from house to house in Salzburg's lake district, kidnapping, torturing and then murdering families. Certainly no funny game. Haneke remade the film in English in 2008.

THE THIRD MAN

'I had paid my last farewell to Harry a week ago, when his coffin was lowered into the frozen February ground, so that it was with incredulity that I saw him pass by, without a sign of recognition, among the host of strangers in the Strand.' Thus wrote Graham Greene on the back of an envelope. There it stayed, for many years, an idea without a context. Then Sir Alexander Korda asked him to write a film about the four-power occupation of postwar Vienna.

Greene had an opening scene and a framework, but no plot. He flew to Vienna in 1948 and searched with increasing desperation for inspiration. Nothing came to mind until, with his departure imminent, Greene had lunch with a British intelligence officer who told him about the underground police who patrolled the huge network of sewers beneath the city, and the black-market trade in penicillin. Greene put the two ideas together and created his story.

Shot in Vienna in the same year, the film perfectly captures the atmosphere of postwar Vienna using an excellent play of shadow and light. The plot is simple but gripping; Holly Martin, an out-of-work writer played by Joseph Cotton, travels to Vienna at the request of his old school mate Harry Lime (played superbly by Orson Welles), only to find him dead under mysterious circumstances. Doubts over the death drag Martin into the black-market penicillin racket and the path of the multinational force controlling Vienna. Accompanying the first-rate script, camera work and acting is a mesmerising soundtrack. After filming one night, director Carol Reed was dining at a *Heuriger* and fell under the spell of Anton Karas' zither playing. Although Karas could neither read nor write music, Reed flew him to London to record the soundtrack. His bouncing, staggering 'Harry Lime Theme' dominated the film, became a chart hit and earned Karas a fortune.

The Third Man was an instant success, and has aged with grace and style. It won first prize at Cannes in 1949, the Oscar for Best Camera for a Black and White Movie in 1950, and was selected by the British Film Institute as 'favourite British film of the 20th century' in 1999. For years, the Burg Kino (p198) has screened the film on a weekly basis.

The film's popularity has spawned the Third Man Private Collection (p83) and fans of the film can follow a short self-guided tour of the city on our Third Man walking tour (p140). True aficionados may want to take the more detailed guided tour run by Vienna Walks, the Third Man Tour (☎ 774 89 01; www.viennawalks.com; departs U4 Stadtpark station Johannesgasse exit; €17), conducted in English every Monday and Friday at 4pm. It covers all the main locations used in the film, including a glimpse of the underground sewers, home to 2.5 million rats. You'll discover that the sewers are not linked, so unfortunately it's impossible to cross the city underground as Harry Lime did in the film.

story of a society enslaved by technology, and *The Last Will of Dr Mabuse* (1932), during which an incarcerated madman spouts Nazi doctrine. Billy Wilder, writer and director of massive hits including *Some Like it Hot*, *The Apartment* and *Sunset Boulevard*, was Viennese, though he moved to the States early in his career. Hedy Lamarr (not to be confused with Hedley Lamarr of *Blazing Saddles* fame) – Hollywood glamour girl and inventor of submarine guidance systems – was also born in Vienna. Klaus Maria Brandauer, star of *Out of Africa* and *Mephisto*, is another native. And Vienna itself has been the star of movies such as *The Third Man*, *The Night Porter* and *Before Sunrise*.

These days, the big name is Haneke, whose films tend to feature large doses of sadism and masochism. His film *The Piano Teacher*, based on the novel by Viennese writer Jelinek, won three awards at Cannes in 2001 and *The White Ribbon*, a dark tale about a family in Germany shortly before WWI, won the Palme d'Or (Cannes' highest prize) in 2009 and was nominated for two Academy Awards.

Documentary maker Ulrich Seidl has made *Jesus, You Know*, following six Viennese Catholics as they visit their church for prayer, and *Animal Love*, an investigation of Viennese suburbanites who have abandoned human company for that of pets. In 2001 he branched into features with *Dog Days* and his latest, *Import Export*, was nominated at Cannes in 2007. Hausner has made several short films and released her first feature, *Lovely Rita*, the story of a suburban girl who kills her parents in cold blood, in 2001. Her most recent film, *Lourdes*, about a wheelchair-bound woman who makes a pilgrimage to Lourdes and finds that she can suddenly walk, received the prize for best film at the 2009 Vienna International Film Festival.

Recently, Austria has been celebrating Viennese-born actor Christoph Waltz. Waltz, a virtual unknown outside Austria and Germany until he was cast in Quentin Tarantino's *Inglourious Basterds*, shot to international fame for his portrayal of the film's pivotal character, SS Colonel Hans Landa. The role won him the 2010 Academy Award for Best Supporting Actor.

NEIGHBOURHOODS

top picks

NEIGHBOURHOODS

To understand Vienna's urban topography, imagine a lake with concentric ripples. The ancient Romans cast the first stone into this lake when they created Vindobona, the military outpost based around Hoher Markt in central Vienna. From the 13th century Vienna was fortified by a wall with turrets and, beyond this, with sloped clearings that made approaching invaders (most famously, the Ottoman Turks) vulnerable to the city's defenders. These clearings metamorphosed into a ring road that today encircles the Innere Stadt. Each section of this ring road has its own name (eg Opernring), but the Viennese simply call it 'Der Ring' or 'Die Ringstrasse'.

Wedged between the Ringstrasse and the next major circular road, the Gürtel, are high density *Vorstädte* (inner suburbs). In medieval times, if you lived in one of these during an attack you either fled or hung around to watch your house burn. Inner suburbs such as Josefstadt and Alsergrund were ravaged by fire in the second Turkish siege of 1683.

Beyond these *Vorstädte* are today's suburbs *(Vororte),* which by European standards have less of an inner-city character. These suburbs give way to Greater Vienna, which is flanked in the north and west by the picturesque Wienerwald (Vienna Woods).

Vienna's city planners have for centuries made all this more easily governable by carving it into administrative districts, each with its own number – today there are 23.

Central Vienna (corresponding roughly to the Innere Stadt district) is a Unesco World Heritage site with medieval, Renaissance, baroque, late-19th century and modern and postmodern architectural masterpieces. Understandably, it can get overrun with visitors in summer, but quiet pockets can always be found (see p64).

Each of Vienna's *Vorstädte* has a unique character and flair – connoisseurs of inner-city life will love exploring these for interesting architecture or to dig up places for eating, drinking, shopping or high-kicking into the night.

Landstrasse – district 03 – is situated across the Wien River from Central Vienna in the southeast and hugs the Danube Canal. For the visitor, the main reason for coming here will be magnificent Schloss Belvedere or to visit the museum dedicated to Friedensreich Hundertwasser. It tends to be low on restaurants and nightlife hotspots.

The districts Wieden (04), Margareten (05), Mariahilf (06) and Neubau (07) form an extraordinarily lively ribbon south and west of the centre (Vorstadt Southwest) that is gradually experiencing 'gentry creep' as affluent Viennese move in. These *Vorstädte* are easily the most exciting in Vienna and you can expect to spend a lot of time in them. Wieden and Mariahilf are blessed with the Naschmarkt, a food market medina of stalls, and with parkland and high-profile attractions around Karlsplatz. Margareten has little in the way of heavyweight sights but exudes strong local flavour. Mariahilf has the bristling and increasingly popular Gumpendorfer Strasse, and Vienna's mainstream shopping strip, Mariahilfer Strasse. Neubau, directly north of this, is in parts alternative, in parts gentrified, such as in the quaint Spittelberg area, and in other quarters more alternative-chic. It's flanked in the east by a Vienna cultural 'must-see': the MuseumsQuartier.

Josefstadt (08) and the Alsergrund (09) in the Vorstadt Northwest neighbourhood have a lively university campus and some quality sights such as Palais Liechtenstein (Liechtenstein Museum). Outside the Gürtel, Schönbrunn (Southwest and the Gürtel) is a glorious baroque palace and gardens, whereas Leopoldstadt east of the Danube Canal – a Jewish quarter in the Middle Ages – has an unusual, oddly abandoned atmosphere and begs rediscovery. In Greater Vienna, the Vienna Woods beckon, along with wine taverns and a handful of good sights.

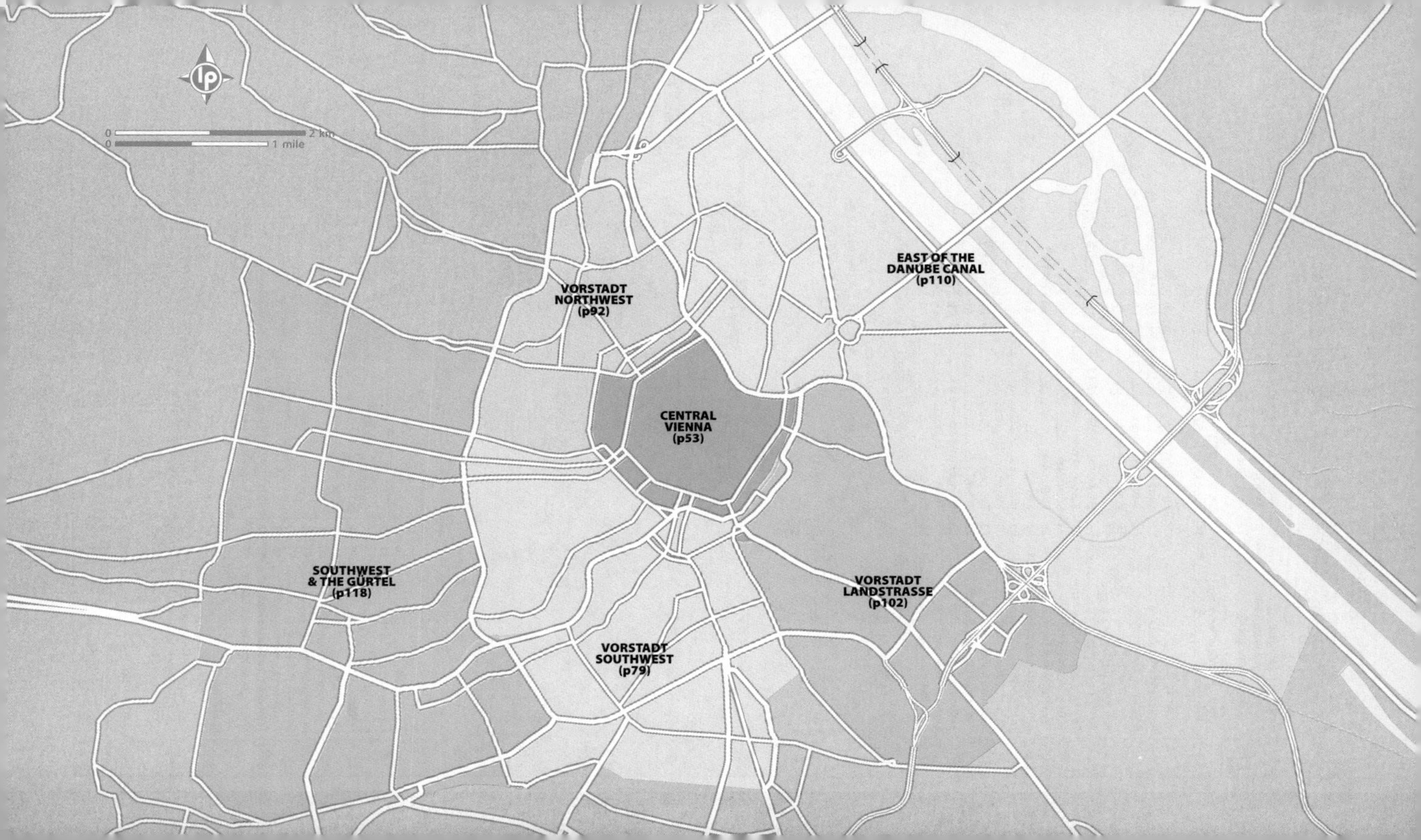
0 2 km
0 1 mile
VORSTADT NORTHWEST (p92)
EAST OF THE DANUBE CANAL (p110)
CENTRAL VIENNA (p53)
SOUTHWEST & THE GÜRTEL (p118)
VORSTADT LANDSTRASSE (p102)
VORSTADT SOUTHWEST (p79)

GREATER VIENNA

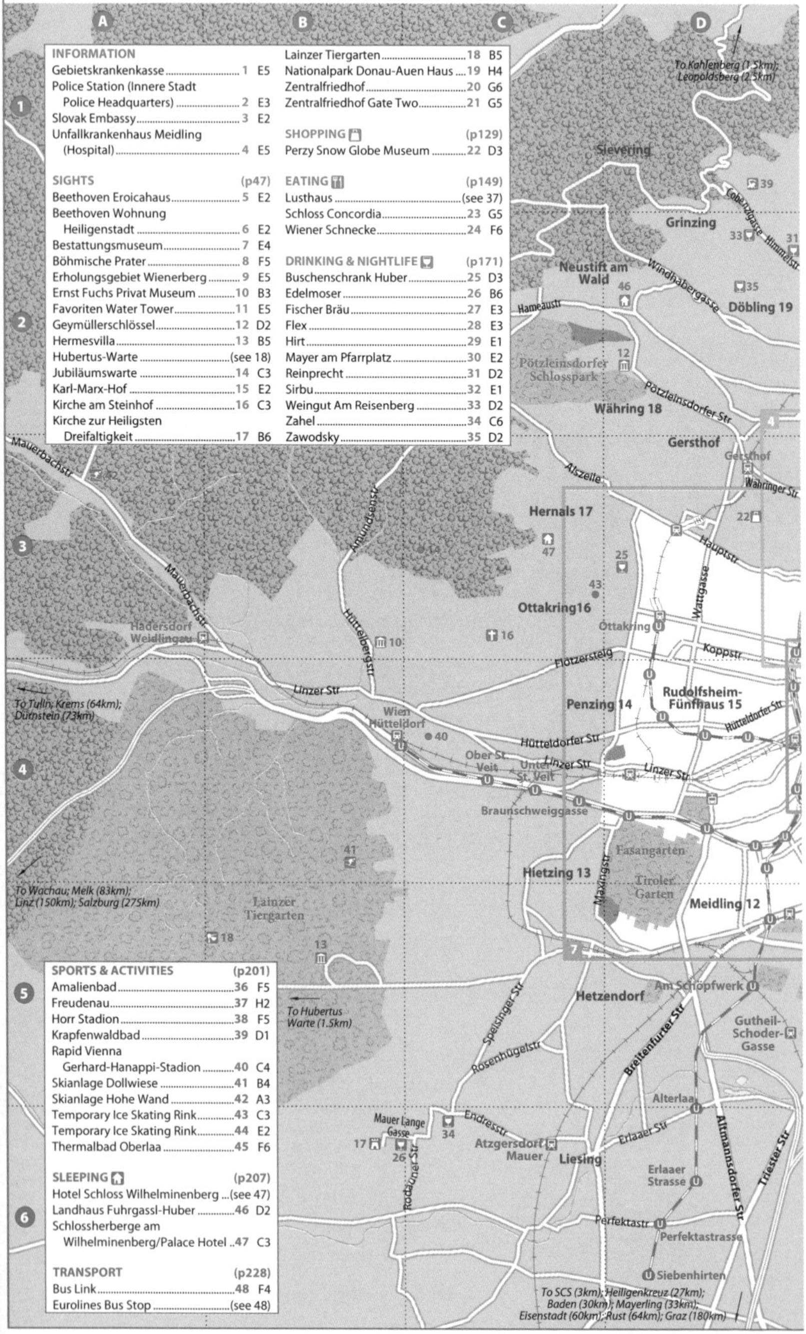

INFORMATION

- Gebietskrankenkasse ... 1 E5
- Police Station (Innere Stadt Police Headquarters) ... 2 E3
- Slovak Embassy ... 3 E2
- Unfallkrankenhaus Meidling (Hospital) ... 4 E5

SIGHTS (p47)

- Beethoven Eroicahaus ... 5 E2
- Beethoven Wohnung Heiligenstadt ... 6 E2
- Bestattungsmuseum ... 7 E4
- Böhmische Prater ... 8 F5
- Erholungsgebiet Wienerberg ... 9 E5
- Ernst Fuchs Privat Museum ... 10 B3
- Favoriten Water Tower ... 11 E5
- Geymüllerschlössel ... 12 D2
- Hermesvilla ... 13 B5
- Hubertus-Warte ... (see 18)
- Jubiläumswarte ... 14 C3
- Karl-Marx-Hof ... 15 E2
- Kirche am Steinhof ... 16 C3
- Kirche zur Heiligsten Dreifaltigkeit ... 17 B6
- Lainzer Tiergarten ... 18 B5
- Nationalpark Donau-Auen Haus ... 19 H4
- Zentralfriedhof ... 20 G6
- Zentralfriedhof Gate Two ... 21 G5

SHOPPING (p129)

- Perzy Snow Globe Museum ... 22 D3

EATING (p149)

- Lusthaus ... (see 37)
- Schloss Concordia ... 23 G5
- Wiener Schnecke ... 24 F6

DRINKING & NIGHTLIFE (p171)

- Buschenschrank Huber ... 25 D3
- Edelmoser ... 26 B6
- Fischer Bräu ... 27 E3
- Flex ... 28 E3
- Hirt ... 29 E1
- Mayer am Pfarrplatz ... 30 E2
- Reinprecht ... 31 D2
- Sirbu ... 32 E1
- Weingut Am Reisenberg ... 33 D2
- Zahel ... 34 C6
- Zawodsky ... 35 D2

SPORTS & ACTIVITIES (p201)

- Amalienbad ... 36 F5
- Freudenau ... 37 H2
- Horr Stadion ... 38 F5
- Krapfenwaldbad ... 39 D1
- Rapid Vienna Gerhard-Hanappi-Stadion ... 40 C4
- Skianlage Dollwiese ... 41 B4
- Skianlage Hohe Wand ... 42 A3
- Temporary Ice Skating Rink ... 43 C3
- Temporary Ice Skating Rink ... 44 E2
- Thermalbad Oberlaa ... 45 F6

SLEEPING (p207)

- Hotel Schloss Wilhelminenberg ... (see 47)
- Landhaus Fuhrgassl-Huber ... 46 D2
- Schlossherberge am Wilhelminenberg/Palace Hotel ... 47 C3

TRANSPORT (p228)

- Bus Link ... 48 F4
- Eurolines Bus Stop ... (see 48)

To Kahlenberg (1.5km); Leopoldsberg (2.5km)
To Tulln; Krems (64km); Dürnstein (73km)
To Wachau; Melk (83km); Linz (150km); Salzburg (275km)
To Hubertus Warte (1.5km)
To SCS (3km); Heiligenkreuz (27km); Baden (30km); Mayerling (33km); Eisenstadt (60km); Rust (64km); Graz (180km)

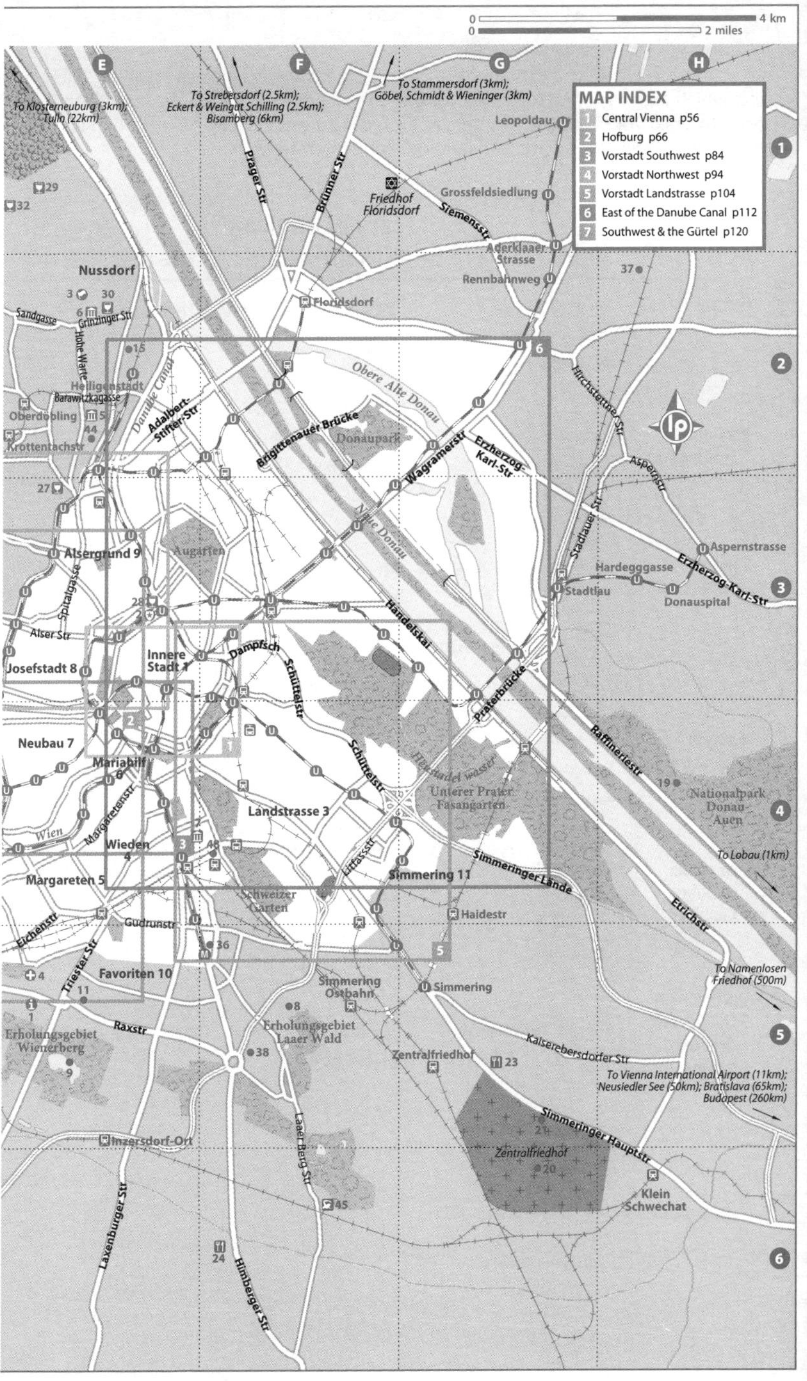
MAP INDEX
1 Central Vienna p56
2 Hofburg p66
3 Vorstadt Southwest p84
4 Vorstadt Northwest p94
5 Vorstadt Landstrasse p104
6 East of the Danube Canal p112
7 Southwest & the Gürtel p120
To Klosterneuburg (3km); Tulln (22km)
To Strebersdorf (2.5km); Eckert & Weingut Schilling (2.5km); Bisamberg (6km)
To Stammersdorf (3km); Göbel, Schmidt & Wieninger (3km)
Leopoldau
Grossfeldsiedlung
Aderklaaer Strasse
Rennbahnweg
Friedhof Floridsdorf
Floridsdorf
Nussdorf
Heiligenstadt
Oberdöbling
Obere Alte Donau
Donaupark
Neue Donau
Augarten
Alsergrund 9
Josefstadt 8
Innere Stadt 1
Neubau 7
Mariahilf 6
Wieden 4
Margareten 5
Landstrasse 3
Favoriten 10
Simmering 11
Stadtlau
Hardegggasse
Donauspital
Aspernstrasse
Unterer Prater Fasangarten
Nationalpark Donau-Auen
To Lobau (1km)
Schweizer Garten
Haidestr
Simmering Ostbahn
Simmering
To Namenlosen Friedhof (500m)
Erholungsgebiet Laaer Wald
Erholungsgebiet Wienerberg
Zentralfriedhof
To Vienna International Airport (11km); Neusiedler See (50km); Bratislava (65km); Budapest (260km)
Inzersdorf-Ort
Klein Schwechat
Prager Str
Brünner Str
Siemensstr
Brigittenauer Brücke
Wagramerstr
Erzherzog-Karl-Str
Hirschstettner Str
Stadlauer Str
Asperstr
Handelskai
Praterbrücke
Raffineriestr
Simmeringer Lände
Etrichstr
Dampfsch
Schüttelstr
Heustadelwasser
Littasstr
Adalbert-Stifter-Str
Danube Canal
Sandgasse
Grinzinger Str
Hohe Warte
Barawitzkagasse
Krottenbachstr
Spitalgasse
Alser Str
Margaretenstr
Wien
Gudrunstr
Eichenstr
Triester Str
Raxstr
Kaiserebersdorfer Str
Simmeringer Hauptstr
Laaer Berg Str
Laxenburger Str
Himberger Str
0 4 km
0 2 miles

ITINERARY BUILDER

The table below allows you to plan a day's worth of activities in any area of the city. Simply select which area you wish to explore, and then mix and match from the corresponding listings to build your day. The first item in each cell represents a well-known highlight of the area, while the other items are more off-the-beaten-track gems.

AREA / ACTIVITIES	Sights	Eating, Drinking & Nightlife	The Arts
Central Vienna	Hofburg (p65) Justizpalast (p74) Jesuitenkirche (p61)	Österreicher im MAK (p156) Loos American Bar (p175) Palais Palffy (p187)	Hofburg Concert Halls (p193) Staatsoper (p195) Porgy & Bess (p190)
Vorstadt Southwest	Karlskirche (p80) MuseumsQuartier (p86) Third Man Private Collection (p83)	Restaurant Collio (p158) Café Drechsler (p179) Rote Bar (p190)	Radiokulturhaus (p195) Schikaneder (p199) Top Kino (p199)
Vorstadt Northwest	Liechtenstein Museum (p96) Servitenkirche (p98) Pathologisch-Anatomisches Bundesmuseum (p93)	Stomach (p165) Halbestadt Bar (p182) Café Concerto (p189)	Wiener Residenzorchester (p196) Vienna's English Theatre (p197) Theater in der Josefstadt (p197)
Vorstadt Landstrasse	Schloss Belvedere (p102) St Marxer Friedhof (p107) KunstHausWien (p106)	Gasthaus Wild (p167) Salm Bräu (p189) Strandbar Herrmann (p183)	Konzerthaus (p194) Arnold Schönberg Center (p193) Arena (p188)
East of the Danube Canal	Riesenrad (p111) Wiener Kriminalmuseum (p114) Donauinsel (p115)	Restaurant Vincent (p168) Tachles (p183) Pratersauna (p188)	Odeon (p194) Kino Unter Sternen (p199)
Southwest & the Gürtel/ Greater Vienna	Schloss Schönbrunn (p119) Friedhof der Namenlosen (p126) Kirche am Steinhof (p126)	Noi (p169) 10er Marie (p184) Reigen (p190)	Orangery (p194) Marionettentheater (p197)

CENTRAL VIENNA

Drinking & Nightlife p174; Eating p154; Shopping p130; Sleeping p209

The Central Vienna neighbourhood (*'der Erste'* or the Innere Stadt) is not only the oldest part of Austria's capital, it is the most spectacular and exciting from the angle of formal culture. It bubbles over with high-profile cultural sights, and if time is limited this is the part of town to explore first. But you're also going to have to do some prioritising because of the sheer number of museums (about 60 in the Innere Stadt) and cultural richness (to help you, we've put together some recommendations – opposite). In size, however, the Innere Stadt is mercifully compact – smaller than Central Park in New York or about twice the size of London's Hyde Park. You can walk across it in less than an hour but spend a couple of lifetimes exploring its many different faces.

The Innere Stadt is a Unesco World Heritage site. It encompasses Roman excavations, Gothic and baroque architecture, as well as neoclassical and revivalist buildings that were erected along the Ringstrasse on its perimeter from the mid-19th century. Sprinkled among these are numerous fine examples of *Jugendstil* (art nouveau) and Secession styles by masters such as Alfred Loos – including some public toilets he designed – and Secession guru Otto Wagner.

The very heart of the Innere Stadt is Stephansplatz, where Vienna's spectacular Gothic cathedral towers, forming the single landmark from which distances from the centre are measured. It is indisputably the most recognisable building in Vienna, even if its Gothic design makes it not necessarily the most popular among Viennese. For the visitor it's useful for orientation because some of the district's most important thoroughfares – Kärntner Strasse, Graben and Rotenturmstrasse – lead from here to other attractions.

East of Stephansplatz are some lovely courtyards, such as Heiligenkreuzerhof, and this area has a musical focus, with the Haus der Musik (House of Music), Mozarthaus and a memorial to Johann Strauss the Younger. It also has a good sprinkling of baroque churches and the Museum für angewandte Kunst (Museum of Applied Arts).

Southwest of Stephansdom is a cultural highlight of another kind: the Hofburg. This monumental palace was home to the Habsburgs for about six centuries and today forms a magnificent ensemble of architecture, state offices and museums set around historic squares. The Spanish Riding School (famous for its performing Lipizzaner horses) is based here and you can view the former imperial apartments and priceless treasures of the Habsburgs, or visit the numerous museums inside and around the Hofburg and its historic squares. An artistic highlight is the Kunsthistorisches Museum (Museum of Art History).

North of Hofburg is a sprinkling of good sights, including Vienna's Rathaus (town hall) and the open spaces around it, the unusual Justizpalast (Palace of Justice), and the national parliament. The vicinity north of Stephansplatz to the Danube Canal takes in the traditional Jewish quarter of town and the lively but tacky 'Bermuda Triangle' of bars and handful of seedy red-light clubs.

While Central Vienna can be easily covered by foot, the U1 and U3 U-Bahn lines conveniently cross the centre. Tram 1 covers all of the Ringstrasse except between Kärntner Ring and Julius-Raab-Platz, where tram 2 takes over. Tram D connects the Ringstrasse with Belvedere (in the Landstrasse neighbourhood).

A DIVIDED CITY

Vienna comprises 23 districts *(Bezirke)*. *Der Erste,* the first district, takes in the Innere Stadt, and the rest fan out from there almost in a spiral. Generally speaking, the higher the district number the further it is from the centre.

Districts not only divide the city geographically, but also socially. They often, but not always, point to social status and wealth. The 13th (Hietzing) and 19th (Döbling) districts are generally regarded as the *crème de la crème,* with the 18th (Währing) and 3rd (Landstrasse) coming close behind. Also-rans include the 8th (Josefstadt) and 9th (Alsergrund). The 15th (Rudolfsheim-Fünfhaus) and 16th (Ottakring) districts attract not only immigrants but also young Viennese looking for ethnic diversity, while the 10th (Favoriten), 11th (Simmering) and 12th (Meidling) are regarded as Vienna's poorer districts.

Addresses come in three parts: district, street name and street number/apartment number in that order – eg 01, Kärntner Strasse 43/12 means flat 12, number 43 on Kärntner Strasse in the first district.

This part of Vienna is so full of sights that it can be tempting to have a guidebook constantly in your hand. Don't forget to put it away at times, though, and take a moment to wander aimlessly and let the Innere Stadt work its magic on you.

STEPHANSPLATZ

Stephansplatz is the heart and soul of Vienna and home to the gloriously Gothic Stephansdom (St Stephan's Cathedral). On the northern flank is the Erzbischöfliches Palais (Archbishop's Palace), which was built in 1640 and now houses the Dom- & Diözesanmuseum. On the corner of Stephansplatz and Graben is the controversial Haas Haus, a modern edifice of glass and steel that arouses the passions of architectural purists but for the rest of us provides a contemporary juxtaposition to history – and some fantastic views from the DO & CO hotel and restaurant inside to the cathedral's unusually patterned roof.

STEPHANSDOM Map pp56-7

☎ 515 52 3540; www.stephanskirche.at; 01, Stephansplatz; admission free; 6am-10pm Mon-Sat, 7am-10pm Sun; U1, U3 Stephansplatz

Vienna's Gothic masterpiece Stephansdom (St Stephen's Cathedral), or Steffl (Little Stephan) as it's locally called, symbolises Vienna like no other building. A church has stood on this site since the 12th century, but little remains of the original structure aside from the Riesentor (Giant's Gate) and Heidentürme (Towers of the Heathens); both features are Romanesque in style. The Riesentor (rumour has it that the gate was named because a mammoth's tibia, considered to be a giant's shin, once hung here) is the main western entrance, topped by a tympanum of lattice patterns and statues. In 1359, at the behest of Habsburg Duke Rudolf IV, Stephansdom began receiving its Gothic makeover and Rudolf earned himself the epithet of 'The Founder' by laying the first stone in the reconstruction.

From the outside of the cathedral, the first thing that will strike you is the glorious tiled roof, with its dazzling row of chevrons on one end and the Austrian eagle on the other; a good perspective of this is from the northeast of Stephansplatz. Inside the cathedral, the magnificent Gothic stone pulpit takes pride of place, fashioned in 1515 by Anton Pilgram. One often overlooked detail is the pulpit's handrailing, which has salamanders and toads fighting an eternal battle of good versus evil up and down its length. The baroque high altar, at the very far end of the nave, shows the stoning of St Stephen. The chancel to its left has the winged Wiener Neustadt altarpiece, dating from 1447; the right chancel has the Renaissance red marble tomb of Friedrich III. Under his guidance the city became a bishopric (and the church a cathedral) in 1469.

Much of the nave is closed to the public during mass, which is held up to

MUSEUM DISCOUNTS

Museum discounts can cut your costs significantly, so definitely keep these in mind (for more on general discount cards such as the Vienna Card, see p233). In general, children up to age 14, 16 or 18 (inclusive) are admitted at the children's rate (often free); concession prices cover senior citizens (over 65), students up to the age of 27 and disabled people.

In municipal and many other museums entry is free for anyone under 19 years. The Wien Museum and numerous others are free for everyone at least one day in the month, usually the first Sunday (see www.wienmuseum.at for a complete list).

Various museum groups offer combined tickets. A useful one is the Sisi Ticket (adult/student/6-18yr/family €22.50/20/13.50/46.90), covering entrance to the Kaiserappartements (p66), Hofmobiliendepot (p89) and a grand tour of Schloss Schönbrunn (p119). Family tickets for this are two adults and three kids.

The Kunsthistorisches Museum has a Schätze der Habsburger (Habsburg Treasures; €18) combined ticket giving entry to the Kunsthistorisches Museum and the Schatzkammer, while the Wiener Museumsmelange combines the two Jewish museums (p63 and p75) with either the Haus der Musik (p58), Mozarthaus (p59) or the KunstHausWien (p106). Art lovers should consider the annual ticket for the Kunsthistorisches Museum (€29), which gives multiple admission for one year after validation to all seven museums in the ensemble – a bargain in anyone's book!

For combined Belvedere museum tickets, see p103.

GUIDED TOURS & MUSIC IN VIENNA'S CATHEDRAL

Guided English-language tours of the Dom explain briefly the background of the cathedral and walk you through its main interior features. The 30-minute tours leave at 3.45pm from April to October and cost €4.50 (for those younger than 14 it's €1.50). The same tours in German leave at 10.30am and 3pm Monday to Saturday and 3pm Sunday. Evening tours in German at 7pm every Saturday from June to September include a brisk climb to the top of the south tower (€10/4). An all-inclusive tour – part audioguide, part with a tour guide (adult plus one child under 14 is €14.50; a senior or student pays €12) – takes in the cathedral interior, catacombs, south tower and the north tower. The most common option is the multilingual audioguide (€4.90) for the cathedral interior.

The Dom website (www.stephanskirche.at) has a program of special concerts and events, but the 10.30am Mass (9.30am during the school holidays around July and August) is something special as it's conducted with full choral accompaniment.

seven times a day, and from July to mid-October the nave can only be visited with a tour.

STEPHANSDOM KATAKOMBEN

Map pp56-7

☎ 515 52 3526; www.stephanskirche.at; 01, Stephansplatz; tours adult/under 14yr €4.50/1.50; 🕑 10-11.30am & 1.30-4.30pm Mon-Sat, 1.30-4.30pm Sun; Ⓤ U1, U3 Stephansplatz

The area on Stephansplatz around the cathedral was originally a graveyard – making it the 'dead centre' of Vienna in a very literal sense. But with plague and influenza epidemics striking Europe in the 1730s, Karl VI ordered the graveyard to be closed and henceforth Vienna buried its dead beneath Stephansdom in the 'New Tombs', which in the 19th century became more wistfully known as *Katakomben* (catacombs). Today they contain the remains of countless victims, who are kept in a mass grave and a bone house. Also on display are rows of urns containing the internal organs of the Habsburgs. One of the many privileges of being a Habsburg was to be dismembered and dispersed after death: their hearts are in the Augustinerkirche in the Hofburg (see p70) and the rest of their bits are in the Kaisergruft (see p62).

CATHEDRAL SOUTH TOWER Map pp56-7

☎ 515 52 3520; www.stephanskirche.at; 01, Stephansplatz; adult/under 14yr €3.50/1; 🕑 9am-5.30pm; Ⓤ U1, U3 Stephansplatz

When the foundation stone for the south tower (Südturm) was laid in 1359, Rudolf IV is said to have used a trowel and spade made of silver – both of which apparently survived among the cathedral treasures until the 15th century before vanishing. Two towers were originally envisaged, but the Südturm grew so high that little space remained for the second. In 1433, after 75 years of toil, the tower reached its final height of 136.7m, and today you can ascend the 343 steps to a cramped platform for one of Vienna's most spectacular views over the rooftops of the Innere Stadt.

CATHEDRAL PUMMERIN Map pp56-7

☎ 515 52 3520; www.stephanskirche.at; 01, Stephansplatz; adult/under 14yr €4.50/1.50; 🕑 8.15am-4.30pm mid-Jan–Jun & Sep-Dec, 8.15am-6pm Jul & Aug; Ⓤ U1, U3 Stephansplatz

With the imperial purse withering and Gothic styles losing their allure, work on a second tower on Stephansdom was abandoned and in 1579 the half-completed north tower (Nordturm) was given a Renaissance cupola. Austria's largest bell, weighing in at a hefty 21 tonnes, is the Pummerin (boomer bell) and was installed here in 1952. The north tower housing it is accessible by lift.

DOM- & DIÖZESANMUSEUM Map pp56-7

☎ 515 52 3689; 01, Stephansplatz 6; adult/under 14yr/family €7/3/16; 🕑 10am-5pm Tue-Sat; Ⓤ U1, U3 Stephansplatz

The Cathedral and Diocesan Museum of Vienna is a treasure trove of religious art pieces spanning a period of more than 1000 years. The collection is blessed with some extraordinary articles – such as the earliest European portrait, that of Duke Rudolph IV (1360), and two Syrian glass vessels (1280–1310) thought to be among the oldest glass bottles in the world – making this museum a must for those interested in religious art.

CENTRAL VIENNA

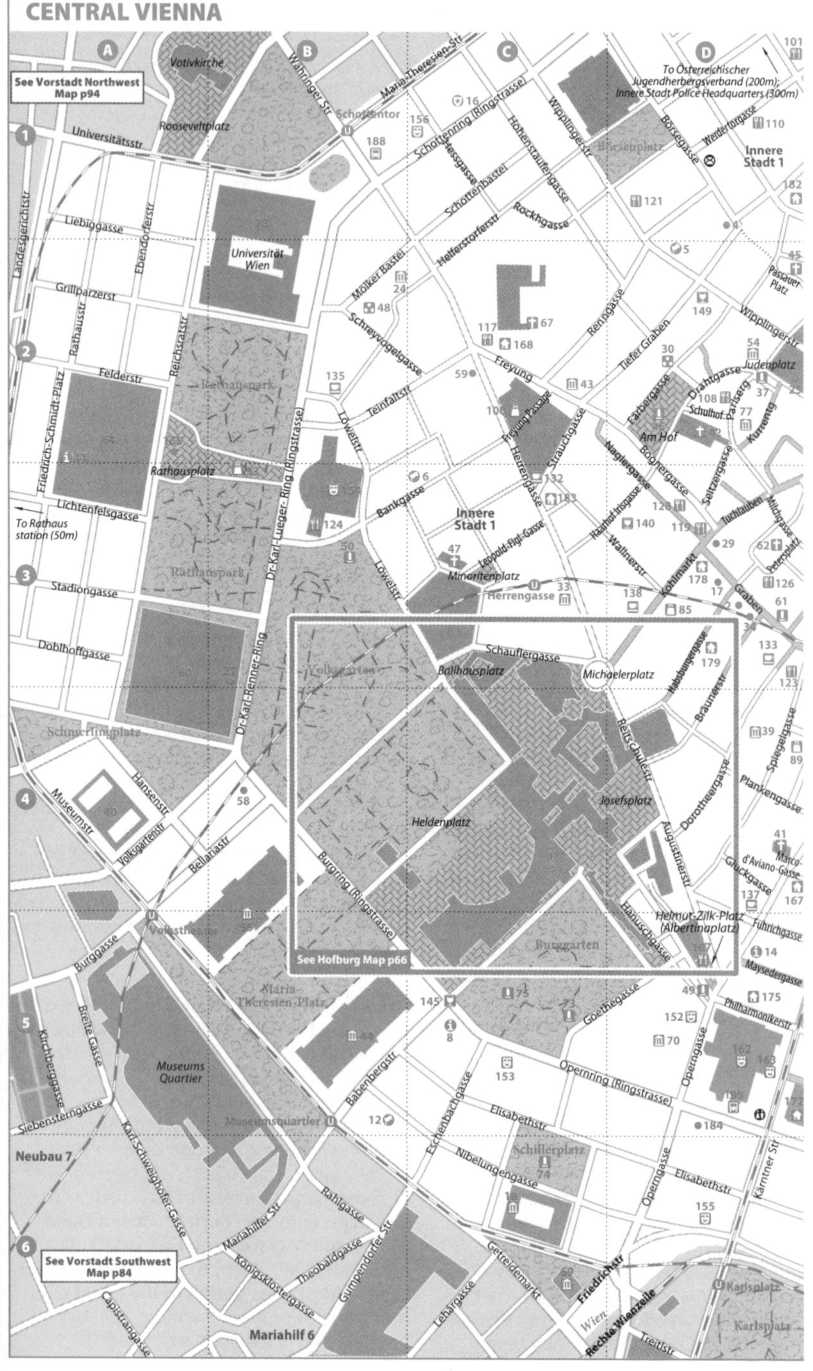

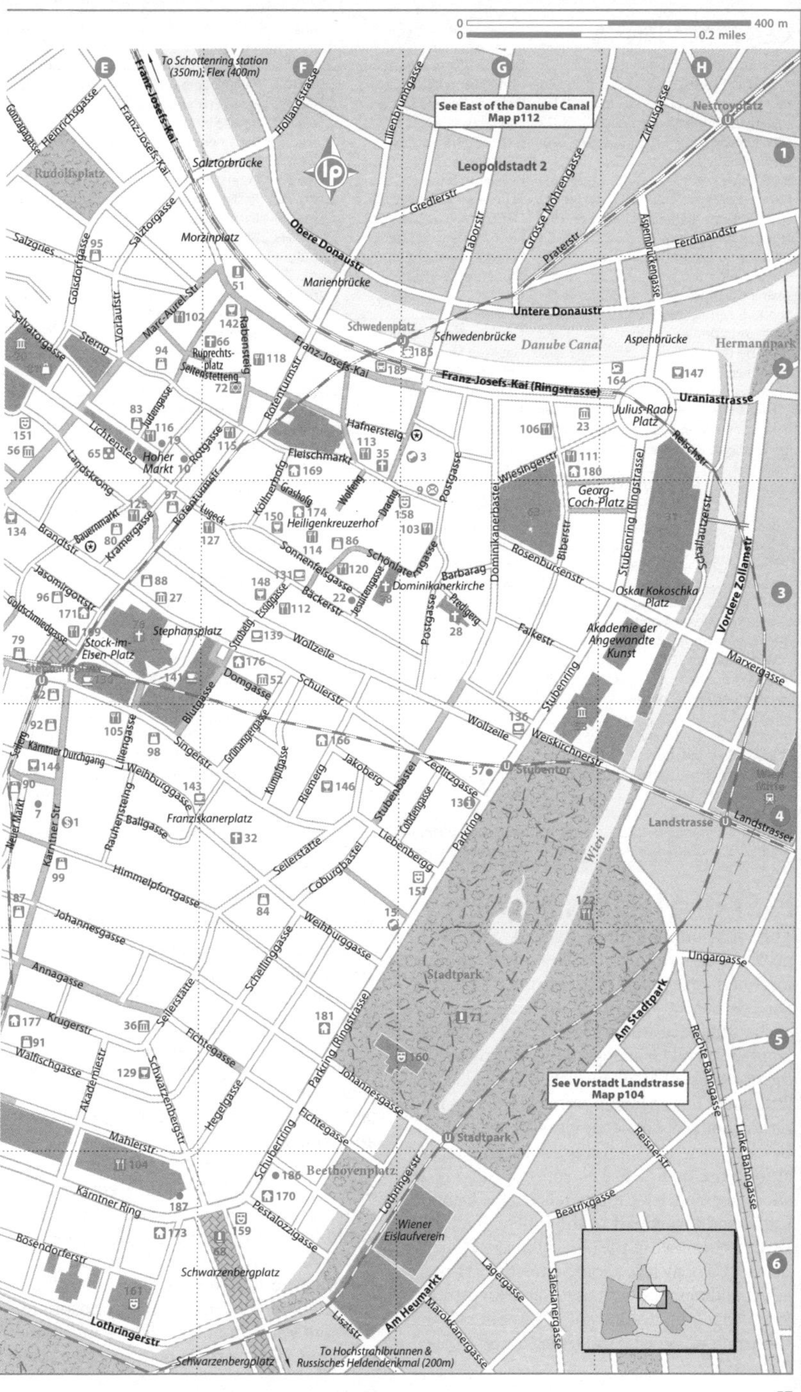

0 400 m
0 0.2 miles
E
F
G
H
1
2
3
4
5
6
To Schottenring station (350m); Flex (400m)
See East of the Danube Canal Map p112
Leopoldstadt 2
Franz-Josefs-Kai
Hollandstrasse
Lilienbrunngasse
Zirkusgasse
Nestroyplatz
Gonzagagasse
Heinrichsgasse
Rudolfsplatz
Salztorbrücke
Gredlerstr
Taborstr
Grosse Mohrengasse
Praterstr
Aspernbrückengasse
Ferdinandstr
Salztorgasse
Morzinplatz
Obere Donaustr
Salzgries
Marienbrücke
Untere Donaustr
Gölsdorfgasse
Vorlaufstr
Marc-Aurel-Str
Rabensteig
Salvatorgasse
Sterng
Ruprechtsplatz
Seitenstetteng
Schwedenplatz
Schwedenbrücke
Danube Canal
Aspenbrücke
Hermannpark
Franz-Josefs-Kai (Ringstrasse)
Uraniastrasse
Julius-Raab-Platz
Rotenturmstr
Judengasse
Hafnersteig
Fleischmarkt
Lichtensteg
Hoher Markt
Rotgasse
Landskrongasse
Wiesingerstr
Georg-Coch-Platz
Stubenring (Ringstrasse)
Reischstr
Kollnerhofg
Grashofg
Postgasse
Heiligenkreuzerhof
Bauernmarkt
Kramergasse
Lugeck
Brandstr
Schönlaterngasse
Sonnenfelsgasse
Rosenbursenstr
Biberstr
Dominikanerbastei
Dominikanerkirche
Barbarag
Predigerg
Jasomirgottstr
Bäckerstr
Essiggasse
Jesuitengasse
Oskar Kokoschka Platz
Schallautzerstr
Vordere Zollamtstr
Goldschmiedgasse
Stock-im-Eisen-Platz
Stephansplatz
Strobelg
Wollzeile
Falkestr
Akademie der Angewandte Kunst
Marxergasse
Domgasse
Schulerstr
Stubenring
Blutgasse
Liliengasse
Singerstr
Grünangergasse
Weiskirchnerstr
Kärntner Durchgang
Weihburggasse
Kumpfgasse
Jakoberg
Stubentor
Riemerg
Stubenbastei
Zedlitzgasse
Cobdengasse
Franziskanerplatz
Rauhensteing
Ballgasse
Landstrasse
Landstrasser
Kärntner Str
Neuer Markt
Seilerstätte
Liebenbergg
Parkring
Himmelpfortgasse
Coburgbastei
Wien
Johannesgasse
Weihburggasse
Ungargasse
Annagasse
Schellinggasse
Stadtpark
Krugerstr
Seilerstätte
Am Stadtpark
Walfischgasse
Fichtegasse
Parkring (Ringstrasse)
Rechte Bahngasse
Schwarzenbergstr
Akademiestr
Hegelgasse
Johannesgasse
See Vorstadt Landstrasse Map p104
Mahlerstr
Schubertring
Fichtegasse
Stadtpark
Linke Bahngasse
Reisnerstr
Beethovenplatz
Lothringerstr
Kärntner Ring
Pestalozzigasse
Beatrixgasse
Wiener Eislaufverein
Bösendorferstr
Schwarzenbergplatz
Lagergasse
Salesianergasse
Lothringerstr
Am Heumarkt
Marokkanergasse
Lisztstr
Schwarzenbergplatz
To Hochstrahlbrunnen & Russisches Heldendenkmal (200m)

CENTRAL VIENNA

INFORMATION

American Express ... 1 E4
Berlitz ... 2 D3
Canadian Embassy ... 3 G2
City Segway Tours ... (see 190)
Cityrama ... 4 D1
DDSG Blue Danube ... (see 185)
French Embassy ... 5 D2
Hop On Hop Off Vienna Line ... (see 190)
Hungarian Embassy ... 6 C3
Inlingua Sprachschule ... 7 E4
Jugendinfo ... 8 C5
Main Post Office ... 9 G3
Niederösterreich Werbung ... 10 E2
Rathaus Information Office ... 11 A2
Ring Tram ... (see 189)
Slovenian Embassy ... 12 B5
Slowakische Zentrale für Tourismus ... 13 G4
Tourist Info Wien ... 14 D5
US Embassy, Consular Section ... 15 F4
Vienna Police Headquarters ... 16 C1

SIGHTS (p53)

Adolf Loos' Public Toilets ... 17 D3
Akademie der Bildenden Künste ... 18 C6
Am Hof ... (see 46)
Ankeruhr – Hoher Markt ... 19 E2
Archiv des Österreichischen Widerstands ... 20 E2
Athena Fountain ... 21 B3
Austrian Academy of the Sciences ... 22 F3
BAWAG Contemporary/ BAWAG Foundation ... 23 G2
Beethoven Pasqualatihaus ... 24 B2
Böhmische Hofkanzlei ... 25 D2
Börse Palais ... 26 C1
Cathedral Pummerin ... (see 76)
Cathedral South Tower ... (see 76)
Dom- & Diözesanmuseum ... 27 E3
Dominikanerkirche ... 28 G3
Dr-Ignaz-Seipel-Platz ... (see 38)
Equitable Palais ... (see 82)
Erste Österrichisches Sparkasse ... 29 D3
Esperanto Museum ... (see 33)
Feuerwehr Zentrale ... 30 D2
Fleischmarkt ... (see 35)
Former Kriegsministerium ... 31 H3
Franziskanerkirche ... 32 F4
Globenmuseum ... 33 C3
Graben ... (see 61)
Grabenhof ... 34 D3
Greek Orthodox Church ... 35 F2
Haus der Musik ... 36 E5
Helmut-Zilk-Platz (Albertinaplatz) ... (see 49)
Holocaust-Denkmal ... 37 D2
Jesuitenkirche ... 38 F3
Jüdisches Museum ... 39 D4
Justizpalast ... 40 A4
Kaisergruft ... 41 D4
Kapuzinerkirche ... (see 41)
Kirche am Hof ... 42 D2
Kunstforum ... 43 C2
Kunsthistorisches Museum ... 44 B5
Maria am Gestade ... 45 D2
Mariensäule ... 46 D2
Minoritenkirche ... 47 C3
Mölker Bastei ... 48 B2
Monument Against War & Fascism ... 49 D5
Monument to Empress Elisabeth ... 50 B3
Morzinplatz & Monument to the Victims of Facism ... 51 F2
Mozarthaus Vienna ... 52 F3
Museum für angewandte Kunst ... 53 G4
Museum Judenplatz ... 54 D2
Naturhistorisches Museum ... 55 B5
Neidhart-Fresken ... 56 E2
Palais Dumba ... 57 G4
Palais Epstein ... 58 B4
Palais Kinsky ... 59 C2
Parlament ... 60 A3
Pestsäule ... 61 D3
Peterskirche ... 62 D3
Postsparkasse ... 63 G3
Rathaus ... 64 A2
Römer Museum – Hoher Markt ... 65 E2
Ruprechtskirche ... 66 F2
Schottenkirche ... 67 C2
Schwarzenbergplatz ... 68 F6
Secession ... 69 C6
Staatsopermuseum ... 70 D5
Stadtpark & Johann Strauss Denkmal ... 71 G5
Stadttempel ... 72 F2
Statue of Franz Josef ... 73 C5
Statue of Friedrich Schiller ... 74 C6
Statue of Mozart ... 75 C5
Stephansdom ... 76 E3
Stephansdom Katakomben ... (see 76)
Uhren Museum ... 77 D2
University Main Building ... 78 B1

SHOPPING (p129)

Altmann & Kühne ... 79 E3
Art Up ... 80 E3
Atelier Naske ... 81 E2
Augarten Wein ... 82 E3
Austrian Delights ... 83 E2
British Bookshop ... 84 F4
Freytag & Berndt ... 85 D3
Freyung Christmas Market ... (see 117)
Heiligenkreuzerhof Christmas Market ... 86 F3
J&L Lobmeyr ... 87 E4
Manner ... 88 E3
Markt Freyung ... (see 117)
Meinl am Graben ... (see 119)

EAST OF STEPHANSPLATZ

The area immediately east of Stephansplatz is a labyrinth of cobblestone alleys and forgotten streets that is a pleasure to wander. Directly behind Stephansdom is an especially enchanting area where the alleys of Blutgasse, Domgasse and Grünangergasse intertwine. To the northeast of Stephansplatz the streets are a little wider but no less appealing; Heiligenkreuzerhof, home of one of the city's most delightful Christmas markets (p147), and Schönlaterngasse are among the quaint places you find here. The wider Fleischmarkt runs parallel to the Danube Canal and forms part of the Innere Stadt that used to be known as the Griechenviertel (Greek quarter). Today it has some attractive art-nouveau buildings. Further east towards Ringstrasse, spaces open up around the Stadtpark and the Museum für angewandte Kunst (Museum of Applied Arts; p60).

HAUS DER MUSIK Map pp56-7

☎ 516 48-0; www.hdm.at; 01, Seilerstätte 30; adult/under 12yr/concession €10/5.50/8.50; 10am-10pm; tram 1, 2 bus 3A

The Haus der Musik is one of Vienna's more unusual museums. Although some of the activities and exhibits could be a little more user-friendly, it manages to explain sound in an amusing and interactive way (in English and German) for both children and adults.

The 1st floor hosts historical archives of the Vienna Philharmonic. Here you can listen to a shortened version of the world-famous New Year's concert, and a bizarre interactive tool allows you to compose your own waltz with the roll of a die. The 2nd floor, called the Sonosphere, is where you can delve into the mechanics of sound. This features plenty of engaging

CENTRAL VIENNA

Mühlbauer 89 D4
Oberlaa 90 E4
Opern Confiserie 91 E5
Österreichische Werkstätten 92 E4
Rathausplatz Christmas Market 93 B3
Shakespeare & Co 94 E2
Unger und Klein 95 E1
Vienna Bag .... (see 131)
Wein & Co 96 E3
Weltladen 97 E3
Woka 98 E4
Wolford 99 E4
Xocolat 100 C2

EATING (p149)
Aubergine 101 D1
Aurelius 102 E2
Beim Czaak 103 G3
Billa Supermarket 104 E6
Billa Supermarket 105 E4
Billa Supermarket 106 G2
Bio-Markt Freyung .... (see 117)
Bitzinger Würstelstand am Albertinaplatz 107 D5
Bodega Marqués 108 D2
DO & CO Stephansplatz 109 E3
EN 110 D1
Expedit 111 G2
Figlmüller 112 F3
Griechenbeisl 113 F2
Hollmann Salon 114 F3
Kiang 115 F2
Limes 116 E2
Markt Freyung 117 C2
Maschu Maschu 118 F2
Meierei im Stadtpark .... (see 122)
Meinl's Restaurant 119 D3
Österreicher im MAK .... (see 53)
Restaurant Bauer 120 F3
Soupkultur 121 D1
Steirereck im Stadtpark 122 G4
Trzesniewski 123 D3
Vestibül 124 B3
Wrenkh 125 E3
Yohm 126 D3
Zanoni & Zanoni 127 F3
Zum Schwarzen Kameel 128 D3

DRINKING & NIGHTLIFE (p171)
1516 Brewing Company 129 E5
Aida 130 E3
Café Alt Wein 131 F3
Café Central 132 C3
Café Hawelka 133 D3
Café Korb 134 E3
Café Landtmann 135 B2
Café Prückel 136 G4
Café Sacher .... (see 175)
Café Tirolerhof 137 D4
Demel 138 D3
Diglas 139 F3
Esterházykeller 140 D3
Haas & Haas 141 E3
Jazzland 142 F2
Kleines Café 143 E4
Loos American Bar 144 E4
Passage 145 C5
Porgy & Bess 146 F4
Urania 147 H2
vis-a-vis 148 F3
Why Not? 149 D2
Zwölf Apostelkeller 150 F3

MUSIC & THE ARTS (p191)
Artis International 151 E2
Bundestheaterkassen 152 D5
Burg Kino 153 C5
Burgtheater 154 B3
Cinemagic 155 D6
De France 156 C1
Gartenbaukino 157 G4
Kammeroper 158 G3
Kasino am Schwarzenbergplatz 159 F6
Kursalon 160 G5
Musikverein 161 E6
Staatsoper 162 D5
Wien-Ticket Pavillon 163 D5

SPORTS & ACTIVITIES (p201)
Badeschiff 164 H2
Wiener Eistraum 165 A2

SLEEPING (p207)
Appartements Riemergasse 166 F4
Aviano 167 D4
Benediktushaus 168 C2
DO & CO .... (see 109)
Holmann Beletage 169 F2
Hotel am Schubertring 170 F6
Hotel am Stephansplatz 171 E3
Hotel Bristol 172 D5
Hotel Imperial 173 E6
Hotel Kaertnerhof 174 F3
Hotel Sacher 175 D5
König von Ungarn 176 F3
Pension am Operneck 177 E5
Pension Nossek 178 D3
Pension Pertschy 179 D3
Pension Riedl 180 G2
Radisson SAS Palais Hotel 181 F5
Schweizer Pension 182 D1
Style Hotel 183 C3

TRANSPORT (p228)
Avis 184 D5
DDSG Blue Danube 185 G2
Europcar 186 F6
Hertz 187 E6
Schottentor Night Bus Stop 188 B1
Schwedenplatz Night Bus Stop 189 F2
Staatsoper Night Bus Stop 190 D5
Twin City Liner .... (see 185)

instruments, interactive toys and touch screens. Here you can test the limits of your hearing and play around with sampled sounds to record your own CD (€7).

Floor 3 covers Vienna's classical composers and is polished off with the 'virtual conductor': a video of the Vienna Philharmonic that responds to a conducting baton and keeps time with your movements.

The museum hosts the occasional children's program – see the website for details.

MOZARTHAUS VIENNA Map pp56-7

☎ 512 17 91; www.mozarthausvienna.at; 01, Domgasse 5; adult/concession & under 14yr €9/7; 10am-7pm; U1, U3 Stephansplatz 1A

Mozarthaus Vienna, the residence where the great composer spent two and a half happy and productive years, is now the city's premiere Mozart attraction. The museum was revamped a few years ago and is well worth a visit for an insight into the life and times of Mozart in Vienna (a total of 10 years). One floor deals with the society of the late 18th century, providing asides into prominent figures in the court and Mozart's life, such as the Freemasons to whom he dedicated a number of pieces. Mozart's vices – his womanising, gambling and ability to waste excessive amounts of money – lend a spicy edge (you can look through some peepholes). Another floor concentrates on Mozart's music and his musical influences. It was here he penned *The Marriage of Figaro,* which went down like a lead balloon in Vienna but was enthusiastically received in Prague. A surreal holographic

top picks

CENTRAL VIENNA FOR CHILDREN

- Haus der Musik (p58)
- Globenmuseum (p71)
- Museum für Völkerkunde (p72)
- Naturhistorisches Museum (p70)
- Neue Burg Museums – Hofjagd und Rüstkammer (p71)
- Spanish Riding School – Morning training (p67)

performance of scenes from *The Magic Flute* is in another room. The final floor is sparsely furnished in period pieces to represent Mozart's apartment. An audio guide is included in the admission price and is an invaluable companion.

MUSEUM FÜR ANGEWANDTE KUNST Map pp56-7

☎ 711 36-0; www.mak.at; 01, Stubenring 5; adult/under 19yr/concession €7.90/free/5.50; 10am-6pm Wed-Sun, 10am-midnight Tue; U3 Stubentor 2

The Museum für angewandte Kunst (Museum of Applied Arts), better known as the MAK, has an extensive collection of household items better described as art. MAK shares its home with the excellent cafe Österreicher im MAK (p156), and the building – a neo-Renaissance construction dating from 1871 – offers some fine features in its own right, especially the ceilings.

Each exhibition room is devoted to a different style or sometimes a region, eg Renaissance, baroque, oriental, historicism, empire, art deco and the distinctive metalwork of the Wiener Werkstätte. The basement houses the Study Collection. Here exhibits are grouped according to the type of materials used: glass and ceramics, metal, wood and textiles. Actual objects range from ancient oriental statues to sofas (note the red-lips sofa). There are some particularly good porcelain and glassware pieces, with casts showing how they're made.

MAK is free on Saturdays, and tours (€2) are available in German at 11am on Saturday and in English at noon on Sunday.

FRANZISKANERKIRCHE Map pp56-7

☎ 512 45 7811; 01, Franziskanerplatz; admission free; 7am-8pm; U1, U3 Stephansplatz

This Franciscan church is a glorious architectural deception. Viewed from outside, it exudes all the hallmarks of an early 17th-century Renaissance style, yet inside it is awash with gold and marble decorative features from the baroque era about 100 years later. The impressive high altar takes the form of a triumphal arch and hidden behind this is Vienna's oldest organ, dating from 1642, built by Johann Wöckherl. This organ is being restored and if all goes according to plan it will be wheezing heavenly tones again from around 2011.

FLEISCHMARKT Map pp56-7

01, Fleischmarkt; U1, U3 Stephansplatz

Around 1700 a gaggle of Greek merchants settled around Fleischmarkt, which gradually became known as the Griechenviertel (Greek quarter). Their favourite meeting place was the Griechenbeisl (see p156), today one of Vienna's most popular (and touristed) *Beisln*. As the community became more established, a few wealthier Greeks spun off towards the Ringstrasse and built larger abodes there. One immigrant, the industrialist and politician Nikolaus von Dumba, commissioned the building of Palais Dumba (Map pp56-7; Parkring 4) in 1866. By the early 20th century, the traditional Greek quarter of Fleischmarkt was being blessed with an attractive cluster of art-nouveau buildings. No 14, built by F Dehm and F Olbricht between 1889 and 1899, exhibits gold and stucco embellishments, while No 7 (Max Kropf; 1899) was the childhood home of Hollywood film director Billy Wilder from 1914 to 1924. Arthur Baron was responsible for Nos 1 and 3 (1910).

GREEK ORTHODOX CHURCH Map pp56-7

☎ 533 38 89; 01, Fleischmarkt 13; admission free; 11am-3pm Mon-Sat, 11am-1pm Sun; U1, U4 Schwedenplatz 1, 2

Built in 1861 at the behest of the Greek community, the interior of Vienna's main Greek Orthodox church is a glittering blaze of Byzantine designs. A ceiling fresco depicting the prophets surrounded by swirls of gold is augmented by a high altar of 13 panels, each of which features sparkling gilding, and a doorway to the inner sanctum. Today, the Greek community in Vienna numbers about 10,000.

BAWAG CONTEMPORARY/BAWAG FOUNDATION Map pp56-7

☎ 534 53-0; www.bawag-foundation.at; 01, Franz-Josefs-Kai 3; admission free; 2-8pm; 1, 2
This gallery, financed by the BAWAG Bank, features contemporary artists from both the international and local scenes, focusing on the generation born in the 1970s. It has a regular influx of temporary exhibitions on display in all media, with works ranging from sculpture pieces to photo exhibitions and film.

DOMINIKANERKIRCHE Map pp56-7

☎ 512 91 74; 01, Postgasse 4; admission free; 7am-7pm; U3 Stubentor 1, 2, 2A
The Dominicans first came to Vienna in 1226, when Leopold VI of Babenberg invited them to settle, but their first church, built on the site of today's Dominikanerkirche, was dismantled during the first Turkish siege in 1529 and the stone used to fortify the city walls. The church you see today was the first baroque church in Vienna and was consecrated in 1634. It was largely the work of Italian architects and artisans and is well worth visiting for its large interior of white stucco and frescos.

DR-IGNAZ-SEIPEL-PLATZ Map pp56-7

01; U1, U3 Stephansplatz
Formerly known as Universitätsplatz (University Sq), this was once the heart of Vienna's old university quarter. Today the Austrian Academy of the Sciences (☎ 515 81-0; www.oeaw.ac.at; Dr-Ignaz-Seipel-Platz 2; admission free; 7am-6pm Mon-Fri) is located inside the Alte-Uni (Old Uni) building. An early university was built here in the 1420s, but the current building has the hallmarks of late-baroque restoration work from the mid-18th century. Opposite is the Jesuitenkirche (☎ 512 5232-0; Dr-Ignaz-Seipel-Platz 1; admission free; 7am-7pm Mon-Sat, 8am-8pm Sun), formerly the university church and dating from 1627. In 1703 this received a baroque makeover by the Italian architect and painter Andrea Pozzo (1642–1709), who created its startling *trompe-l'œil* dome and other ceiling frescos. Walk beyond the 'dome' to visually destroy Pozzo's illusion.

STADTPARK & JOHANN STRAUSS DENKMAL Map pp56-7

01, 03; U4 Stadtpark D
Opened to the public in 1862, the Stadtpark (City Park) is an enjoyable recreational spot with winding paths and a pond – it's great for strolling or relaxing in the sun and a favourite lunchtime escape for Innere Stadt workers. The park spans the Wien River, which empties into the Danube Canal, and part of it extends into Landstrasse (p102). Of the several statues inhabiting the park (including Schindler, Bruckner and Schubert), the most recognisable is the Johann Strauss Denkmal, a golden statue of Johann Strauss the Younger under a white arch.

POSTSPARKASSE Map pp56-7

☎ 534 53 33088; www.ottowagner.at; 01, Georg-Coch-Platz 2; museum adult/under 10yr/concession €5/free/3.50; 9am-5pm Mon-Fri, 10am-5pm Sat; U1, U4 Schwedenplatz 1, 2
The celebrated Post Office Savings Bank building is the work of Otto Wagner, who oversaw its construction between 1904 and 1906, and again from 1910 to 1912. The *Jugendstil* design and choice of materials were innovative for the time, with the grey marble facade held together by 17,000 metal nails, and an interior filled with sci-fi aluminium heating ducts and naked stanchions. The small museum at the back of the main savings hall hosts temporary exhibitions focusing on design – anything from office buildings to nifty kitchenware.

FORMER KRIEGSMINISTERIUM Map pp56-7

01, Stubenring 1; U1, U4 Schwedenplatz 1, 2
Today occupied by federal ministries, the former Kriegsministerium (Imperial War Ministry) is a rather austere military building from 1913. It makes an interesting contrast to Otto Wagner's quirky Postsparkasse directly opposite. Wagner in fact pitched for the project but his plans were knocked back for not meeting the criteria. In the end, an extra floor had to be added to Ludwig Bauman's design to support the hideously overdimensional eagle adorning the facade.

SCHWARZENBERGPLATZ Map pp56-7

01, 03; U4 Stadtpark or Karlsplatz
Forming a square that crosses the Ringstrasse and spills into the Landstrasse

district (see p102), Schwarzenbergplatz is dominated in the north by a statue of Karl von Schwarzenberg, leader of the Austrian and Bohemian troops in the Battle of Leipzig (1813). The southern stretch of the square sports the stony fountain Hochstrahlbrunnen and behind this is the Russisches Heldendenkmal (Russian Heroes' Monument). The fountain was commissioned in 1873 to commemorate Vienna's first water mains; a dedication in Russian on the monument reads: 'Eternal glory to the heroes of the Red Army who fell in battle for the freedom and independence of the people of Europe against German-Fascist invaders'. As far as war memorials go, this one is remarkably elegant and attractive.

KÄRNTNER STRASSE & AROUND

Creating the main link between Stephansplatz and the Staatsoper, Kärntner Strasse began life as a thoroughfare for traders entering and leaving Vienna, in the 1970s becoming the city's first pedestrian zone and prime shopping street. The parallel Neuer Markt, the former flower market, today has the vicinity's main attraction, the Kaisergruft (Imperial Burial Vault). The centre of the square is adorned with a replica of Georg Raphael Donner's beautiful Providentia Fountain (1739). The original figures proved too risqué for Maria Theresia and had to be removed in 1773 – since 1921 they have resided in Lower Belvedere (see p103).

KAISERGRUFT Map pp56-7

☎ 512 68 53; 01, Neuer Markt; adult/under 14yr/concession €5/2/4; 10am-6pm; U1, U3 Stephansplatz 2A

The Kaisergruft beneath the Kapuzinerkirche (Church of the Capuchin Friars) is the final resting place of most of the Habsburg royal family (the hearts and organs reside in Augustinerkirche and Stephansdom, respectively). Opened in 1633, it was instigated by Empress Anna (1585–1618), and her body and that of her husband, Emperor Matthias (1557–1619), were the first to be entombed. Since then, all but three of the Habsburg dynasty found their way here: the last emperor, Karl I, was buried in exile in Madeira, and Marie Antoinette (daughter of Maria Theresia) still lies in Paris. The remains of Duc de Reichstadt, son of Napoleon's second wife, Marie Louise, were transferred to Paris as a publicity stunt by the Nazis in 1940.

Fashions change over time, and this also goes for a decent Habsburg farewell. Tombs range from the sleek and unadorned to the fiddly and pompously baroque, such as the huge double sarcophagus containing Maria Theresia and Franz Stephan. The tomb of Charles VI is also striking – both of these are the work of Balthasar Moll.

AKADEMIE DER BILDENDEN KÜNSTE

Map pp56-7

☎ 588 16-0; www.akademiegalerie.at, in German; 01, Schillerplatz 3; adult/under 10yr/concession €6/free/3.50; 10am-6pm Tue-Sun; U1, U2, U4 Karlsplatz D, 1, 2, 62

The Akademie der bildenden Künste (Academy of Fine Arts) is an often underrated art space. Its gallery concentrates on the classic Flemish, Dutch and German painters, and includes important figures such as Hieronymus Bosch, Rembrandt, Van Dyck, Rubens, Titian, Francesco Guardi and Cranach the Elde, to mention a handful. The supreme highlight is Bosch's impressive and gruesome *Triptych of the Last Judgement* altarpiece (1504–08), with the banishment of Adam and Eve on the left panel and the horror of Hell in the middle and right panels. The building itself has an attractive facade and was designed by Theophil Hansen (1813–91), of Parlament fame. It still operates as an art school and is famous for turning down Adolf Hitler twice and accepting Egon Schiele (though the latter was happy to leave as quickly as possible). Directly in front of the academy is a statue of Friedrich Schiller, 18th-century German playwright.

Audio guides are available for an extra €2, and tours (€3, in German only) take place at 10.30am every Sunday from October to June.

SECESSION Map pp56-7

☎ 587 53 07; www.secession.at; 01, Friedrichstrasse 12; exhibition & frieze adult/concession €8.50/5, exhibition only €5/4; 10am-6pm Tue-Sun; U1, U2, U4 Karlsplatz

In 1897, 19 progressive artists broke away from the Künstlerhaus and the conservative artistic establishment it represented and formed the Vienna Secession (*Sezession;* p37).

Their aim was to present current trends in contemporary art and shake off historicism. Among their number were Klimt, Josef Hoffman, Kolo Moser and Joseph M Olbrich (a former student of Wagner). Olbrich was given the honour of designing the new exhibition centre of the Secessionists. It was erected just a year later and combined sparse functionality with stylistic motifs.

The building is certainly a move away from the Ringstrasse architectural throwbacks. Its most striking feature is a delicate golden dome rising from a turret on the roof that deserves better than the description 'golden cabbage' accorded it by some Viennese. Other features are the Medusa-like faces above the door with dangling serpents instead of earlobes, minimalist stone owls gazing down from the walls and vast ceramic pots supported by tortoises at the front.

The 14th exhibition (1902) held in the building featured the famous *Beethoven Frieze,* by Klimt. This 34m-long work was intended as a temporary display, little more than an elaborate poster for the main exhibit, Max Klinger's Beethoven monument. It was bought at the end of the exhibition by a private collector and transported – plaster, reeds, laths and all – in eight sections to the buyer's home. In 1973 the government purchased the frieze and since 1983 it has been on display in the basement. Multilingual brochures in the room explain the various graphic elements, which are based on Richard Wagner's interpretation of Beethoven's ninth symphony. The small room you enter before viewing the frieze tells the story of the building. It served as a hospital during WWI and was torched by the retreating Germans during WWII (the gold dome survived the fire). The ground floor is still used as it was originally intended: presenting temporary exhibitions of contemporary art.

STAATSOPERMUSEUM Map pp56-7

☎ 514 44 2250; 01, Goethegasse 1; adult/under 19yr/senior €3/2/2.50, with Staatsoper tour €6.50/3.50/5.50; 🕑 10am-6pm Tue-Sun; Ⓤ U1, U2, U4 Karlsplatz 🚊 D, 1, 2, 62

This shrine to Viennese high culture covers the last 50 years of the Staatsoper. It relies mostly on photographs to take you through highlights such as Karajan's eight-year reign as director. Opera lovers who don't understand German will enjoy the aura and being surrounded by the portraits of operatic greats; others with a passing interest will like the occasional gem, such as Dame Margot Fonteyn's stub-toed ballet slipper. A visit to this museum is best combined with a tour of the Staatsoper (p195).

HELMUT-ZILK-PLATZ (ALBERTINAPLATZ) Map pp56-7

01; Ⓤ U1, U3 Stephansplatz, U4 Karlsplatz

This attractive square wedged between the Staatsoper and the Albertina (p70) is the site of the troubling work Monument Against War and Fascism, by Alfred Hrdlicka, created in 1988. This series of pale blocklike sculptures commemorates Jews and other victims of war and fascism. The dark, squat shape wrapped in barbed wire represents a Jew scrubbing the floor; the greyish block originally came from the Mauthausen concentration camp.

STEPHANSPLATZ TO HOFBURG

The vicinity between Stephansplatz and Hofburg is linked by the two busy pedestrian-only streets Graben and Kohlmarkt. The latter ends at Michaelerplatz and Michaelertor, one of the Hofburg's major gates. Shops – some really expensive shops – several art-nouveau architectural highlights and the Jüdisches Museum (Jewish Museum) are the main attractions. Enthusiasts of antiques will enjoy wandering 'off-piste' in the antique quarter between Seilergasse and Habsburgergasse.

JÜDISCHES MUSEUM Map pp56-7

☎ 535 04 31; www.jmw.at; 01, Dorotheergasse 11; adult/concession & child €6.50/4; 🕑 10am-6pm Sun-Fri; Ⓤ U1, U3 Stephansplatz

Occupying three floors of Palais Eskeles, Vienna's Jüdisches Museum uses holograms and an assortment of objects to document the history of Jews in Vienna, from the first settlements at Judenplatz in the 13th century to the present. The ground floor is filled with the Max Berger collection: a rich compilation of Judaica. Temporary exhibitions are a key feature of the museum and 21 holograms depict the history of the Jewish people in Vienna. The third floor 'Schaudepot' contains a vast assortment of Tora crowns, plates, shofars and other valuables confiscated by the

PEACEFUL POCKETS

The Innere Stadt can fill with people in summer, but a few quiet corners can be found:

Blutgasse to Stubenbastei Directly east of Stephansplatz is an intertwining set of streets, many of which are laid in cobblestones.

Heiligenkreuzerhof and Schönlaterngasse Northeast of Stephansplatz, twisting Schönlaterngasse (lane of the beautiful lanterns) is lined with tall baroque buildings and connects to Heiligenkreuzerhof, a quiet residential courtyard and site of the city's most authentic Christmas market (p147).

Ruprechtsplatz and around North of Stephansplatz is the old Jewish quarter and oldest church, Ruprechtskirche (p76).

Maria am Gestade and around North of Stephansplatz, the fine Maria am Gestade Gothic church (p76) proudly stands guard over a flight of steps leading to quiet Concordiaplatz.

Between Am Hof and Judenplatz A tight, interlocking bunch of streets decorated with fancy facades is just northwest of Stephansplatz.

Nazis in 1938. An audio guide is included in the price, and free tours on Sunday (in German) are conducted at 2pm and 3pm on the temporary exhibitions, and at 4pm on all exhibitions. A combined ticket of €10/6 per adult/concession & child allows entry to the museum, the Stadttempel (p77) and the Museum Judenplatz (p75).

GRABEN Map pp56-7

01; U1, U3 Stephansplatz

Branching off from Stock-im-Eisen-Platz (a small square adjoining Stephansplatz), Graben literally began life as a ditch dug by the Romans to protect Vinodoba. In 1192 Leopold V filled in the ditch and built a defensive city wall that ended in Freyung, using as finance the ransom paid by archrival Richard the Lionheart, who at that time was being kept under lock and key in a castle near Dürnstein, on the Danube.

Two fascinating landmarks on Graben are the writhing, towering Pestsäule (Plague Column), and Adolf Loos' public toilets, which are in the *Jugendstil* design. The Pestsäule commemorates the end of the plague and was erected in 1692. It was designed by Johann Bernhard Fischer von Erlach – don't miss this, as it is one of the finest in Europe.

Architectural highlights to look out for on Graben include the neo-Renaissance Equitable Palais at No 3; the ornate inner courtyard is tiled with Hungarian Zsolnay ceramics. The blackened and aged stump encased in glass on the building's eastern corner was where apprentice journeyfolk during the Middle Ages would hammer nails into the stump to ensure a safe homeward journey. Other buildings are the neoclassical revivalist Erste Österreichisches Sparkasse (1836), on the corner of Tuchlauben, complete with a gilded bee symbolising thrift and industriousness, and the *Jugendstil* Grabenhof (1876) at No 14, built by Otto Wagner using the plans of Otto Thienemann.

PETERSKIRCHE Map pp56-7

☎ 533 64 33; www.peterskirche.at, in German; 01, Petersplatz; admission free; 10am-8pm Mon-Fri, 9am-9pm Sat & Sun; U1, U3 Stephansplatz 1A, 2A, 3A

The Peterskirche (Church of St Peter), situated just north of Graben, was built in 1733 according to plans of the celebrated baroque architect Johann Lukas von Hildebrandt. This was not the first baroque church in Vienna (the Dominikanerkirche (p61) has that honour), nor is it considered the finest (the Karlskirche (p80) with its glass elevator to the cupola, pips it at the post). But don't pass without at least a glimpse at its interior highlights: a fresco on the dome painted by JM Rottmayr and a golden altar depicting the Martyrdom of Saint John Nepomuk.

HOFBURG & AROUND

With the Habsburg's predilection for pomp, and with Vienna's historical roots as an imperial capital and bastion of the Occident, this was a city built to impress. It's worth bearing in mind that if the Ottoman Turks had taken Vienna in the second siege in the late 17th century, much of Europe would have lain at their feet. The Hofburg, whipped up and constantly revamped from the 13th century, is the ultimate display of Austria's former imperial power. It was home to the Habsburg rulers from Rudolph I in 1279 until the Austrian monarchy collapsed under Karl I in 1918, and today houses the offices of the Austrian president and an ensemble of extraordinary museums. Picturesque parkland flanks it on both sides.

ROMAN RUINS – MICHAELERPLATZ

Map p66

U3 Herrengasse 2A, 3A

Ringed by gorgeous architecture, Michaelerplatz is centred on Roman ruins that are reputed to have been a brothel for soldiers. This cobblestoned circular 'square' is often packed with snap-happy travellers, ticket touts and *Fiaker* (horse-drawn carriages), and on hot summer days the throng of people and the smell of *Pferdekacke* (horse crap) can be overwhelming. Notwithstanding the crowds, and the experience of Vienna lifted from the pages of a travel brochure in pungent Odorama, Michaelerplatz is one of the prettiest squares in the city.

MICHAELERKIRCHE Map p66

533 80 00; www.michaelerkirche.at, in German; 01, Michaelerplatz; admission free; 7am-10pm; U3 Herrengasse 2A, 3A

The Michaelerkirche dates from the 13th century and, not counting the Roman ruins, is the oldest building on Michaelerplatz. The most interesting aspect of the church is its burial crypt, which you can see on 40-minute bilingual German/English tours at 11am and 1.30pm Monday to Saturday between Easter and October. Out of respect

ORIENTATION IN THE HOFBURG

The Hofburg (Map p66) is a jigsaw puzzle of absurdly monumental buildings designed to impress. This was especially the Habsburg's intention when it came to monarchs who visited Austria's most famous family. As a mere mortal, your first reaction might be to feel stunned by it all: weeping at this glory, walking backwards on your knees between Habsburg monuments or simply keeling over feet up and waving your legs in splendid awe are probably among the least appropriate responses in this modern age.

South (left if you are facing the Hofburg) of Michaelerplatz is the pretty square, Josefsplatz, named after Joseph II. It gained celluloid immortality in the film *The Third Man* as it was here, outside Palais Pallavicini (Josefsplatz 5), that Harry Lime faked his own death. An equestrian monument to Emperor Josef II stands in the middle of the square. On or close to Josefsplatz are the Albertina (p70), Augustinerkirche (p70) and the Nationalbibliothek (p71).

Approaching the Hofburg from Michaelerplatz (and entering through a portal once reserved exclusively for the Kaiser) you pass through the Michaelertor and neobaroque Michaelertrakt. The Michaelerplatz side of the building is lined with statues of Hercules in various acts of subjugating creatures, and on each side of the entrance you find evocative fountains depicting the Power of the Land and Power of the Sea. You get the idea – lots of rippling muscle and deep metaphors. The entrance leads into a beautiful domed area. On the left of the hall is the Spanish Riding School (p67) and its visitor centre.

Straight ahead, you reach the large courtyard In der Burg, with its monument to Emperor Franz, the last in a long line of Holy Roman emperors after Napoleon brought about the collapse of the Reich in 1806. Entrance to the Kaiserappartements (p66) is from this courtyard.

The oldest part of the Hofburg is the Schweizerhof (Swiss Courtyard), named after the Swiss guards who used to protect its precincts. This is reached via the Renaissance Swiss Gate on the left, which dates from 1553. The 13th-century courtyard gives access to the Burgkapelle (Royal Chapel; p67) and the Schatzkammer (Imperial Treasury; p67). The buildings encircling the Schweizerhof are collectively known as the Alte Burg (Old Palace).

Continuing straight ahead, you reach Heldenplatz (Hero's Sq) and the Neue Burg, built between the second half of the 19th century and WWI. Around this time, events caught up with the Habsburgs and plans for a second wing mirroring the curving facade on the southwest side of Heldenplatz never eventuated, giving the square a lopsided appearance. The Neue Burg houses the Museum für Völkerkunde (p72) and the three Neue Burg Museums (p71). The balcony holds the infamous distinction of being the place from which Hitler addressed a rally during his triumphant 1938 visit to Vienna after the Anschluss.

Facing each other with eternal stares on Heldenplatz are the monuments to Prince Eugene of Savoy (closest to the Neue Burg) and Archduke Karl (Charles of Austria). Anton Fernkorn, the sculptor of both, is rumoured to have gone loony over his failure to correctly balance the Prince Eugene statue; the steed's tail rests on the ground to provide stability.

Finally, after passing through the Burgtor (Palace Gate; 1821–24), you reach Maria-Theresien-Platz, where a statue of Maria Theresia is flanked by the Kunsthistorisches Museum (p69) and the Naturhistorisches Museum (p70).

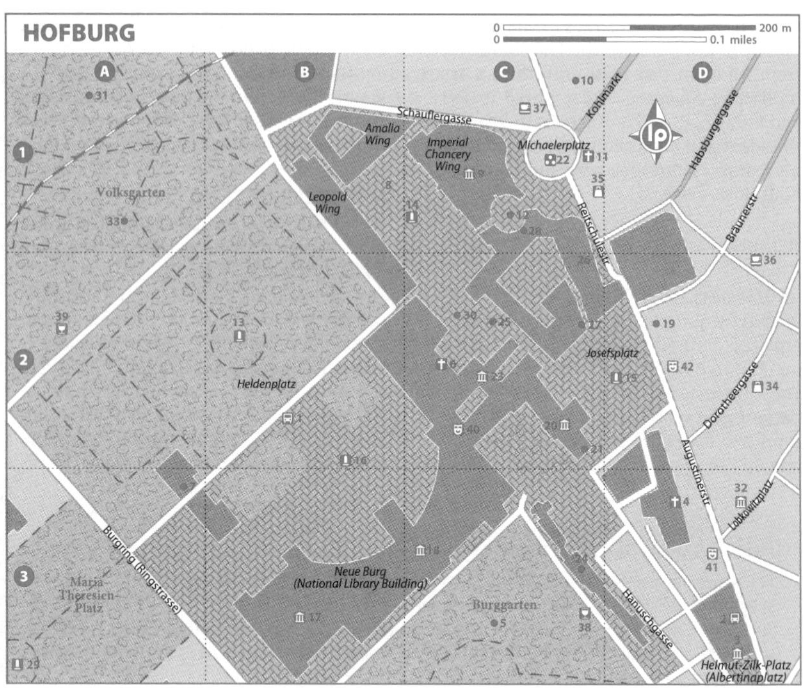

for the dead, taking photos is not allowed. Understandably, death itself is the theme of the tours, which take you past coffins that have rusted away to reveal their occupants, others with glass covers, and to a viewing of several noble mummies preserved by the rarefied air of the crypt. Only the well-off and noble were buried in the crypt, and unlike the catacombs in Stephansdom, it wasn't used for plague victims.

LOOS HAUS Map p66

01, Michaelerplatz 3; 8am or 9am-3pm Mon-Wed & Fri, 9am-5.30pm Thu; U1, U3 Stephansplatz

Designed by Adolf Loos, this modernist gem put Franz Josef's nose seriously out of joint when it was completed in 1911. Its intentionally simple facade offended the emperor so deeply that he ordered the curtains pulled on all palace windows overlooking the building. Critics described it as a 'house without eyebrows', referring to its lack of window detail, and work had to be stopped until Loos agreed to add 10 window boxes. Today it is widely accepted as a work of genius and houses a bank on the ground floor and temporary exhibition halls on the upper floors.

KAISERAPPARTEMENTS Map p66

533 75 70; www.hofburg-wien.at; 01, Innerer Burghof, Kaisertor; adult/under 19yr/student €9.90/5.90/8.90; 9am-5.30pm Sep-Jun, 9am-6pm Jul & Aug; U3 Herrengasse 2A, 3A

The Kaiserappartements (Imperial Apartments) were once the official living quarters of Franz Josef I and Empress Elisabeth (or Sisi as she was affectionately named). The first section, known as the Sisi Museum, is devoted to Austria's most beloved empress. It has a strong focus on the clothing and jewellery of Austria's monarch – if your interest in a pretty dress is limited, you may find the reconstruction of Sisi's luxurious Pullman coach more interesting. The windows mimic the movement of the train, and the original can be viewed inside the Technisches Museum (p123). Part of this first section also has a replica of her personal fitness room complete with rings and bars, testament to her obsession with keeping slim. Many of the empress's famous portraits are on show, as is her death

HOFBURG

INFORMATION

Oldtimer Bus Tours ... 1 B2
Redbus City Tours ... 2 D3

SIGHTS (p64)

Albertina ... 3 D3
Augustinerkirche ... 4 D3
Burggarten ... 5 C3
Burgkapelle ... 6 C2
Burgtor ... 7 A3
Ephesos Museum ... (see 18)
Hofjagd und Rüstkammer Collection ... (see 18)
In der Burg ... 8 B1
Kaiserappartements ... 9 C1
Loos Haus ... 10 C1
Michaelerkirche ... 11 C1
Michaelertor & Michaelertrakt ... 12 C1
Monument to Archduke Karl ... 13 B2
Monument to Emperor Franz ... 14 C1
Monument to Emperor Josef II ... 15 D2
Monument to Prince Eugene of Savoy ... 16 B2
Museum für Völkerkunde ... 17 B3
Nationalbibliothek ... (see 18)
Neue Burg Museums ... 18 C3
Österreichisches Filmmuseum ... (see 41)
Palais Pallavicini ... 19 D2
Papyrus Museum ... (see 18)
Prunksaal ... 20 C2
Prunksaal Entrance ... 21 C2
Roman Ruins – Michaelerplatz ... 22 C1
Sammlung Alter Musikinstrumente ... (see 18)
Schatzkammer ... 23 C2
Schmetterlinghaus ... 24 C3
Schweizerhof ... 25 C2
Silberkammer ... (see 9)
Sisi Museum ... (see 9)
Spanish Riding School ... 26 C2
Spanish Riding School Entrance (Training Session Viewing) ... 27 C2
Spanish Riding School Office ... 28 C1
Statue of Maria Theresia ... 29 A3
Swiss Gate ... 30 C2
Temple of Theseus ... 31 A1
Theatermuseum ... 32 D3
Volksgarten ... 33 A1

SHOPPING (p129)

Dorotheum ... 34 D2
Loden-Plankl ... 35 C1

DRINKING & NIGHTLIFE (p171)

Café Bräunerhof ... 36 D2
Café Griensteidl ... 37 C1
Palais Palffy ... (see 42)
Palmenhaus ... 38 C3
Volksgarten Pavillon ... 39 A2

MUSIC & THE ARTS (p191)

Hofburg Concert Halls ... 40 C2
Österreichisches Filmmuseum ... 41 D3
Palais Palffy ... 42 D2

mask, made after her assassination in Geneva in 1898.

The adjoining Silberkammer (Silver Depot) collection is included in the entry price. The largest silver service here can take care of 140 dinner guests. Audio guides – available in 11 languages – are also included in the admission price. Admission including a tour of either the Silberkammer or the Sisi Museum and Kaiserappartements costs €12.40 for adults, €11.40 for students and €6.90 for children.

SCHATZKAMMER Map p66

☎ 525 24-0; www.khm.at; 01, Schweizerhof; adult/under 19yr/concession €12/free/9; 10am-6pm Wed-Mon; U3 Herrengasse; 2A, 3A

The Schatzkammer (Imperial Treasury) contains secular and ecclesiastical treasures of priceless value and splendour – the sheer wealth of this collection of crown jewels is staggering. As you walk through the rooms you see magnificent treasures such as a golden rose, diamond studded Turkish sabres, a 2680-carat Colombian emerald and, the highlight of the treasury, the imperial crown.

The wood-panelled Sacred Treasury has a collection of rare religious relics, some of which can be taken with a grain of salt: fragments of the True Cross, one of the nails from the Crucifixion, a thorn from Christ's crown and a piece of tablecloth from the Last Supper.

Audio guides in German, English, Italian and French cost €3 (the shorter highlight audio tour is free) and are very worthwhile. A combined 'Treasures of the Habsburgs' ticket, which includes the Kunsthistorisches Museum, costs €18. Allow anything from 30 minutes to two hours for the Schatzkammer.

BURGKAPELLE Map p66

☎ 533 99 27; www.hofburgkapelle.at, in German; 01, Schweizerhof; admission €1.50; 11am-3pm Mon-Thu, 11am-1pm Fri; U3 Herrengasse; 2A, 3A

The Burgkapelle (Royal Chapel) originally dates from the 13th century and received a Gothic makeover from 1447 to 1449, but much of this disappeared during the baroque fad. The vaulted wooden statuary survived and is testament to those Gothic days. This is where the Vienna Boys' Choir Mass (p194) takes place every Sunday at 9.15am between September and June. The chapel is sometimes closed to visitors in July and August, so check ahead in those months.

SPANISH RIDING SCHOOL Map p66

☎ 533 90 31; www.srs.at; 01, Michaelerplatz 1; performances €23-143; U3 Herrengasse; 2A, 3A

The world-famous Spanish Riding School (Spanische Hofreitschule) is a Viennese institution truly reminiscent of the imperial Habsburg era. This unequalled equestrian show is performed by Lipizzaner stallions formerly kept at an imperial stud established at Lipizza (hence 'Lipizzaner'; see p68). These graceful stallions perform an equine ballet to a program of classical music while the audience watches from pillared balconies – or cheaper standing room – and the chandeliers shimmer above.

There are many different ways to see the Lipizzaner. Performances are the top-shelf variant, and for seats at these you will need to book several months in advance. The website has the performance dates and you can order tickets online. As a rule of thumb, performances are at 11am on Saturday and Sunday from mid-February to June and late August to December. For standing room, book at least one month in advance. During the summer break, special 'Piber meets Vienna' performances are held for tourists.

Visitors to the 'Morgenarbeit' morning training sessions (adults/student & child/senior/family €12/6/9/24; 10am-noon Tue-Sat Jan-Jun & mid-Aug–Dec – check website for exact dates) can drop in for part of a session and leave whenever they want to. Guided tours (adult/student & child/senior €16/8/13; 2pm, 3pm & 4pm Tue-Sun) held in English and German take you into the performance hall, stables and other facilities, and a combined morning training & tour (adult/student & child/senior €26/12/20) is another option.

The visitor centre (9am-4pm Tue-Fri, till 7pm Friday on performance days) on Michaelerplatz sells all tickets, and morning training tickets can also be bought at Gate 2 on Josefsplatz during training sessions.

THEATERMUSEUM Map p66

☎ 525 24 610; www.theatermuseum.at, in German; 01, Lobkowitzplatz 2; adult/under 19yr/concession €4.50/free/3.50; 10am-6pm Tue-Sun; U1, U2, U4 Karlsplatz 3A

The baroque Lobkowitz palace, which houses the Theatermuseum, is as much a delight to see as the museum itself. Built between 1691 and 1694, it was at the cutting edge of the baroque movement and

THE WHITE HORSE IN HISTORY

The Lipizzaner stallions date back to the 1520s, when Ferdinand I imported the first horses from Spain for the imperial palace. His son Maximilian II imported new stock in the 1560s, and in 1580 Archduke Charles II established the imperial stud in Lipizza (Lipica, today in Slovenia), giving the horse its name. Austria's nobility had good reason for looking to Spain for its horses: the Spanish were considered the last word in equine breeding at the time, thanks to Moors from the 7th century who had brought their elegant horses to the Iberian Peninsula. Italian horses were added to the stock around the mid-1700s (these too had Spanish blood) and by the mid-18th century the Lipizzaner had a reputation for being Europe's finest horses.

The original baroque horses were not white or light grey, but of various colours. In fact, it only became fashionable to breed white stallions during the 19th century, when Arab and various other horses were re-introduced into the line and the horses carefully selected.

Over the centuries, natural catastrophe, but more often war, caused the Lipizzaner to be evacuated from their original stud in Slovenia on numerous occasions. One of their periods of exile from the stud in Lipica was in 1915 due to the outbreak of WWI. Some of the horses went to Laxemburg (just outside Vienna), and others to Bohemia in today's Czech Republic (at the time part of the Austro-Hungarian Empire). When the Austrian monarchy collapsed in 1918, Lipica passed into Italian hands and the horses were divided between Austria and Italy. The Italians ran the stud in Slovenia, while the Austrians transferred their horses to Piber, near Graz, which had been breeding military horses for the empire since 1798 – mostly at that time stallions crossed with English breeds. Today, Piber still supplies the Spanish Riding School with its white stallions.

Things got no easier for the Lipizzaner after WWI, with Europe being carved into ever-smaller pieces. Austrians, Hungarians, Czechs, Italians and Yugoslavs developed their own studs, and even Romanians had their own Lipizzaner lineages. When WWII broke out, Hitler's cohorts goose-stepped in and requisitioned the Piber stud in Austria and started breeding military horses and – spare the thought! – pack mules there. They also decided to bring the different studs in their occupied regions together under one roof, and Piber's Lipizzaner wound up in Hostau, situated in Bohemia.

Fearing the Lipizzaner would fall into the hands of the Russian army as it advanced towards the region in 1945 (and amid rather odd fears that the pirouetting stars would be eaten), American forces seized the Lipizzaner and other horses in Hostau and transferred them to the safety of rural Upper Austria. The 'rescue' of the Lipizzaner was the basis for a rather kitsch Walt Disney film from 1963, *The Miracle of the White Stallions*. In 1952 our equine friends were finally returned to Piber but as a result of this turbulent history there are Lipizzaner lineages in a handful of European countries, including Slovenia, of course, which in 2007 issued 20-cent coins with a Lipizzaner imprint.

GETTING THE MOST OUT OF THE KUNSTHISTORISCHES MUSEUM

To really make the most of this top attraction, set aside at least three hours. Even better, if you've got the time, buy an annual ticket (€29; see p54), valid for all seven related museums, and spread your visits over several days. The seven museums are the Museum of Ethnology, Theatermuseum, Neue Burg, Wagenburg, Schatzkammer and the Theseus Temple (contemporary art), which is being restored. The combined 'Treasures of the Habsburgs' ticket, which includes the Schatzkammer, costs €18. Admission to the Kunsthistorisches Museum includes the Neue Burg museums and vice versa (p71).

Audio guides, tours & books

Audio guides in English, German and Italian cost €3 and are well worth the investment. A regular program of free tours (conducted in German) is published every two months and available from the service desk. The service desk also has a useful plan of the museum (€0.50), and the museum shop sells some informative and colourful books in various languages about the museum's works – including the excellent *The Kunsthistorisches Museum Vienna* (€12.90).

The Building

Once planning began in the 1850s to revamp Ringstrasse, the Habsburgs sniffed their chance to unite their large art collection under one worthy roof. The German architect Gottfried Semper (1803–79) and the Austrian Karl Freiherr von Hasenauer (1833–94) designed the building in a neo-Renaissance style, and it was opened in 1891. When you enter, a circular recess in the ceiling allows a view into the domed hall, and halfway up the staircase you reach Antonio Canova's (1757–1822) *Theseus and the Minotaur* from 1819 (predating the museum). Beyond that you can take up position to admire the fresco paintings depicting a veritable pantheon of European masters (Dürer, Rembrandt and Raphael, to name a few). Diagrams on each side of the hall indicate who painted what. The ceiling is the work of Hungarian Mihály Munkácsy (1844–1900), after Hans Makart (1840–84) had completed the semicircular lunettes but died before he could get to the ceiling. Gustav Klimt (1862–1918), his younger brother Ernst Klimt (1864–92) and Franz Matsch (1861–1942) did the paintings broken by the columns.

Orientation

The Egyptian & Oriental collection is located on the right (west wing) as you enter, but first admire the view to the dome and the fresco paintings. The west wing is closed indefinitely for restoration, but usually houses the decorative arts of the Kunstkammer (Cabinet of Curiosities). The Gemäldegalerie (Picture Gallery) on the first floor is the most important part of the museum. The east wing is devoted to German, Dutch and Flemish paintings from masters such as Pieter Bruegel the Elder (1525–69), Albrecht Dürer (1471–1528), Peter Paul Rubens (1577–1640) and Rembrandt (1606–69), whereas the west wing includes painters such as Titian (about 1485–1576), Raphael (1483–1520), Caravaggio (1571–1610) and many others whose works can be fully appreciated with the audio guides.

took its name from the noble family who occupied the esteemed halls from 1753 onwards. The Eroicasaal, with frescos dating from 1724–29, is its decorative highlight; the banquet hall is where Beethoven conducted the first performance of his Third Symphony.

The palace has temporary and permanent exhibitions on the history of Austrian theatre, but a little German is needed to fully appreciate it. The permanent collection is devoted to Gustav Mahler and regularly changes themes. A small room hidden towards the back of the 1st floor contains an ensemble of puppets from puppeteer Richard Teschner. These works of intricate detail range from magicians to orang-utans and are vaguely reminiscent of Java's *Wayang Golek* wooden puppets. They are often used in performances; inquire at the ticket desk for times.

KUNSTHISTORISCHES MUSEUM

Map pp56-7

☎ 525 24-0; www.khm.at; 01, Maria-Theresien-Platz; adult/under 19yr/concession €12/free/9; 10am-6pm Tue-Sun, 10am-9pm Thu; U2 Museumsquartier D, 1, 2

One of the unforgettable experiences of being in Vienna will be a visit to the Kunsthistorisches Museum (Museum of Art History), brimming with works by Europe's finest painters, sculptors and artisans. The museum has sculptures from classical times (and some copies) in its Egyptian-Oriental collection, antiques, a coin collection, and decorative curiosities from the Renaissance and baroque epochs (this section was closed for long-term restoration at the time of publication). These alone would be reason to set aside half a day or more for the museum, but the Picture Gallery takes it one echelon higher to offer a breathtaking window into mainly Flemish, Dutch, Italian and German works from the 16th and 17th centuries – the time when the Habsburgs went on a collecting frenzy.

NATURHISTORISCHES MUSEUM

Map pp56-7

☎ 521 77-0; www.nhm-wien.ac.at; 01, Burgring 7; adult/under 19yr/student €10/free/5; 9am-6.30pm Thu-Mon, 9am-9pm Wed; U2, U3 Volkstheater D, 1, 2

The Naturhistorisches Museum (Museum of Natural History) is the scientific counterpart of the Kunsthistorisches Museum and almost as sensational, with extraordinary exhibits on minerals, meteorites and assorted animal remains in jars, as well as some fascinating Stone Age Venus figurines. Highlights of the gemstone collection in Room IV are the Colombian emerald, believed to be a present from the Aztec ruler Montezuma to the Spanish conquistador Hernán Cortés, and the bouquet of precious stones presented to Franz Stephan by Maria Theresia. Two 'must sees' of the museum are the 25,000-year-old statuette Venus of Willendorf, entertainingly presented in her own wooden hut with light and sound effects (and Palaeolithic hunter poised on her roof), and the 32,000 BC statuette Fanny from Stratzing (the oldest figurative sculpture in the world). When not on tour, the original 'Dancing Fanny' is situated sublimely in a case on the left as you enter room 11. It's an odd nickname that comes from her unusual pose, supposedly reminiscent of the Austrian ballerina Fanny Elssler. There's a kids' corner for those between five and 14 years.

ALBERTINA Map p66

☎ 534 83-0; www.albertina.at; 01, Helmut-Zilk-Platz 1; adult/under 19yr/student/senior €9.50/free/7/8; 10am-6pm Thu-Tue, 10am-9pm Wed; U1, U2, U4 Karlsplatz 3A

Once used as the Habsburg's imperial apartments for guests, the Albertina now houses the greatest collection of graphic art in the world. The collection, founded in 1768 by Maria Theresia's son-in-law Duke Albert von Sachsen-Teschen, consists of an astonishing 1.5 million prints and 50,000 drawings, including 145 Dürer drawings (the largest collection in the world), 43 by Raphael, 70 by Rembrandt and 150 by Schiele. There are loads more by Leonardo da Vinci, Michelangelo, Peter Paul Rubens, Michael Bruegel, Paul Cézanne, Pablo Picasso, Henri Matisse, Gustav Klimt and Oskar Kokoschka.

The enormous collection of graphics, architectural sketches, photographs, prints and drawings from the archive are used as the basis for temporary exhibits on a particular theme, and these have been augmented since 2009 by a sensational permanent collection of paintings in the Masterworks of Modern Art section, which is a who's who of 20th-century and contemporary art – Chagal, Nolde, Jawlensky and very many more.

The Österreichisches Filmmuseum (p199) is also in the Albertina.

VOLKSGARTEN Map p66

01, Dr-Karl-Renner-Ring; admission free; 6am-10pm Apr-Oct, 6am-8pm Nov-Mar; U3 Volkstheater, Herrengasse 46 2A, 48A

Spreading out between the Burgtheater and Heldenplatz, the Volksgarten (People's Garden) is great for relaxing among dignified rose bushes and even more dignified statues. A monument to Empress Elisabeth is in the northeast corner, not far from the Temple of Theseus, an imitation of the one in Athens (commissioned by Napoleon), and the club Volksgarten (p188).

BURGGARTEN Map p66

01, Burgring; admission free; 6am-10pm Apr-Oct, 6am-8pm Nov-Mar; U2 Museumsquartier, U2, U3 Volkstheater D, 1, 2 2A, 57A

Tucked behind the Hofburg, the Burggarten (Castle Garden) is a leafy oasis amid the hustle and bustle of the Ringstrasse and Innere Stadt. The marble statue of Mozart is the park's most famous tenant, but there's also a statue of Franz Josef in military garb. Lining the Innere Stadt side of the Burggarten is the Schmetterlinghaus and the ever-popular bar Palmenhaus (p174).

AUGUSTINERKIRCHE Map p66

☎ 533 70 99; 01, Augustinerstrasse 3; admission free; U1, U3 Herrengasse 2A, 3A

The Augustinerkirche (Augustinian Church) dates from the 14th century and is one of the older parts of the Hofburg. The vaulted ceiling testifies to its unmistakably Gothic origins, and the sparse interior was converted to baroque in the 17th century before being restored to original Gothic in

1784. The stone high altar is neo-Gothic, dating from 1870. On the right as you enter is a pyramid-shaped tomb containing Maria Theresia's daughter Archduchess Maria Christina, designed by Antonio Canova (of *Theseus and the Minotaur* fame, see p69). The Augustinerkirche, however, is most famous for being where the hearts of 54 Habsburg rulers are kept. The urns containing them can be viewed in the Herzgrüftel (Little Heart Crypt; tour adult/child €2.50/1.75; approx 12.30pm Sun, following Mass, other days by appt). The church hosts regular evening classical music concerts, and the 11am Mass on Sunday is celebrated with a full choir and orchestra; the choir practices on a regular basis and times are posted on the church door.

NEUE BURG MUSEUMS Map p66

525 24-0; 01, Heldenplatz; adult/under 19yr/concession €12/free/9; 10am-6pm Wed-Sun; D, 1, 2 2A

Instruments of all shapes and sizes are on display at the Sammlung Alter Musikinstrumente (Collection of Ancient Musical Instruments), the first of three-museums-in-one in the Neue Burg. The forward-thinking Archduke Ferdinand of Tyrol started the whole thing by collecting rare instruments and this now ranks among the finest Renaissance collections in the world. It will be a highlight for the musically inclined: there are horns shaped like serpents and violins with carved faces, and a few of the historic instruments can be played (pianists can grab their chance to knock out a tune on something unusual).

The admission price includes entry to two adjoining collections. The Ephesos Museum contains artefacts from Ephesus and Samothrace, supposedly donated (some say 'lifted') by the Sultan in 1900 after a team of Austrian archaeologists excavated the famous site in Turkey. The highlight of the museum are figures from 161 AD in a frieze honouring the defeat of the Parthians by Lucius Verus and his Roman army. Noted as one of the finest museums of its kind in the world, the Hofjagd und Rüstkammer (Arms and Armour) collection dates mostly from the 15th and 16th centuries and has some superb examples of ancient armour. This is one place that will enthral adults and kids alike.

Audio guides are available for €3 and admission to the Kunsthistorisches Museum includes the Neue Burg museums (p69).

top picks

IT'S FREE – CENTRAL VIENNA

- Hofburg squares, gardens & monuments (p65)
- BAWAG Contemporary/BAWAG Foundation (p61)
- Justizpalast (p74)
- Augustinerkirche (p70)
- Stephansdom – the nave (p54)
- Museum für angewandte Kunst (p60; Sat free)
- Archiv des Österreichischen Widerstands (p77)
- University Main Building (p73)
- Ringstrasse (p75 and p134)

NATIONALBIBLIOTHEK Map p66

534 10-0; www.onb.ac.at; 01, Josefsplatz 1; adult/under 19yr/concession/family €7/free/4.50/12.50; 10am-6pm Tue, Wed, Fri-Sun, 10am-9pm Thu; U3 Herrengasse 2A, 3A

The Nationalbibliothek (National Library) was once the imperial library and is now the largest library in Vienna. The real reason to visit these esteemed halls of knowledge is to gaze on the Prunksaal (Grand Hall). Commissioned by Charles VI, this baroque hall was the brainchild of Johann Bernhard Fischer von Erlach, who died the year the first brick was laid, and finished by his son Joseph in 1735. Leather-bound scholarly tomes line the walls, and the upper storey of shelves is flanked by an elegantly curving wood balcony. Rare ancient volumes (mostly 15th century) are stored within glass cabinets, with pages opened to beautifully illustrated passages of text. A statue of Charles VI stands guard under the central dome, which itself has a fresco by Daniel Gran depicting the emperor's apotheosis.

Combined tickets for the Prunksaal, Globenmuseum (p71), Esperanto Museum (p72) and Papyrus Museum cost adult/concession €12/9.50, and are valid for seven days.

GLOBENMUSEUM Map pp56-7

534 10 710; www.onb.ac.at; 01, Herrengasse 9, 1st fl; adult/under 19yr/concession/family €5/free/3/8; 10am-6pm Tue, Wed, Fri-Sun, 10am-9pm Thu; U3 Herrengasse 2A, 3A

Part of the Nationalbibliothek (National Library) collection of museums, this small museum situated inside a former palace

(Palais Mollard) is dedicated to cartography. Among the collection of 19th-century globes and maps are a couple of gems a few centuries older. Look for the globe made for Emperor Karl V by Mercator in 1541. An interactive model of this alongside the real one allows you to zoom in on the 16th-century world for close-ups that get a little rough.

PAPYRUS MUSEUM Map p66

☎ 534 10 420; www.onb.ac.at; 01, Heldenplatz, Neue Burg; adult/under 19yr/concession/family €3/free/2.50/4.50; 10am-6pm Tue, Wed, Fri-Sun, 10am-9pm Thu; U3 Herrengasse 2A, 3A

Part of the Nationalbibliothek museum ensemble, the Papyrus Museum displays a collection of 200 fragments of ancient writing on papyrus. Papyrus was used for writing in ancient Egypt and the museum focuses on this, and cultures that influenced ancient Egypt, as well as fragments of writing on other media such as parchment and clay. One of its highlights is a fragment of musical notation on pottery depicting the choral ode from *Orestes,* a tragedy written by the Greek Euripides.

ESPERANTO MUSEUM Map pp56-7

☎ 534 10 730; www.onb.ac.at; 01, Herrengasse 9, ground fl; adult/under 19yr/concession/family €3/free/2.50/4.50; 10am-6pm Tue, Wed, Fri-Sun, 10am-9pm Thu; U3 Herrengasse 2A, 3A

The oft-overlooked Esperanto Museum is mostly devoted to the artificial language created by Dr Ludvik Zamenhof back in 1887 and is part of the national library ensemble of museums. The first book in Esperanto, written by Dr Zamenhof himself, is displayed in the museum, which also covers several other ways of scissor-jumping the language barrier: a media terminal even goes briefly into the language used by the Klingons of *Star Trek* fame (reciting lines from Shakespeare's *Hamlet*).

MINORITENKIRCHE Map pp56-7

☎ 533 41 62; 01, Minoritenplatz; admission free; 8am-6pm Apr-Oct, 8am-5pm Nov-Mar; U3 Herrengasse

The Minoritenkirche (Minorite Church) is a 13th-century Gothic church that, like many in Austria, later received a baroque facelift. If you think the tower looks a little stubby, you're right on the button: it was 'shortened' by the Turks in 1529. The most noteworthy piece inside is a mosaic copy of da Vinci's *Last Supper,* commissioned by Napoleon. The church hosts classical concerts and choir recitals throughout the year; schedules are often posted outside. Expect to pay about €20.

MUSEUM FÜR VÖLKERKUNDE Map p66

☎ 534 30-0; www.ethno-museum.ac.at; 01, Heldenplatz; adult/under 19yr/concession €8/free/6; 10am-6pm Wed-Mon; D, 1, 2 2A

You can impress your children by taking them to the Museum für Völkerkunde (Museum of Ethnology) – it was revamped a few years ago and exudes a lightness of mood and has a thoughtful use of space that adults will appreciate too. Exhibits are on non-European cultures and divided into regions and nationalities, covering such countries as China, Japan and Korea, and also Polynesian, Native American and Inuit cultures.

SCHMETTERLINGHAUS Map p66

☎ 533 85 70; www.schmetterlinghaus.at; 01, Burggarten; adult/3-6yr/student/senior €5.50/3/4.50/5; 10am-4.45pm Mon-Fri, 10am-6.15pm Sat & Sun Apr-Oct, 10am-3.45pm Nov-Mar; U1, U2, U4 Karlsplatz D, 1, 2, 62

Sharing the Habsburg's personal *Jugendstil* glasshouse (1901) with the Palmenhaus bar (p174), the Schmetterlinghaus (Butterfly House) is for the butterfly-mad only. There are hundreds of butterflies and the shop stocks a great range of butterfly paraphernalia, but the air is hot and unbearably humid, the species range fairly limited and it's quite a small display area. It's located in the Burggarten, directly behind the Neue Burg.

NORTH OF HOFBURG

The area north of the Hofburg takes in Vienna's Rathaus (town hall) in the northwest, as well as a northern quarter of the Innere Stadt from Michaelerplatz to Schottentor peppered with palaces and churches. Freyung and Am Hof are historic squares in this interesting part of town, which date back to Roman times.

PARLAMENT Map pp56-7

☎ 401 10 2400; www.parlament.gv.at; 01, Dr-Karl-Renner-Ring 3; tours adult/under 19yr/concession €4/1/2; U2, U3 Volkstheater D, 1, 2, 46, 49

The Parlament building opposite the Volksgarten strikes a governing pose over the Ringstrasse. Its neoclassical facade and Greek pillars, designed by Theophil Hansen in 1883, are striking, and the beautiful Athena Fountain, sculpted by Karl Kundmann, which guards the building offsets it magnificently.

The visitor centre (admission free; 8.30am-6.30pm Mon-Fri, 9.30am-4.30pm Sat) directly behind Athena is where you can find out about the history of Austrian politics and how parliament runs from a multimedia show of video clips and interactive screens.

SCHOTTENKIRCHE Map pp56-7

534 98 600; 01, Freyung; church admission free, museum adult/child/student €5/1/4; 11am-5pm Tue-Sat; U2 Schottentor 1A

At the northern end of Herrengasse, the Schottenkirche (Church of the Scots) was founded by Benedictine monks probably originating from Scotia Maior (Ireland); the present facade dates from the 19th century. The interior has a beautifully frescoed ceiling and terracotta-red touches. Although the main nave can only be entered during services at noon and 6pm to 7pm daily, it's possible to peek through the gates. A small art and artefacts museum in the adjoining monastery displays religious pieces from the church and monastery, but of more interest is the church shop (10am-6pm Mon-Fri, 10am-5pm Sat), which stocks homemade schnapps, honey and jams.

On Fridays Freyung is transformed into a farmers market (p158), from where organic produce from Lower Austria finds its way into the larders of Viennese.

RATHAUS Map pp56-7

525 50; www.wien.gv.at; 01, Rathausplatz; admission free; tours 1pm Mon, Wed & Fri; U2 Rathaus D, 1, 2

For sheer grandness, the Rathaus (City Hall) steals the show on Ringstrasse. This neo-Gothic concoction, completed in 1883 by Friedrich von Schmidt, was modelled on Flemish city halls. Its main spire soars to 102m, if you include the pennant held by the knight at the top. You're free to wander through the seven inner courtyards, but you must join a guided tour to see the interior, with its red carpets, gigantic mirrors and frescos (tours leave from the Rathaus information office on Friedrich-Schmidt-Platz). The largest of these inner courtyards sometimes hosts concerts.

Rathausplatz is the sight of some of the city's most frequented events, including the Christkindlmarkt (p147), Musikfilm Festival (p18) and the Wiener Eistraum (Vienna Ice Dream; p203).

TOURS OF PARLAMENT

Tours of the parliament lasting almost one hour are conducted at 11am, 2pm, 3pm and 4pm Monday to Thursday, at 11am, 1pm, 2pm, 3pm and 4pm on Friday, and on the hour between 11am and 4pm on Saturday from September to mid-July. The rest of the year tours are on the hour between 11am and 4pm Monday to Saturday. A combined ticket for a tour of Parlament and entrance to Palais Epstein costs adult/concession & child €7/3.

PALAIS EPSTEIN Map pp56-7

401 10 2400; www.palaisepstein.at; 01, Dr-Karl-Renner-Ring 1; tours adult/under 19yr/concession €4/1/2; tours 11am & 2pm Sat mid-Sep–mid-Jul; D, 1, 2, 46, 49 48A

Designed by Theophil von Hansen, the same architect who created the plans for Austria's national Parlament, Palais Epstein started life as home to the prominent Jewish Epstein family before being sold in 1873 to plug financial problems. It later became the infamous Soviet Union headquarters during the 'four men in a jeep' period after WWII – nicknamed the 'Gateway to Siberia' because around 1000 Austrians passed through its doorways on their deportation route to Siberia. Today it houses part of the Austrian national parliament and you can take tours – the only way to see inside – through its hallowed halls (the glass atrium rises an impressive four floors) and visit its *bel étage* rooms. With a filigree ceiling of gold lacework and circular frescos (Hansen based it on detail in the Santa Maria dei Miracoli in Venice), the *Spielzimmer* (play room) is one highlight. A ticket for a two-hour tour of the palace and the parliament costs adult/concession & child €7/3. No tours leave when the parliament is in session.

UNIVERSITY MAIN BUILDING Map pp56-7

4277-0; www.univie.ac.at; 01, Dr-Karl-Lueger-Ring 1; admission free; 7am-10pm Mon-Fri, 7am-7pm Sat; U2 Schottentor 37, 38, 40, 41, 42, 43, 44

Founded in 1365, Vienna's venerable university was the first in the German-speaking countries. Today it has about 85,000 students, and at some time or another they all drop by the main university building. Grand Duke Rudolph IV (1339–65) used Paris' Sorbonne as his inspiration, and it was just as well he wasn't around in 1520 during the Reformation, because in that year his 'Sorbonne' was shoe-horned into the Church. In fact, occasional head-clinching between Church and secular institutions over the centuries is a feature of Vienna's university history. When Maria Theresia squeezed the Church out of Austrian universities during the Enlightenment in the mid-18th century, she almost made the uni trim and fit for the modern age. 'Almost' because ironically the first woman was admitted only in 1897. During the Nazi era, about half the professors and tutors had to pack their bags, either because of their politics or 'race'.

One-hour tours (☎ 427 71 7524; 🕑 in English 11.30am Sat, in German 10.30am Sat & 6pm Thu; adult/senior & student €5/3.50) take you through the late-19th century neo-Renaissance and neobaroque arcades, reading room and, when possible, decorative main ceremonial chamber. They leave from the porter's office in the entrance hall.

Directly opposite the university is the Votivkirche (see p99), and also the Mölker Bastei, one of the couple of remaining sections of the old city walls.

JUSTIZPALAST Map pp56-7

☎ 521 52-0; Schmerlingplatz 11; 🕑 8am-4pm Mon-Fri; Ⓤ U2, U3 Volkstheater 🚋 46 🚌 2A, 48A

Completed in 1881, the Justizpalast is home to the supreme court. It's an impressive neo-Renaissance building that – as long as you're not being dragged in wearing handcuffs – is also interesting inside. To enter, you pass through airport-type security. Inside, the 23m-high central hall is a majestic ensemble of staircase, arcades, glass roofing and an oversized statue of Justitia poised with her sword and law book. In July 1927, after members of the right-wing Front Fighters paramilitary group were unexpectedly acquitted here of killing two people during a demonstration, an outraged crowd stormed the building and started burning Justitia's court records. Flames were soon licking out of the windows, prompting 600 police guards to open fire on the demonstrators. At least 89 people were killed and hundreds wounded. In 1945, the commander of the four occupying Allied powers had his office here. The canteen on the top floor is open to the general public and has great views across the Hofburg.

KUNSTFORUM Map pp56-7

☎ 537 33 26; www.bankaustria-kunstforum.at; 01, Freyung 8; adult/17-27yr/senior/family €9/6/7.50/20; 🕑 10am-7pm Sat-Thu, 10am-9pm Fri; Ⓤ U3 Herrengasse 🚌 2A, 3A

The private Kunstforum museum gets about 300,000 visitors each year, and for good reason – it stages an exciting program of changing exhibitions that focus on a specific theme, often (but not always) with a modern and postmodern skew. One in recent years focused on food in still life art, with 90 works from the 16th to the 20th century, some by Cézanne and Picasso.

AM HOF Map pp56-7

01; Ⓤ U3 Herrengasse, U2 Schottentor 🚌 1A

Am Hof, off Bognergasse, is where the Babenberg monarchs (p22) resided in a fortress before rulers moved to the site of the Hofburg in the late 13th century. Roman excavations can be seen at the Feuerwehr Zentrale (Fire Brigade Centre; ☎ 505 87 47-0; 01, Am Hof 9; closed for conservation works). Nearby at No 11 a gold-painted cannonball is embedded in the facade, a relic from the 1683 Turkish siege. The former Jesuit monastery Kirche Am Hof (☎ 533 83 94; admission free; 🕑 8am-noon, 4.30-6pm Mon-Sat, 7am-7pm Sun), on the southeast side, has a baroque facade adapted from its fire-damaged Gothic predecessor and the hugely expansive nave is lined with white pillars and topped with gold badges. It was here in 1806 that a royal herald announced the end of the Holy Roman Empire, ruled by the Habsburgs for about 500 years. The Mariensäule (Mary's Column) in the centre of the square is dedicated to the Virgin Mary and was erected in 1667.

BEETHOVEN PASQUALATIHAUS Map pp56-7

☎ 535 89 05; 01, Mölker Bastei 8; adult/under 19yr/concession €2/free/1; 🕑 10am-1pm & 2-6pm Tue-Sun; Ⓤ U2 Schottentor 🚋 37, 38, 40, 41, 42, 43, 44

Beethoven made the 4th floor of this house his residence from 1804 to 1814 (he apparently occupied around 80 places in his 35 years in Vienna, but thankfully not all of them are museums!) and during that time composed Symphonies 4, 5 and 7 and the opera *Fidelio,* among other works. His two rooms (plus another two from a neighbouring apartment) have been converted into a museum, which is lightly filled with photos, articles and a handful of his personal belongings. The house is named after its long-time owner Josef Benedikt Freiherr von Pasqualati.

PALAIS KINSKY Map pp56-7

01, Freyung 4; ⌚ 10am-6pm Mon-Fri; Ⓤ U2 Schottentor 🚌 1A

Built by Hildebrandt in 1716, Palais Kinsky has a classic baroque facade and its highlight is an elaborate three-storey stairway off to the left of the first inner courtyard, with elegant bannisters graced with statues at every turn. The ceiling fresco is a fanciful creation filled with podgy cherubs, bare-breasted beauties and the occasional strongman. The palace now contains art shops and upmarket restaurants.

JEWISH QUARTER TO THE CANAL

The old Jewish quarter is centred on Judenplatz, north of Stephansplatz. It begins from the north-east corner of Am Hof and can be reached from there via a collection of quaint, cobblestone streets and quiet corners. Lined with intricate baroque and 19th-century buildings, Judenplatz was for centuries the centre of the Jewish ghetto, and excavations have uncovered a medieval synagogue dating from 1420, which has subsequently been turned into the Museum Judenplatz.

Between Judenplatz and Schottenring (to the north) the streets are less appealing. The section of the Innere Stadt between Judenplatz and the Danube Canal has some major draws, though, especially on Passauser Platz, Hoher Markt and Ruprechtsplatz. As you get near the canal you pass through an area dubbed the 'Bermuda Triangle' for its plentiful bars. During the day, it's quiet. At night, it heaves with drunken revellers and can get unappetising.

MUSEUM JUDENPLATZ Map pp56-7

☎ 535 04 31; www.jmw.at; 01, Judenplatz 8; adult/concession €4/2.50; ⌚ 10am-6pm Sun-Thu, 10am-2pm Fri; 🚌 2A, 3A

The main focus of the city's second Jewish museum is the excavated remains of a

VENNA'S RINGSTRASSE

The Ringstrasse, or the Ring as it's known locally, is a wide, tree-lined boulevard encircling much of the Innere Stadt along the line of the former 16th-century city walls. Originally these walls had the extra protection of a ditch or moat, beyond which a wide, sloped clearing allowed defenders to hurl the heavy stuff at their exposed invaders. Anyone living in the *Vorstädte* (inner suburbs) outside the fortress was expected to flee inside it as the invading forces approached, or take their chances on the land. In this regard, Vienna was a medieval city like many others in Europe that had anything of value inside its walls worth protecting – Vienna had a great deal.

By the mid-19th century, the fortress had become an anachronism and the clearings had turned into *Glacis* (exercise grounds and parkland). In stepped Emperor Franz Josef I. His idea was to replace them with grandiose public buildings that would better reflect the power and the wealth of the Habsburg Empire.

The Ringstrasse was laid out between 1858 and 1865, and in the decade afterwards most of the impressive edifices that now line this busy thoroughfare were already under construction. Franz Josef had extremely deep pockets to match his elaborate plans – consider this for an architectural shopping list: Börse Palais (1877; Map pp56-7), Staatsoper (built 1861–69; p195), Musikverein (1867–69;), MAK (1868–71; p60), Akademie der bildenden Künste (1872–76; p62), Naturhistorisches Museum (1872–81; p70), Rathaus (1872–83; p73), Kunsthistorisches Museum (1872–91; p69), Parlament (1873–83; p72), Universität Wien (1873–84; p73), Burgtheater (1874–88; p196), Justizpalast (1875–81; p74) and the Heldenplatz section of the Hofburg's Neue Burg (1881–1908; p71).

WWI intervened and the empire was lost before Franz Josef's grand scheme was fully realised. A further wing of the Hofburg had been planned (which would have sat directly on the Ringstrasse, taking up what is now the Volksgarten), and the palace and the giant museums opposite were to be linked by a majestic walkway, rising in arches over the Ring. It never happened.

To fully appreciate the sheer scale of the endeavour, walk at least some of the Ringstrasse. The whole ring is about 5km but the grandest section, between the university and the opera, is less than 2km. See p134 for more.

medieval synagogue that once stood on Judenplatz. Built around 1420, it didn't last long: Duke Albrecht V's 'hatred and misconception' led him to order its destruction in 1421. The basic outline of the synagogue can still be seen, illuminated with subdued lighting. A small model of the building completes the picture. After entering the museum you get headphones and descend into a film room to watch an informative 12-minute video on Judaism, the synagogue and the Jewish quarter. Next up are excavations, after which you can search the databases for lost relatives or friends if you wish. A combined ticket (adult/concession & child €10/6) allows entry to the museum, the Stadttempel (p77) and Jüdisches Museum (p63).

HOLOCAUST-DENKMAL Map pp56-7

01, Judenplatz; 2A, 3A

The focal point of Judenplatz is the Holocaust-Denkmal, a pale, bulky memorial to the 65,000 Austrian Jews who perished in the Holocaust. Designed by British sculptor Rachel Whiteread and unveiled in 2000, the 'nameless library' – a structure in the shape of a library where the spines of books face inwards – represents the untold stories of Holocaust victims and has the names of Austrian concentration camps written across its base. On the north side of Judenplatz is the former Böhmische Hofkanzlei (Bohemian Court Chancery). Walk around to Wipplingerstrasse to see its striking facade by Johann Bernhard Fischer von Erlach.

ANKERUHR – HOHER MARKT Map pp56-7

01, Hoher Markt; U1, U3 Stephansplatz 1A, 2A 3A

Vienna's oldest square (once the centre of the Roman outpost) is home to the Ankeruhr (Anker Clock), an art-nouveau masterpiece created by Franz von Matsch in 1911 and named after the Anker Insurance Co, which commissioned it. Over a 12-hour period, figures slowly pass across the clock face, indicating the time against a static measure showing the minutes. Figures range from Marcus Aurelius (the Roman emperor who died in Vienna in AD 180) to Josef Haydn, with Eugene of Savoy, Maria Theresia and others in between. Details of who's who are on a plaque on the wall below. People flock here at noon, when all the figures trundle past in succession and organ music from the appropriate period is piped out.

RÖMER MUSEUM – HOHER MARKT

Map pp56-7

535 56 06; 01, Hoher Markt 3; adult/under 19yr/concession €4/free/3; 9am-6pm Tue-Sun; U1, U3 Stephansplatz 1A, 2A 3A

Who knows what the Romans would make of their former outpost today being hidden beneath a restaurant on Hoher Markt, but the small expanse of Roman ruins dating from the 1st to the 5th century are thought to be part of the officers' quarters of the Roman legion camp at Vindobona. You can see crumbled walls and tiled floors and a small but selective exhibit on artefacts found during the excavations. The ruins are part of the 'Wien Museum' municipal museum ensemble of Vienna.

RUPRECHTSKIRCHE Map pp56-7

535 60 03; www.ruprechtskirche.at, in German; 01, Seitenstettengasse 5; admission free; 10am-noon Mon-Fri, 3-5pm Mon, Wed & Fri; U1, U3 Stephansplatz 1A, 2A 3A

A few steps north of Ruprechtsplatz, Ruprechtskirche (St Rupert's Church) dates from about 1137 or earlier, making it the oldest church in Vienna. The lower levels of the tower date from the 12th century, the roof from the 15th century and the iron Renaissance door on the west side from the 1530s. What makes this church attractive is its unusually simple exterior of ivy-clad stone walls in cobblestoned surrounds. The interior is just as sleek and worth viewing, with a Romanesque nave from the 12th century.

MARIA AM GESTADE Map pp56-7

533 95 94-0; http://maria-am-gestade.redemptoristen.at, in German; 01, Passauer Platz; U1, U3 Stephansplatz 1A, 2A 3A

Originally a wooden church built by Danube boatsmen around 880, Maria am Gestade (Maria on the Riverbank) today is a shapely Gothic beauty of stone assembled from the 14th century. Because of the steep ground, the nave was built narrower than the choir (and with a slight bend). When Napoleon came to town from 1805, he used it as a store for his weapons and stall for his horses. The interior, with its high vaulted Gothic ceiling and pretty stained glass behind a winged Gothic altar, can only be viewed during services, held at 7am and 11am Monday to Saturday, and from 7am to noon Sunday. The church is on a picturesque flight of steps in a quiet corner of town.

STADTTEMPEL Map pp56-7

☎ 531 04 170; www.ikg-wien.at; 01, Seitenstettengasse 4; hrs vary; U1, U4 Schwedenplatz 1, 2 2A

The Stadttempel (City Synagogue), Vienna's main synogogue, was completed in 1826 after *Toleranzpatent* reforms by Joseph II in the 1780s granted rights to Vienna's Jews to practise their religion. This paved the way for improved standing for Jews in the broader community and a rise in fortunes. Built in an exquisite Biedermeier style, the main prayer room is flanked by 12 ionic columns and rises into a cupola. It seats about 500 people. Visitors of the Jewish faith can phone the synagogue (Hebrew, English and German spoken) for more information about services. Arrive early to register with security, and bring your passport.

One-hour tours (☎ 535 04 31 130; adult/concession €3/2; 11.30am & 2pm) for general visitors are conducted by the Jewish Museum (meet outside the synagogue); these take you past a 2002 memorial to the Jewish victims of the Shoa and into the main hall. The Stadttempel is included in the combined ticket for the Jüdisches Museum (p63) and Museum Judenplatz (p75).

MORZINPLATZ Map pp56-7

01; U1, U4 Schwedenplatz 1, 2 2A

Situated on the Danube Canal between Salztorbrücke and Marienbrücke, Morzinplatz is dominated by the Monument to the Victims of Fascism (1985), on the site of the former Gestapo headquarters during the Nazi era. The monument features the Star of David and the pink triangle, representing the Jewish and homosexual victims of the Nazis.

UHREN MUSEUM Map pp56-7

☎ 533 22 65; www.wienmuseum.at; 01, Schulhof 2; adult/under 19yr/concession €4/free/2; 10am-6pm Tue-Sun; U3 Herrengasse 1A, 2A, 3A

The municipal Uhren Museum (Clock Museum) loudly ticks away time from its location behind the Kirche Am Hof. Opened in 1921 in the Hafenhaus, one of Vienna's oldest buildings, its three floors are weighed down with an astounding 21,200 clocks and watches, ranging from the 15th century to a 1992 computer clock. Its collection of Biedermeier and *belle époque* models will, for most, steal the show. The peace and quiet is shattered at the striking of the hour, so those with sensitive ears should avoid these times. Admission and guided tours at 10am and 11am on the first and third Sunday of the month are free.

NEIDHART-FRESKEN Map pp56-7

☎ 535 90 65; 01, Tuchlauben 19; adult/child/student/senior €6/free/3/4; 10am-1pm Tue, 2-6pm Tue & Fri-Sun; 2A, 3A

An unassuming house on Tuchlauben hides quite a remarkable decoration: the oldest extant secular murals in Vienna. The small frescos, dating from 1398, tell the story of the minstrel Neidhart von Reuental (1180–1240) and life in the Middle Ages in lively and jolly scenes. The frescos have lost some colour and are patchy in parts, but are in superb condition considering their age. Neidhart is a municipal museum.

ARCHIV DES ÖSTERREICHISCHEN WIDERSTANDS Map pp56-7

☎ 228 94 69; www.doew.at; 01 Wipplingerstrasse 8; admission free; 9am-5pm Mon-Thu; 2A, 3A

Housed in the Altes Rathaus (Old City Hall), the Austrian Resistance Archive documents the little-known antifascist resistance force that operated during the Nazi regime; some 2700 resistance fighters were executed by the Nazis and thousands more sent to concentration camps. The exhibition gives in-depth analysis of the Nazi doctrines on homosexuality, 'unworthy' citizens, concentration camps and forced labour, and there are many of the photos and memorabilia detailing the time before and after the Anschluss. It is a disturbing but highly worthwhile exhibition.

FROM SQUARE TO SQUARE IN THE INNERE STADT

Walking Tour

1 Zollamtsteg

This is a pedestrian crossing of the Wien River that together with the Bogenbrücke from 1900 forms a sublime and unusual backdrop: green railway bridges cross diagonally, a perfect motif for a creative photograph of passing trains.

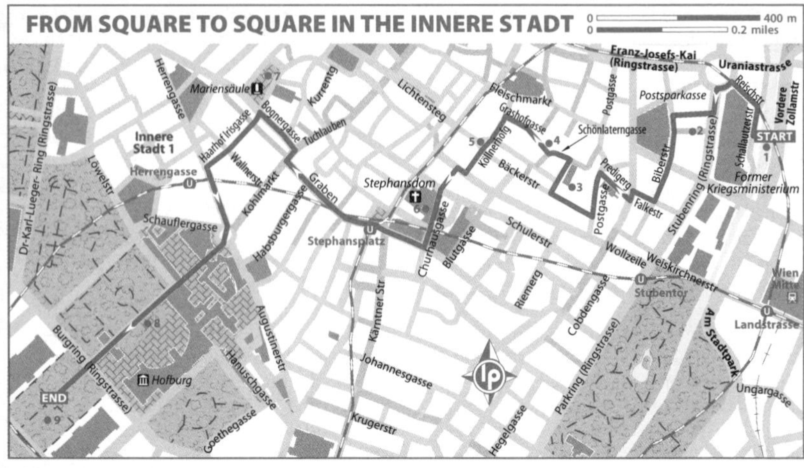

WALK FACTS

Start Zollamtsteg
End Maria-Theresien-Platz
Distance 3km
Time 90 minutes
Exertion Easy
Fuel stop Beim Czaak (p157)

2 Georg-Coch-Platz
Separating Otto Wagner's *Jugendstil* Postsparkasse (p61) building from the pompous former Kriegsministerium (p61), this inauspicious patch offers an impressive vista of contrasting early-20th-century architecture.

3 Dr-Ignaz-Seipel-Platz
Formerly known as Universitätsplatz and one of Vienna's most interesting squares, Dr-Ignaz-Seipel-Platz (p61) is named after an Austrian chancellor, Ignaz Seipel (1876–1932), who was in power from 1926 to 1929. The son of a *Fiaker* driver, he became a university professor and theologian who melded an anti-Marxist block during the Red Vienna period (see p27).

4 Heiligenkreuzerhof
Dating from the late 17th and early 18th centuries, this remarkable part of Vienna gets its name from the Cistercian foundation that settled here (explaining the baroque, domed chapel at the entrance from Schönlaterngasse). The foundations of this picturesque square go back to the 12th century.

5 Lugeck
Spiked by a statue of Johannes Gutenberg (1400–68), who invented mechanical typesetting, this square was probably a lookout on the old fortress around the 13th century. A cheesy old ditty goes, 'Lugeck I happened upon, where merchants were going to and fro, in colourful clothing speaking in foreign tongues'.

6 Stephansplatz
From Stephansplatz all distances from the centre of the capital are measured. It's home to Stephansdom (p54), Vienna's Gothic cathedral. The square is very many things, but rarely is it quiet.

7 Am Hof
With the Mariensäule at its centre, Am Hof (p74) is something of a Cinderella square: oft-overlooked, yet the lanes and streets around it are well worth exploring.

8 Heldenplatz
Situated inside the Hofburg (p65), contiguous to the many Hofburg squares, Heldenplatz is where political events are traditionally held. Hitler held one here in 1938 to an ecstatic crowd.

9 Maria-Theresien-Platz
The highlight of Maria-Theresien-Platz comes in the weeks leading up to Christmas, when a Christkindlmarkt (p147) opens and you can stand around drinking mulled wine near the statue of plump Maria Theresia.

VORSTADT SOUTHWEST

Drinking & Nightlife p178; Eating p158; Shopping p143; Sleeping p212

The high-density *Vorstädte*, Vienna's inner suburbs, are very much the places where the Viennese live, work and go to play, and the experience of going deeper into them (ie away from the Ringstrasse) can be likened to pressing up a river. Things begin normally enough, but at some point you may realise you've entered something akin to an urban heart of darkness, where *Vorstadt* patriarchs hold court to gritty regulars in divy *Beisl* (beer houses) or coffee houses, the Viennese passion for wry humour ascends to its highest form, and Viennese life takes on that character it is famous for – alternating between the mundane, the morbid and, quite frankly, the bizarre. Sometimes these *Vorstädte* are even normal.

Wieden (the 4th district), Margareten (the 5th), Mariahilf (the 6th) and Neubau (the 7th) form a southwest area of the inner city overflowing with shops, sights and entertainment venues. These are wonderful areas for eating, drinking and making merry.

Wieden, particularly around Karlsplatz, has a good sprinkling of sights on the cusp of the Innere Stadt. The main city museum (Wien Museum) is here, and so too is the Naschmarkt, Vienna's food-stall paradise hugging the Wien River. In and around the junction of Schliefmühlgasse and Margaretenstrasse is a concentration of bars and clubs that place this area high on the list of destinations for a good night out. This borderland between Wieden and Margareten is currently also the part with the most alternative vibe.

Margareten has a very close-knit feel and, as with all *Vorstädte*, changes in character every few blocks. Housing becomes less dense before it almost loses character altogether and vanishes into the oblivion of the busy Gürtel at the former Südbahnhof (currently being resurrected as Vienna's main train station). You will find lots of shops and places to eat and drink here too.

Striding across the Wien River north into Mariahilf, you enter a part of the district around Gumpendorfer Strasse that was once run-down and from a town planning point of view more gum than tooth; today it is enjoying a new lease of life with the advent of scruffy-chic bars and shops, especially on the stretch east of the Haus des Meeres, a sea-life museum inside a *Flakturm* (air raid shelter; see p107). A southern portion of the district also takes in one side of Naschmarkt.

Further north, 'the fifth' ends abruptly at Mariahilfer Strasse, the equivalent of London's Oxford St. Westbahnhof/BahnhofCity Wien West presides over the top (west) end of the street (although the street continues beyond this somewhat), and the Innere Stadt end of Mariahilfer Strasse leads into the MuseumsQuartier, Vienna's constellation of open space and culture that is packed with museums. Connoisseurs in the art of people-watching will love the MuseumsQuartier. Here you can see students, office workers, men with sharp shoes and sideburns, women with alternative-chic accessories, pallid couch potatoes experimenting with natural light early evening in summer, and playful kids – all enjoying the MuseumsQuartier's potpourri of options. Much of Vienna comes here to relax.

All of the MuseumsQuartier is actually in the Neubau district, directly backing onto Spittelberg, once a separate district of narrow cobblestone streets and Biedermeier houses (and vice of all unsavoury sorts). Today it has been made pretty, real estate has developed less-than-quaint price tags, and it has a handful of shops, bars and restaurants. At Christmas Spittelberg is transformed into one of the city's most patronised markets, with craft stalls aplenty and city workers sipping *Glühwein* (mulled wine). A stroll around Neubau takes you beyond this into a lively district of idiosyncratic secondhand and alternative shops around Neubaugasse.

The U-Bahn line U4 runs along the Wien River, providing a useful west–east connection. From there it's a short walk either north or south of Naschmarkt into other districts. Bus 13A connects Margareten's Pilgramgasse with the Neubau district.

Together, these inner-city districts are vibrant, rich in cultural sights and even richer in Viennese everyday life – it's a part of town you might find yourself spending much of your time in.

HITLER IN VIENNA

Born in Braunau am Inn, Upper Austria, in 1889, with the name Adolf Schicklgruber (his father changed the family name when they moved to Germany in 1893), Adolf Hitler moved to Vienna when he was just 17. Six unsettled, unsuccessful, poverty-stricken years later he abandoned the city and moved to Munich to make a name for himself. He later wrote in *Mein Kampf* that his Vienna years were 'a time of the greatest transformation that I have ever been through. From a weak citizen of the world I became a fanatical anti-Semite'. Whether this had anything to do with being twice rejected by the Akademie der bildenden Künste (Academy of Fine Arts), who dismissed his work as 'inadequate', he did not say. Even though he was convinced that proper training would have made him into a very successful artist, these rejections caused Hitler to write to a friend that perhaps fate may have reserved for him 'some other purpose'. This 'purpose' became all too clear to everyone over time.

Hitler briefly returned to Vienna in 1938 at the head of the German army and was greeted by enthusiastic crowds on Heldenplatz. He left a day later.

SOUTH OF MARIAHILFER STRASSE

South of the busy but characterless Mariahilfer Strasse, Gumpendorfer Strasse is well-seeded with interesting shops and drinking and eating spots, while the Naschmarkt on the Linke Wienzeile and Rechte Wienzeile (alongside the Wien River) pulls hungry Viennese from all over town. East of this, Karlsplatz is a straggling composite of green spaces and busy streets, but is dense with sights, among them the Wien Museum, Otto Wagner's Stadtbahn Pavillons and also the 'must-see' baroque Karlskirche.

KARLSKIRCHE Map pp84-5

☎ 712 44 56; www.karlskirche.at, in German; 04, Karlsplatz; adult/under 10yr/concession €6/free/4; 9am-noon & 1-6pm Mon-Sat, 1-5.30pm Sun; U1, U2, U4 Karlsplatz

Karlskirche (Church of St Charles Borromeo) rises at the southeast corner of Resselpark and is the finest of Vienna's baroque churches. This dramatic structure was built between 1716 and 1739, after a vow by Karl VI at the end of the 1713 plague. It was designed and commenced by Johann Bernhard Fischer von Erlach and completed by his son Joseph. The enormous twin columns at the front are modelled on Trajan's Column in Rome and show scenes from the life of St Charles Borromeo (who helped plague victims in Italy), to whom the church is dedicated. The huge oval dome reaches 72m. The admission price includes entrance to Museo Borromeo and a small museum with a handful of religious art and clothing purportedly from the saint, but the highlight is the lift to the dome for a close-up view of the intricate frescos by Johann Michael Rottmayr. The altar panel is by Sebastiano Ricci and shows the Assumption of the Virgin. In front of the church is a pond, replete with a Henry Moore sculpture from 1978.

WIEN MUSEUM Map pp84-5

☎ 505 87 47-0; www.wienmuseum.at; 04, Karlsplatz 5; adult/under 19yr/student/concession €6/free/3/4; 10am-6pm Tue-Sun; U1, U2, U4 Karlsplatz D, 1, 2, 62 4A

The Wien Museum provides an insightful snapshot of the development of Vienna from prehistory to the present day, putting the city and its personalities in a meaningful context. Exhibits are spread over three floors, including spaces for two temporary exhibitions. Begin on the ground floor from the right as you enter. This section traces the history of the city from 5600 BC to the end of the Middle Ages, and as well as featuring medieval helms with bizarre ornamentations it has a large collection of sandstone figures that were removed from Stephansdom in the mid-19th century. The 1st floor covers the Renaissance and baroque eras and has a fascinating model of the city in its medieval heyday. Both Turkish sieges are well represented. The 2nd floor begins with the Biedermeier era and works its way through the 20th century. A second model of the Innere Stadt shows the Ringstrasse developments and is augmented by some insightful period photographs.

NASCHMARKT Map pp84-5

06, Linke Wienzeile/Rechte Wienzeile btwn Getreidemarkt & Kettenbrückengasse; 6am-7.30pm Mon-Fri, 6am-6pm Sat; U4 Kettenbrückengasse

Vienna's famous market and eating strip began life as a farmers market in the 18th century, when the fruit market on Freyung was moved here. Interestingly, a law passed in 1793 said that fruit and vegetables arriving in town by cart had to be sold on Naschmarkt, while anything brought in by boat could be sold from the decks. The fruits of the Orient poured in, the predecessors of the modern-day sausage stand were erected and sections were set aside for coal, wood and farming tools and machines. Officially, it became known as Naschmarkt ('munch market') in 1905, a few years after Otto Wagner bedded the Wien River down in its open-topped stone and concrete sarcophagus. This Otto Wagnerian horror was a blessing for Naschmarkt, because it created space to expand. A close shave came in 1965 when there were plans to tear it down – it was saved, and today the Naschmarkt is not only the place to shop for food but has an antique market each Saturday.

STADTBAHN PAVILLONS Map pp84-5

☎ 505 87 478 5177; 04, Karlsplatz; adult/under 19yr/concession €2/free/1; 10am-6pm Tue-Sun Apr-Oct; U1, U2, U4 Karlsplatz D, 1, 2, 62 4A

Peeking above the Resselpark at Karlsplatz are two of Otto Wagner's finest designs, the Stadtbahn Pavillons. Built in 1898 at a time when Wagner was assembling Vienna's first public transport system (1893–1902), the pavilions are gorgeous examples of *Jugendstil*, with floral motifs and gold trim on a structure of steel and marble. The west pavilion now holds an exhibit on Wagner's most famous works, the Kirche am Steinhof (p126) and Postsparkasse (p61), which fans of *Jugendstil* will love. The eastern pavilion is now home to Club U (p174).

top picks

VORSTADT SOUTHWEST FOR CHILDREN

- Haus des Meeres (p82)
- Zoom (p88)
- Dschungel Wien (p89)
- Hofmobiliendepot – play area (p89)
- Wien Museum (p80)

GENERALI FOUNDATION Map pp84-5

☎ 504 98 80; www.gfound.or.at; 04, Wiedner Hauptstrasse 15; adult/concession €6/3; 11am-6pm Tue, Wed, Fri-Sun, 11am-8pm Thu; U1, U2, U4 Karlsplatz 62

The Generali Foundation is a fine gallery that picks and chooses exhibition pieces from its vast collection – numbering around 1400 – to create new themes. The majority of its ensemble covers conceptual and performance art from the mid-to-late 20th century. The entrance to the exhibition hall is towards the back of a residential passageway. Guided tours in German, which take place at 6pm on Thursdays, cost €2. Tuesday is free for students, and from 6pm Thursday entry costs €3 for everyone.

KUNSTHALLE PROJECT SPACE Map pp84-5

☎ 521 89 33; www.kunsthallewien.at; 04, Treitlstrasse 2; admission free; 4pm-midnight; U1, U2, U4 Karlsplatz D, 1, 2, 62

Once the Kunsthalle had taken up its new residence in the MuseumsQuartier, this glass cube was built on the site. Its doors were thrown open in 2001 to temporary exhibitions of up-and-coming artists. The website tells you what's on (and any variation in times). After the exhibition, chill out at the Kunsthallencafé (p178) next door.

SCHUBERT STERBEWOHNUNG Map pp84-5

☎ 581 67 30; www.wienmuseum.at; 04, Kettenbrückengasse 6; adult/under 19yr/concession €2/free/1; 10am-1pm & 2-6pm Wed & Thu; U4 Kettenbrückengasse 59A

Here, in his brother's apartment, Franz Schubert spent his dying days (40 to be precise) in 1828. While dying of either typhoid fever or syphilis he continued to compose, scribbling out a string of piano sonatas and his last work, *Der Hirt auf dem Felsen* (The Shepherd on the Rock). The apartment (Schubert's Death Apartment) is fairly bereft of personal effects but does document these final days with some interesting *Schubi* knick-knacks and sounds.

BESTATTUNGSMUSEUM off Map pp84-5

☎ 501 95-0; www.bestattungwien.at, in German; 04, Goldeggasse 19;adult/concession €4.50/2.50; noon-3pm Mon-Fri; D 13A

The Bestattungsmuseum is devoted to the noble art of undertaking. By no means

IN MARGARETEN WITH AUSTRIA'S QUEEN OF CRIME

A serial killer stalks the streets of Margareten in Vienna's southwest Vorstadt. Orlando, a transvestite sporting a Sisi hairdo, almost becomes the killer's second victim. Katharina Kafka, a waiter with a Gypsy background from the cafe Cuadro becomes involved in the search for the killer. Murder, mayhem and lots of reality just a stone's throw from where the city planner Otto Wagner gave the Wien River its concrete shoes (or at least its concrete cladding): this is the starting point for *Schön Tod* (which roughly translates as Dead Pretty), the 13th crime novel by Edith Kneifl, Austria's Queen of Crime. The book has been shortlisted for the Wiener Krimi-Preis (Vienna Crime Prize).

Edith Kneifl sweeps through the door of Cuadro dressed against double-digit subzero temperatures in a formidable winter coat. 'Margareten is changing' she tells us over coffee just a few paces from where Orlando almost comes unstuck. A reason for the change might stem from Vienna's architectural firm Coop Himmelb(l)au opening an atelier in the district, she believes. These days the workshops, sweatshops and working class housing of Margareten are becoming a favoured haunt for young artists and designers.

Edith Kneifl is one of the district's most high-profile fans. 'Margareten has the flavour of a big city', she says, 'and when you get closer to the Gürtel it gets wild and more multicultural. This mix of ethnic groups in the Vorstadt pans out well in Vienna'. Later she points to time she spent living in cities including San Francisco and New York – cities larger than Vienna where she says she developed a taste for a mix of different ethnic cultures.

Chandler, Hammet, the Swede Stieg Larsson and Sara Paretsky, cofounder of the American Sisters of Crime movement, are names that come up when we talk about crime-writing greats. 'For a long time our male colleagues here copied Chandler and Hammett, taking as their heroes men who prowled the streets as chain-smoking lone wolves. Our heroes are more realistic, ordinary women who have everyday problems, like problems with a husband or the children.'

Kneifl was a qualified and practicing psychologist before becoming a full-time author. In one anthology she compiled, *Tatort Wien* (Crime Scene Vienna), 16 Viennese woman writers litter the works with dead men, mostly husbands and lovers. This, she says with a hearty laugh, was not really intended, it just turned out that way.

One of the interesting aspects of *Schön Tod* is that it includes local Margareten characters who exist in real life: Stefan Gergely, the owner of Cuadro and other restaurants, crops up. So too does Frau Klaric from a second-hand shop on Margaretenplatz. And many, many more. 'It was an experiment to see whether this would work. I've never had real people in my novels until now', she says.

Later that morning she takes us around landmarks in Margareten. Some of these are the scenes of her fictional crimes ('The park where the body was found is just along there'). We pass the Pischinger shop, which sells the working-class competitor to Vienna's more famous 'Manner' wafers. We drop into Fredys Feuerhalle on Margaretenstrasse – formerly a *Beisl* and today a kiosk where tough-as-nut regulars down beer and skol the hard stuff. We go past one of Vienna's hottest tips for hams (Thum Schinkenmanufaktur) and we look into Frau Poldi's drugstore, seemingly a remnant from the age of laudanum and headache powders and destined to be lost to the district when Poldi eventually retires.

'The father of Herr Gergely', Edith Kneifl says later, referring to Cuadro's owner, 'invented the effervescent tablet'. And then she bids farewell, jumping onto a bus, which disappears with bronchial coughs in the freezing cold across town planner Otto Wagner's river-in-concrete-shoes. It was cold in Margareten that day – damned cold, and the drunks were staring at nothing, clinging frozen to their bottles…

The places mentioned:

- Cuadro (p162)
- Midinette (Map pp84-5; 05, Margaretenstrasse 84) Frau Klaric's antiques and second-hand store, with an interesting second-hand fashion store next door.
- Fredys Feuerhalle (Map pp84-5; 05, Margaretenstrasse 97) For drinks on the run. We found it an acquired taste.
- Thum Schinkenmanufaktur (Map pp84-5; ☎ 544 25 41; http://thum-schinken.at; 05, Margaretenstrasse 126) Small but fine store with Mangalitza ham and very many other varieties.
- Pischinger Abholmarkt (Map pp84-5; 05, Pilgramgasse 24) We find its wafers tastier than Vienna's more-famous Manner brand.

in the same gruesome league as the Pathologisch-Anatomisches Bundesmuseum (p93) or the Josephinum (p93), it nevertheless includes intriguing photos, documents and paraphernalia retelling the history of undertaking in a city famous for its macabre side.

HAUS DES MEERES Map pp84-5

☎ 587 14 17; www.haus-des-meeres.at; 06, im Esterhazypark, Fritz-Grünbaumplatz 1; adult/under 6yr/6-15yr/concession €12.50/4/5.90/9.60; 9am-6pm Fri-Wed, 9am-9pm Thu; U3 Neubaugasse 13A, 14A

What the 'House of the Sea' lacks is the chance for visitors to spring into the shark tank for some thrashing and splashing. There are probably insurance reasons for this not being a hands-on (or rather, feet-off) museum but a staff member does negotiate the tank at 6pm Thursday. While the museum is unlikely to blow you away instantly, you can get an interesting glimpse into the world of lizards, sharks, crocodiles and snakes, with a few fish and creepy-crawlies tossed in. The shark and piranha feeding sessions at 3pm Wednesday and Sunday are strong draws, and another is the reptile feeding at 10am Sunday and 7pm Thursday. There's a glass tropical house filled with lithe monkeys and a small rainforest. It occupies the inside of a Flakturm (p107), giving you a chance to see the interior of one of these monoliths.

HAYDNHAUS Map pp84-5

☎ 596 13 07; 06, Haydngasse 19; adult/under 19yr/concession €4/free/3; 🕑 10am-1pm & 2-6pm Tue-Sun; Ⓤ U3 Zieglergasse 🚌 57A

Though modest, the exhibition in Haydn's last residence was revamped in 2009 and focuses on Vienna as well as London during the late 18th and early 19th centuries. Haydn lived in Vienna during the heady times of Napoleon's occupation. His small garden, open to the public, is modelled on the original.

OTTO WAGNER BUILDINGS Map pp84-5

06, Linke Wienzeile & Köstlergasse; Ⓤ U4 Kettenbrückengasse

Something of a problem zone due to flooding, the Wien River needed regulating in the late 19th century. It would be more accurate to say that its last semblance of being a natural river was utterly and completely obliterated. At the same time, Otto Wagner had visions of turning the area between Karlsplatz and Schönbrunn into a magnificent boulevard. The vision blurred and the reality is a gushing, concrete-bottomed creek (a shocking eyesore designed by Wagner) and a couple of attractive Wagner houses on the Linke Wienzeile. Majolika-Haus at No 40 (1899) is the prettiest as it's completely covered in glazed ceramic to create flowing floral motifs on the facade. The second of these *Jugendstil* masterpieces is a corner house at No 38, with reliefs from Kolo Moser and shapely bronze figures from Othmar Schimkowitz. Nearby is a third house, simpler than these, at Köstlergasse 3 and, finally, you can put Wagner's functionality to the test by descending into his Kettenbrückengasse U-Bahn station.

THIRD MAN PRIVATE COLLECTION

Map pp84-5

☎ 586 48 72; 04, Pressgasse 25; adult/10-16yr/concession €7.50/4/6; 🕑 2-6pm Sat; Ⓤ U4 Kettenbrückengasse

The hours of this private museum may be limited, but fans of the quintessential film about Vienna from 1948 (and voted best British film of the 20th century by the British Film Institute) will enjoy perusing the posters, *Third Man* paraphernalia and the other 3000 or so objects on show here. Stills on the walls illustrate the craftwork of Australian-born cinematographer Robert Krasker, who received an Oscar. The museum indirectly covers aspects of Vienna before and after 'Harry Lime Time' as well as the film itself.

ANOTHER CIVILIZATION

The inner suburbs of Vienna (the *Vorstädte*) have always had a special place in Vienna's urban fabric. Each began in its own way – a convent in Landstrasse, the gentry building estates in Alsergrund – but in Vienna at the turn of the 20th century the inner suburbs had pretty much come to be seen as a strange civilisation in their own right. It had a lot to do with the industrial age.

The capital reflected the social divisions of the day. The Innere Stadt was largely the residential preserve of the aristocracy, whereas the upper middle class gravitated to the newly developed Ringstrasse. Beyond that, less well-off middle classes filled the *Vorstädte* and the working classes poured into the outer fringes of these and the suburbs beyond the Gürtel. The *Vorstädte* were where the different levels of society rubbed shoulders. Fred Heller, a Jewish journalist and writer, characterised them in 1918 as marginal places with dark landscapes along the tram lines. Others saw them as anarchic, pathological places, dull, joyless, but often crawling with vice – which sounds more like a description of what's just outside the Gürtel today.

VORSTADT SOUTHWEST

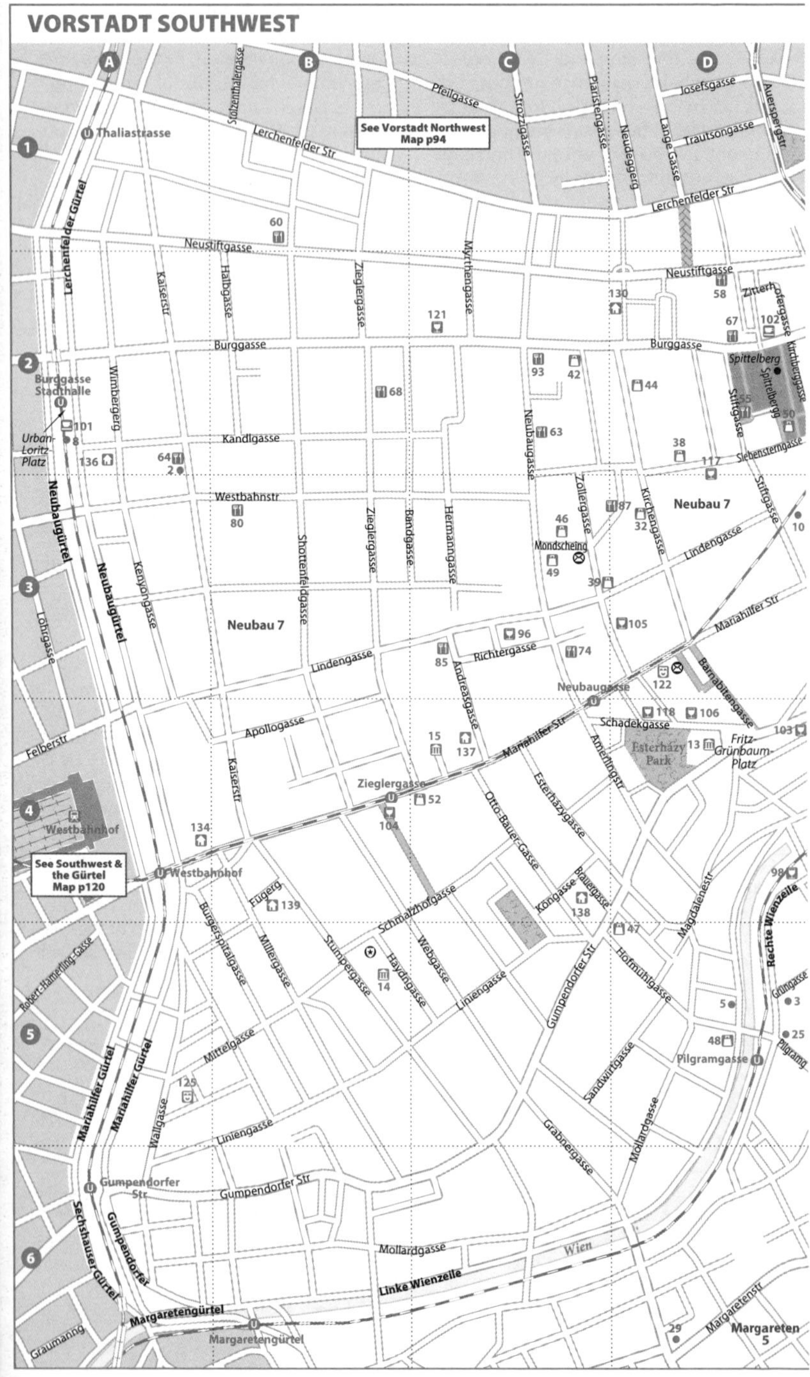

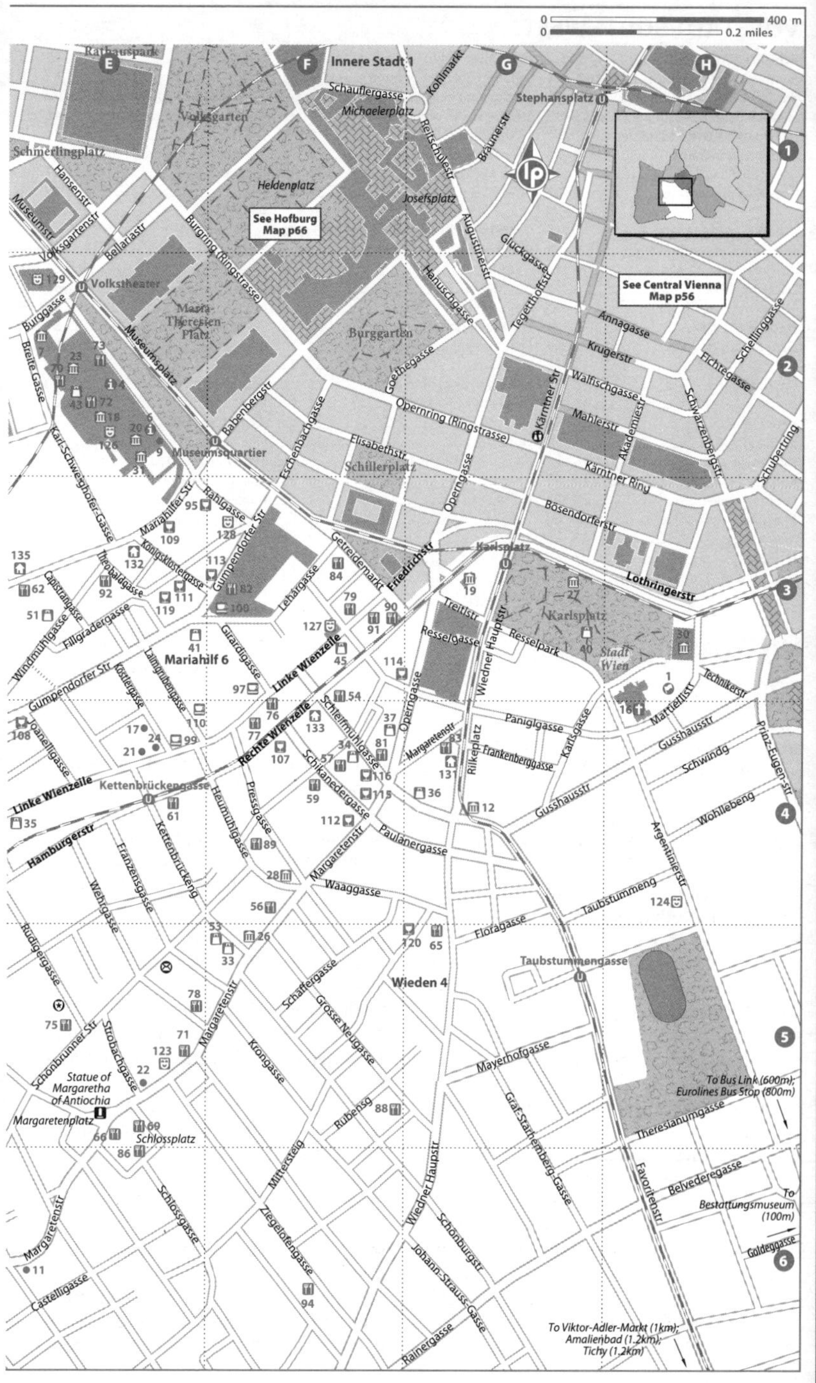

Innere Stadt 1
Mariahilf 6
Wieden 4
Volksgarten
Heldenplatz
Burggarten
Schillerplatz
Karlsplatz
Maria-Theresien-Platz
Museumsquartier
See Hofburg Map p66
See Central Vienna Map p56
Stephansplatz
Volkstheater
Karlsplatz
Kettenbrückengasse
Taubstummengasse
Kärntner Str
Opernring (Ringstrasse)
Burgring (Ringstrasse)
Kärntner Ring
Lothringerstr
Linke Wienzeile
Rechte Wienzeile
Wiedner Hauptstr
Margaretenstr
Favoritenstr
Margaretenplatz
Schlossplatz
Statue of Margaretha of Antiochia
To Bus Link (600m); Eurolines Bus Stop (800m)
To Bestattungsmuseum (100m)
To Viktor-Adler-Markt (1km); Amalienbad (1.2km); Tichy (1.2km)
0 400 m
0 0.2 miles

VORSTADT SOUTHWEST

INFORMATION

Australian Embassy ... 1 H3
Bizeps ... 2 A2
Faktor i ... 3 D5
MQ Point (MuseumsQuartier Information Centre) ... 4 E2
Rosa Lila Villa ... 5 D5
WienXtra-Kinderinfo ... 6 E2

SIGHTS (p79)

Architekturzentrum Wien ... 7 E2
Bücherei Wien ... 8 A2
Dschungel Wien ... 9 E2
Flakturm ... 10 D3
Fredys Feuerhalle ... 11 E6
Generali Foundation ... 12 G4
Haus des Meeres ... 13 D4
Haydenhaus ... 14 B5
Hofmobiliendepot ... 15 C4
Karlskirche ... 16 H4
Köstlergasse 3 ... 17 E4
Kunsthalle ... 18 E2
Kunsthalle Project Space ... 19 G3
Leopold Museum ... 20 E2
Majolika-Haus ... 21 E4
Midinette ... 22 E5
MUMOK ... 23 E2
Naschmarkt ... (see 45)
No 38 Linke Wienzeile ... 24 E4
Pischinger Abholmarkt ... 25 D5
Schubert Sterbewohnung ... 26 F5
Stadtbahn Pavillons ... 27 G3
Third Man Private Collection ... 28 F4
Thum Schinkenmanufaktur ... 29 D6
Wien Museum ... 30 H3
Zoom ... 31 E2

SHOPPING (p129)

Buchhandlung Walther König ... (see 4)
Das Möbel ... (see 102)
Das Studio ... 32 D3
Fair Kleidung ... 33 F5
Flo Vintage Mode ... 34 F4
Flohmarkt ... 35 E4
gabarage upcycling design ... 36 G4
Göttin des Glücks ... 37 F4
Holzer Galerie ... 38 D2
Hot Dogs ... 39 C3
Karlsplatz Christmas Market ... 40 G3
Lichterloh ... 41 E3
Lollipop ... 42 C2
Lomoshop ... 43 E2
Mon Ami ... (see 111)
Mot Mot ... 44 D2
Naschmarkt ... 45 F3
Park ... 46 C3
Phili's - With Love ... 47 D5
Piccini Piccolo Gourmet ... (see 79)
Rave Up ... 48 D5
Shu! ... 49 C3
Spittelberg Christmas Market ... 50 D2
Teuchtler ... 51 E3
Thalia ... 52 C4
Wie Wien ... 53 F5

EATING (p149)

Amacord ... 54 F3
Amerlingbeisl ... 55 D2
Aromat ... 56 F4
Babettes ... 57 F4
Bankok ... 58 D2
Beograd ... 59 F4
Billa Supermarket ... 60 B1
Billa Supermarket ... 61 E4
Billa Supermarket ... 62 E3
Billa Supermarket ... 63 C2
Biomarkt Maran ... 64 A2
Chang Asian Noodles ... 65 G5
Cuadro ... 66 E5
Die Burgermacher ... 67 D2
Do-An ... (see 76)
Gaumenspiel ... 68 B2
Gergely's ... 69 E5
Glacis Beisl ... 70 E2

MUSEUMSQUARTIER & AROUND

The MuseumsQuartier, or MQ, makes the heady claim to be among the world's 10 largest cultural complexes and a place where 'baroque meets cyberspace'. Despite the obvious hype, this cultural district is absolutely idiosyncratic and unique. It has about 60,000 sq metres of exhibition space, and houses the Leopold Museum, Museum moderner Kunst (MUMOK; Museum of Modern Art), Kunsthalle, Zoom, Architekturzentrum Wien, Tanzquartier Wien and numerous cafes and restaurants. Towards the front of the complex and behind it (behind the Kunsthalle) is Quartier 21, spaces with clusters of shops and temporary exhibitions, and near its Mariahilfer Strasse entrance is Dschungel Wien, a theatre for children. Surprisingly, people still live here – in apartments.

The MQ has succeeded in the tough act of bringing together heritage and the avante garde. The historic part consists of former stables dating from 1725, designed by Johann Bernhard Fischer von Erlach. These housed a reputed 600 horses, and contained two rooms just for the emperor's personal stock – one for the white stallions, the other for the black. The rectangular Haupthof is used for happenings and hosts both a winter and summer program of events (see the website www.m-q.at for details). It's especially popular during the summer months when everyone gets to work on tans while reposed on postmodern seating that each year is painted a different colour.

Behind the MQ are the cobblestone streets of Spittelberg. Elsewhere in Neubau, take a stroll along streets such as Zollergasse, Kirchengasse, Neubaugasse and Lindengasse, where the shopping is fabulous and off-beat.

LEOPOLD MUSEUM Map pp84-5

☎ 525 70-0; www.leopoldmuseum.org; 07, Museumsplatz 1; adult/under 7yr/student/senior/family (2 adults & 3 children under 18yr) €10/free/6.50/7.50/20; 10am-6pm Fri-Mon & Wed, 10am-9pm Thu; U2 Museumsquartier, U2, U3 Volkstheater 2A, 48A

Although choosing which area of the MQ to visit first is a question of taste, the Leopold is easily the most popular. This museum is named after Rudolf Leopold, a Viennese ophthalmologist who, on buying his first Egon Schiele (1890–1918) for a song as a young student in 1950, started to amass a huge private collection of mainly 19th-century and modernist Austrian artworks. In 1994 he sold the lot – 5266 paintings – to the Austrian government for

VORSTADT SOUTHWEST

Haas Beisl ... 71 E5
Halle ... 72 E2
Kantine ... 73 E2
Maschu Maschu II ... 74 C3
Motto ... 75 E5
Naschmarkt Deli ... 76 F4
Neni ... 77 F4
ON ... 78 E5
Piccini Piccolo Gourmet ... 79 F3
Podium ... 80 B3
Point of Sale ... 81 F4
Ra'mien ... 82 F3
Restaurant Collio ... 83 G4
Saigon ... 84 F3
Schon Schön ... 85 C3
Shanghai Tan ... (see 82)
Silberwirt ... 86 E6
St Josef ... 87 D3
Tancredi ... 88 F5
Ubl ... 89 F4
Umar ... 90 F3
Urbanek ... 91 F3
Vapiano ... 92 E3
Zu den Zwei Liesln ... 93 C2
Zum Alten Fassl ... 94 F6

DRINKING & NIGHTLIFE (p171)
Aux Gazelles ... 95 E3
Blue Box ... 96 C3
Café Drechsler ... 97 F3
Café Leopold ... (see 20)
Café Rüdigerhof ... 98 D4
Café Savoy ... 99 E4
Café Sperl ... 100 F3
Café Willendorf ... (see 5)
Canetti ... 101 A2
Club U ... (see 27)
Das Möbel ... 102 D2
Ebert's Cocktail Bar ... 103 D4
Elektro Gönner ... 104 B4
Europa ... 105 D3
Futuregarden Bar & Art Club ... 106 D4
Goodmann ... 107 F4
Joanelli ... 108 E4
Kunsthallencafé ... (see 18)
Lutz ... 109 E3
Mango Bar ... 110 E4
Mon Ami ... 111 E3
Orange One ... 112 F4
Phil ... 113 F3
Rotes Bar ... (see 129)
Roxy ... 114 F3
Schikaneder ... 115 F4
Sekt Comptoir ... 116 F4
Siebensternbräu ... 117 D2
Tanzcafé Jenseits ... 118 D4
Titanic ... 119 E3
Top Kino Bar ... (see 128)
Wieden Bräu ... 120 G5
Wirr ... 121 C2

MUSIC & THE ARTS (p191)
English Cinema Haydn ... 122 D3
Filmcasino ... 123 E5
Radiokulturhaus ... 124 H4
Raimund Theater ... 125 A5
Schikaneder ... (see 115)
Tanzquartier Wien ... 126 E2
Theater an der Wien ... 127 F3
Top Kino ... 128 F3
Volkstheater ... 129 E2

SPORTS & ACTIVITIES (p201)
Kletteranlage Flakturm ... (see 13)

SLEEPING (p207)
Altstadt ... 130 D2
Das Triest ... 131 G4
Das Tyrol ... 132 E3
Hotel Drei Kronen ... 133 F4
Hotel Fürstenhof ... 134 A4
Österreichischer Jugendherbergswerk ... 135 E3
Pension Carantania ... 136 A2
Pension Hargita ... 137 C4
Pension Kraml ... 138 C4
Westend City Hostel ... 139 B4

€160 million (sold individually, the paintings would have made him €574 million), and the Leopold Museum was born.

The building is in complete contrast to the MUMOK, with a white, limestone exterior, open space (the 21m-high glass-covered atrium is lovely) and natural light flooding most rooms. Considering Rudolf Leopold's love of Schiele, it's no surprise the museum contains the largest collection of the painter's work in the world. The collection also includes Schiele drawings and graphics, but the originals are so sensitive to light that they are rarely exhibited. Copies, however, are frequently on show.

Other artists well represented include Albin Egger-Lienz (1868–1926), Richard Gerstl (1883–1908) and Austria's third-greatest expressionist, Kokoschka (1886–1980). Works by Loos, Hoffmann, (Otto) Wagner, Waldmüller and Romako are also on display.

Audio guides (bring your passport for ID) in English and German are available for €3, as are free guided tours in German at 3pm on Saturday and Sunday and at 6pm Thursday. A joint ticket covering the Leopold and the Kunsthistorisches Museum costs adult/concession €17/11. On the top floor is Café Leopold (p180).

MQ TICKETS & INFORMATION

The MQ is a constellation of top-ranking museums with a focus on the 20th and 21st centuries. If you plan to see several of them, pick up one of the combined tickets. These are available from the MQ Point (☎ 523 58 81-17 31, within Austria 0820-600 600; www.mqw.at; 07, Museumsplatz 1; 10am-7pm).

- MQ Kombi Ticket (€25) includes entry into every museum except Zoom (which only has a reduced ticket price), and 30% discount on performances in the Tanzquartier Wien
- MQ Art Ticket (€21.50) allows admission into the Leopold Museum, MUMOK and Kunsthalle, and reductions for Zoom and the Tanzquartier
- MQ Duo Ticket (€17) covers admission into the Leopold Museum and MUMOK and has the Zoom and Tanzquartier reductions (a flexible version allows you to choose two from any of the museums)
- MQ Family Ticket (2 adults & 2 children under 13 €29) offers entry to MUMOK and the Leopold Museum, with the Zoom and Tanzquartier reductions

MUMOK Map pp84-5

☎ 525 00-0; www.mumok.at; 07, Museumsplatz 1; adult/student & under 19yr/senior €9/free/7.20; 10am-6pm Fri-Wed, 10am-9pm Thu; U2 Museumsquartier, U2, U3 Volkstheater 49 2A, 48A

The dark basalt edifice and sharp corners of the Museum moderner Kunst (Museum of Modern Art) are a complete contrast to the MQ's historical sleeve. Inside, MUMOK is crawling with Vienna's finest collection of 20th-century art, centred on fluxus, nouveau realism, pop art and photo-realism. The best of expressionism, cubism, minimal art and Viennese Actionism (p42) is represented in a collection of 9000 works that are rotated and exhibited by theme – but take note that sometimes all this Actionism is packed away to make room for temporary exhibitions. On any visit you might glimpse: wearily slumped attendant (not part of any exhibit), photos of horribly deformed babies, a video piece of a man being led by a beautiful woman across a pedestrian crossing on a dog leash, naked bodies smeared with salad and other delights, a man parting his own buttocks, flagellation in a lecture hall, and an ultra close-up of a urinating penis. The heavy stuff comes later. Other well-known artists represented throughout the museum – Picasso, Paul Klee, René Magritte, Max Ernst and Alberto Giacometti – are positively tame in comparison.

KUNSTHALLE Map pp84-5

☎ 521 89 33; www.kunsthallewien.at; 07, Museumsplatz 1; Hall 1 adult/under 13yr/concession €7.50/free/6, Hall 2 €6/free/4.50, combined ticket €10.50/8.50; 10am-7pm Fri-Wed, 10am-9pm Thu; U2 Museumsquartier U2, U3 Volkstheater 49, 2A, 48A

Situated between the Leopold and MUMOK, the Kunsthalle (Art Hall) is a collection of exhibition halls used to showcase local and international contemporary art. While it lacks the sheer architectural impact of the Tate Modern in London or the Centre Pompidou in Paris, its high ceilings, open planning and functionality have helped the venue leapfrog into the ranks of the top exhibition spaces in Europe. Programs, which run for three to six months, rely heavily on photography, video, film, installations and new media. Weekend visits cost €1 more, but German-language guided tours are included. The Saturday tours (Halle 1 at 3pm, Halle 2 at 4pm) focus on a theme, while Sunday tours (same times) give an overview.

ARCHITEKTURZENTRUM WIEN Map pp84-5

☎ 522 31 15; www.azw.at; 07, Museumsplatz 1; one exhibition adult/student €7/4.50, two exhibitions €9/6.50; 10am-7pm; U2 Museumsquartier, U2, U3 Volkstheater 49 2A, 48A

The Architekturzentrum Wien (Vienna Architecture Centre) takes up much of the MQ north of MUMOK, collectively encompassing three halls used for temporary exhibitions, a library and a cafe. Exhibitions focus on international architectural developments, and change on a regular basis. The extensive library is open to the public 10am to 5.30pm Monday, Wednesday and Friday and until 7pm on Saturday and Sunday. The centre also organises regular walking tours through Vienna on Sunday (in German), covering various architectural themes. You need to book ahead; see the website for dates and prices.

The separately run Design Forum (☎ 524 49 49-0; www.designforum.at; 07, Museumsplatz 1; adult/concession €2/1; 10am-6pm Mon-Fri, 11am-6pm Sat & Sun) is what its name suggests – exhibitions on Austrian design.

ZOOM Map pp84-5

☎ 524 79 08; www.kindermuseum.at, in German; 07, Museumsplatz 1; programs 8.30am-4pm Tue-Sun, ticket office 8am-4pm Mon-Fri, 9.30am-3.30pm Sat & Sun; U2 Museumsquartier U2, U3 Volkstheater 2A

Zoom children's museum is an arts and crafts session with a lot of play thrown in. Children are guided through themed pro-

top picks

IT'S FREE – VORSTADT SOUTHWEST

- Museumsquartier – Courtyard (p86)
- Naschmarkt & Otto Wagner Buildings (p80) and (p83)
- Spittelberg (p79)
- Leopold Museum guided tours (in German; p86)

A GENTRIFIED CLAY PIT

You couldn't guess it today but the gentrified eastern part of Mariahilf around Windmühlengasse and the Museums-Quartier was once a clay pit for making terracotta tiles, giving the area its long-disappeared name 'Laimgrube'. A steep section ending at the Wien River was also called 'Saugraben' (Sow's Trench) or the more familiar 'An der Wien'. All the streets with 'mühl' in their names (such as Schleifmühlgasse) had mills on them. Orchards and vineyards also dotted the area down into the hollow of the Wien River, but today the only hints remaining of this landscape are some narrow lanes and numerous flights of stairs just off Mariahilfer Strasse. (Rahlgasse leads to several interesting eating and drinking options.)

The clay pit gradually encroached into Spittelberg, which then shed its origins as a picturesque blend of meadows and farmhouses outside the city walls. By the mid-17th century, it was dubbed Crobotendörfl (Croatian Village) for its large number of Croatians. When the Turks occupied Spittelberg (and got no further) in that fateful autumn of 1683, Spittelberg's houses were virtually demolished – either by the locals who didn't want them falling into Turkish hands or during the attack. By the mid-19th century Spittelberg was notorious for street prostitution. But even vice, it seems, has a use-by date and in the 21st century Spittelberg's cobblestone streets of fallen angels are prime real estate.

grams and have the chance to make, break, draw, explore and be creative. The museum consists of 'Exhibition', a section with a new exhibition every six months (free entry), a 'Studio' (child €5, one adult free, two adults €3.50) for budding Picassos, and sections 'Lab' (multimedia; child €5, adults free) and 'Ocean' (play activities to stimulate coordination, social and cognitive abilities; child €3, one adult free, two adults €2.50). To avoid a screaming disappointment – or a long day's sulk into bedtime – book ahead. Programs, aimed at kids from eight months to 14 years, last about 1½ hours and spots can be reserved from the ticket office.

DSCHUNGEL WIEN Map pp84-5

☎ 522 07 2020; www.dschungelwien.at; 07, Museumsplatz 1; adult/under 18yr €12/7.50; U U2 Museumsquartier, U2, U3 Volkstheater 2A

This theatre for children mostly has performances in German, but every now and again it stages dance or a performance in English. Performance times for the regular shows are generally at 10am or 10.30am and again at 2.30pm as well as at 4.30pm daily. Adults pay children's prices for matinee performances.

HOFMOBILIENDEPOT Map pp84-5

☎ 524 33 570; www.hofmobiliendepot.at; 07, Andreasgasse 7;adult/under 19yr/concession/family €6.90/4.50/5.50/16; 10am-6pm Tue-Sun; U U3 Zieglergasse

Ostensibly, the Hofmobiliendepot is storage space for furniture not displayed in the Hofburg, Schönbrunn, Schloss Belvedere and other Habsburg residences, plus a smattering of late-20th-century furniture thrown in. Covering four floors, the collection is a highlight for those whose first love is furniture design; for the rest of us it's very interesting and worthwhile. Biedermeier aficionados will gravitate to the 3rd floor, where over a dozen rooms are beautifully laid out in the early 19th-century style, and a few dozen chairs from the era can be tested by visitors. In all, it's the most comprehensive collection of Biedermeier furniture in the world. The 4th floor displays *Jugendstil* furniture from the likes of Wagner, Loos and Hoffmann.

This, one of the more underrated museums in the city, is included in the Sisi Ticket (p54).

BÜCHEREI WIEN Map pp84-5

☎ 400 08 4500; www.buechereien.wien.at; 07, Urban-Loritz-Platz; 11am-7pm Mon-Fri, 11am-5pm Sat; U U6 Burggasse-Stadthalle 6, 18

Vienna's central city library straddles the U6 line, its pyramidlike steps leading up to the enormous main doors, which are two storeys tall. At the top of the library is the cafe Canetti (p181), which has far-reaching views to the south.

TWO MONASTERIES & A WALTZ TO THE KARLSKIRCHE

Walking Tour

1 Volkstheater

The Volkstheater (p197) building dates from the turn of the 20th century and is the everyperson counterpart to the more highbrow Burgtheater (p196). It is built in a neoclassical revivalist style.

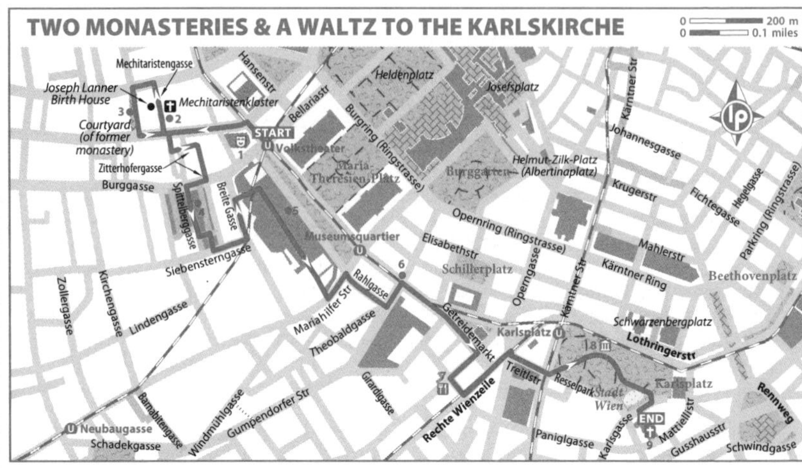

> **WALK FACTS**
>
> Start Volkstheater
> End Karlskirche
> Distance 3.5km
> Time Two hours
> Exertion Easy
> Fuel stop Naschmarkt (p161)

2 Mechitaristengasse

The cobblestone Mechitaristengasse has two interesting landmarks. One is the Mechitaristenkloster (Mechitaristen Seminary; ☎ 523 64 17; 07, Mechateristengasse 4; 🕑 by prior arrangement), housing Armenian Catholic monks who arrived here from Trieste (Italy) in 1805. The museum has a collection of some 40,000 coins, which can be viewed along with the elegant library by prior arrangement. Mechitaristengasse 5 is the birth house of the cofounder of the Vienna Waltz, composer Joseph Lanner (1801–43).

3 Monastiri (former monastery)

Vienna has an abundance of historic courtyards and this is arguably the most attractive in the Neubau district. The site was originally a monastery but today the building and passage are lined with a bakery, cafe and restaurant, with outdoor eating in summer.

4 Spittelberg

The quaint cobblestone streets of Spittelberg have come a long way since the Turks all but razed the area in 1683. For many years, lowlifers (students, artists etc) predominated here. Its attractive Biedermeier houses set the tone today, though surprisingly many of them are still rundown or even empty.

5 MuseumsQuartier

With its large courtyard, abundance of museums and handful of good places to eat and drink, the MuseumsQuartier (p86) has developed since 1998 into one of Europe's most dynamic cultural spaces, with events held in the courtyard throughout the year. The architecture is a vibrant mix of baroque and modern. Parts of the MQ are former imperial stables completed in 1725.

6 Corner of Getreidemarkt and Gumpendorfer Strasse

This part of Vienna originally consisted of vineyards and orchards that sloped to the Wien River. From this corner you can see the Karlskirche towering in the distance and the filigree golden dome of the Secession building (p62), housing the famous frieze by Gustav Klimt.

7 Naschmarkt

This market, with its spectacular location, dates back to the late 18th century. After a narrow escape in the hands of developers, it's home to a vast array of stalls; many of the larger food 'stands', such as Neni (p160), are multilevel and offer some of the most delicious food in town.

8 Stadtbahn Pavillons

Wherever you look in this part of town, you find the architectural signature of Otto Wagner. He 'tamed' the unruly Wien River, and designed these two *Jugendstil* pavilions (p81), which are among his best designs and date from 1898, when Vienna was getting its first public transport system.

9 Karlskirche

Rising in a magnificent pile of baroque splendor, the Karlskirche (p80) is Vienna's finest baroque church and was completed in 1738. An inside elevator allows you to soar into the cupola for a close-up of Johann Michael Rottmayr's frescos. Scary stuff.

VORSTADT NORTHWEST

Drinking & Nightlife p181; Eating p164; Shopping p147; Sleeping p213

North of Neubau, the inner city district of Josefstadt (the 8th) and Alsergrund (the 9th) form the northwestern and northern borders of the suburbs flanking the Innere Stadt. Josefstadt is short on sights but has a healthy sprinkling of eating and drinking spots, while Alsergrund has both in abundance.

As far as the Vorstädte go, Josefstadt is a young one. It was only in the mid-17th century that city housing and shops sprouted out of the meadows, fields and vineyards here. From the late 17th century, after the Turks were beaten back for the second time, a clutch of nobles and the well-off gradually discovered the pleasures of Vorstadt living. The reason for this late discovery was simple enough – from 1704 Leopold I started building his new fortification (today's Gürtel, a major road) that made living outside the fortress (today's Ringstrasse) a more attractive proposition for the well-heeled. There was also the advantage of space – enough space to sink a fortune into opulent, expansive palaces. An example of this is Josefstadt's Palais Schönborn (not to be confused with Schloss Schönbrunn), now a museum for folklore.

In Alsergrund in 1588, in a garden near Schottentor, Vienna's first potato was planted by the famous Dutch botanist Karl Clusius (aka Charles de l'Ecluse; see p99), who did more for the spud in Europe than any man or woman before or after. Like Josefstadt, Alsergrund received a good sprinkling of palaces from the 18th century after the real money realised the Ottoman Turks were in no state to sack them anymore – today Alsergrund's palace-museum Palais Liechtenstein testifies to the grand dreams of this baroque moment of 'Now I get it!'

From around the mid-19th century less well-off middle classes moved into Josefstadt, especially in the south and the west around the Gürtel, where even today you find the grittier or sleazy parts. The closer you move towards the Ringstrasse, the more the architecture takes on a Biedermeier flavour.

Alsergrund, with its Palais Liechtenstein, the Sigmund Freud Museum and some interesting churches, is strong on sights. But the transformation since 1998 of the district's old Allgemeines Krankenhaus (Altes AKH for short; a former hospital) into a large university campus has injected new life into a district that had always soaked up a substantial student population from the university main building (p73). Today you also find lots of bars and cheap restaurants packed with students, their graduate tutors and young professors. If you're here from the US, the UK or elsewhere for academic reasons, you've got the good fortune to be on one of the world's most interesting campuses. In contrast to this, and also in Alsergrund, is the unusual Fernwärme – a waste incinerator transformed into a colourful landmark by Friedensreich Hundertwasser.

The U6 runs along the Gürtel from Westbahnhof, and the most useful tram connection in the neighbourhood is the No 5 from Westbahnhof and the D from the Ringstrasse towards Liechtenstein Park.

ALTES AKH & JOSEFSTADT

Situated on the southern edge of Alsergrund where it borders on Josefstadt, the Altes AKH university campus exists through an interesting turn of events. The site, along with many of the buildings, was originally a 17th-century poor house, which Joseph II turned into a general hospital in the late 18th century. The courtyard areas 1 to 7 are all part of Emperor Joseph's hospital, designed by Joseph Gerl and opened in 1784. Courtyards were added in the early 19th century, and today these have been complemented by modern buildings. The result is a contemporary campus that forms a microdistrict, with a Pathological Anatomy Museum, another museum on its flanks dedicated to the history of medicine, a prayer house that is now an attractive memorial to Jews, a great children's playground, and supermarket, restaurants and bars where

top picks

VORSTADT NORTHWEST FOR CHILDREN

- Altes AKH – playground (above)
- Pathologisch-Anatomisches Bundesmuseum (p93)
- Liechtenstein Museum – gardens (p96)

students, staff and anyone else can eat, buy and imbibe. It even has its own Christkindlmarkt (see p147) in Hof 1 (Courtyard 1). With its interconnecting courtyards, the campus is an attractive, peaceful and at night sometimes even raucous quarter to explore or relax in.

Some interesting streets to explore in Josefstadt are its main street, Josefstädter Strasse, and those around the second-hand and antique stores on Piaristengasse and Lange Gasse.

top picks

IT'S FREE – VORSTADT NORTHWEST

- Altes AKH & Bethaus (opposite and below)
- Liechtenstein Museum – gardens (p96)
- Piaristenkirche (p96)
- Servitenkirche & Servitenviertel (p98)

JOSEPHINUM Map pp94-5

☎ 427 76 3401; 09, Währinger Strasse 25; adult/concession €2/1; ⌚ admission 9am-4pm Mon & Tue, 10am-6pm Wed-Sat, tour 11am Thu; 🚊 37, 38, 40, 41, 42

The prime exhibits of the Museum of Medical History on the 1st floor of the building are ceroplastic and wax specimen models of the human frame, created more than 200 years ago by Felice Fontana and Paolo Mascagni. They were used in the Academy of Medico-Surgery, an institution instigated by Joseph II in 1785 to improve the skills of army surgeons who lacked medical qualifications. Three rooms of this gory lot will make you feel like you've wandered onto the set of a horror movie. A book is open at 'The Common Causes of Sadism', another depicts common positions of those who hang themselves. Hold down your breakfast and take a wander through this intriguing exhibition. It includes a large collection of medical instruments (plus a first aid kit more likely to be a last resort), photos and an interesting collection of paintings depicting operations.

PATHOLOGISCH-ANATOMISCHES BUNDESMUSEUM Map pp94-5

☎ 406 86 72; www.narrenturm.at; 09, Spitalgasse 2; adult/under 19yr €2/free; ⌚ 3-6pm Wed, 8-11am Thu, 10am-1pm 1st Sat of month; 🚊 5, 33, 37, 38, 40, 41, 42

Housed in the Narrenturm (Fool's Tower), which served as an insane asylum from 1784 to 1866, the Pathologisch-Anatomisches Bundesmuseum (Pathological Anatomy Museum) is not for the weak of heart. Filled with medical oddities and abnormalities preserved in jars of formaldehyde, plus the odd wax model with one grisly disease or another, the museum definitely will take your breakfast to the edge. Tours (adult/concession & under 14yr €4/3) last 45 minutes but there are no set times – just roll up and ask, or call ahead. The Narrenturm itself dates from 1784 and is a delightfully circular, neoclassical design by the Franco-Austrian Isidore Canevale (1730–86).

BETHAUS Map pp94-5

09, Spitalgasse 2, Courtyard 6 – Altes AKH; admission free; 🚊 5, 33, 37, 38, 40, 41, 42

This tiny Jewish prayer house, replete with an atrium roof, is a moving aspect of the Altes AKH university campus. It was built in 1903 for Jewish patients of the hospital and in 1938 the Nazis unleashed their terror upon it. The building was completely revamped in the 1970s (a transformer was housed here for many years), and today it has been resurrected as art and also as a memorial. The transparent floor chronicles the fate of the prayer house, one level depicts Max Fleischer's original design from 1903, above that is a text from the Gestapo about the pogroms of 1938 against Vienna's Jews, the third layer is a plan of the transformer station, and the atrium roof is a glass version of Fleischer's original roof. Bulgarian-born artist Minna Antova was responsible for these artistic features, which successfully capture a mood of vulnerability. Mostly it's locked, but you can see inside.

MUSEUM FÜR VOLKSKUNDE Map pp94-5

☎ 406 89 05; www.volkskundemuseum.at; 08, Laudongasse 15-19; adult/child/student/family €5/free/2/9; ⌚ 10am-5pm Tue-Sun; 🚊 5, 33 🚌 13A

Housed in turn-of-the-18th-century Palais Schönborn, this folklore museum gives a taste of 18th- and 19th-century rural dwellings, and is stocked with handcrafted sculptures, paintings and furniture from throughout Austria and its neighbouring countries. Many of the pieces have a religious or rural theme, and telltale floral motifs are everywhere. Temporary exhibitions regularly feature.

VORSTADT NORTHWEST

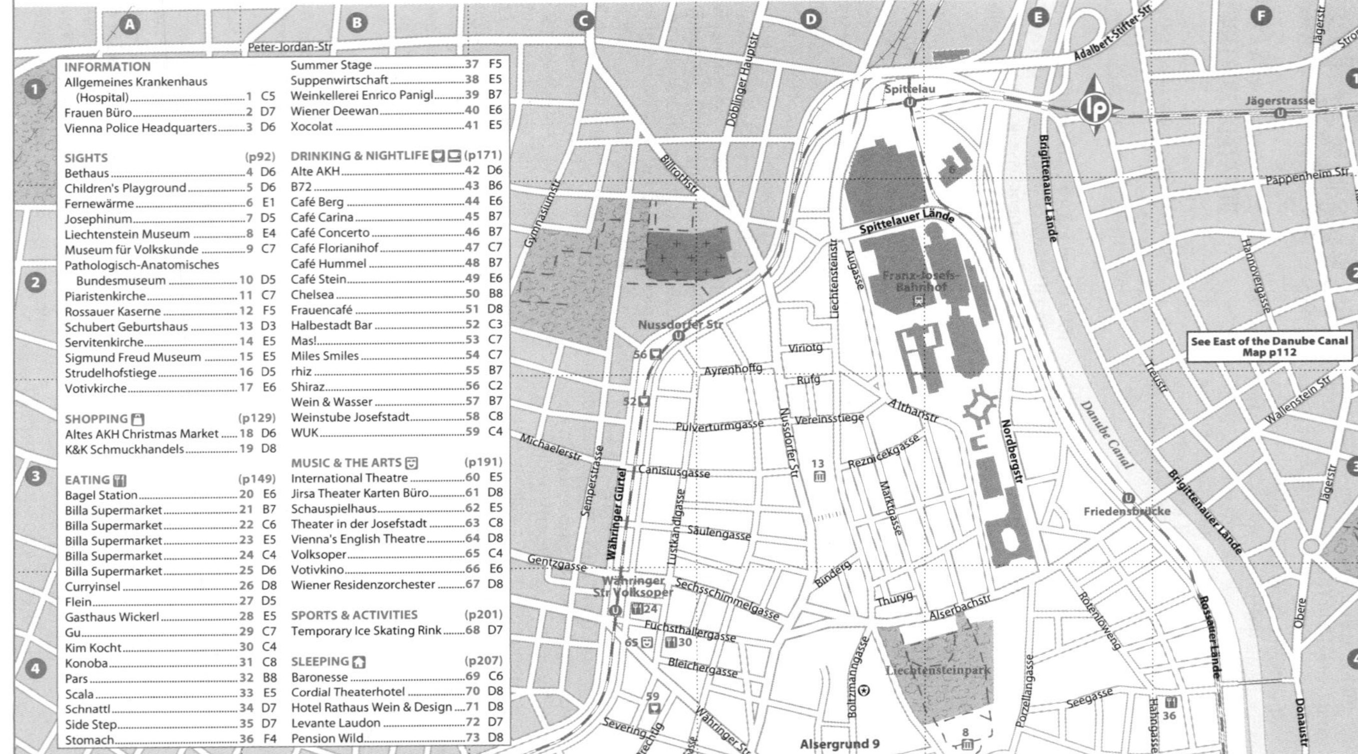
INFORMATION
Allgemeines Krankenhaus (Hospital) 1 C5
Frauen Büro 2 D7
Vienna Police Headquarters 3 D6
SIGHTS (p92)
Bethaus 4 D6
Children's Playground 5 D6
Fernewärme 6 E1
Josephinum 7 D5
Liechtenstein Museum 8 E4
Museum für Volkskunde 9 C7
Pathologisch-Anatomisches Bundesmuseum 10 D5
Piaristenkirche 11 C7
Rossauer Kaserne 12 F5
Schubert Geburtshaus 13 D3
Servitenkirche 14 E5
Sigmund Freud Museum 15 E5
Strudelhofstiege 16 D5
Votivkirche 17 E6
SHOPPING (p129)
Altes AKH Christmas Market 18 D6
K&K Schmuckhandels 19 D8
EATING (p149)
Bagel Station 20 E6
Billa Supermarket 21 B7
Billa Supermarket 22 C6
Billa Supermarket 23 E5
Billa Supermarket 24 C4
Billa Supermarket 25 D6
Curryinsel 26 D8
Flein 27 D5
Gasthaus Wickerl 28 E5
Gu 29 C7
Kim Kocht 30 C4
Konoba 31 C8
Pars 32 B8
Scala 33 E5
Schnattl 34 D7
Side Step 35 D7
Stomach 36 F4
Summer Stage 37 F5
Suppenwirtschaft 38 E5
Weinkellerei Enrico Panigl 39 B7
Wiener Deewan 40 E6
Xocolat 41 E5
DRINKING & NIGHTLIFE (p171)
Alte AKH 42 D6
B72 43 B6
Café Berg 44 E6
Café Carina 45 B7
Café Concerto 46 B7
Café Florianihof 47 C7
Café Hummel 48 B7
Café Stein 49 E6
Chelsea 50 B8
Frauencafé 51 D8
Halbestadt Bar 52 C3
Mas! 53 C7
Miles Smiles 54 C7
rhiz 55 B7
Shiraz 56 C2
Wein & Wasser 57 B7
Weinstube Josefstadt 58 C8
WUK 59 C4
MUSIC & THE ARTS (p191)
International Theatre 60 E5
Jirsa Theater Karten Büro 61 D8
Schauspielhaus 62 E5
Theater in der Josefstadt 63 C8
Vienna's English Theatre 64 D8
Volksoper 65 C4
Votivkino 66 E6
Wiener Residenzorchester 67 D8
SPORTS & ACTIVITIES (p201)
Temporary Ice Skating Rink 68 D7
SLEEPING (p207)
Baronesse 69 C6
Cordial Theaterhotel 70 D8
Hotel Rathaus Wein & Design 71 D8
Levante Laudon 72 D7
Pension Wild 73 D8
0 400 m
0 0.2 miles
Peter-Jordan-Str
Döblinger Hauptstr
Billrothstr
Gymnasiumstr
Spittelau
Adalbert-Stifter-Str
Jägerstrasse
Jägerstr
Stromstr
Pappenheim Str
Raffaelgasse
Hannovergasse
Brigittenauer Lände
Spittelauer Lände
Franz-Josefs-Bahnhof
Liechtensteinstr
Augasse
Nussdorfer Str
Viriotg
Rufg
Ayrenhoffg
Vereinsstiege
Althanstr
Pulverturmgasse
Reznicekgasse
Nordbergstr
Marktgasse
Michaelerstr
Semperstrasse
Währinger Gürtel
Canisiusgasse
Lustkandlgasse
Säulengasse
Gentzgasse
Währinger Str Volksoper
Sechsschimmelgasse
Binderg
Thuryg
Alserbachstr
Fuchsthallergasse
Bleichergasse
Boltzmanngasse
Liechtensteinpark
Porzellangasse
Seegasse
Hahngasse
Rotenloweng
Rossauer Lände
Friedensbrücke
Danube Canal
Treustr
Wallenstein Str
Obere
Donaustr
Severing
Prechtlg
Gasse
Währinger Str
Alsergrund 9
See East of the Danube Canal Map p112

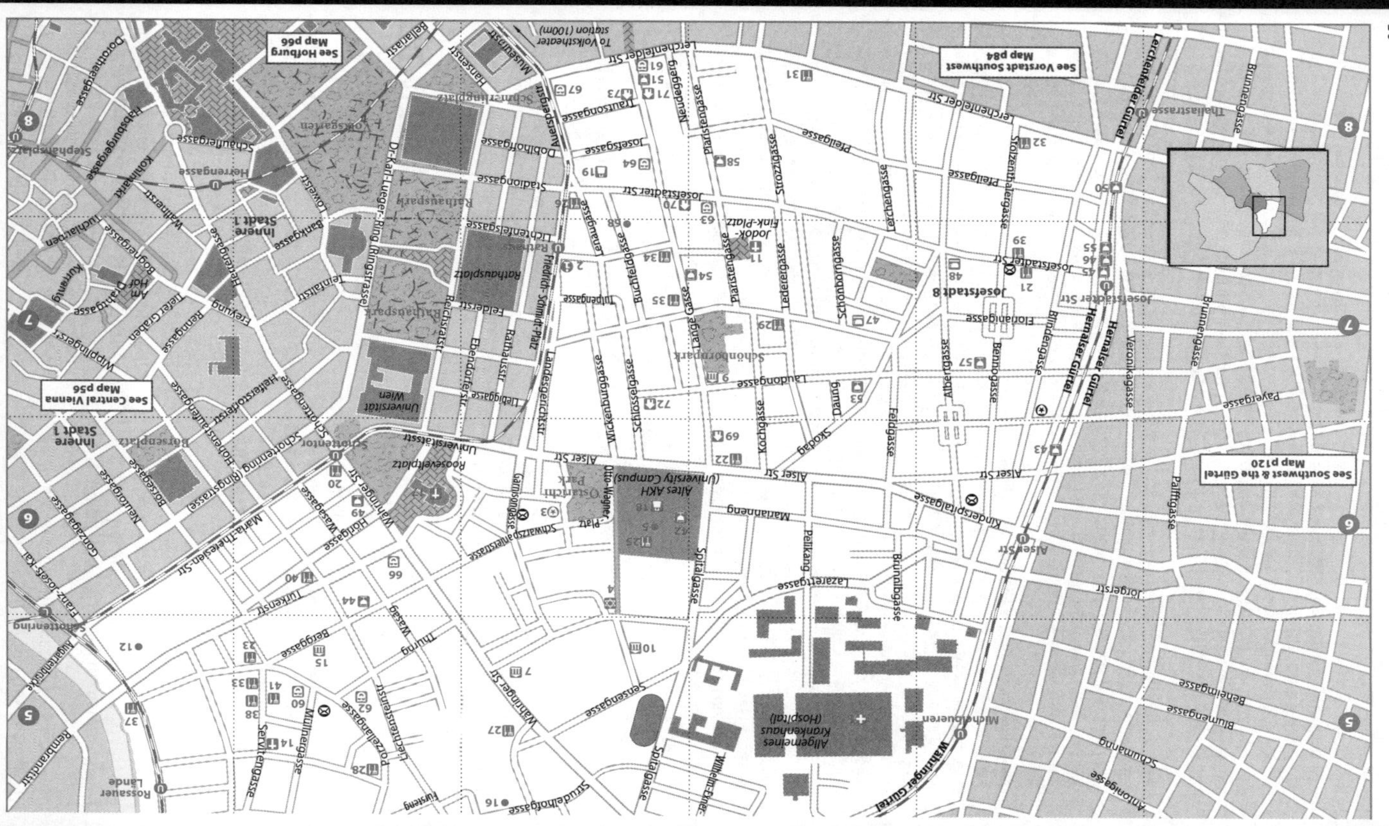
See Central Vienna Map p56
See Hofburg Map p66
See Vorstadt Southwest Map p84
See Southwest & the Gürtel Map p120
To Volkstheater station (100m)
Innere Stadt 1
Josefstadt 8
Allgemeines Krankenhaus (Hospital)
Altes AKH (University Campus)
Universität Wien
Rathausplatz
Rathauspark
Volksgarten
Börsenplatz
Schönbornpark
Jodok-Fink-Platz
Rossauer Lände
Schottenring
Schottentor
Rathaus
Herrengasse
Stephansplatz
Alser Str
Josefstädter Str
Michelbeuern
Thaliastrasse
Währinger Gürtel
Hernalser Gürtel
Lerchenfelder Gürtel
Dr-Karl-Lueger-Ring (Ringstrasse)
Schottenring (Ringstrasse)
Maria-Theresien-Str
Franz-Josefs-Kai
Währinger Str
Universitätsstr
Alser Str
Josefstädter Str
Lerchenfelder Str
Landesgerichtsstr
Friedrich-Schmidt-Platz
Auerspergstr
Museumstr
Lange Gasse
Laudongasse
Skodag
Kochgasse
Feldgasse
Albertgasse
Florianigasse
Schlösselgasse
Wickenburggasse
Spitalgasse
Lazarettgasse
Pelikang
Marianneng
Kinderspitalgasse
Sensengasse
Strudelhofgasse
Liechtensteinstr
Porzellangasse
Servitengasse
Müllnergasse
Berggasse
Türkenstr
Hörlgasse
Wasagasse
Freyung
Herrengasse
Wallnerstr
Kohlmarkt
Habsburgergasse
Dorotheergasse
Wipplingerstr
Renngasse
Tiefer Graben
Börsegasse
Neutorgasse
Gonzagagasse
Hohenstaufengasse
Helferstorferstr
Schottengasse
Bankgasse
Löwelstr
Teinfaltstr
Reichsratsstr
Ebendorferstr
Rathausstr
Felderstr
Liebiggasse
Lichtenfelsgasse
Stadiongasse
Doblhoffgasse
Schmerlingplatz
Hansenstr
Bellariastr
Tulpengasse
Buchfeldgasse
Lenaugasse
Piaristengasse
Lederergasse
Strozzigasse
Schönborngasse
Lerchengasse
Pfeilgasse
Stolzenthalergasse
Benngasse
Blindengasse
Veronikagasse
Brunnengasse
Payergasse
Palffygasse
Jörgerstr
Schumanng
Antonigasse
Blumengasse
Beheimgasse
Brünnlbadgasse
Josefsgasse
Trautsongasse
Neudeggerg
Daung
Rooseveltplatz
Otto-Wagner-Platz
Schwarzspanierstrasse
Garnisongasse
Spitalgasse
Wilhelm-Exner-
Rembrandtstr
Augartenbrücke
Thurng
Wasag
Fuxsteig
Stephansplatz
Schauflergasse
Kurrentg
Am Hof
Drahtgasse
Bognergasse
Tuchlauben

PIARISTENKIRCHE Map pp94-5

☎ 405 04 25; www.mariatreu.at, in German; 08, Jodok-Fink-Platz; admission free; 8am-6pm; J 13A

The Piaristenkirche (Church of the Piarist Order), or Maria Treu Church, is notable for two interior features: its ceiling frescos and its organ. The stunning frescos, completed by Franz Anton Maulbertsch in 1753, depict various stories from the Bible, while the organ holds the distinction of being used by Anton Bruckner for his entry examination into the Music Academy.

ALSERGRUND – NORTH OF THE ALTES AKH

The lion's share of Alsergrund is located north of the Altes AKH university campus and takes in a handful of top sights. Highlights are the Liechtenstein Museum and the Sigmund Freud Museum, but look out for the architectural oddity of Hundertwasser's decorative touches to Vienna's towering waste incinerator.

If going between Liechtenstein Palace and the Altes AKH, the quickest route is via Strudlhofgasse and Strudlhofstiege (p101), an impressive set of *Jugendstil* steps designed in 1910.

LIECHTENSTEIN MUSEUM Map pp94-5

☎ 319 57 670, concert bookings 319 57 67-252; www.liechtensteinmuseum.at; 09, Fürstengasse 1; adult/under 16yr €10/free; 10am-5pm Fri-Tue; D 40A

Until 1938, the royal family of Liechtenstein resided in Vienna, but after the Anschluss they bid a hasty retreat to their small country squeezed between Austria and Switzerland. They didn't manage to take everything with them, and it was only near the end of WWII that they transferred their collection of baroque masterpieces to Vaduz.

SIGMUND FREUD – A MAN WHO CHANGED OUR MINDS

Frau Scholz-Strasser, what does the Sigmund Freud Museum say to us as visitors? The museum is absolutely unique because here you can get a feel for Freud's original waiting room and his surroundings in the 19th century – where Freud changed and redefined our understanding of human beings. On the one hand, visitors get a great deal of information about Freud's life, his work and his social environment, and on the other hand it's a place you can feel. Some people say they can still feel Freud's breath in the rooms. Exhibitions look at the theories of Freud and the conditions under which his theories took shape. For example, once we held an exhibition on Freud's neighbours in the building – neighbours who vanished from 1938 after Hitler annexed Austria.

Which aspects of the museum are crucial for our understanding of Freud and his time? Definitely the waiting room. Also crucial is 20-minute film footage with a commentary by Freud's daughter, Anna. This shows Sigmund Freud and the family in private circumstances in the Vienna of the 1930s, Freud going into exile with the help of Marie Bonaparte, and his final one and a half years in London. The film's only shown here and in London – it's never been shown on TV or in the cinema.

How long is needed for a visit? We suggest about one hour or more. There's a 50-minute audio guide, but also written guides available in the shop for anyone wanting to delve even deeper. We've also got about 300 written exhibits, so there's a lot to read if you want to. Plan on spending at least one and a half hours in that case. Many of our visitors come to feel the aura of the house, though. They drop by for 15 minutes and are happy with that.

What can we still learn today from Sigmund Freud? His theories of the unconscious showed that we human beings aren't in control of ourselves as much as we like to believe. He developed a model that says overcoming the drive of aggression must be a cultural achievement. But he also doubted whether we human beings were really capable of achieving this, and he leaves the question open. Second, he was a dynamic scientist – he constantly revised his theories in his own lifetime and stood by this idea of revision. He's received a lot of flak for that.

Is the human being a dangerous creature in Freud's view? Human beings have an unimaginably strong urge for pleasure, an addiction if you like. Eros, the urge for life, and Thanatos, the death drive, are things that Freud saw as two complementary and interacting aspects of human beings. They are connected with one another, but when these get out of balance, when these disconnect, human beings go off the rails and find no way back – there's an unmitigated eruption of the death drive, and the result can be a compulsion to commit massacre and genocide. Eros, on the other hand, stands for resolution, bliss, endless happiness. Human beings carry both of these within them. It's a highly complex, dark theory for which Freud has often been criticised.

TOURS & EVENTS IN THE LIECHTENSTEIN MUSEUM

Guided tours of temporary exhibitions in the Liechtenstein Museum (in German) cost €4 and begin at 3pm Friday and 11.30am Sunday. Each Sunday a visit is combined with a classical concert. The price for both (€30) includes entry to the permanent and temporary exhibitions, a guided tour at 1.30pm, lunch or coffee and cake between 11am and 2pm in the palace restaurant, and the concert itself, held at 11am and again at 3pm in the Hercules Hall.

After many years collecting dust in depot vaults, this private collection of Prince Hans-Adam II of Liechtenstein is now on display, with around 200 paintings and 50 sculptures dating from 1500 to 1700.

This was built as a palace, not a museum, so orientation is the key. On the ground floor near the western staircase (left as you enter), is the **Gentlemen's Apartment Library**, a magnificent neoclassical hall containing about 100,000 books, frescos by Johann Michael Rottmayr and a templelike empire clock dating from 1795. From the library you pass through the Italian-styled **Sala Terrena** to galleries I to III, which have changing exhibitions. You can also enter these from alongside the eastern staircase (near the cloak room). After that, climb the eastern staircase, which, like its western counterpart, is decorated with Rottmayr frescos uncovered during restoration work in 2003.

Upstairs is the **Herkulessaal** (Hercules Hall) – so named for the Hercules motifs within its ceiling frescos by renowned Roman painter Andrea Pozzo (1642–1709). Surrounding the hall on three sides, beginning from the eastern staircase (right) and culminating at the western staircase, are galleries IV to X with the permanent collection of the palace. And what a collection this is!

Did Freud foresee the Nazi atrocities? Clearly, in my view. In 1932 Albert Einstein was asked by the League of Nations to select one person and discuss a topic with this person in correspondence. He chose Sigmund Freud. Einstein's question was: 'Is there a way of freeing people from the calamity of war?' In his letter, Freud anticipated both the terror of the Nazis and WWII without naming these as such. After 1933, when Hitler came to power in Germany, Freud's books were burned by the Nazis.

The title of one of Freud's books is *Jokes and their Relation to the Unconscious.* Did Sigmund Freud have a lighter side? He had humour and an acute ability to use language. He also had a tremendous amount of empathy, especially when dealing with people who were experiencing mental suffering. His empathy, along with the use of psychoanalytical techniques, was undoubtedly a precondition for his psychoanalysis.

What aspects of Freud do you find odd? His conservative image of women, for which he's been sharply criticised in the 20th century and today. The image of women in his theories is one-dimensional. The other is his view of homosexuality, which he saw as a deviation from 'normal' sexual behaviour. Although many of his patients and friends were eccentric or unusual women – Marie Bonaparte, or Lou Andreas-Salomé for instance, the daughter of a Russian general – Freud took a one-dimensional view of women in his theories.

Was Freud himself ever a licentious man? No, he got engaged, married his wife, Martha, and that was pretty much it.

What would Freud think and do in today's Vienna? But first of all, what would he say about it? Probably that it's too loud, too fast, too hectic.

Has he got a favourite *Beisl*? We know that Freud never really frequented the beer houses. His wife cooked for him, he conducted his sessions and retreated into the private sphere for meals. The *Beisln* were more for writers and literary figures, philosophers, people who weren't working regular hours. We do have photos of him in *Heurigen,* though. We've got three or four taken in the wine taverns in the Vienna Woods, although he didn't drink wine in these. He loved the vineyards, always had summer houses up there, and went on long walks. Then he'd drop into a *Heuriger*.

A favourite coffee house? Café Korb in the first district. Not a lot has changed there in 100 years.

Would we find Sigmund Freud today in the Hofburg or in the 'MUMOK' Museum for Modern Art? Freud's a Hofburg type. He had virtually no interest in contemporary art or architecture. We're often asked, 'Why didn't he take an interest in Egon Schiele or other expressionists?' He simply didn't. He would have liked the classical exhibits in the Ephesos Museum in the Hofburg, and being in the national library. Sigmund Freud was quite conservative in that regard.

An interview with Inge Scholz-Strasser, Director of the Sigmund Freud Museum (p98) *and Chairperson of the Board of Directors of the Sigmund Freud Privatstiftung.*

Seven galleries intertwine to provide a trip through 200 years of art history, starting in 1500 with early Italian panel paintings in Gallery IV. Gallery V is dedicated to late-Gothic and Renaissance portraits; Raphael's *Portrait of a Man* (1503) is a highlight here. The centrepiece of the upper floor is Gallery VII, which is home to Peter Paul Rubens' *Decius Mus* cycle (1618). Consisting of eight almost life-size paintings, the cycle depicts the life and death of Decius Mus, a Roman leader who sacrificed himself so that his army could be victorious on the battlefield. Gallery VIII is totally devoted to Rubens and Flemish baroque painting, and even more Rubens are on display in Gallery IX – this time his portraits – alongside Van Dyck and Frans Hals. The sheer exuberance and life captured by Rubens in his *Portrait of Clara Serena Rubens* (1616, Gallery VIII) is testament to the great artist's talent. Gallery X gives you a soft landing of ivory craftwork and Dutch still life, but also contains the world's most valuable piece of furniture – the Florentine Badminton Cabinet, made for the British nobleman Henry Somerset, the 3rd Duke of Beaufort in the 1720s.

The gardens of the palace offer a green space that are ideal for letting the kids run riot in a historical landscaped garden. This began life as a baroque garden in the late 17th century and was transformed into an English garden (ie lots of water, big trees, more of a wild look) in the 18th century. Its hybrid of continental baroque and English landscaping today comes from the 19th century.

SIGMUND FREUD MUSEUM Map pp94-5

☎ 319 15 96; www.freud-museum.at; 09, Berggasse 19; adult/concession & child/senior €7/4.50/5.50; 9am-6pm Jul-Sep, 9am-5pm Oct-Jun; D

Sigmund Freud is a bit like the telephone – once it happened, there was no going back. The apartment where he lived and worked from 1891 till his forced departure from Vienna with the arrival of the Nazis in 1938 is now a museum devoted to the father of psychoanalysis. It contains a number of his possessions, and Freud's obsessions – travelling, smoking and collecting ancient art – are well represented; Egyptian and Buddhist statues are everywhere. Notes (in English) illuminate the offerings and audio guides (€2) are available at the ticket desk. The 2nd floor is used for temporary exhibitions.

SERVITENKIRCHE Map pp94-5

☎ 317 61 95-0; www.rossau.at, in German; 09, Servitengasse 9; admission free; Mass only; U4 Rossauer Lände D

Dominating the Serviten quarter – a small confluence of cobblestone streets lined with bars, restaurants and shops a few blocks from the Ringstrasse – the Servitenkirche was built in 1677 and is the only church outside the Innere Stadt to survive the second Turkish siege of 1683. Its baroque interior and oval nave were inspired by the Karlskirche, but unfortunately it's only open for Mass (see the website); outside of this you'll have to make do with peering through iron railings. The adjoining monastery is an oasis of calm, in particular its inner courtyard (entry is through the door on the left).

FERNWÄRME Map pp94-5

☎ 313 26-0; 09, Spittelauer Lände 45; admission free; tours by appt; U4, U6 Spittelau D

The Fernwärme is a typically Viennese brainchild. Inside this is mostly a mundane incinerator. Outside it is a visual bonanza of colours topped by a glistening chimney stack that culminates in an Arabesque

CAFÉ KORB – SLIPPING INTO FREUD'S HANGOUT

OK, so it's a bad pun, but to round off your Freudian experience head for Freud's local, the Café Korb (Map pp56-7; ☎ 533 72 15; www.cafekorb.at, in German; 01, Brandstätte 9; light dishes €4-8.50; 8am-midnight Mon-Sat, 11am-11pm Sun; U1, U3 Stephansplatz;). Café Korb has always been a family-run place. Over the years, though, it has morphed from Freud's hangout, to a joint with a bowling alley in the cellar, and into its current manifestation incorporating an art lounge downstairs (the bowling alley has survived) and some pimped-up, postmodern toilets. It also has occasional events with an art edge, making this one of Vienna's most interesting coffee houses. By the way, the writer Elfriede Jelinek once claimed it had the best apple strudel in town, strudel that a scribe from *Time* magazine has also sung the praise of.

KARL CLUSIUS – A MAN AND HIS POTATOES

An odd fact about Alsergrund is its role in the history of the humble potato. In 1588, in a garden near Schottentor, Vienna's first potato was planted by Karl Clusius (aka Charles de l'Ecluse). Clusius was a famous Dutch botanist lured to Vienna by the Habsburgs, and his work on propagating the – at the time – exotic potato was significant to its success in Europe.

While he had green fingers with spuds (and, before that, tulips in his native Holland, triggering a phenomenon known as 'tulip fever'), his life in the Alsergrund garden turned into a rather bleak affair. Before arriving, Clusius came down with dropsy at the age of 24 (he was cured with chicory). When he was 39 he fell off a horse on the Iberian Peninsula (yes, where the famous Lipizzaner originated) and broke his right arm. Shortly afterwards, he fell off again and broke his right leg. Once in Alsergrund, he dislocated his left foot. Eight years later, he dislocated his right hip. The doctors didn't pick this one up and he hobbled around his potato garden on crutches for a long time, which caused his hip to break, induced chronic constipation (through long periods of immobility) and triggered *Steinschmerzen* (probably kidney or gall stones). By all reports he wasn't a happy man in the Habsburg's services, and after 14 years in Alsergrund he hobbled off to the Dutch city of Leiden (which literally means suffering) to take a post as professor. He died there in 1609.

As one 19th-century encyclopaedia on herbal medicine put it: 'A shame that a man who achieved so much should become the first martyr of botany'.

golden bulb. It's the work of – you've probably guessed by now – Friedensreich Hundertwasser and is best admired not from the cool distance of a train or tram. Inside, in the foyer, free exhibitions are put on by or about local artists while, each summer, open-air concerts are held in the yard – including some in conjunction with Jazz Fest Wien (see p17). With luck, you can jag a tour and find out more about this wonderfully pimped rubbish dump.

SCHUBERT GEBURTSHAUS Map pp94-5

☎ 317 36 01; 09, Nussdorfer Strasse 54; adult/under 19yr/concession €2/free/1; 10am-1pm & 2-6pm Tue-Sun; tram 37, 38

The house where Schubert was born in 1797, in the kitchen, was known at that time as *Zum roten Krebsen* (The Red Crab), but Schubert probably didn't remember much about that – he and his family crawled off to greater things when he was five. Apart from his trademark glasses, the house is rather short on objects. But 'Schubertologists' might like to trek here, especially to catch the occasional concert. Bizarrely, a couple of rooms of the house are given over to Adalbert Stifter (1805–68) and his Biedermeier paintings. Apart from being born into the same epoch (more an achievement of their mothers than the men of arts), the two men had absolutely nothing to do with each other.

ROSSAUER KASERNE Map pp94-5

09, Rossauer Lände 1; U-Bahn U2, U4 Schottenring tram 31

This huge red-brick complex, today housing the police, Defence Department and Vienna's traffic office, has an impeccable pedigree. It was originally built as barracks after the 1848 revolution. It's a rather fanciful affair replete with pseudo-Medieval turrets and massive entranceways and has been restored after being damaged in bombing during WWII.

VOTIVKIRCHE Map pp94-5

09, Rooseveltplatz; admission free; 9am-1pm & 4-6pm Tue-Sat, 9am-1pm Sun; U-Bahn U2 Schottentor tram 37, 38, 40, 41, 42, 43, 44

In 1853 Franz Josef I survived an assassination attempt when a knife-wielding Hungarian failed to find the emperor's neck through his collar. The Votivkirche (Votive Church) was commissioned in thanks for his lucky escape; in stepped Heinrich von Ferstel with a twin-towered neo-Gothic construction, completed in 1879. The rather bleak interior is bedecked with frescos and bulbous chandeliers, and the tomb of Count Niklas Salm, one of the architects of the successful defence against the Turks in 1529, is in the Baptismal Chapel. The prize exhibit of a small church museum (☎ 406 11 92; adult/concession €3.90/2.90; 4-6pm Mon-Fri, 10am-1pm Sat) is the Antwerp Altar from 1460.

MAINLY PALACES
Walking Tour

1 Galerie am Roten Hof
Vienna has a substantial Russian émigré population and Galerie am Roten Hof (☎ 406 31 07; www.amrotenhof.at; 08, Piaristengasse 1; 1-7pm Mon-Fri, 11am-3pm Sat) is one of its cultural spots. This private gallery has contemporary Russian art and occasional events to celebrate Easter and other dates of note.

WALK FACTS

Start Piaristengasse
End Servitenkirche
Distance 3.2km
Time 90 minutes
Exertion Easy
Fuel stop Gasthaus Wickerl (p165)

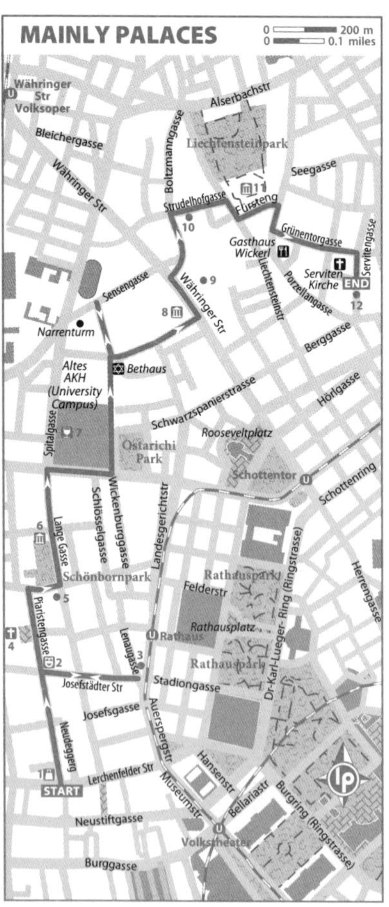

2 Theater in der Josefstadt
The first theatre sprang up here in 1788. It was resurrected in the Biedermeier style by Josef Georg Kornhäusel and reopened to the tune of Beethoven's 'Die Weihe des Hauses' (the Inauguration of the House). Beethoven directed the piece, which was especially written for this theatre (see p197).

3 Palais Auersperg
Palaces sprouted from the ground in the inner northwest like mung beans once the Turkish threat seemed under control. Palais Auersperg (08, Auerspergstrasse 1) dates from about 1708. In the 1720s it received a baroque makeover from Johann Lukas von Hildebrandt, of Schloss Belvedere fame. Today the only way to view its splendid baroque interior is to receive an invitation to one of the opulent functions often held here.

4 Piaristenkirche
The Piaristenkirche (p96) has an organ used by Anton Bruckner and some sensational 18th century frescos – the finest in this part of town.

5 Palais Damian
Taking its name from its one-time owner Karl von Damian, who began building it in the Vorstadt from 1700, this palace at Lange Gasse 53 grew over time and became a sanatorium in the mid-19th century. During WWII the Vienna Boys' Choir resided here. Today there is little to see inside as it houses government department offices.

6 Palais Schönborn
Today housing the Museum für Volkskunde (p93), this is another of Johann Lukas von Hildebrandt's works, dating from 1706–11. The arcaded garden was used for theatre performances, and to keep the garden green a pipeline was laid from Ottakring. Later, in 1760, it received its neoclassical gable.

7 Altes AKH
The Altes AKH campus (p92) is one of the most interesting you will find anywhere. It has some lovely courtyards, and beyond the main Courtyard 1 you find the Bethaus (Courtyard 6; p93) memorial and the Narrenturm (p93).

8 Josephinum

One of Vienna's more unusual attractions, the Josephinum (p93) takes you into medical history with models of human anatomy and all sorts of interesting books on fascinating subjects like sadomasochism. You have to really like human bodies in all their beauty and ugliness to love this.

9 Palais Clam-Gallas

Today housing the French Cultural Institute, this palace (Währinger Strasse 32-36) was built in 1834–35 in a neoclassical revivalist style with gardens. Immediately after WWII, US troops occupied it, then the French turned it into what it is today. The restaurant Flein is conveniently close (see p165).

10 Strudlhofstiege

This *Jugendstil* staircase (p92) from 1910 forms a winding cascade of steps into Liechtensteinstrasse and has two fountains integrated into it. At night the Strudelhofstiege is lit up gloriously. It's named after Peter von Strudel, who took Vienna into the high baroque period in the late 16th and early 17th centuries.

11 Palais Liechtenstein

Today housing the Liechtenstein Museum (p96) this magnificent palace was built between 1690 and 1712. The extensive gardens, originally baroque and transformed into an English landscape in the 19th century, are an exercise in manicured perfection.

12 Serviten quarter

This quarter of the northwestern *Vorstadt* is easily among Vienna's most attractive. The cobblestone Servitenstrasse is dominated by the Servitenkirche (p98) and alongside it is a wonderful cloister where you can contemplate your weary feet.

VORSTADT LANDSTRASSE

Drinking & Nightlife p183; Eating p167; Sleeping p214

Landstrasse (the 3rd), the largest of the districts inside the Gürtel, is flanked by the Danube Canal to the east and Wieden to the west. The district has two distinct characters. Close to the Ringstrasse it's splitting at the seams with 19th-century buildings, while its southern vicinities are filled with working-class housing. The main street linking these two urban personalities is Landstrasse Hauptstrasse, an artery leading south from Wien Mitte railway station. This is where airport trains arrive and depart, and by 2012 a glass-cubelike construction will have cleaned up what is at present a messy building site. The part of Landstrasse Hauptstrasse up to and around the Rochusgasse U-Bahn station is the most interesting. There's also a farmers market here at Rochusplatzand a cluster of other eating spots.

Landstrasse Hauptstrasse in the south vanishes into the Landstrasse Gürtel, but the district itself (unlike other Vorstadt districts) continues beyond this before reaching Simmering, a suburb on Vienna's southern fringe. Here you find the Gasometer, four enormous gas tanks transformed into a complex of student apartments, shops and an entertainment venue.

Inner Landstrasse has some good sights such as works by Friedensreich Hundertwasser, but the real highlight is Schloss Belvedere and the palace gardens. Landstrasse is an interesting district in its different personalities, and you can easily hop over to it from the section of the Ringstrasse in the Innere Stadt between Schwarzenbergplatz and the Danube Canal.

Landstrasse Wien Mitte (U3 & U4) and Rochusplatz (U3) are the most convenient U-Bahn stations on Landstrasse Hauptstrasse, whereas tram D from the Ringstrasse takes you via Belvedere to Südbahnhof (future Hauptbahnhof).

SCHLOSS BELVEDERE & AROUND

Belvedere is considered one of the world's finest baroque palaces. Designed by Johann Lukas von Hildebrandt, it was built for the brilliant military strategist Prince Eugene of Savoy, conqueror of the Turks in the Austro-Turkish War of 1716–18 and hero to a nation. The Unteres (Lower) Belvedere was built first (1714–16), with an orangery attached, and was the prince's summer residence. Connected to it by a long, landscaped garden is the Oberes (Upper) Belvedere (1721–23), the venue for the prince's banquets and other big bashes.

Considered together, the Belvedere residences were at the time almost more magnificent than the imperial residence, the Hofburg. This irked the Habsburgs, especially as the prince was able to look down onto the city from the elevated vantage point of the Oberes Belvedere. It was therefore with some satisfaction that Maria Theresia was able to purchase the Belvedere after the prince's death. It then became a Habsburg residence and was most recently occupied by the Archduke Franz Ferdinand, who started a court there to rival his uncle's (Franz Josef I) in the Hofburg.

LANDSTRASSE – THE SCARLET DERBY

The Viennese began settling the Landstrasse when a convent for nuns was established in the district not far from Stubentor U-Bahn station, but from around 1200 the centre had developed in the vicinity of Rochusplatz and the Rochuskirche (Map pp104-5). From around 1400 today's busy Rennweg was lined with vineyards, and from 1600 a shooting range for practice was set up along it, which got its name from – punters take note here – the local horse race (*Rennen* means a race). From 1382 to 1534 the 'Scharlachrennen' (probably best translated as the Scarlet Derby) used to be held on the main street.

OBERES BELVEDERE Map pp104-5

☎ 795 57-0; www.belvedere.at; 03, Prinz-Eugen-Strasse 27; adult/under 19yr/student/senior €9.50/free/6.50/7.50; 10am-6pm; D

Oberes Belvedere is one of those 'must sees' for visitors to Vienna, and quite rightly too. First, its collection of art offers a deep insight into Austrian artists in particular, and secondly this baroque palace is a sublime masterpiece whose interior allows you to drift with the ebb and flow of the ages, from the historic to the modern. Herculean figures supporting columns greet you in the entrance lobby and exploits of Alexander the Great flank the stairs climbing from the entrance to the 1st floor.

Highlights are paintings by Gustav Klimt, including his famous *The Kiss* (1908) and *Judith* (1901), as well as Biedermeier works by Ferdinand Georg Waldmüller (1793–1865) and modern artists of the calibre of Hans Makart (1840–84), Friedensreich Hundertwasser (1928–2000), Fritz Wotruba (1907–75) and many more.

The west wing of Upper Belvedere showcases some stunning late-Gothic sculpture and panels, beginning from 1400 to the 16th century. The baroque era finds expression in the evocative and sometimes disturbing paintings of Johann Michael Rottmayr (1654–1730) and Paul Troger (1698–1762), and the bizarrely grimacing sculptured heads of Franz Xaver Messerschmidt (1736–83).

While visiting the Upper Belvedere, try to see the elaborately stuccoed and frescoed Marmorsaal (Marble Hall), offering superb views over the palace gardens and Vienna.

Headphones with a commentary in English can be hired for €4; 30-minute tours costs €3.

UNTERES BELVEDERE Map pp104-5

☎ 795 57-0; www.belvedere.at; 03, Rennweg 6; adult/under 19yr/student/senior €9.50/free/6.50/7.50; 10am-6pm Thu-Tue, 10am-9pm Wed; 71

Built between 1714 and 1716, Lower Belvedere is a treat of baroque delights. Highlights include Prince Eugene's former residential apartment and ceremonial rooms, the Groteskensaal (Hall of the Grotesque; now the museum shop), a second Marmorsaal (Marble Hall), the Marmorgalerie (Marble Gallery) and the Goldenes Zimmer (Golden Room). Temporary exhibitions are held here and in the redesigned Orangery, with a walkway offering views over Prince Eugene's private garden and to Oberes Belvedere. Audio guides in English cost €3.50.

The Prunkstall (attached to the Orangery) houses a collection of Austrian medieval art, which comprises religious scenes, altarpieces and statues. Often it's only open between 10am and noon due to lack of staff.

BELVEDERE COMBINED TICKETS

The Belvedere is home to the Österreichische Galerie (Austrian Gallery), split between the Unteres Belvedere and the Orangery, which combine to house special exhibitions, and Oberes Belvedere, housing primarily Austrian art from the Middle Ages to the present. A combined ticket (adult/under 19yr/student/senior €13.50/free/9.50/10.50) allows entry to Oberes Belvedere, Unteres Belvedere, the Orangery, Prunkstall, Augarten Contemporary (in Leopoldstadt; see p111) and the Prunkräume and is valid for more than one day. Pick up information from the palace itself or check the website.

The 20er Haus, part of the Belvedere ensemble, is currently being reconstructed and will one day reopen as a forum for art from 1945 to the present.

GARDENS

03, Rennweg/Prinz-Eugen-Strasse; D, 71

The long garden between the two Belvederes was laid out in classical French style and has sphinxes and other mythical beasts along its borders. Opening times of the garden vary almost monthly. Core hours to keep in mind are from 6.30am to at least 8pm from March to mid-August, and to at

STOLEN TREASURES

After the Anschluss in 1938 many Jewish families were forced to flee the country, following which the Nazis seized their property. The Bloch-Bauers were one such unfortunate family, and in among their substantial collection were five Klimt originals, including the *Portrait of Adele Bloch-Bauer I* (1907).

The stolen paintings hung in the Oberes Belvedere until early 2006, when a US Supreme Court ruled the Austrian government must return the paintings to their rightful owner, Adele Bloch's niece and heir Maria Altmann. Austria believed it was entitled to the paintings because Adele Bloch, who died in 1925, had specified they be donated to the national gallery; however, her husband, who died in exile in 1945, wanted them returned to his family.

The paintings arrived in the US to much joy, while Austria mourned the loss of part of its cultural heritage. The government was offered the chance to buy the paintings, but the US$100 million price tag was regarded as too steep. It was actually a bargain – the *Portrait of Adele Bloch-Bauer I* alone fetched US$135 million at auction, at the time the highest price paid for a painting. It now hangs in the New York Neue Galerie, a museum devoted to German and Austrian art.

VORSTADT LANDSTRASSE

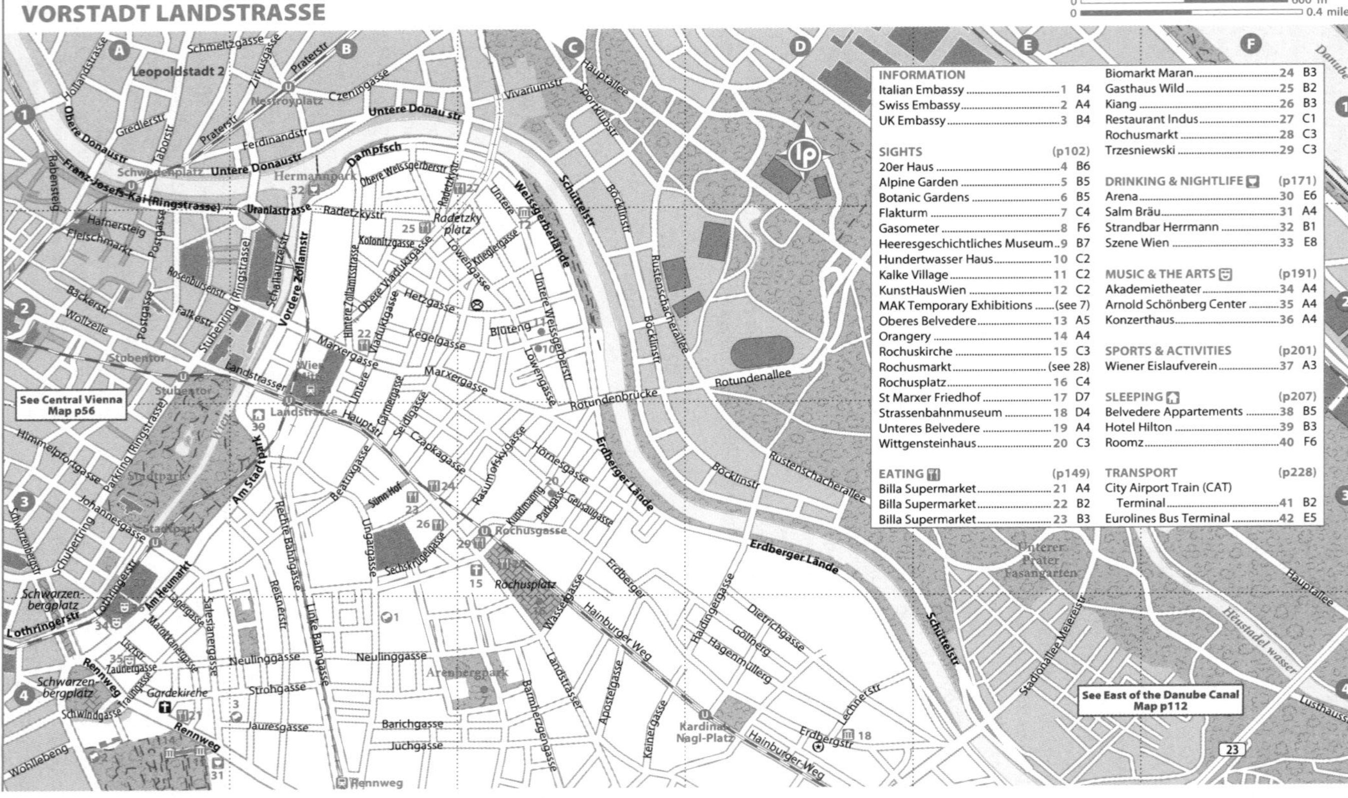

INFORMATION		
Italian Embassy	1	B4
Swiss Embassy	2	A4
UK Embassy	3	B4

SIGHTS	(p102)	
20er Haus	4	B6
Alpine Garden	5	B5
Botanic Gardens	6	B5
Flakturm	7	C4
Gasometer	8	F6
Heeresgeschichtliches Museum	9	B7
Hundertwasser Haus	10	C2
Kalke Village	11	C2
KunstHausWien	12	C2
MAK Temporary Exhibitions	(see 7)	
Oberes Belvedere	13	A5
Orangery	14	A4
Rochuskirche	15	C3
Rochusmarkt	(see 28)	
Rochusplatz	16	C4
St Marxer Friedhof	17	D7
Strassenbahnmuseum	18	D4
Unteres Belvedere	19	A4
Wittgensteinhaus	20	C3

EATING	(p149)	
Billa Supermarket	21	A4
Billa Supermarket	22	B2
Billa Supermarket	23	B3
Biomarkt Maran	24	B3
Gasthaus Wild	25	B2
Kiang	26	B3
Restaurant Indus	27	C1
Rochusmarkt	28	C3
Trzesniewski	29	C3

DRINKING & NIGHTLIFE	(p171)	
Arena	30	E6
Salm Bräu	31	A4
Strandbar Herrmann	32	B1
Szene Wien	33	E8

MUSIC & THE ARTS	(p191)	
Akademietheater	34	A4
Arnold Schönberg Center	35	A4
Konzerthaus	36	A4

SPORTS & ACTIVITIES	(p201)	
Wiener Eislaufverein	37	A3

SLEEPING	(p207)	
Belvedere Appartements	38	B5
Hotel Hilton	39	B3
Roomz	40	F6

TRANSPORT	(p228)	
City Airport Train (CAT) Terminal	41	B2
Eurolines Bus Terminal	42	E5

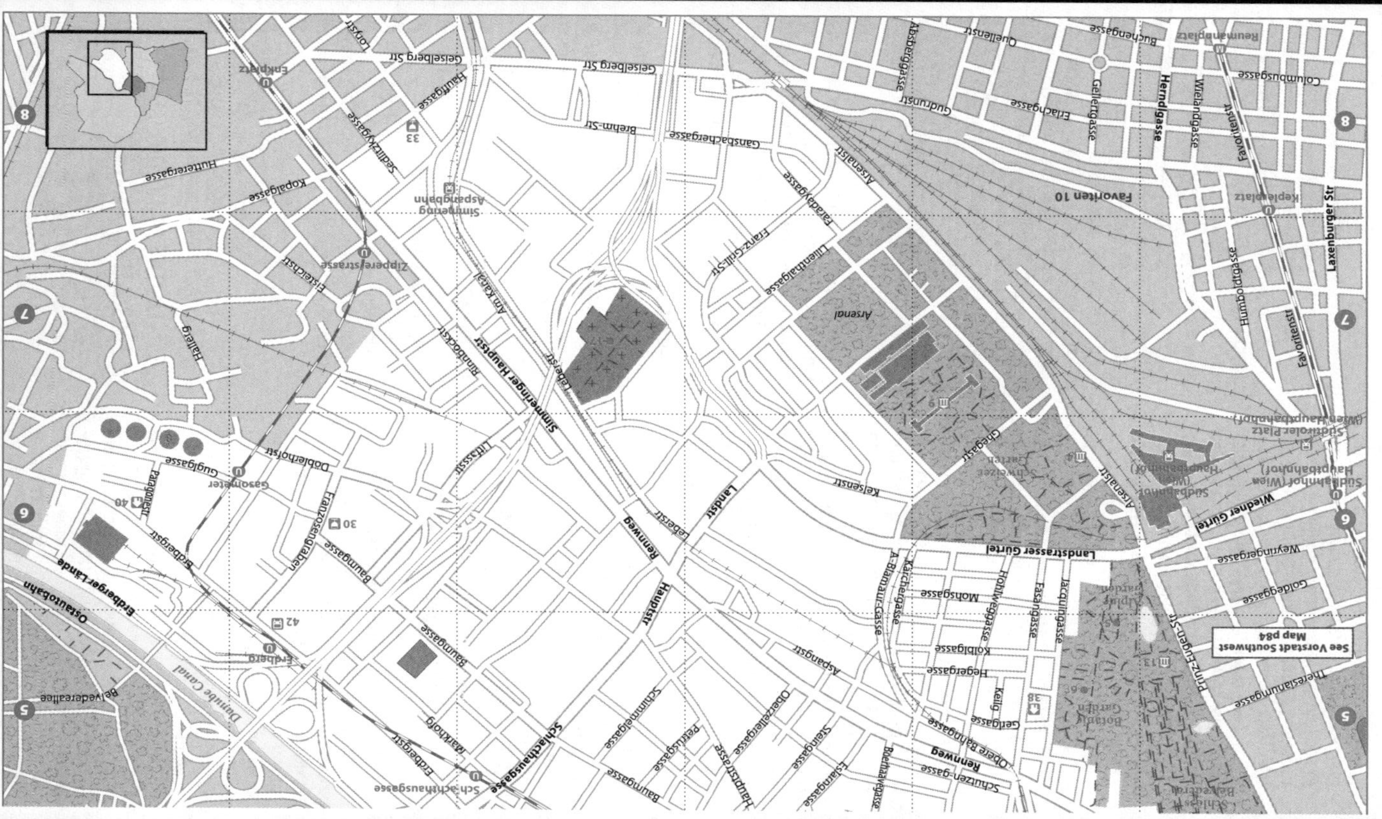
Ostautobahn
Erdberger Lände
Danube Canal
Belvederealllee
Erdbergstr
Paragonstr
Guglgasse
Gasometer
Döblerhofstr
Franzosengraben
Baumgasse
Erdberg
Schlachthausgasse
Markhofg
Hallerg
Hutterergasse
Kopalgasse
Eisteichstr
Zippererstrasse
Enkplatz
Sedlitzkygasse
Lorystr
Hauffgasse
Geiselberg Str
Simmering Aspangbahn
Rinnböckstr
Litfassstr
Simmeringer Hauptstr
Am Kanal
Leberstr
Rennweg
Hauptstr
Landstr
Schimmelgasse
Petrusgasse
Hauptstrasse
Oberzellergasse
Steingasse
Aspangstr
Brehm-Str
Gansbachergasse
Franz-Grill-Str
Lilienthalgasse
Faradaygasse
Arsenalstr
Kelsenstr
Arsenal
A-Blamauer-Gasse
Karchergasse
Boerhaavegasse
Schützen-gasse
Obere Bahngasse
Gerlgasse
Hegergasse
Kolbigasse
Mohsgasse
Hohlweggasse
Fasangasse
Jacquingasse
Landstrasser Gürtel
Ghegastr
Schweizer Garten
Botanic Garden
Alpine Garden
Schloss Belvedere
Prinz-Eugen-Str
Absberggasse
Gudrunstr
Quellenstr
Erlachgasse
Gellertgasse
Favoriten 10
Herndlgasse
Buchengasse
Wielandgasse
Humboldtgasse
Favoritenstr
Keplerplatz
Reumannplatz
Columbusgasse
Laxenburger Str
Südbahnhof (Wien Hauptbahnhof)
Südtiroler Platz (Wien Hauptbahnhof)
Wiedner Gürtel
Weyringergasse
Goldeggasse
Theresianumgasse
See Vorstadt Southwest Map p84

top picks

IT'S FREE – VORSTADT LANDSTRASSE

- Schloss Belvedere – gardens (p103)
- Hundertwasser Haus (below)
- St Marxer Friedhof (opposite)
- Gasometer (opposite)

least 6pm the rest of the year. South of the Oberes Belvedere is a small Alpine Garden (Map pp104-5; adult/concession €3.20/2.50; 10am-6pm Apr-Jul), which has 3500 plant species and a bonsai section. North from here is the much larger Botanic Gardens (Map pp104-5; admission free; 9am-1 hr before dusk) belonging to the Vienna University.

HEERESGESCHICHTLICHES MUSEUM

Map pp104-5

795 61-0; www.hgm.or.at; 03, Arsenal; adult/under 10yr/concession/family €5.30/free/3.30/7.30; 9am-5pm; 18 69A

In the wake of the 1848 rebellion, Franz Josef I decided his defences needed strengthening and ordered the building of the Arsenal. This large collection of barracks and a munitions depot was completed in neo-Byzantine style in 1856. Its handsome facade belied the true purpose of the building: it was a fortress built to discourage any further uprisings. At the same time Franz Josef established the Heeresgeschichtliches Museum (Museum of Military History) within the Arsenal, making it the oldest public museum in Vienna.

Inside, the vaulted ceilings, frescos and Moorish columns make it an interesting place to visit, even if your interest in military matters is fleeting. The exhibition is a little dated, but it covers some interesting wars that give an insight into Vienna – such as the two Turk sieges. The Sarajevo Room contains the car in which heir to the throne Franz Ferdinand (1863–1914) was murdered in July 1914 while in the Bosnian capital – the event that triggered WWI.

PRINCE EUGENE

One of Austria's greatest military heroes wasn't even a native of the country. Prince Eugene of Savoy (1663–1736) was born in Paris and after being informed he was too short to be accepted into the French army he left France in 1683 to join the Habsburg forces. Eugene arrived just in time to help beat off the Turkish forces besieging Vienna. He was given his own regiment and within 10 years was promoted to field marshal. His skills as a military strategist were evident in his victories against the Turks at Zenta in 1697 and during the campaign in the Balkans from 1714 to 1718, which finally drove the Turks out of all but a small corner of Europe. His capture of the fortress at Belgrade in 1718 was instrumental in ending that war. Prince Eugene's skills as a statesperson were also employed in the War of the Spanish Succession, when he negotiated with his former homeland.

BETWEEN RENNWEG & THE CANAL

The vicinity north of Rennweg and along the canal has a sprinkling of sights of a more low-key nature. Hundertwasser enthusiasts will find Vienna's main museum dedicated to him in the part of Landstrasse close to the Innere Stadt and canal. Just south of these is Wittgensteinhaus, an Adolf Loos design.

HUNDERTWASSER HAUS Map pp104-5

03, Löwengasse & Kegelgasse; 1, 0

This residential block of flats was designed by Hundertwasser, Vienna's radical architect and lover of uneven surfaces. It is now one of Vienna's most prestigious addresses, even though it only provides rented accommodation and is owned by the city of Vienna. It's not possible to see inside, but you can cross the road to visit the Kalke Village (www.kalke-village.at; 9am-7pm), also the handiwork of Hundertwasser, created from an old Michelin factory. It contains overpriced cafes, souvenir shops and art shops, all in typical Hundertwasser fashion with colourful ceramics and a distinct absence of straight lines.

KUNSTHAUSWIEN Map pp104-5

712 04 95; www.kunsthauswien.com; 03, Untere Weissgerberstrasse 13; adult/11-18yr/concession €9/4.50/7, incl temporary exhibitions adult/concession & child €12/9; 10am-7pm; 1, 0

The KunstHausWien (Art House Vienna), with its bulging ceramics, lack of straight lines and colourful tilework, is another of Hundertwasser's inventive creations. The art house is something of a paean in honour of the artist, illustrating his paintings, graphics, tapestry, philosophy, ecology and architecture. The gallery also puts on quality temporary exhibitions featuring other artists. Be sure to wander to the rooftop where you'll find a shady patch of grass under the grove of trees.

Monday is half-price day (unless it's a holiday) and guided tours in German of the permanent exhibition leave at noon on Sundays and are included in the price.

top picks

VORSTADT LANDSTRASSE FOR CHILDREN

- Heeresgeschichtliches Museum (opposite)
- Strassenbahnmuseum (below)
- Schloss Belvedere – gardens (p103)

ST MARXER FRIEDHOF Map pp104-5

03, Leberstrasse 6-8; 🕑 7am-7pm Jun-Aug, 7am-6pm May & Sep, 7am-5pm Apr & Oct, 7am-dusk Nov-Mar; 🚊 71 🚌 74A

Also known as the Biedermeier cemetery, after the period in which all 6000 graves were laid out, St Marxer Friedhof (Cemetery of St Marx) is a pilgrimage site for Mozart aficionados. In December 1791 Mozart was buried in an unmarked grave with none of his family present. Over time the site was forgotten and his wife's search for the exact location was in vain. The search did, however, bear one fruit: a poignant memorial, Mozartgrab, made from a broken pillar and a discarded stone angel was erected in the area where he was most likely buried. In May the cemetery is blanketed in lilies and is a sight to behold.

STRASSENBAHNMUSEUM Map pp104-5

☎ 786 03 03; www.wiener-tramwaymuseum.org, in German; 03, Erdbergstrasse 109; adult/under 15yr/concession €6/free/5; 🕑 10am-5pm Sat & Sun May-Sep; Ⓤ U3 Schlachthausgasse 🚊 18 🚌 77A

With around 80 trams, the Strassenbahnmuseum is one of the largest of its kind in the world. Avid train- and tram-spotters will love it; the extensive collection ranges from an 1871 horse-drawn trolley to the latest Porsche-designed tram seen on Vienna's streets today, and a couple of buses are thrown in for good measure. Many of the shiny examples can be explored from the inside.

GASOMETER Map pp104-5

www.wiener-gasometer.at; 03, Guglgasse 6-14; 🕑 9.30am-7pm Mon, Tue, Thu & Fri, 9.30am-8pm Wed, 10am-6pm Sat; Ⓤ U3 Gasometer

These four round, brownstone gas containers, measuring 75m tall and each big enough to house the Riesenrad, supplied gas to the city from 1899 to 1969. Today they have been redeveloped into 615 apartments, a students' hostel, an adjacent event hall and a cinema, but it's the fairly average shopping complex that predominates. Four different architectural groups were involved in this project for urban renewal, one for each gasometer and each with an atrium.

French star architect Jean Nouvelle gave his monolith nine towers rising rib-like to its atrium, the Viennese architectural group Coop Himmelb(l)au gave Gasometer B a

FLAKTÜRME

It can be quite a shock – and a little unnerving – to walk around a corner and be confronted with a gigantic relic from WWII, a *Flakturm* (flak tower). Built from 1943 to 1944 as a defence against air attacks, these bare monolithic blocks stand like sleeping giants among the residential districts of Vienna. Apart from their air-defence capabilities, they were built to house up to 30,000 troops, had an underground hospital and munitions factory and could control their own water and power supplies. They were built to last too: with 5m-thick walls of reinforced concrete, they are almost impossible to pull down. So they remain standing as an uncomfortable reminder of the Nazi era, featureless but for four circular gun bases at the top corners (these protrusions are strangely reminiscent of Mickey Mouse's ears).

Six flak towers still exist; two in Augarten (p111); one just off Mariahilfer Strasse in Esterházypark, housing the Haus des Meeres (p82); and another behind the MuseumsQuartier in the Stiftskaserne (Map pp84-5). Of the last two in Arenbergpark (Map pp104-5), one is used by MAK for temporary exhibitions (☎ 711 36-231; open 2pm to 6pm on Sundays from May to November); admission (€5.50) includes a guided tour through one of these WWII dinosaurs, so even if you're not interested in what's on show, it's worth paying the entrance fee.

shield (part of the gasometer is a student residence, part an events location), Gasometer C was redesigned by the Viennese Manfred Wehdorn in a fairly traditional design, and Austrian Wilhelm Holzbauer moved away from the idea of a central area by creating three arcing spaces. The idea is great, especially seen from a passing train, but the reality inside the most lively section (the shops close to the U-Bahn) just resembles an outer suburban shopping mall with offices thrown in – which much of it is.

WITTGENSTEINHAUS Map pp104-5

☎ 713 31 64; 03, Parkgasse 18; admission free; 10am-noon & 3-4.30pm Mon-Thu; U3 Rochusgasse

Designed by Paul Engelmann – a student of Adolf Loos – and the philosopher Ludwig Wittgenstein, this building has strict lines and a stepped design reminiscent of the Bauhaus style. It's now occupied by the Bulgarian embassy and can be viewed at set times or by prior appointment. Taking photographs is forbidden, though.

FROM BAROQUE TO HUNDERTWASSER

Walking & Tram Tour

1 Palais Schwarzenberg

Backing onto Schwarzenbergplatz is Palais Schwarzenberg, cocreated by Johann Bernhard Fischer von Erlach and his son Joseph in the early 18th century. They based it on a baroque palace from 1697 that was designed by Johann Lukas von Hildebrandt, the architect responsible for Belvedere. Today it is a luxury hotel.

2 Belvedere Gardens

While Oberes Belvedere (p102) and Unteres Belvedere (p103)were the work of Hildebrandt, Belvedere Gardens (free admission), which lend themselves to a stroll, were laid out by gardener and *maître fontainier* (master of fountains) Dominique Girard (1680–1738).

3 Hauptbahnhof Wien & Bahnorama

A tremendously impressive pile of rubble – worthy of industrial art – existed on the main site of the former Südbahnhof at the time of research. This is destined to become the new Hauptbahnhof Wien (main train station), easing into service from 2012. Until 2015 (when it should be completed), visitors can scale a spruce tower (yes, it will later be reused) to a 40m viewing platform. This, the Bahnorama, opening late 2010, will have exhibitions on the new station.

WALK FACTS

Start Palais Schwarzenberg
End KunstHausWien
Transport 0 (between Fasangasse & Sechskrügelgasse)
Distance 5.5km (1.2km by tram)
Time Three hours
Exertion Easy
Fuel stop Trzesniewski (p167)

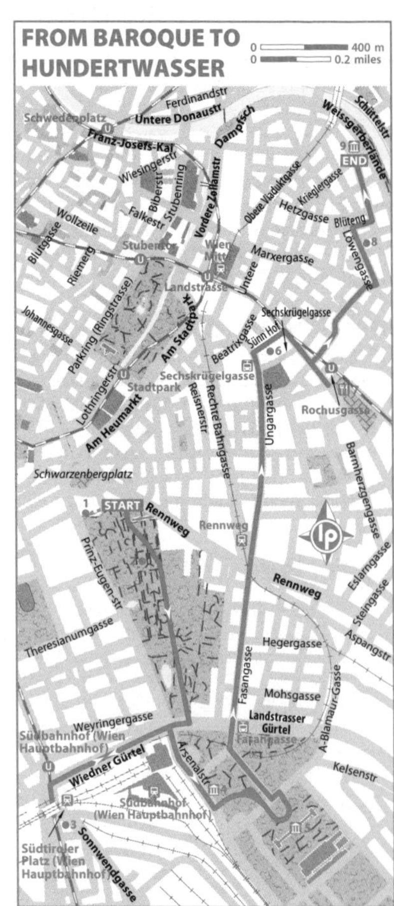

4 20er Haus
Originally a pavilion for the 1958 World Expo stood on this site. It was transported here and used as a modern museum by the MUMOK (p88) until that shifted into the MuseumsQuartier. Today it is the site of the revamped 20er Haus, opening in 2010 with contemporary art and works by Austrian sculptor Fritz Wotruba.

5 Heeresgeschichtliches Museum
The museum (p106) is housed in the massive former neo-Byzantine arsenal dating from 1856. Take a wander around and explore the impressive grounds.

6 Sünn Hof
For this leg of the tour, jump on tram O to Sechskrügelgasse. Extending between Ungarstrasse and Landstrasse Hauptstrasse (at the Mercure Hotel near Ungargasse 13), this is an elegant Biedermeier yard with a few shops, a couple of restaurants and the Mercure Hotel itself. From the early 19th century it was used by tradespeople.

7 Rochusmarkt
Rochusplatz is home to the Rochusmarkt (p167), the main market in the district. Drop into one of the eateries here to replenish your strength and get into some people-watching.

8 Hundertwasser Haus
Created from the former Michelin factory, the residential Hundertwasser Haus (p106) shows all the wobbly hallmarks of the man who designed it, Friedensreich Hundertwasser.

9 KunstHausWien
Quotations are everywhere in the KunstHausWien (p106), the main museum for Hundertwasser. Some of his pronouncements are annoyingly didactic or smack of old hippydom ('each raindrop is a kiss from heaven'), but they're often thought-provoking.

EAST OF THE DANUBE CANAL

Drinking & Nightlife p183; Eating p168; Shopping p147; Sleeping p214

The East of the Danube Canal neighbourhood takes in the districts Leopoldstadt (the 2nd district) and Brigittenau (the 20th), and sections of Floridsdorf (the 21st) and Donaustadt (the 22nd). Of most interest to the casual visitor is Leopoldstadt and, beyond that, Donaustadt, which forms part of an area known locally as Transdanubia (a Hungarian term for 'across the Danube').

Foremost among the attractions in this neighbourhood is the Prater, Vienna's large, central, green oasis, which also hosts the city's second symbol, the giant Riesenrad (Ferris wheel). Also popular is the Donauinsel (Danube Island), a recreational playground with river beaches, water sports and kilometres of walking, cycling, and in-line-skating tracks. The Alte Donau (Old Danube), another big draw, is an arm of the Danube long ago cut off from the river. The remainder of Donaustadt, east of the Alte Donau, can be safely ignored by the casual visitor as residential sprawl, with its wide streets and 1950s apartment blocks.

Leopoldstadt, the closest of the four districts to the Innere Stadt, is by far the most interesting historically and culturally. Home to European Jews for centuries, in recent years it has become one of the city's more ethnically diverse districts (see p110). Brigittenau, situated just north of Leopoldstadt, is mostly a residential area partly built on land reclaimed during late-19th-century work to regulate the Danube River.

Praterstern (U1 & U2) is the main public transport link through Leopoldstadt to the Prater, with the U1 continuing on to the Donauinsel. Tram No 1 is a useful link between the southern portions of the Prater and the Ringstrasse.

LEOPOLDSTADT

If New York's Statue of Liberty symbolises the freedom to choose a better life, Vienna's Riesenrad in the Prater asserts your right to rotate senselessly through the air and have a great time doing it. Either way, it's a fantastic experience.

In addition to the Prater, Leopoldstadt also boasts the baroque Augarten parkland, the site of one museum that is part of the Schloss Belvedere (p102) ensemble, and a couple of smaller museums – the strangest of which is devoted to Viennese criminal history. It's an interesting district to explore on foot, especially in the vicinity between Taborstrasse and Augarten.

PRATER Map pp112-13

www.wiener-prater.at; admission free; U1, U2 Praterstern

The Prater itself is a term often describing two distinct areas of parkland, which together comprise the city's favourite outdoor playground: the Würstelprater, and a stretch of green woodland park on its outskirts taking in the Unterer Prater.

The Würstelprater (Map pp112-13; or Volksprater as it's also known) is a large amusement park with all sorts of funfair rides, ranging from modern big dippers to merry-go-rounds and test-your-strength machines that could easily date from the early 20th century. Bumper cars, go-karts, haunted houses, games rooms and

LEOPOLDSTADT'S JEWISH HERITAGE

Leopoldstadt started life as a walled Jewish ghetto in 1624 under the watchful eye of Ferdinand II, but the district gained its name from Leopold I, the notoriously anti-Semite Habsburg who dispelled Jews from a ghetto in the area in 1670, destroyed their synagogue and replaced it with the Leopoldkirche (Map pp112-13).

Long the scapegoats of the city, Jews had gradually been moving back after their expulsion in the 15th century (see p23) and resettling the area. By the 18th and 19th centuries, the city was experiencing an influx of immigrant Jews, particularly from Eastern Europe. The area saw overcrowding and some of the worst conditions in the city, but this was nothing compared to the barbaric treatment later meted out under the Nazis, who expelled all Jews and left behind a desolate district.

The beginning of the 21st century has seen a new influx, and Jews now share Leopoldstadt with immigrants from Turkey and the Balkans, who have arrived in recent decades; Karmelitermarkt (p168), the district's busy food market, is the place to find kosher and halal food and a healthy ethnic diversity.

minigolf attractions abound, as do hotdog and candy-floss stands.

Rides in the Prater sideshow cost around €1 to €5. Colourful, bizarre, deformed statues of people and creatures are located in the centre of the parkland as well as on and around Rondeau and Calafattiplatz.

The 60 sq km of woodland park taking in the Unterer Prater may be more appealing to some. Formerly the royal hunting grounds of Joseph II, this (along with what today has become the Würstelprater) was first opened to the public in 1766. Viennese flock to this park to walk, run, cycle, in-line skate or simply soak up the sun in the open green fields or tree-shaded alleys. Even though this park attracts a multitude of people, it's still possible to find a private patch of green, particularly in its southwestern reaches.

Austria's largest football venue, Ernst-Happel-Stadion (p205), is also in the Prater. It's a grim but little-known fact that after Hitler invaded Poland in 1939, Viennese with Polish blood were imprisoned beneath one of the stands, and at other times during the Nazi era Jews were assembled here before being deported. Close to the Riesenrad begins the 4km Liliputbahn (minirailway) connecting the Würstelprater with Ernst-Happel-Stadion.

RIESENRAD Map pp112-13

☎ 729 54 30; www.wienerriesenrad.com; 02, Prater 90; adult/3-14yr/family €8.50/3.50/21; 9am-11.45pm May-Sep, 10am-9.45pm Mar, Apr & Oct, 10am-7.45pm Nov-Feb; U1 Praterstern; 0, 5, 21

The Riesenrad is a towering, modern symbol of Vienna. Built in 1897 by Englishman Walter B Basset, the wheel rises to 65m and takes about 20 minutes to rotate its 430-tonne weight one complete circle – giving you ample time to snap some fantastic shots of the city spread out at your feet. It survived bombing in 1945 and has had dramatic lighting and a cafe at its base added.

This icon achieved celluloid fame in *The Third Man,* in the scene where Holly Martins finally confronts Harry Lime; and also featured in the James Bond flick *The Living Daylights,* and *Before Sunrise,* directed by Richard Linklater. The latter is an intriguing film featuring a lot of Vienna.

A ticket for the Riesenrad includes entry into the Panorama, a collection of disused wheel-cabins filled with models depicting scenes from the city's history, including Roman Vienna and the Turkish invasions.

RIESENRAD COMBINED TICKETS

The various combination tickets for the giant Ferris wheel (below), a magic show on Riesenradplatz known as Miraculum, Donauturm (p116), Liliputbahn (below) and Schönbrunn's Tiergarten (p122) can be good value, especially if you have kids. The Riesenrad plus Miraculum show costs adult/child €11.50/7, Riesenrad plus Liliputbahn costs €9.90/4.20, Riesenrad plus Tiergarten costs €16.50/7, and Riesenrad plus Donauturm costs €11/6.10.

AUGARTEN Map pp112-13

www.kultur.park.augarten.org, in German; 03, Obere Augartenstrasse; 6am-dusk Apr-Oct, from 6.30am Nov-Mar; 31; 5A

This picturesque park from 1775 is dotted with open meadows and criss-crossed by tree-lined paths. You can kick a ball in one section, let the kids stage a riot in a playground in another, visit a porcelain factory (p114) or art exhibition (below) or watch a film in summer at Kino Unter Sternen (p199) in July and August. The Vienna Boys' Choir also practises here, inside the Palais Augarten (Augarten Palace). Kids are likely to find the most captivating features of the park to be the austere Flaktürme (flak towers; Map pp104-5) in its northern and western corners. For more about Flaktürme, see p107. Locals are understandably protective of their *Erlustigungsort* (recreational space), which has come under threat by several construction plans over the years (see p114).

AUGARTEN CONTEMPORARY/ GUSTINUS AMBROSI-MUSEUM

Map pp112-13

☎ 216 86 1621; www.belvedere.at; 02, Scherzergasse 1a; adult/concession €5/3.50; 11am-7pm Thu-Sun; 2, 5

Sculptures by Austrian-born Gustinus Ambrosi (1893–1975) are the highlight of the works displayed inside the Atelier section of this museum in the western corner of the Augarten. Alongside his works are sculptures by other European artists from the 20th and 21st centuries, while the Augarten Contemporary, part of the same museum, features temporary exhibits from international artists.

EAST OF THE DANUBE CANAL

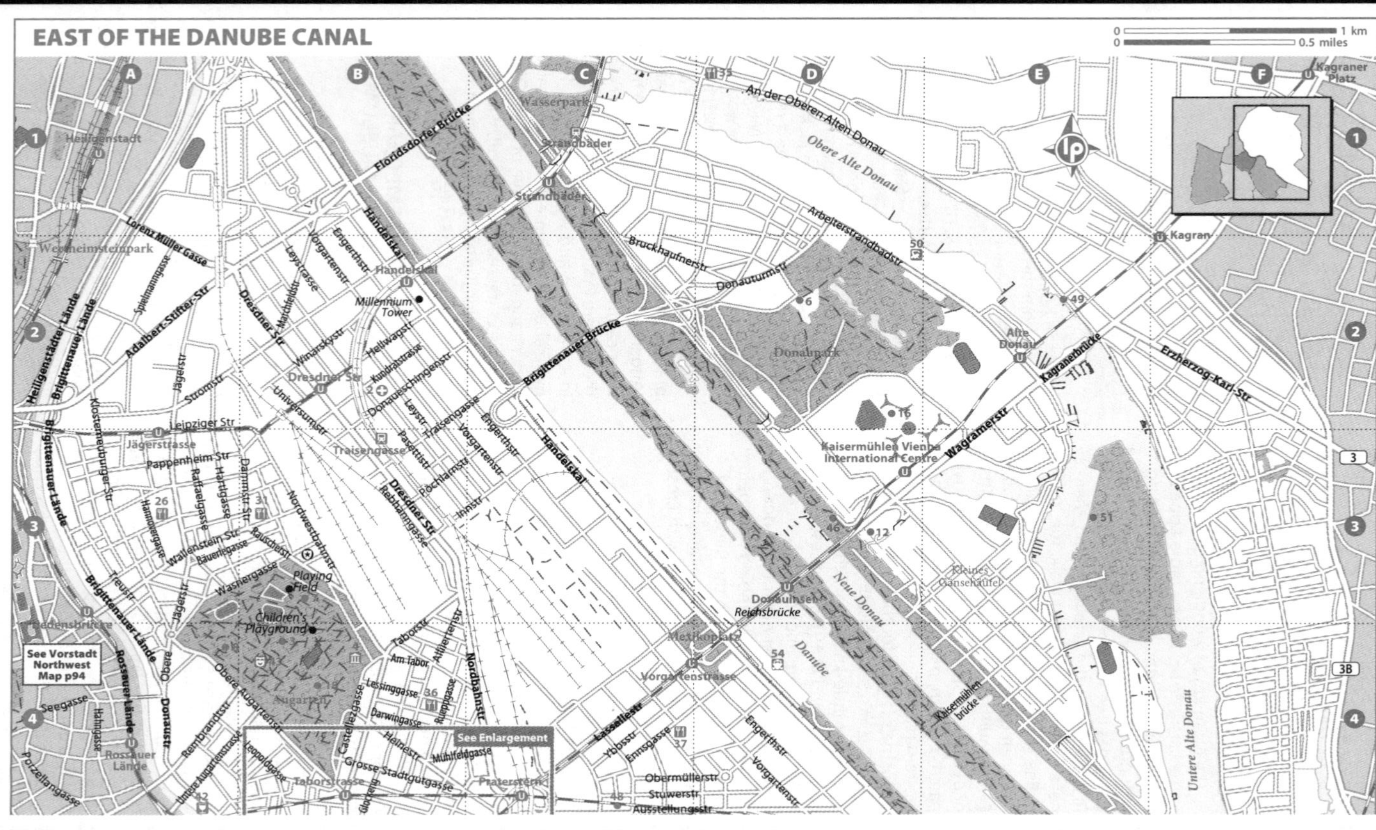

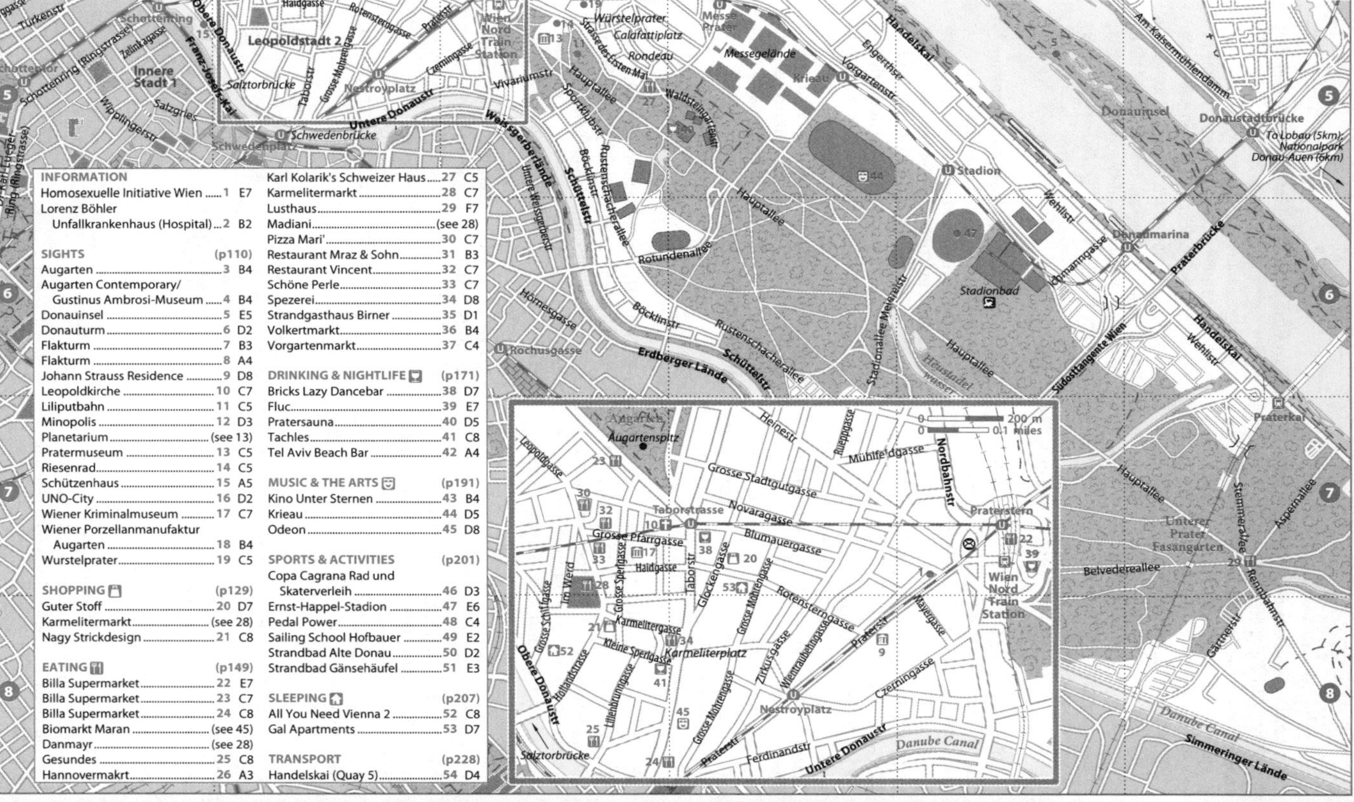
INFORMATION
Homosexuelle Initiative Wien 1 E7
Lorenz Böhler Unfallkrankenhaus (Hospital)...2 B2
SIGHTS (p110)
Augarten 3 B4
Augarten Contemporary/ Gustinus Ambrosi-Museum 4 B4
Donauinsel 5 E5
Donauturm 6 D2
Flakturm 7 B3
Flakturm 8 A4
Johann Strauss Residence 9 D8
Leopoldkirche 10 C7
Liliputbahn 11 C5
Minopolis 12 D3
Planetarium ......(see 13)
Pratermuseum 13 C5
Riesenrad 14 C5
Schützenhaus 15 A5
UNO-City 16 D2
Wiener Kriminalmuseum 17 C7
Wiener Porzellanmanufaktur Augarten 18 B4
Wurstelprater 19 C5
SHOPPING (p129)
Guter Stoff 20 D7
Karmelitermarkt ......(see 28)
Nagy Strickdesign 21 C8
EATING (p149)
Billa Supermarket 22 E7
Billa Supermarket 23 C7
Billa Supermarket 24 C8
Biomarkt Maran ......(see 45)
Danmayr ......(see 28)
Gesundes 25 C8
Hannovermakrt 26 A3
Karl Kolarik's Schweizer Haus 27 C5
Karmelitermarkt 28 C7
Lusthaus 29 F7
Madiani ......(see 28)
Pizza Mari' 30 C7
Restaurant Mraz & Sohn 31 B3
Restaurant Vincent 32 C7
Schöne Perle 33 C7
Spezerei 34 D8
Strandgasthaus Birner 35 D1
Volkertmarkt 36 B4
Vorgartenmarkt 37 C4
DRINKING & NIGHTLIFE (p171)
Bricks Lazy Dancebar 38 D7
Fluc 39 E7
Pratersauna 40 D5
Tachles 41 C8
Tel Aviv Beach Bar 42 A4
MUSIC & THE ARTS (p191)
Kino Unter Sternen 43 B4
Krieau 44 D5
Odeon 45 D8
SPORTS & ACTIVITIES (p201)
Copa Cagrana Rad und Skaterverleih 46 D3
Ernst-Happel-Stadion 47 E6
Pedal Power 48 C4
Sailing School Hofbauer 49 E2
Strandbad Alte Donau 50 D2
Strandbad Gänsehäufel 51 E3
SLEEPING (p207)
All You Need Vienna 2 ......52 C8
Gal Apartments 53 D7
TRANSPORT (p228)
Handelskai (Quay 5) 54 D4

UP IN THE TREES

The Augarten is an oddly multifunctional baroque space in Leopoldstadt that departs from the usual concept of immaculately manicured gardens. Baroque purists will keel over at the two monstrous Flaktürme (p107), built during WWII, inside the gardens. This *Erlustigungsort* (recreational space) for everyperson envisaged by Joseph II has often come under threat: in the early 1970s there were plans to build a school, old-age home and childcare centre on it (this plan was abandoned); and in 1999 plans for a new sports field for the Jewish sports association SC Hakoah were quashed after challenge by protesters. Most recently, plans by the Vienna Boys' Choir to build a concert hall on the Augartenspitz near Taborstrasse have led to protesters occupying the site. Work on the hall was supposed to begin in 2009 but the protests have caused delays. When protesters were forcibly removed from a campsite on the Augartenspitz in March 2010, they climbed into the trees and occupied them. Despite protests, though, this time it really looks like building work will go ahead on the Augartenspitz.

Entry to the Atelier is included in the Schloss Belvedere ticket (adult/senior/student/child €13.50/10.50/9.50/free; see p102).

WIENER PORZELLANMANUFAKTUR AUGARTEN Map pp112-13

☎ 211 24-200; www.augarten.at; 02, Obere Augartenstrasse 1, Schloss Augarten; tours adult/under 10yr/concession €12/3/6; 9.30am-5pm Mon-Fri; 31 5A

Vienna's Porcelain Factory is the second-oldest porcelain manufacturer in Europe. It produces exquisite pieces featuring plenty of fanciful flourishes, which you can buy in the shop (see p141). One-hour tours of the premises are available daily at 10am, when you can learn about the process of turning white kaolin, feldspar and quartz into delicate creations through the process of moulding, casting, luting, glazing and painting.

PLANETARIUM Map pp112-13

☎ 729 54 94; www.planetarium-wien.at, in German; 02, Oswald-Thomas-Platz 1; adult/under 18yr €8/6; U1 Praterstern 0, 5

The Planetarium, Vienna's extraterrestrial and interstellar viewfinder, is located on the edge of the Würstelprater behind the Riesenrad. Shows – normally at 9.30am or 10am, 11am, 3pm and 6pm or 7pm – change on a regular basis, but usually focus on how the Earth fits into the cosmological scheme of things. All shows are in German only, though.

WIENER KRIMINALMUSEUM Map pp112-13

☎ 214 46 78; www.kriminalmuseum.at, in German; 02, Grosse Sperlgasse 24; adult/under 18yr/concession €5/2/4; 10am-5pm Thu-Sun; 2 5A

The Vienna Crime Museum is another interesting chapter in the Viennese obsession with death. It takes a tabloid-style look at crimes and criminals in Austria and dwells on murders in the last 100 years or so with particularly grisly relish; there are skulls of earlier criminals, and even an 18th-century head pickled in a jar. Other displays include death masks of convicted murderers and weapons supposedly used to carry out the murders.

JOHANN STRAUSS RESIDENCE Map pp112-13

☎ 214 01 21; www.wienmuseum.at; 02, Praterstrasse 54; adult/under 19yr/concession €2/free/1; 10am-1pm & 2-6pm Tue-Sun; U1 Nestroyplatz 5A

Strauss the Younger called Praterstrasse 54 home from 1863 to 1878 and composed *the* waltz, 'The Blue Danube', under its high ceilings. Inside you'll find an above-average collection of Strauss and ballroom memorabilia, including an Amati violin said to have belonged to him and oil paintings from his last apartment, which was destroyed

top picks

EAST OF THE DANUBE CANAL FOR CHILDREN

- Riesenrad (p111)
- Planetarium (above)
- Augarten playground (p111)
- Alte Donau (opposite)
- Donauinsel (opposite)
- Minopolis (p116)

top picks

IT'S FREE – EAST OF THE DANUBE CANAL

- Würstelprater & Unterer Prater (p110)
- Donauinsel (below)
- Augarten (p111)

during WWII. The rooms are bedecked in period furniture from Strauss' era. The residence is a municipal museum.

PRATERMUSEUM Map pp112-13

☎ 726 76 83; 02, Oswald-Thomas-Platz 1; adult/under 19yr/concession €2/free/1; 10am-1pm & 2-6pm Fri-Sun; U1 Praterstern 0, 5, 21

Sharing the same building as the Planetarium, this municipal museum traces the history of the Würstelprater and its woodland neighbour. For all the life and splendour the Prater has seen, unfortunately its museum has only a rather dull mix of photos and stories, mainly from the 19th century. The antique slot machines, some of which are still functioning, are the museum's saving grace.

DONAUSTADT

The largest of Vienna's districts, Donaustadt (the 22nd), features the straightened Danube River, the elongated Donauinsel and the Danube's arcing backwaters, now used as recreational areas. Otherwise it is characterised by seemingly endless blocks of residential housing and the modern UNO-City, where the UN bases some of its institutions.

DONAUINSEL Map pp112-13

22; U1 Donauinsel

The svelte Danube Island stretches some 21.5km from opposite Klosterneuburg in the north to the Nationalpark Donau-Auen in the south and splits the Danube in two, creating a separate arm from the main river known as the Neue Donau (New Danube). It was created in 1970 and is Vienna's prime aquatic playground, with long sections of beach (don't expect much sand) perfect for swimming, boating and a little waterskiing. The tips of the island are designated FKK (*Freikörperkultur;* free body culture) zones reserved for nudist bathers, who also enjoy dining, drinking, walking, biking and in-line skating *au naturel;* it's quite a sight. Concrete paths run the entire length of the island, and there are bicycle and in-line-skate rental stores. Restaurants and snack bars are dotted along the paths, but the highest concentration of bars – collectively known as Sunken City and Copa Cagrana – is near Reichsbrücke and the U1 Donauinsel stop. In late June the island hosts the Donauinselfest (Danube Island Festival; p17). For more information on outdoor activities, see p202).

ALTE DONAU Map pp112-13

22, Untere Alte Donau; U1 Alte Donau U6 Untere Alte Donau

The Alte Donau, a landlocked arm of the Danube, is separated from the Neue Donau by a sliver of land. One third of it lies in Floridsdorf. It carried the main flow of the river until 1875, when artificial flood precautions created the linear course of the Danube that you see today. Now the 160-hectare water expanse is a favourite of Viennese sailing and boating enthusiasts, and also attracts swimmers, walkers, fishermen and, in winter (if it's cold enough), ice skaters. Alongside free access points to the Alte Donau are almost a dozen city-owned bathing complexes that are open (approximately) from May to September. The biggest of these is the Strandbad Gänsehäufel (p204) complex, on an island jutting out into the Alte Donau. The island also has a nudist section, swimming pools and lake access.

LOBAU Map pp50-1

22, S7, 907, S80, 910 Lobau

This one is for those who want to go off-piste in summer. The Lobau is at the southern extremes of Donaustadt, and comprises an area of dense scrub and woodland that is home to the western extension of the Nationalpark Donau-Auen, a couple of industrial sights and an abundance of small lakes. In summer, Vienna's alternative crowd flock to the Lobau for skinny-dipping.

NATIONALPARK DONAU-AUEN Map pp50-1

☎ 400 04 9495; www.donauauen.at; 22, Dechantweg 8; 10am-6pm Wed-Sun early Mar-late Oct; 91A, 93A

Established in 1996, the Donau-Auen National Park covers around 9300 hectares and runs in a thin strip on both sides of the Danube, extending from the edge of Vienna to the Slovakian border. About 60% is forested and approximately 25% comprises lakes and waterways. The park was created to protect an environment threatened by a hydroelectric power station in Hainburg. You'll find plentiful flora and fauna, including 700 species of fern and flowering plants, and a high density of kingfishers (feeding off the 50 species of fish found in the waterways here). A Nationalparkhaus (National Park Office) is situated on the northern entrance to the park and offers a series of tours – see the website and register in advance; some are free, others cost for adults/children about €10/5. Boat tours (☎ 400 04 9480; adult/child €10/4; departs 9am May-Oct) into the national park leave from Salztorbrücke and last 4½ hours; booking necessary.

DONAUTURM Map pp112-13

☎ 263 35 72; www.donauturm.at; 22, Donauturmstrasse 4; adult/under 14yr €5.90/4.30; 10am-10pm; U1 Kaisermühlen Vienna International Centre 20B

At 252m the Danube Tower in Donaupark is Vienna's tallest structure – next highest is the Millennium Tower at 202m. Its revolving restaurant at 170m allows fantastic panoramic views of the city and beyond – the food tends to be tried and trusted Viennese favourites. Tickets covering entrance to the Donauturm and Riesenrad cost for adult/child €11.40/5.90. The adventurous can bungee jump off the side of the tower – see the website for details.

UNO-CITY Map pp112-13

☎ 260 60 3328; www.unvienna.org; 22, Wagramer Strasse 5; adult/child/concession €6/2/4; 11am & 2pm Mon-Fri; U1 Kaisermühlen Vienna International Centre

UNO-City, or Vienna International Centre as it is officially known, is home to a variety of international organisations, but mainly houses the UN's third-largest office in the world. Multilingual guided tours lasting about one hour take you through conference rooms and exhibitions on UN activities and give you an insight into what goes on behind usually closed doors. The complex was the picture of modernism way back in 1979 when it was built; today it looks less than fab. It does have a rather glamorous extraterritorial status, though, so bring your passport when visiting.

MINOPOLIS Map pp112-13

☎ 0810 970 270; www.minopolis.at, in German; 22, Wagramerstrasse 2; adult/child €6/15, 2hrs before closing adult/child €free/6; 2-7pm Fri, 1-7pm Sat & Sun May-Sep, 2-7pm Fri, 10am-6pm Sat & Sun Oct-Apr; U1 Kaisermühlen Vienna International Centre

This city theme park offers children the chance to play grown-up for the day. The 6000-sq-m park of streets, buildings, shops and cars includes 26 stations that provide information and activities on various occupations, such as journalist, fire fighter, and doctor. Children are given Eurolinos, the money of Minopolis, to spend or save as they see fit, and while it's commercially orientated entertainment, children seem to love it.

FROM THE DANUBE CANAL THROUGH LEOPOLDSTADT

Walking Tour

1 Schwedenbrücke

The ugly concrete bridge linking the 'island' of Leopoldstadt began life as a wooden structure in 1819 and 100 years later was named Schwedenbrücke in thanks to Sweden for the assistance it provided to the children of Vienna following WWI.

2 Odeon

The Odeon (p194) theatre was built in the 1880s in an Italian neoclassical revivalist style, but it was so badly damaged during WWII that this space lay idle for four decades before being resuscitated in the 1980s and used for theatre, opera and dance.

3 Wiener Kriminalmuseum

The small but worthwhile Wiener Kriminalmuseum (p114) is tacky and tabloid, a little bit bloodthirsty and gruesome, and somehow very Viennese in its macabre exhibits.

4 Karmelitermarkt

Leopoldstadt has an expansive, sometimes even deserted feel, but this cannot be said

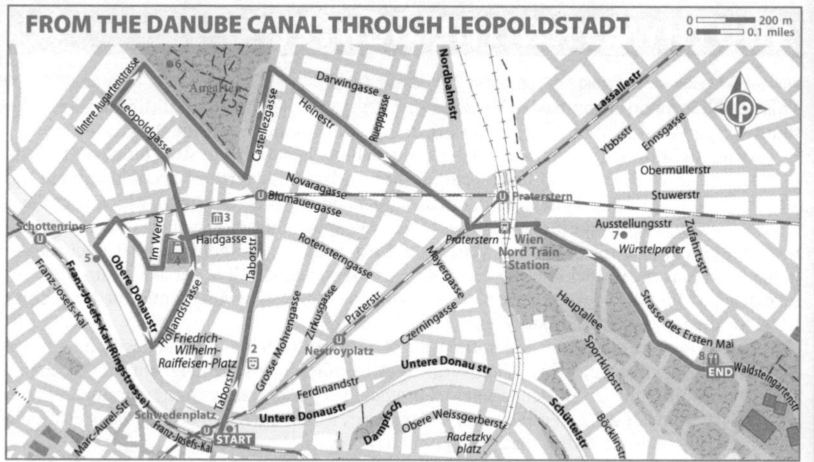

WALK FACTS

Start Schwedenbrücke
End Prater
Distance 7km
Time 3 hours
Exertion Moderate
Fuel stop Karl Kolarik's Schweizer Haus (p169)

about the Karmelitermarkt (p168), a bustling but not overcrowded farmers market with stalls, restaurants, and food with more tradition than you might reckon with – *Wurst* made from horse meat (see p169) – for the brave or old fashioned.

5 Schützenhaus

Situated on the Danube Canal, this Otto Wagner building from 1908 was originally the Kaiserbad (Imperial Baths), later torn down to make room for Wagner's building to control a weir. There have been plans to turn the rundown house into a cafe, but nothing has come of these yet.

6 Augarten

The genteel Augarten (p111) is Vienna's oldest baroque garden, having taken shape on the drawing board of city fathers and mothers from 1712 before opening its doors to the public in 1775. Sights to explore here include two Flaktürme, the Augarten Contemporary/Gustinus Ambrosi-Museum (p111), and the Wiener Porzellanmanufaktur Augarten (p114).

7 Würstelprater

Another tacky but fun attraction, the Würstelprater (p111) is the riotous side of the open spaces of the Prater parkland and home to all kinds of rides, but especially the Riesenrad (p111), Vienna's giant Ferris wheel.

8 Karl Kolarik's Schweizer Haus

If the stomach's screaming out for a fix of pork hocks, this is the place for them. You can wash them down with Budweiser beer on tap. Karl Kolarik's Schweizer Haus (p169) has even been doing a beer-laced chocolate of late – you get the idea: it's a favourite address for hearty Bohemian fare indoors or outdoors.

SOUTHWEST & THE GÜRTEL

Drinking & Nightlife p184; Eating p169; Shopping p148; Sleeping p215

This neighbourhood encompasses Meidling (the 12th) and Hietzing (the 13th), which lie to the southwest of Westbahnhof, and extends north in a swath along or outside the Gürtel.

The highlight of this neighbourhood is easily Schloss Schönbrunn, stretching southwards in very well-to-do Hietzing but bordering right on Meidling. North of Schönbrunn are the workers' suburbs Rudolfsheim-Fünfhaus (the 15th) and Penzing (the 14th), which begin just west of the Gürtel and have inner vicinities close to Westbahnhof. Going north of Penzing, you reach Ottakring (the 16th), another workers' suburb with an immigrant feel, relatively dense housing and an occasional good restaurant or drinking venue. All of these are fairly low on formal sights for the visitor, but are no less worthy for exploring if you're interested in getting a feel for the texture of suburban Vienna.

Situated right on the Gürtel and at the time of publication being upgraded with new shops and offices tagged BahnhofCity Wien West, Westbahnhof forms the neighbourhood's major railway transport hub. Until Vienna's new *Hauptbahnhof* (main train station) is gradually eased into service from late 2012, Westbahnhof will remain Vienna's most important hub for national and international trains. After that, it will only have regional connections.

North of Westbahnhof, the Gürtel takes on a sleazy character. Much of the Gürtel around the inner suburbs of Vienna is dotted with red-light clubs, but here the constellation reaches meltdown. Women may not always feel comfortable along the Neubaugürtel section, but it's worth persisting – the part around Josefstädter Strasse U-Bahn station has some good drinking and nightlife venues in the vaults beneath the railway line, and west of here around Brunnenmarkt in Ottakring are some good shopping, eating and drinking options. This vicinity is packed with Turkish immigrants. The main transport link along here is the U6, whereas trams 52 and 58 link Schönbrunn and Westbahnhof.

The further west you go from the Gürtel, the more spacious Vienna becomes, until eventually you reach the outer portions of Greater Vienna. The majority of your time, however, will be spent exploring the palace and gardens of Schönbrunn. While there, take a wander around the backstreets of old Hietzing; Biedermeier and modernist villas by Adolf Loos, Josef Hoffmann and Friedrich Ohmann are scattered throughout the area (particularly along Gloriettegasse and Lainzer Strasse).

SCHÖNBRUNN & AROUND

In terms of offering a display of imperial wealth, Schloss Schönbrunn and its adjoining garden are second only to Versailles. For all its grandiose proportions today, however, this baroque palace is in fact the downsized version of the imperial palace originally planned.

The name comes from the Schöner Brunnen (Beautiful Fountain), which was built around a spring discovered when Emperor Matthias (1557–1619) went out hunting and struck water instead. A pleasure palace was built here by Ferdinand II in 1637, only to be razed by the Turks in 1683. Soon after, Leopold I commissioned Johann Bernhard Fischer von Erlach to build a luxurious summer palace. Fischer von Erlach came up with hugely ambitious plans for one that would dwarf Versailles and be situated on the hill where the Gloriette now stands. The imperial purse winced and a 'less elaborate' building was constructed. It was finished in 1700.

Maria Theresia, upon her accession to the throne in 1740, chose Schönbrunn as the seat for her family and her court. The young architect Nicolas Pacassi was commissioned to renovate and extend the palace to meet her requirements, and work was carried out from

HIGHWAY TO HELL – THE GÜRTEL

The Gürtel, the broad 'belt' of bitumen road surrounding the *Vorstädte*, started life as a fortifying wall in 1704, but it never really fulfilled its true calling. Instead, it became a toll and customs barrier, while also making the wealthy feel secure enough to build palaces in the previously vulnerable inner suburbs. Unlike the Ringstrasse, it has always lacked serious money, being an eyesore at best and a hotbed of vice at most times. Despite partially successful citizens' initiatives to pimp it up in the area around Westbahnhof, the Gürtel retains a jaded, low-life character.

TICKETS FOR SCHLOSS SCHÖNBRUNN

If you plan to see several sights at Schönbrunn, it's worth purchasing one of the available combined tickets. Prices vary according to whether it's summer season (April to October) or winter. The best way to get a ticket is to buy it in advance on the internet (www.schoenbrunn.at). Print the ticket yourself and present it when you enter. (For the Sisi Ticket, see p54).

The summer season Classic Pass (adult/under 19yr/concession/family €17.90/10.90/16/38.90) is valid for a grand tour of Schloss Schönbrunn and visits to the Kronprinzengarten (Crown Prince Garden), Irrgarten & Labyrinth (Maze & Labyrinth), Gloriette with viewing terrace and Hofbackstube Schönbrunn (Court Bakery Schönbrunn; ☎ 24 100-300; per person €8.90; 🕑 10am-5pm, shows on the hour, mid-Mar–Oct) with the chance to watch apple strudel being made and enjoy the result with a cup of coffee. A Classic Pass 'light' (€13.90/9.50/13.50/33) excludes the Apple Strudel Show. The Court Bakery Schönbrunn can be viewed separately (it's inside Café Residenz). The summer Gold Pass (adult/under 19yr/concession €36/18/36) includes the Grand Tour, Crown Prince Garden, Tiergarten, Palmenhaus, Wüstenhaus, Wagenburg, Gloriette, Maze & Labyrinth, and Court Bakery Schönbrunn. The Winter Pass (adult/under 19yr & concession €25/12) includes the Grand Tour, Tiergarten, Palmenhaus, Wüstenhaus, Wagenburg, Gloriette and Maze & Labyrinth.

1744 to 1749. The interior was fitted out in rococo style, and the palace then had some 2000 rooms, as well as a chapel and a theatre. Like most imperial buildings associated with Maria Theresia, the exterior was painted her favourite colour, known as *Schönbrunngelb* (Schönbrunn yellow).

The Habsburgs were not the only famous residents here, as Napoleon took it over from 1805 to 1809. The last in the Habsburg line, Karl I, was the one who turned out the lights for the Habsburgs when he abdicated in the Blue Chinese Salon in 1918. After that the palace became the property of the new republic. Bomb damage was suffered during WWII, restoration of which was completed in 1955.

SCHLOSS SCHÖNBRUNN Map pp120-1

☎ 811 13-0; www.schoenbrunn.at; 13, Schloss Schönbrunn; Imperial Tour with audio adult/under 19yr/concession €9.50/6.50/8.50, Grand Tour with audio €12.90/8.90/11.40, Grand Tour with German guide €14.40/9.90/12.90; 🕑 8.30am-6pm Jul-Aug, 8.30am-5pm Apr-Jun & Sep-Oct, 8.30am-4.30pm Nov-Mar; Ⓤ U4 Schönbrunn, U4 Hietzing 🚋 10, 58 🚌 10A

While Schloss Belvedere (see p102) is mostly about the stupendous art collection and a handful of grand rooms, a tour of Schloss Schönbrunn focuses on the palace itself – especially the Habsburg residents. This means grand rooms and background on the habits and quirks of Austria's famous family.

Of the 1441 rooms within the palace, 40 are open to the public. The Imperial Tour takes you into 26 of these, and in the last room those on a Grand Tour show their tickets again and continue through the remaining rooms. Note that the Grosse Galerie (Great Gallery), part of both tours, is being restored until late 2012. Despite the rather steep prices, both tours are well worth doing for an insight into the people and the opulence of the baroque age. Because of the popularity of the palace, tickets are stamped with a departure time, and there may be a time lag before you're allowed to set off in summer, so buy your ticket straight away and explore the gardens while you wait.

SCHLOSS SCHÖNBRUNN GARDENS

Map pp120-1

13, Schloss Schönbrunn; admission free; 🕑 6am-dusk Apr-Oct, 6.30am-dusk Nov-Mar; Ⓤ U4 Schönbrunn, U4 Hietzing 🚋 10, 58 🚌 10A

The beautifully tended formal gardens of the palace, arranged in the French style, are a symphony of colour in the summer and a combination of greys and browns in winter; all seasons are appealing in their own right. The grounds, which were opened to the public by Joseph II in 1779, hide a number of attractions in the tree-lined avenues that were arranged according to a grid and star-shaped system between 1750 and 1755. From 1772 to 1780 Ferdinand Hetzendorf added some of the final touches to the park under the instructions of Joseph II: fake Roman ruins in 1778; the Neptunbrunnen (Neptune Fountain), a riotous ensemble from Greek mythology, in 1781; and the crowning glory, the Gloriette (rooftop access adult/child/student €2/1.40/1.70; 🕑 9am-7pm Jul & Aug, 9am-6pm Apr-Jun

SOUTHWEST & THE GÜRTEL

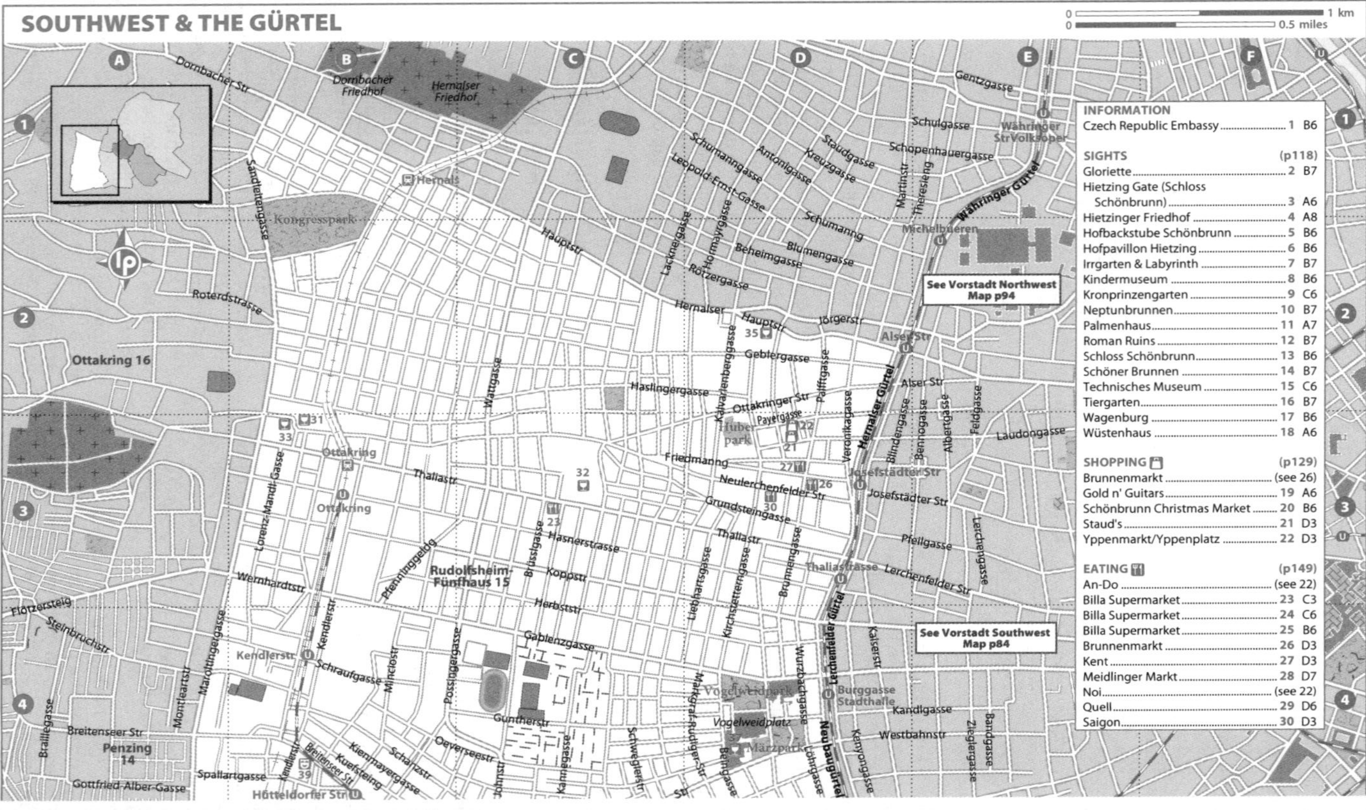

INFORMATION
Czech Republic Embassy 1 B6

SIGHTS (p118)
Gloriette 2 B7
Hietzing Gate (Schloss Schönbrunn) 3 A6
Hietzinger Friedhof 4 A8
Hofbackstube Schönbrunn 5 B6
Hofpavillon Hietzing 6 B6
Irrgarten & Labyrinth 7 B7
Kindermuseum 8 B6
Kronprinzengarten 9 C6
Neptunbrunnen 10 B7
Palmenhaus 11 A7
Roman Ruins 12 B7
Schloss Schönbrunn 13 B6
Schöner Brunnen 14 B7
Technisches Museum 15 C6
Tiergarten 16 B7
Wagenburg 17 B6
Wüstenhaus 18 A6

SHOPPING (p129)
Brunnenmarkt (see 26)
Gold n' Guitars 19 A6
Schönbrunn Christmas Market 20 B6
Staud's 21 D3
Yppenmarkt/Yppenplatz 22 D3

EATING (p149)
An-Do (see 22)
Billa Supermarket 23 C3
Billa Supermarket 24 C6
Billa Supermarket 25 B6
Brunnenmarkt 26 D3
Kent 27 D3
Meidlinger Markt 28 D7
Noi (see 22)
Quell 29 D6
Saigon 30 D3

DRINKING & NIGHTLIFE (p171)
10er Marie 31 B3
Bach 32 C3
Buschenschrank Stippert 33 B3
Café Gloriette (see 2)
Lo:sch 34 D6
Metropol 35 D2
Reigen 36 B6
Stadthalle 37 D4
U4 38 C7
Yppenplatz (see 22)
MUSIC & THE ARTS (p191)
Breitenseer Lichtspiele 39 B4
Marionettentheater 40 B6
Orangery 41 C6
Schlosstheater Schönbrunn (see 13)
SLEEPING (p207)
Altwienerhof 42 D6
Boutiquehotel Stadthalle 43 D5
Do Step Inn 44 D5
Wombat's 45 D5
Wombat's 46 D5
TRANSPORT (p228)
Westbahnhof Airport Bus Stop 47 D5
Schloss Schönbrunn
Auer-Welsbach-Park
Main Entrance
Palace Entrance
Meidling Gate
Maria Theresia Gate
Maxing Gate
Meierei Gate
Tiroler Garten
Fasangarten
Hietzinger Friedhof
Penzinger Friedhof
Meidling 12
Hietzing 13
Westbahnhof
Mariahilfer Gürtel
Linke Wienzeile
Schönbrunner Schlossstr
Hadikgasse
Hietzinger Kai
Grünbergstr
Altmannsdorfer Str
Wienerbergstr
Triester Str
Matzleinsdorfer Platz
Gaudenzdorfer Gürtel
Margaretengürtel

top picks

IT'S FREE – SOUTHWEST & THE GÜRTEL

- Schloss Schönbrunn Gardens (p119)
- Hietzinger Friedhof (opposite)
- U6 – Along the Gürtel (opposite)
- Hofpavillon Hietzing (opposite)

& Sep, 9am-5pm Oct) in 1775. The view from the Gloriette, looking back towards the palace with Vienna shimmering in the distance, ranks among the best in Vienna. It's possible to venture onto its roof, but the view is only marginally superior.

The original Schöner Brunnen, from which the palace gained its name, now pours through the stone pitcher of a nymph near the Roman ruins. The garden's 630m-long Irrgarten (maze; adult/child/student €2.90/1.70/2.40; 9am-7pm Jul & Aug, 9am-6pm Apr-Jun & Sep, 9am-5pm Oct) is a classic hedge design based on the original maze that occupied its place from 1720 to 1892; adjoining this is the Labyrinth, a playground with games, climbing equipment and a giant mirror kaleidoscope.

To the east of the palace is the Kronprinzengarten (Crown Prince Garden; adult/child/student €2/1.40/1.70; 9am-6pm Jul & Aug, 9am-5pm Apr-Jun, Sep & Oct), a replica of the baroque garden that occupied the space around 1750.

KINDERMUSEUM Map pp120-1

811 13 239; www.schoenbrunn.at/kinder, in German; 13, Schloss Schönbrunn; adult/under 19yr/concession/family €6.50/4.90/5/17; 10am-5pm Sat, Sun & school holidays; U4 Schönbrunn, U4 Hietzing 10, 58 10A

Schönbrunn's Children's Museum does what it knows best: imperialism. Activities and displays help kids discover the day-to-day life of the Habsburg court, and once they've got an idea, they can don princely or princessly outfits and start ordering the serfs (parents) around. Other rooms devoted to toys, natural science and archaeology all help to keep them entertained. Guided tours (adult/child/family €6.50/4.90/17) in German are a regular feature, departing at 10.30am, 1.30pm and 3pm (in English by appointment only).

WAGENBURG Map pp120-1

525 24-0; 13, Schloss Schönbrunn; adult/under 19yr/concession €6/free/4; 9am-6pm Apr-Oct, 10am-4pm Nov-Mar; U4 Schönbrunn 10A

The Wagenburg (Imperial Coach Collection) is *Pimp My Ride* imperial style. On display is a vast array of carriages, including Emperor Franz Stephan's coronation carriage, with its ornate gold plating, Venetian glass panes and painted cherubs. The whole thing weighs an astonishing 4000kg. Also look for the dainty child's carriage built for Napoleon's son, with eagle-wing-shaped mudguards and bee motifs.

PALMENHAUS Map pp120-1

877 50 87406; 13, Maxingstrasse 13b; adult/student & under 18yr €4/3; 9.30am-6pm May-Sep, 9.30am-5pm Oct-Apr; U4 Hietzing 10, 58, 60

Travellers from London or fresh from a London spell may think they're experiencing *déjà vu* on sighting the Palm House. This was built in 1882 by Franz Segenschmid as a replica of the one in London's Kew Gardens. Inside is a veritable jungle of tropical plants from around the world. A combined ticket for the Palmenhaus and Wüstenhaus (below) costs €6 per person.

TIERGARTEN Map pp120-1

877 92 94; www.zoovienna.at; 13, Maxingstrasse 13b; adult/senior & child €14/6; 9am-6.30pm Apr-Sep, 9am-5.30pm Mar & Oct, 9am-5pm Feb, 9am-4.30pm Nov-Jan; U4 Hietzing 10, 58, 60

Founded in 1752 as a menagerie by Franz Stephan, the Schönbrunn Tiergarten is the oldest zoo in the world. It houses some 750 animals of all shapes and sizes, including giant pandas that arrived in 2003. A batch of emus, armadillos and baby Siberian tigers joined them in 2006. Thankfully most of the original cramped cages have been updated and improved. The zoo's layout is reminiscent of a bicycle wheel, with pathways as spokes and an octagonal pavilion at its centre. The pavilion dates from 1759 and was used as the imperial breakfast room. Feeding times are staggered throughout the day – maps on display tell you who's dining when.

WÜSTENHAUS Map pp120-1

877 92 94 390; 13, Maxingstrasse 13b; adult/child & student & senior €4/2.50; 9am-6pm

May-Sep, 9am-5pm Oct-Apr; U4 Hietzing 10, 58, 60

The small Wüstenhaus (Desert House) near the Palmenhaus makes good use of the once disused Sonnenuhrhaus (Sundial House) to re-create arid desert scenes. There are four sections – Northern Africa and the Middle East, Africa, the Americas, and Madagascar – with rare cacti and live desert animals, such as the naked mole rat from East Africa. A combined ticket for the Palmenhaus (opposite) and Wüstenhaus costs €6 per person.

TECHNISCHES MUSEUM Map pp120-1

899 98-0; www.technischesmuseum.at; 14, Mariahilfer Strasse 212; adult/under 19yr/ concession €8.50/free/7; 9am-6pm Mon-Fri, 10am-6pm Sat & Sun; 52, 58

The Technical Museum has been around since 1918 and today is a modern museum dedicated to advances in the fields of science and technology. There are loads of hands-on gadgets allowing you to conduct experiments to demonstrate one or another phenomenon, but the most interesting aspect of the museum is its displays from past ages. A Mercedes Silver Arrow from 1950, a model-T Ford from 1923 and penny-farthing bicycles to name a few. Its musical instrument collection is small and focuses mainly on keyboard instruments, so if this is your main interest, head for the Neue Burg museums (p71) instead. The permanent exhibition is complemented by temporary ones, and overall it's an interesting museum for the average visitor, but of course anyone with an engineering mind will absolutely love it. Das Mini section has loads of kids toys and activities and is specifically aimed at two- to six-year-olds.

HOFPAVILLON HIETZING Map pp120-1

13, Schönbrunner Strasse; U4 Hietzing 10, 58, 60

Built between 1898 and 1899 by Otto Wagner as part of the public transport system, the Hofpavillon Hietzing was originally designed as a private station for the imperial court. The elaborate wood-panelled interior is suitably regal and was designed by Wagner in conjunction with Josef Olbrich. Its white facade, decorated with wrought ironwork, is easily spotted just east of the U4 Hietzing stop. It is in poor shape and closed for renovation.

top picks

SOUTHWEST & THE GÜRTEL FOR CHILDREN

- Kindermuseum (opposite)
- Technisches Museum (below)
- Tiergarten (opposite)

HIETZINGER FRIEDHOF Map pp120-1

877 31 07; 13, Maxingstrasse 15; admission free; 7am-8pm May-Aug, 7am-7pm Apr & Sep, 7am-6pm Mar & Oct, 8am-5pm Nov-Feb; 10, 60 56B, 58B, 156B

Aficionados of Vienna's Secessionist movement will want to make the pilgrimage to the Hietzinger cemetery to pay homage to some of its greatest members. Klimt, Moser and Wagner are all buried here. Others buried in the cemetery include Engelbert Dollfuss, leader of the Austro-Fascists, assassinated in 1934, and composer Alban Berg.

BELOW THE BELT & ALONG THE GÜRTEL

Walking Tour

1 Schloss Schönbrunn Gardens

This part of Vienna was called Katterburg in the 14th century and consisted of a mill and vineyards, later morphing under Maximilian II into hunting grounds. From 1695 the predecessor to the Schloss Schönbrunn Gardens (p119) was carved out by Frenchman Jean Trehet and given a baroque form by later masters.

2 Palmenhaus

The Habsburgs were a worldly bunch who liked nothing better than to collect things – this included countries, but also plants of the world, and in the late 19th century under Kaiser Franz Joseph I the royal collection was brought together here, in the Palmenhaus (Palm House; opposite).

3 Gloriette

A walk along the perimeter of the Tiergarten (opposite) is not only a step back into mother nature, it illustrates one of the former functions of the palace gardens – bagging game. On reaching Gloriette (p119) another purpose dawns on you – looking down upon your baroque

WALK FACTS

Start Schloss Schönbrunn – Main entrance
End Yppenmarkt/Yppenplatz
Transport 52, 58 (Winckelmannstrasse to Westbahnhof), U6 (between Westbahnhof & Josefstädter Strasse)
Distance 8km
Time Three hours
Exertion Moderate
Fuel stop Kent (p170)

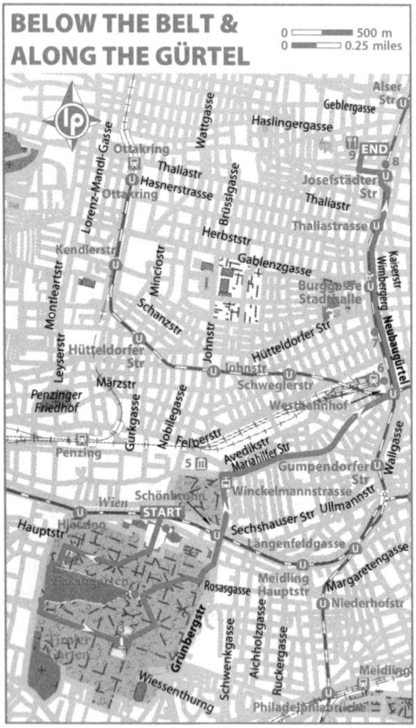

BELOW THE BELT & ALONG THE GÜRTEL

0 500 m
0 0.25 miles

splendour and at the rabble in the suburbs beyond. This is one of Vienna's finest views.

4 Neptunbrunnen

Monumental Neptune Fountain is on the main axis of the gardens. It forms a grotto and borrows from Greek mythology, with Neptune playing the lead, accompanied by a cast of sea nymphs, sea horses and other mythological elements.

5 Technisches Museum

The Technical Museum (p123) is housed inside a reinforced concrete, neoclassical revivalist design dating from 1913. The building symbolises the technology it houses, being the last word in the use of electricity in its day. Inside, an atrium offers light relief from monumentalism.

6 BahnhofCity Wien West & Westbahnhof

Vienna's public transport hub has been redesigned to retain its 1950s look, but has an atrium, hotel and all sorts of shops. The Östereichische Bundesbahnen (ÖBB) says it brings together travel, work and shopping. Thankfully, it leaves out the pimps on the sex strip, but perhaps they could be retrained as information-point staff.

7 The Gürtel

The western Gürtel has long been a problem zone for the city – pimps, slum goddesses plying the oldest trade in the world, human trafficking, rubbernecking drivers, drugs, ugly railway station – you name it. Hopefully, the new BahnhofCity Wien West complex might change things.

8 Josefstädter Strasse Stadtbahnbögen

From the turn of the 20th century, after creating the Stadtbahn (city railway), Otto Wagner created some of the finest *Jugendstil* stations. Today the section of the viaduct around the Josefstädter Strasse Stadtbahnbögen (city railway arches) has morphed into a string of drinking dens, most notably Rhiz (see p181).

9 Yppenmarkt/Yppenplatz

With Brunnenmarkt (p170) and places like Staud's (p148), Noi (p169) and An-Do (p170), the area around Yppenplatz is hustling, bustling and a treat for gourmet pursuits. Hang out here, explore the places and enjoy!

GREATER VIENNA

Drinking & Nightlife p185; Eating p169; Sleeping p216

Greater Vienna takes in a large swathe of suburbia surrounding the city in the south, west and the north. There are 11 districts outside the Gürtel, which separates the inner suburbs (*Vorstädte*) from suburban Vienna (*Vororte*) and each has its own flavour and tone. While portions of the suburbs close to – but outside – the Gürtel retain an almost inner-city character, neighbourhoods become low rise as you move out further. (For ease of use, we've included suburbs close to the Gürtel in the west in the neighbourhood Southwest & the Gürtel; see p118.)

Favoriten and Simmering, two of three districts making up Vienna's southern fringe have a handful of large parks and the city's moody Zentralfriedhof (Central Cemetery). Liesing, in Vienna's southwestern corner, is a sprawling district with a grouping of *Heurigen* in its Mauer neighbourhood and easy access to the Wienerwald (see p126) and the wild Lainzer Tiergarten (Lainzer Zoo). Continuing north, Penzing, Ottakring and Hernals stretch from close to the Gürtel to the Wienerwald. Fairly similar to each other, they encompass the spacious housing suburbs that crawl into the Wienerwald and the dense mix of Turk, Serb, Croat and African immigrant communities closer to the Gürtel.

To the north of Hernals, Währing and Döbling form two of Vienna's wealthier districts. The outer reaches of Döbling are covered in vineyards and *Heurigen*. Some are unashamedly touristy while others are traditional and *Gemütlch* (cosy). Even though it falls outside the city limits, we've included Klosterneuburg in this section as it is close enough to enjoy as an afternoon outing from the city.

Floridsdorf, Vienna's most northerly district, is solidly working class, with few attractions, but it does produce over 30% of the city's wines. Its neighbourhoods Strebersdorf and Stammersdorf hog the most attention and are well known for their traditional *Heurigen* (wine taverns; p173). Just outside the city limits – but still with public transport connections to Floridsdorf – is Bisamberg, a rounded hill rising from the flat plain. It's criss-crossed with walking and cycling paths and covered in vineyards, making it a lovely day's outing for wine and nature enthusiasts.

SOUTHERN VIENNA

Apart from the art-nouveau Amalienbad (see p204) on bustling, multicultural Reumannplatz, the main attraction in the southern suburbs is the Zentralfriedhof (Central Cemetery).

ZENTRALFRIEDHOF Map pp50-1

☎ 760 41-0; 11, Simmeringer Hauptstrasse 232-244; admission free; information office 8am-3pm Mon-Sat, cemetery 7am-8pm May-Aug, 7am-7pm Apr & Sep, 7am-6pm Mar & Oct, 8am-5pm Nov-Feb; tram 6, 71

The cemetery has three gates: the first is opposite Schloss Concordia (p170) and leads to the old Jewish graves; the second, the main gate, directs you to the tombs of honour and the cemetery's church, Dr Karl Lueger Kirche; the third is closer to the Protestant and new Jewish graves. The information centre and map of the cemetery are at Gate Two.

The Ehrengräber (Tombs of Honour) are just beyond Gate Two and, besides the clump of famous composers, includes Hans Makart, sculptor Fritz Wotruba, architects Theophil Hansen and Adolf Loos, and the man of Austrian pop, Falco (Hans Hölzel).

Behind Dr Karl Lueger Kirche, at the far end of the cemetery, are simple plaques devoted to those who fell in the world wars.

BÖHMISCHE PRATER Map pp50-1

10, Laaer Wald; bus 68A

This tiny, old-fashioned version of the Würstelprater (p110), is a short ride from Reumannplatz. Riding the merry-go-rounds and testing your strength on 'strongman' machines here is like stepping back to Victorian times, and a quaint reminder that entertainment like this had a mechanical edge before we started testing our strength and mettle with online games.

FAVORITEN WATER TOWER Map pp50-1

☎ 599 59 31006; 10, Windtenstrasse 3; tram 1

Built in 1889, this tall tower is all that remains of a pumping station that brought water from the Alps to Vienna. Its striking yellow- and red-brick facade is decoratively topped with turrets; tours are occasionally offered. Just south of the tower is the Erholungsgebiet Wienerberg, once the site of Europe's largest brickworks and now a public park.

FRIEDHOF DER NAMENLOSEN

Map pp50-1

☎ 0664-623 56 64; 11, Alberner Hafen; 🚌 76A

This 'Cemetery of the Nameless', situated on the outskirts of Vienna alongside the Danube, was established in 1900 by volunteers to bury the grey, unknown dead (often suicides or accident victims) who washed up on the shores of the blue Danube. Fans of the film *Before Sunrise* will recognise it as one of the places where the two protagonists Céline and Jesse spend time before destiny takes them to other places, other callings.

WESTERN VIENNA

The western suburbs of Vienna boast a masterpiece of Otto Wagner, the Kirche am Steinhof, situated dramatically in the grounds of a psychiatric hospital. In addition to this, the Lainzer Tiergarten wildlife park and the Hermesvilla are drawcards, and there are opportunities for hiking in the forests.

KIRCHE AM STEINHOF Map pp50-1

☎ 910 60 11 007; 14, Baumgartner Höhe 1; church tours adult/under 15yr/concession €6/free/4; 🕑 tours 3-4pm Sat, public admission 4-5pm Sat; 🚌 47A, 48A

The splendour and mood of this Otto Wagner creation set in the grounds of the Psychiatric Hospital of the City of Vienna make it one of his most fascinating works. This distinctive art-nouveau church was built from 1904 to 1907; Moser chipped in with the mosaic windows, and the roof is topped by a copper-covered dome that earned the nickname *Lemoniberg* (lemon mountain) from its original golden colour. The design illustrates Wagner's love of sharp edges and functionality, even down to the sloping floor to allow good drainage; despite this, it is a highly moving piece of church architecture. The grounds and many of the buildings of the hospital themselves were built in the art-nouveau style, and tours Jugendstil Führung am Lemoniberg (adult/under 15yr/concession €10/free/6; 🕑 3.30-5pm Fri Apr-Sep) start from the director's office and take you through highlights, including Wagner's masterpiece.

LAINZER TIERGARTEN Map pp50-1

13, Hermesstrasse; free; 🕑 8am-dusk; 🚌 60B 🚊 60

At 25 sq km, the Lainzer Zoo is the largest (and wildest) of Vienna's city parks. The 'zoo' refers to the abundant wild boar, deer, woodpeckers and squirrels that freely inhabit the park, and the famous Lipizzaner horses that summer here. Apart from the extensive walking possibilities through lush woodland, attractions of the park include the Hermesvilla (below) and the Hubertus-Warte (508m), a viewing platform on top of Kaltbründlberg.

HERMESVILLA Map pp50-1

☎ 804 13 24; 13, Lainzer Tiergarten; adult/concession & under 19yr €5/2.50; 🕑 10am-6pm Tue-Sun late-Mar–Oct; 🚌 60B 🚊 60

The Hermesvilla was commissioned by Franz Josef I and presented to his wife as a gift when he tried to patch up their failing marriage. Built by Karl von Hasenauer

WIENERWALD – THE VIENNA WOODS

The Vienna Woods, a 45km stretch of forested hills fringing the capital from the northwest to the southeast, was immortalised in 'Tales from the Vienna Woods', the concert waltz by Johann Strauss (the son) in 1868. For the Viennese though – and the visitor – the Vienna Woods are mostly a place to escape into the great outdoors. The city council has a website (www.wien.gv.at/english/leisure/hiking) with nine city walks, a couple of which take you into the forest. You'll need about three hours to do the 7.2km 'Stadtwanderweg 4' (city hiking trail 4), which is a nice way of reaching the Jubiläumswarte (opposite). Grab some picnic supplies, jump on tram 49 to Bahnhofstrasse, and walk in the direction of the tram to Rosentalgasse, then follow the signs. From the Jubiläumswarte the trail is mainly through suburbs, so it's nicer to return the way you came. For a walk in the north with *Heurigen*-galore, see p136.

Another way of exploring the Wienerwald on your own is on one of the scores of marked mountain-bike trails. The website www.mbike.at (in German) has routes listed and mapped.

Ticks, which can carry Lyme disease and tick-borne encephalitis, are a problem in the Vienna Woods; if you plan to do summer hiking or mountain biking, play it safe and get vaccinations against encephalitis.

between 1882 and 1886, with Klimt and Makart on board as interior decorators, the villa is plush – it's more a mansion than simply a 'villa'. Empress Elisabeth's bedroom is well over the top, with the walls and ceiling covered in motifs from Shakespeare's *A Midsummer Night's Dream*.

For all its opulence and comforts, the villa unfortunately did not have the desired effect: Elisabeth never really took to the place and rarely ventured back to Vienna. She did, however, name it after her favourite Greek God. Hermesvilla is a municipal museum.

ERNST FUCHS PRIVAT MUSEUM

Map pp50-1

☎ 914 85 75; www.ernstfuchs-zentrum.com; 14, Hüttelbergstrasse 26; adult/concession €11/6; 10am-6pm Tue-Fri & Sun; 35B, 148, 152

This small museum about 2km north of the U4 Hütteldorf stop is devoted to Ernst Fuchs' fantastical paintings, etchings and sculptures. The works have a, shall we say, drug-induced look about them, and what may be more interesting to the visitor is the villa housing the collection. Built by Wagner in 1888, it was saved from ruin by Fuchs and restored to its former glory in 1972. In the gardens (visible from the road) are some interesting statues, ceramics and the ornate Brunnenhaus created by Fuchs. At No 28 is another fine villa designed by Wagner.

JUBILÄUMSWARTE Map pp50-1

16, Pelzer Rennweg; 46B, 148

Rising above the Wienerwald's green canopy, the concrete Jubiläumswarte offers sweeping views from the uppermost platform that take in most of Vienna; on a windy day the climb to the top can be quite an adrenalin rush. You can walk here and back in less than three hours – see the Wienerwald – The Vienna Woods (opposite) boxed text for more.

NORTHERN VIENNA

As in the west, the northern suburbs of Vienna extend into the Vienna Woods, and their main attraction is wine and woods. This is a good area to explore for its *Heurigen*. The affluent districts of Währing and Döbling reach well into the hills north of the city. Four of the city's popular wine villages – Neustift am Walde, Sievering, Grinzing and Nussdorf – are all in this northern section. While many wine taverns in Grinzing and an ever-increasing number in Neustift am Walde cater to busloads of tour groups with unbearable folk music and tacky shows, it would be a shame to dismiss the entire region as a *Heurigen* no-go area. Nussdorf is particularly atmospheric, with a string of traditional *Heurigen* along its main street, Kahlenberger Strasse. Beethoven spent a good portion of his time in the area, residing in various houses, including one on Pfarrplatz, now a *Heuriger*, Mayer am Pfarrplatz, and an apartment nearby. A good way to take in a stretch of the north is on a hike from Kahlenberg to Nussdorf (see p136).

BEETHOVEN WOHNUNG HEILIGENSTADT Map pp50-1

☎ 370 54 08; 19, Probusgasse 6; adult/under 19yr/concession €2/free/1; 10am-1pm & 2-6pm Tue-Sun; D 38A

The musical anomaly that one of the world's greatest composers would turn stone deaf left its mark on Heiligenstadt, as it was here – or more accurately, from the mineral waters located here – Beethoven sought a cure. In this apartment the musical wonder wrote his second symphony. Although the exhibits, including a death mask of Beethoven, are of more interest to buffs, this apartment combines well with a visit to Mayer am Pfarrplatz (p185) and Karl-Marx-Hof (below).

KARL-MARX-HOF Map pp50-1

19, Heiligenstädter Strasse 82-92; U4 Heiligenstadt D

Opposite the U4 Heiligenstadt U-Bahn station, architecture fans and neo-socialists will be excited to find one of the crowning achievements of Red Vienna (p27): the Karl-Marx-Hof. Stretching for almost 1km along Heiligenstädter Strasse, this colossal housing project in pale pink and yellow was built by Karl Ehn, a student of Otto Wagner, between 1927 and 1930. It originally contained some 1600 flats, plus community facilities and inner courtyards. In 1934 it was the centre of the Social Democratic resistance during the civil war, and has since been restored.

KAHLENBERG Map pp50-1

19, Höhenstrasse; 38A

As any proud Pole will tell you, it wasn't the Viennese who drove back the Turks in the second siege in September 1683, it was a force of Polish and German troops under the command of the Polish king, Jan III Sobieski. Mass was conducted on Kahlenberg before the troops rode down into Vienna's *Vorstädte*.

At 484m, Kahlenberg offers fantastic views across Vienna to the Lesser Carpathians hills of Slovakia. Today the St Josephs Kirche on Kahlenberg is run by Polish priests, and alongside the church is a modern hotel and restaurant complex.

A more peaceful spot with similar views is Leopoldsberg (19, Höhenstrasse; 38A), 1km further along Höhenstrasse. Atop this peak is a small fortified church and cafe. A pleasant alternative to taking the bus back down from either of these is to set off by foot through the vineyards to Nussdorf; see p136 for more information.

GEYMÜLLERSCHLÖSSEL Map pp50-1

479 31 39; 18, Pötzleinsdorfer Strasse 102; adult/under 19yr/concession €7.90/free/5.50; 11am-6pm Sun May-Nov; 41 41A

The Geymüllerschlössel, named after its first owner, the banker and merchant Johann Jakob Geymüller, is arguably the finest example of Biedermeier architecture in Austria. Built around 1808 by an unknown architect, it is a mixture of Gothic, Indian and Arabic styles characteristic of the times. The interior, embellished with floral designs and graceful lines, is perfectly preserved. It houses the MAK's (p60) collection of around 160 Viennese clocks dating from 1760 to the second half of the 19th century, and furniture from the period 1800 to 1840. It's a fair way out from the centre and best combined with a walk in the Wienerwald (p126) nearby.

BEETHOVEN EROICAHAUS Map pp50-1

505 8747 85 173; 19, Döblinger Hauptstrasse 92; adult/under 19yr/concession €2/free/1; 37 10A, 39A

For the brief time Beethoven spent at Eroicahaus (the summer of 1803), his work production was grandiose: it was here that he wrote Symphony No 3, *Eroica*. The house is rather empty, however, and no personal effects of the great composer are present, but you can listen to *Eroica* and gaze at a few watercolours and maps. The Eroicahaus is a municipal museum, and is open by appointment only.

KIRCHE ZUR HEILIGSTEN DREIFALTIGKEIT Map pp50-1

888 50 03; www.georgenberg.at; 23, Georgsgasse/Rysergasse; admission free; 2-8pm Sat, 9am-4.30pm Sun; 60A

The stack of concrete blocks that form the Kirche zur Heiligsten Dreifaltigkeit (Holy Trinity Church) is an unusual work of art. Some will find this industrial piece with little warmth exceptionally ugly, while others will see it as a triumph of the contemporary over conformity. But there's no doubting its powerful presence. It's more commonly known as 'Wotrubakirche' after its architect, Fritz Wotruba, who completed it in 1976.

SHOPPING

top picks

What's your recommendation? www.lonelyplanet.com/vienna

SHOPPING

Don't even think about visiting Vienna without hitting the shops. The boutique scene – particularly along Kirchengasse, Neubaugasse and Lindengasse in Neubau – is exploding with affordable, young designers' spaces selling quality creations you'll never see on anyone else – for a partial list of shops check out www.7tm.at. Neubau's northern edge also brims with the city's idiosyncratic *Altwaren* (old wares) shops (rummaging through secondhand treasures and trash is de rigeur) and *Jugendstil* (art nouveau) showrooms filled with both furniture and jewellery, though the supreme is the famous *Flohmarkt* (see the boxed text, p142), adjacent to the Naschmarkt. At this huge Saturday flea market crammed with bargain hunters, the dusty contents of suburban attics mix with genuinely valuable and handsome old pieces to make for a quintessentially Viennese shopping experience. Another such experience is bidding on authentic antique furniture, jewellery and art at famed local auction house Dorotheum (see p141). For excellent gallery-hopping or shopping for period and contemporary art, antique guns, porcelain and armour, hit the streets between the Dorotheum and Albertinaplatz.

In the tiny Innere Stadt Hoher Markt area and Bauernmarkt and around you'll find more fashion and small boutiques, many selling locally designed clothes, accessories or food, such as designers' cooperative Art Up (p132). Outside the Ring, your best bets for a pleasant afternoon's shopping are Mariahilf and Neubau – particularly Neubaugasse and Westbahnstrasse – and Josefstädter Strasse, where you'll find plenty of quirky one-offs and interesting boutiques.

Kärntner Strasse and Mariahilfer Strasse are the prime high streets, with international heavyweights and little you can't find at home, but off the main drag you'll discover a few winners selling local specialities such as porcelain, ceramics, handmade dolls, wrought-iron work and leather goods.

Reviews in this chapter are grouped by neighbourhood, and ordered by the type of product on sale.

PRACTICALITIES

Opening Hours

Most shops are open between 9am and 6.30pm Monday to Friday and until 5pm on Saturday. Some have extended hours on Thursday or Friday until around 8pm or 9pm; some shops open on Sunday afternoon. Opening hours are included for listings in this chapter only where they differ from standard business hours.

Consumer Taxes

Mehrwertsteuer (MWST; value-added tax) is set at 20% for most goods. Prices are displayed inclusive of all taxes, even (usually) service charges in hotels and restaurants.

All non-EU visitors are entitled to a refund of the MWST on purchases over €75.01. To claim the tax, a tax-refund cheque must be filled out by the shop at the time of purchase (you'll need to show your passport), which must then be stamped by border officials when you leave the EU. Vienna airport has a counter for payment of instant refunds. Check www.globalrefund.com for more details about how to obtain a refund – it is best claimed upon departing the EU, as otherwise you'll have to track down an international refund office or make a claim by post. After a handling fee is deducted, refunds normally amount to 13% of the purchase price.

Bargaining

Bargaining is a no-no in shops, although you can certainly haggle when buying secondhand. It's a must at the *Flohmarkt* (see p142).

CENTRAL VIENNA

BRITISH BOOKSHOP Map pp56-7 Books

☎ 512 19 45-0; www.britishbookshop.at; 01, Weihburggasse 24; 🚋 1, 2

The British Bookshop has the largest selection of English reference and teaching books in Vienna. There's also a well-ordered, extensive fiction section, children's books and DVDs.

FREYTAG & BERNDT Map pp56-7 Books, Maps

☎ 533 86 85; www.freytagberndt.at; 01, Kohlmarkt 9; Ⓤ U3 Herrengasse 🚌 2A, 3A

There is no better place for maps and travel guides than Freytag & Berndt. There's an exhaustive collection of guides and maps to Vienna and Austria (including some superbly detailed walking maps) and guides to Europe and the world (many in English).

SHAKESPEARE & CO Map pp56-7 Books

☎ 535 50 53; www.shakespeare.co.at; 01, Sterngasse 2; 9am-9pm Mon-Sat; 2A, 3A

This beautifully cluttered bookshop in a charming area just off Judengasse stocks Vienna's best collection of literary and hard-to-find titles in English – history, culture, classic and modern fiction – with a wide range of titles about Austria and by Austrian writers displayed separately. The personalised and friendly service makes this the best place in town to come for your train and plane reading needs.

LODEN-PLANKL Map p66 Clothing

☎ 533 80 32; www.plankl.at; 01, Michaelerplatz 6; 10am-6pm Mon-Sat Mar-Jun, Sep-Dec, 10am-5pm Jan, Feb, Jul & Aug; U3 Herrengasse 2A, 3A

Christopher Plummer wannabes alert: kit yourself out Von Trapp family style at this 180-year-old institution full of handmade embroidered dirndls and blouses, capes, high-collared jackets and deer-suede and loden (a traditional fabric made from boiled and combed wool) coats. Modern variations share racks with traditional designs, but you're likely to find more nostalgic charm in the trad stuff.

ALTMANN & KÜHNE Map pp56-7 Confectionery

☎ 533 09 27; 01, Graben 30; U1, U3 Stephansplatz

top picks

CHOCOLATE & CAKES

- **Café Sacher** (p176) Its eponymous cake graces thousands of tourists' 'must do in Vienna' lists.
- **Demel** (p176) A famed *Konditorei* (cake shop) with a *Jugendstil* (art nouveau) interior and a peekable cake-designing studio out back.
- **Aida** (p175) Magnificent retro interiors and fabulous cakes and sweets.
- **Oberlaa** (above) Gloriously packaged chocolates and biscuits.
- **Altmann & Kühne** (above) World-famous bonbons made using a 100-year-old recipe.

This charming small shop has a touch of the old world about it, partly due to the handmade packaging of its chocolates and sweets, designed by Wiener Werkstätte in 1928. Altmann & Kühne have been producing handmade bonbons for more than 100 years using a well-kept secret recipe.

OBERLAA Map pp56-7 Confectionery

☎ 513 29 36; www.oberlaa-wien.at; 01, Neuer Markt 16, 8am-8pm; U1, U3 Stephansplatz

Some locals swear that Oberlaa sells the best confectionery in Vienna (in the face of some stiff competition). That's a tough one, but it no doubt offers the most beautifully packaged chocolates, and no other local macaroon measures up to its 'LaaKronen' – brightly coloured in flavours like pistachio, lemon and strawberry, available singly or in gorgeous boxed sets. There are seven other branches around town.

OPERN CONFISERIE Map pp56-7 Confectionery

☎ 512 19 10; 01, Kärntner Strasse 47; 9am-7pm Mon-Sat, 11am-6pm Sun; U1, U2, U4 Karlsplatz D, 1, 2 59A, 62

An old-fashioned confectionery store in the midst of buzzing Kärntner Strasse, with a dizzying array of handmade truffles, many-shaped marzipan, and brightly coloured fruit *gelées*. Look out for Austrian-made Bachhalm handmade chocolate bars, with chunky ingredients – from standards like pistachio to more-challenging taste concepts such as rose petal and shitake mushroom.

XOCOLAT Map pp56-7 Confectionery

☎ 535 43 63; www.xocolat.at; 01, Freyung 2; 10am-6pm Mon-Fri, 10am-5pm Sat, noon-5pm Sun; U3 Herrengasse 1A

Decadence within opulence – it's a palace of chocolate inside a palace. Housed in the magnificent Freyung Passage in the Palais Ferstel, this upmarket *Konditorei* (cake shop) offers 40-odd varieties of beautifully decorated handmade chocolates, some of which qualify as tiny edible works of art. You can also visit the factory where the chocolates are made; see p165.

ART UP Map pp56-7 Fashion & Accessories

☎ 535 50 97; www.artup.at; 01, Bauernmarkt 8; 11.30am-6.30pm Mon-Fri, 11am-5pm Sat; U1, U3 Stephansplatz

Take the temperature of Vienna's contemporary design scene at Art Up, which works on a cooperative model allowing the designers who stock their work here (around 40 when we popped in) to get a foothold in the fashion world. The model makes for an eclectic collection – elegant fashion pieces rub alongside quirky accessories (Astroturf tie or handbag, anyone?) as well as ceramics and bigger art pieces. It's a testament to the liveliness of the fashion and design scenes in Vienna, given new vigour by students coming out of the city's fashion schools and driven by a burgeoning confidence in the quality of home-grown talent.

MÜHLBAUER Map pp56-7 Fashion & Accessories

☎ 512 22 41; www.muehlbauer.at; 01, Seilergasse 10; U1, U3 Stephansplatz

Adorning Viennese heads since 1903, Mühlbauer embodies the spirit of fun that hat-wearing in the 21st century should be all about: cool without being unapproachable, glamorous without being stuffy. Cloches, pillboxes, caps and even bonnets – designs nod to the traditional but with colours and detailing that are oh so now.

VIENNA BAG Map pp56-7 Fashion & Accessories

☎ 513 11 84; www.vienna-bag.com; 01, Bäckerstrasse 7; U1, U3 Stephansplatz 1A, 2A, 3A

Vienna Bag has been making its funky and practical handbags and satchels since 2001. In both black and brightly coloured varieties, they're not only strong, lightweight and washable but chic as well.

WELTLADEN

Map pp56-7 Fashion & Accessories, Gifts

☎ 535 28 86; www.weltlaeden.at; 01, Lichtensteg 1; U1, U4 Schwedenplatz 1, 2

Carrying fair trade everything – bags, plates, coffee, small furnishings, jewellery, sculptures and accessories, scarves and spices – Weltladen lets you shop with a conscience. With seven outlets throughout Vienna you'll probably stumble into one on your visit, but this is the most central location.

WOLFORD Map pp56-7 Fashion & Accessories

☎ 512 87 31; www.wolford.com; 01, Kärntner Strasse 30; U1, U3 Stephansplatz

Perhaps the best-known Austrian brand in the fashion world, Wolford (founded in 1949) is renowned for high-quality hosiery. Here you'll find a huge range – including fishnets in all colours of the rainbow and imaginatively patterned tights, stay-ups, stockings and knee-highs – as well as body stockings and swimwear. There are a number of Wolford branches scattered around town.

AUSTRIAN DELIGHTS Map pp56-7 Food, Gifts

☎ 532 16 61; www.austriandelights.at; 01, Judengasse 1a; 11am-7pm Mon-Fri, 11am-6pm Sat; U1, U3 Stephansplatz

Stocking Austrian-made items by mainly small producers, here you'll find regional specialities – fine confectionery, local wine, schnapps and cognac, jams, jellies, chutneys, honey, vinegars and oils – that you can't find anywhere else in the capital. Be sure to check out its sparkling and still Schilcher wines made from Blauer Wildbacher grapes, an acidic but fruity off-pink-coloured tipple rarely found outside Austria. Most of it is manufactured by hand or, as the owner says, 'items Austrian grandmothers made through the ages'. Samples of many food items are available to taste.

MANNER Map pp56-7 Food, Gifts

☎ 513 70 18; www.manner.com; 01, Stephansplatz 7; 10am-6pm Sun-Mon, 9.30am-8.30pm Sat; U1, U3 Stephansplatz

Even *Manner* – Vienna's favourite sweet since 1898, a glorious concoction of wafers and hazelnut cream – has its own concept store now decked out in the biscuit's signature peachy pink. Buy the product in every imaginable variety and packaging combination (tip: it's a fab snack to carry around sightseeing). There's a second location at Vienna airport (☎ 7007 335 40; Terminal C; open 7am to 8pm daily).

MEINL AM GRABEN Map pp56-7 Food, Wine

☎ 532 33 34; www.meinlamgraben.at; 01, Graben 19; 8am-7.30pm Mon-Fri, 9am-6pm Sat; U1, U3 Stephansplatz 1A, 2A, 3A

You've arrived at Vienna's most prestigious providore, part of the famed Meinl's Restaurant (p154). Quality European foodstuffs like chocolate and confectionery dominate the ground floor, and impressive cheese and cold meats beckon upstairs. The top-end wine shop stocks European and Austrian wine and fruit liqueurs; or pop down to the cellar to indulge in a glass at

(continued on page 141)

THE CAPITAL REVEALED: ON FOOT & WHEELS

Vienna wows with its architectural splendour, vibrant green spaces, sparkling waterways and romantic alleys, and it begs you to probe further. Discovering the city's charms is easy; it's packed with options for every age and interest. You can kick back and relax on public transport, walk around the city centre or work up an appetite for another slice of decadence on a suburban hike or bike ride. Or jump on board a tram and whirl around the city centre, rolling past majestic icons and dazzling structures every few stops, from the jagged white spires of the Votivkirche to the extraordinary Burgtor leading the way to the cluster of *Fiaker* (Viennese horses and carriages). Take a short amble to the bordering hills and – boom – you're encircled by the vineyards within the city limits, where wine taverns, odes to Beethoven and sweeping views pepper your easy hike. The legendary Danube hides off to the east but exposes itself as you glide on two wheels across bridges, roam an island straddling the river and the canal, and marvel at a rubbish incinerator doubling as a work of art. Finally, the silver screen flickers into vibrant technicolour as you uncover Graham Greene's inspiration and trace Harry Lime's haunts from legendary film *The Third Man*.

Trams on Schwarzenbergplatz

RICHARD NEBESKY

DO-IT-YOURSELF RINGSTRASSE TRAM TOUR

Enjoy the quintessential Vienna experience and tool around the Ringstrasse in a charming streetcar, gaping at the city's palatial monuments. Avoid the tourist crowds (and save heaps of euros) by taking the local rather than the special ring tram. Be sure to transfer from tram route 1 to 2 at the Opera station (stop 8 below), but you'll want to hop off for those photo ops anyway, right?

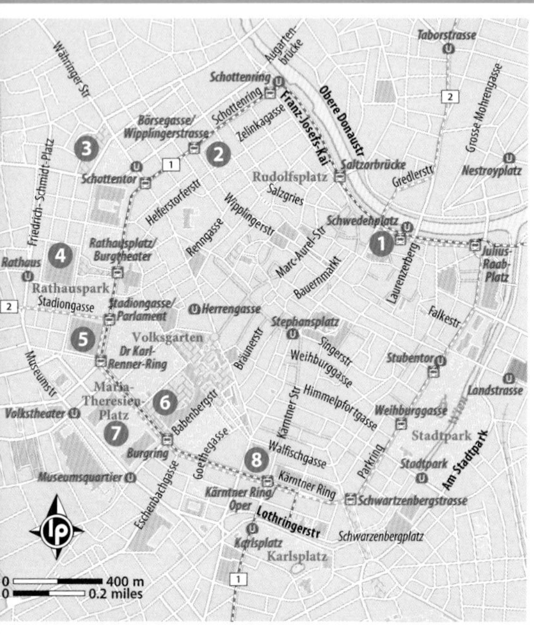

KRZYSZTOF DYDY

VIENNASLIDE/ALAMY

WAYNE WAL

DIANA MAYFIELD

❶ Monument to the Victims of Fascism

Take some time to reflect upon WWII in Austria at the sombre block of sculptures and Star of David at the former Gestapo headquarters site (p77), before crossing Rotenturmstrasse to hop on tram 1 heading towards Stefan-Fadinger-Platz.

❷ Börse Palais (Stock Exchange)

On your left will emerge Vienna's stock exchange, a handsome structure bedecked in dusty brick with white trimmings, designed by renowned Ringstrasse architect Theophil von Hansen.

❸ Votivkirche

Pulling into Schottentor station you'll be accosted on your right by two stone-carved steeples reaching for the sky – this marvellous neo-Gothic structure (p99) is quite reminiscent of France's Chartres Cathedral.

❹ Rathaus & Rathausplatz

When the spires of an arresting Flemish-Gothic edifice beckon your gaze on the right, you will have reached the Town Hall and square (p73), site of the annual Life Ball, Christmas Markets, Musikfilm Festival and Vienna Ice Dream.

❺ Parlament & Athena Fountain

The neoclassical facade of Austria's parliament (p72), with its majestic Greek pillars, will spill into view on the right, flanked by the Athena Fountain – the four figures lying at her feet represent the Danube, Inn, Elbe and Vltava, the four key rivers of the Austro-Hungarian Empire.

❻ Burgtor

A majestic testament to Austria's 1813 triumph over Napoleon in Leipzig, the Burgtor (Palace Gates; p65) will loom into view on the left – the Roman gate leads the way to the Hofburg (Imperial Palace).

❼ Maria-Theresien Platz

Directly opposite the Burgtor is a square anchored by a statue of Empress Maria Theresia, the only female to ascend to the Austrian throne. Note the bundle of papers clasped in her left hand – these are the Pragmatic Sanctions of 1713, which made it possible for women to rule the empire (p65).

❽ Staatsoper

The marvellous neo-Renaissance State Opera House (p195) impresses the masses today, but when it was originally built the Viennese dubbed it 'the *Königgrätz* of architecture', likening it to the 1866 military disaster of the same name.

MUSIC, WINE & THE DANUBE

From hilltop Kahlenberg to cobblestoned Nussdorf, this moderate meander provides panoramic views of the Danube and Vienna, as you wander past vineyards and Beethoven monuments. And when you feel parched, convivial Heurigen *(wine taverns) come to the rescue.* Prost! *(Cheers!)*

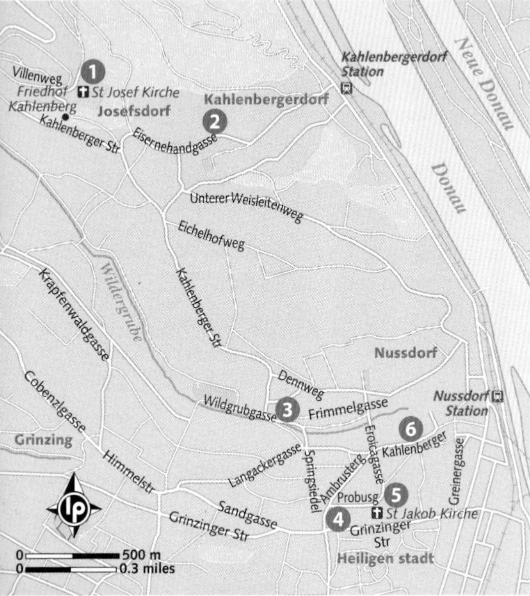

1 Kahlenberg

Take bus 38A to Kahlenberg, where you will be met with sweeping panoramic views of the Danube, Vienna and the expansive vineyards below. Follow the windy Kahlenberger Strasse downhill, passing the tiny Friedhof Kahlenberg cemetery hidden among the trees. Admire the awesome view at the junction before turning left onto Eisernenhandgasse.

2 Hirt

Head downhill to this secluded *Heuriger* (p185) to soak up those views while sampling a little local wine and grabbing a bite. To get back onto Kahlenberger Strasse head steeply uphill to Unterer Weisleitenweg, a dirt path that heads left through vineyards.

3 Beethoven Memorial

Continue down Kahlenberger Strasse until houses start to appear and the road makes a sharp right. Immediately after Frimmelgasse, turn left for the 1863 Beethoven Ruhe, a bust of the late composer. Beethoven used to take tranquil walks around this area (hence the

AMANA IMAGES INC/ALAMY

DIANA MAYI

RICHARD NEBESKY

name of the memorial – *Ruhe* means calm/ peaceful). Cross Schreiberbach, the small stream just south of the memorial, and head south on Springsiedel.

4 Beethoven Wohnung Heiligenstadt

Turning left into Rudolf-Kassner-Gasse, right into Ambrustergasse, and left into Probusgasse, you will come across a picturesque street lined with immaculate town houses, including the composer's former home (p127), where he wrote his second symphony.

5 Mayer am Pfarrplatz

The tiny square at the far end of the street is home to this authentic, peaceful *Heuriger* (p185) set in a Biedermeier house where Beethoven once lived, and one of the oldest churches in the Viennese suburbs, the 17th-century St Jakob Kirche (open 1.30pm to 4.30pm), which has Roman foundations.

6 Nussdorf

From Pfarrplatz, take Eroicagasse (named after Beethoven's Third Symphony) north to Kahlenberger Strasse and into *Heurigen*-filled Nussdorf. Stop by Kierlinger (at 19, Kahlenberger Strasse 20; open 3.30pm to midnight), which consistently wins awards for its Rheinriesling and Weissburgunder (pinot blanc).

DIANA MAYFIELD

KRZYSZTOF DYDYNSKI

CYCLING VIENNA'S PARKLANDS & WATERWAYS

This bike tour takes in Vienna's favourite park and its biggest waterways. With no strenuous hills – and for the most part following well-marked cycle lanes – it can be tackled by almost anyone at their own pace.

3

RICHARD NEBESKY

8

RICHARD NEBESKY

7

RICHARD NEBESKY

1 Schwedenplatz

From Schwedenplatz, a busy plaza and transport hub, head north along the Danube Canal's western bank – not via the main road, but down on the canal-hugging cycle and running path. Past the lively, al-fresco Summer Stage (p165) near Rossauer Brücke, take the cycle ramp on your left and climb above the canal.

2 Fernwärme

Continue until the world's most fantastical city waste incinerator (p98) – the psychedelic Hundertwasser-adorned landmark – comes into view. Remodelled by Hundertwasser in 1991, the structure burns rubbish while channelling high temperatures to heat water, which is then pumped back into the city.

3 Donauinsel

Follow the sign to Donauinsel (Danube Island; p115), crossing the canal via Gürtelbrücke to Leipzigerstrasse until it hits Universumstrasse, then turn left. At Winarskystrasse turn right and follow the path to Nordbahnbrücke, which spans the Danube and Neue Donau (New Danube).

4 Strandgasthaus Birner

At the eastern end of Nordbahnbrücke the path drops onto Arbeiterstrandbadstrasse; turn left onto Birnersteig over the footbridge for a much-needed pit stop at this tiny eatery (p169) overlooking the Alte Donau.

5 Donauturm

Head back and turn left onto Arbeiterstrandbadstrasse until it cuts into Donaupark. Take the *second* sign to the Donauturm, Vienna's tallest (252m) structure (p116). The futuristic landmark looks like a TV tower on the Viennese skyline but actually transmits cellular and radio signals only.

6 UNO-City

Follow the path between the skyscraper cluster (p116), a series of colossal 1970s-era curved buildings home to the UN's third largest offices. At Reichsbrücke turn right and revel in the thrill of gliding across the soaring bridge over the Neue Donau to Donauinsel. Once on the island, go left on any path that appeals.

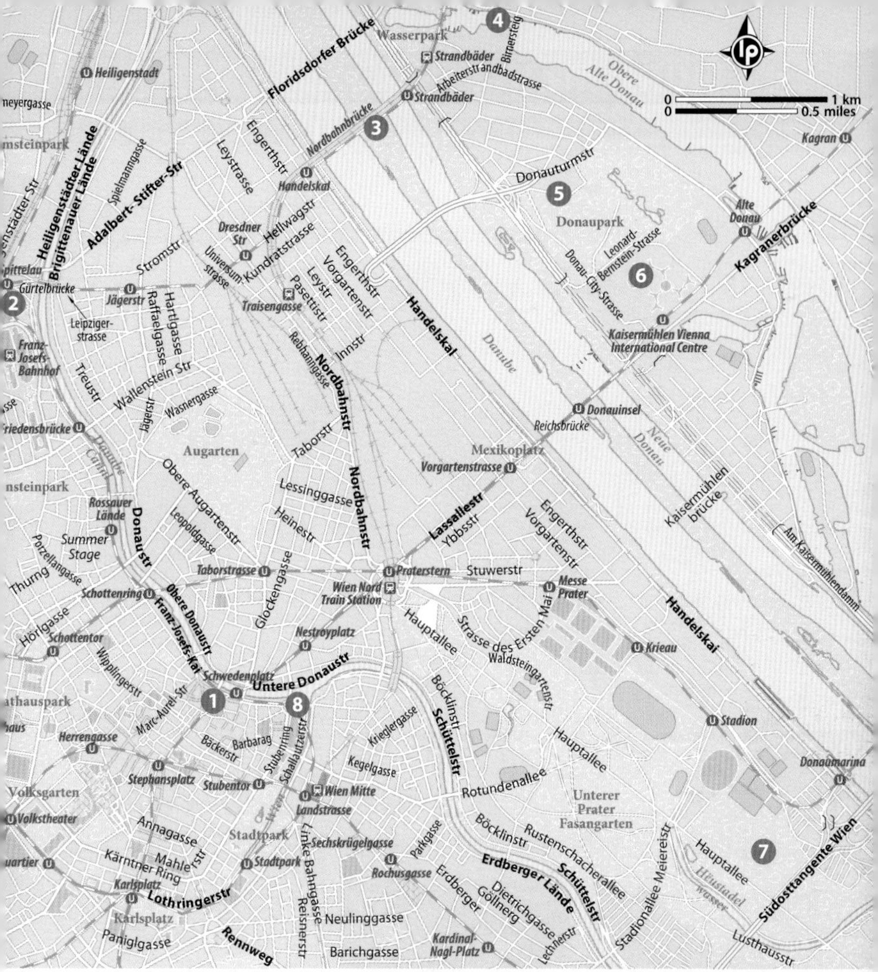

⑦ Prater

Continue until Praterbrücke, cross the Danube again and follow signs to the Prater (p110), Vienna's favourite outdoor playground and home of the Riesenrad (Ferris wheel; p111) and the Würstelprater amusement park. Take in a swirl on the famous wheel or a silly spin on the bumper cars. Then continue along Hauptallee, the park's main thoroughfare, until you reach the end station of tram 1.

⑧ Urania

Turn left onto Rotunden Allee, cross the canal on Rotundenbrücke and turn right until you hit this canalside drinking spot (p174), perfect for reflecting on the day's ride over a coffee or beer.

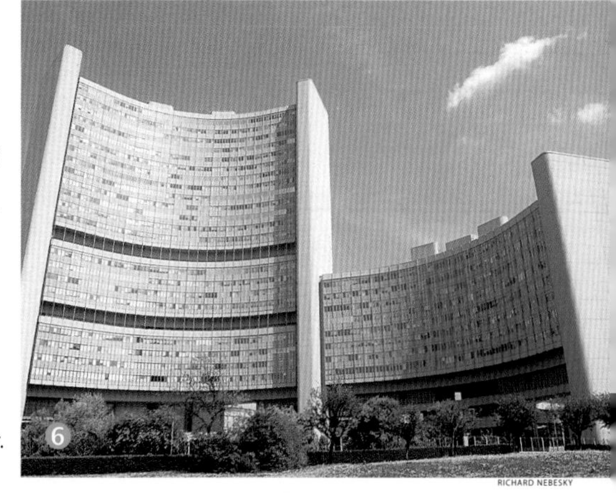

RICHARD NEBESKY

THE THIRD MAN

Harry Lime and Holly Martins' cat-and-mouse chase across the post-WWII, rubble-filled capital is both haunting and moody, with superb dialogue, a scintillating confrontation on the Riesenrad and glimpses of Vienna's most recognised landmarks. Step onto the set with our do-it-yourself ramble.

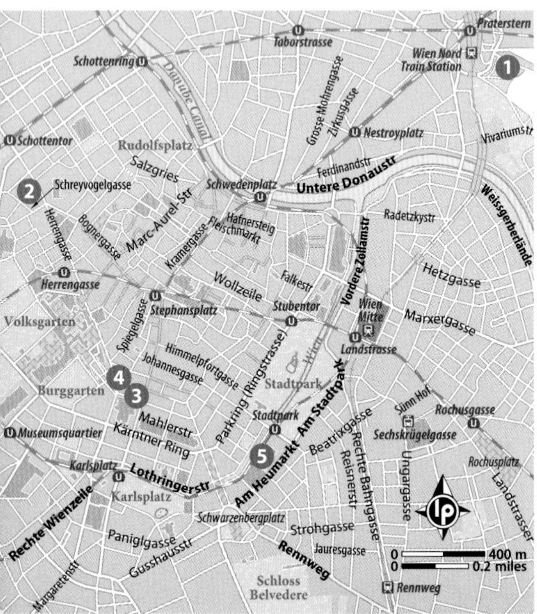

1 Riesenrad

Ride the same giant Ferris wheel (p111) on which Lime berates Martins about his concern for the 'ants' below – from the top, the creatures below do indeed appear insect-sized.

2 Schreyvogelgasse 8

From Praterstern, take the U1 metro line to Schottentor, head towards the Rathaus and turn left onto Schreyvogelgasse. In the electrifying scene with the cat, Martins sees a 'dead man walking' when he glimpses a flash of Lime's face in the shadow of this doorway.

3 Hotel Sacher

The iconic Sacher Hotel (p209), Martins' hotel in the film and the home of Vienna's most famous pastry, was screenwriter Greene's inspiration: at lunch here the author chatted with British intelligence about penicillin smuggling in the city's sewers.

4 Café Mozart

Though the cafe scenes in the film were filmed elsewhere due to wartime damage, this one right across from the Sacher (at Albertinaplatz 2; it's open from 8am to midnight) was Greene's favourite; he worked on drafts of his screenplay here.

5 Beethovenplatz

Head down Krugerstrasse, turn left on Seilerstätte, then right onto Fichtegasse. The pensive Beethoven-in-bronze, sculpted by German Caspar Clemens, flashes across the screen at the start of the film.

5

MAN/IMAGEBROKER

3

RICHARD NEBESKY

1

RICHARD

(continued from page 132)

Meinl's Weinbar (11am-midnight Mon-Sat) in a chilled, classy atmosphere.

AUGARTEN WIEN

Map pp56-7 Glassware & Porcelain

512 14 94; www.augarten.at; 01, Stock-im-Eisen-Platz 3; 9.30am-5pm Mon-Fri; U1, U3 Stephansplatz

Wiener Porzellanmanufaktur Augarten makes Vienna's finest porcelain; the most delicate of ornaments, vases and dinnerware with traditional hand-painted designs; prices start at around €80 for a small vase and go way up. Tours of the factory are available; see the website for details.

J & L LOBMEYR

Map pp56-7 Glassware & Porcelain

512 05 08; www.lobmeyr.at; 01, Kärntner Strasse 26; 10am-7pm Mon-Fri, 10am-6pm Sat; U1, U3 Stephansplatz

Sweep up the beautifully ornate wrought-iron staircase to one of Vienna's most lavish retail experiences. The somewhat cluttered collection of Biedermeier pieces, Loos-designed sets, fine/arty glassware and porcelain on display here glitters from the lights of the chandelier-festooned atrium. The firm has been in business since the beginning of the 19th century, when it exclusively supplied the imperial court; these days, production is more focused towards *Werkstätte* pieces.

ÖSTERREICHISCHE WERKSTÄTTEN

Map pp56-7 Glassware & Porcelain

512 24 18; www.austrianarts.com; 01, Kärntner Strasse 6; U1, U3 Stephansplatz

Established in 1945, Österreichische Werkstätten is dedicated to selling work made by Austrian companies and designed by Austrian designers. Look out for Kisslinger, a family glassware company since 1946, with Klimt- and Hundertwasser-styled designs; Peter Wolfe's more traditional Tirol-style designed glassware; and of course the world-renowned Riedel wineglasses.

ATELIER NASKE

Map pp56-7 Jewellery

316 39 31; www.goldkunst.at, in German; 01, Wipplingerstrasse 7; 2.30-6.30pm Wed & Thu, 3.30-6.30pm Mon & Tue; U1, U3 Stephansplatz

Elke Naske's passion for jewellery is intoxicating. Delicate butterfly pendants, perfectly sculpted rings, cufflinks embedded

top picks

SHOPPING STRIPS

- Josefstädter Strasse An old-fashioned shopping street filled with idiosyncratic shops selling anything from *Altwaren* (old wares) to gemstones.
- Kärntner Strasse The Innere Stadt's main shopping street and a real crowd-puller.
- Kohlmarkt A river of high-end glitz, flowing into a magnificent Hofburg view.
- Neubaugasse & Lindengasse A secondhand-hunter's paradise, lined with unusual shops.
- Mariahilfer Strasse Vienna's largest shopping street, with plenty of high-street names and masses of people.

ALTWAREN AUCTIONS

Although you may never dream of dropping into Sotheby's for a quick browse, when in Vienna it seems perfectly natural to inspect what's on offer at the Dorotheum (Map p66; 515 60-0; www.dorotheum.com; 01, Dorotheergasse 17; 10am-6pm Mon-Fri, 9am-5pm Sat; 2A, 3A). Among the largest auction houses in Europe, this is the apex of Vienna's *Altwaren* (old wares)—consumer culture, the Flohmarkt's wealthy uncle. Something between a museum and the fanciest car-boot sale you ever saw, the rooms are filled with everything from antique toys and tableware to autographs, antique guns and Old Masters paintings.

The stock changes weekly, and not everything is priced sky-high – there are also affordable household ornaments up for grabs. On the 2nd floor is the Freier Verkauf section, a massive antique gallery where you can buy on the spot at marked prices.

Auction proceedings are fun to watch even if you don't intend to buy, and scheduled dates for auctions and viewings are available online (or at the ground-floor reception). If you lack the confidence to bid, you can commission an agent to do it for you. The hammer price usually excludes *Mehrwertsteuer* (MWST; value-added tax); you'll have to pay this but you may be able to claim it back later (see p130).

with precious stones, and more are all painstakingly hand-tapped. Commission her for a piece and she'll make an initial model of it in (less expensive) silver, just to make sure it fits or hangs correctly and suits you unequivocally.

WOKA Map pp56-7 Lighting

☎ 513 29 12; www.woka.at; 01, Singerstrasse 16; U1, U3 Karlsplatz

Get a feel for the spectacular Wiener Werkstätte aesthetic and Bauhaus, art deco and secessionist design, with its accurate reproductions of lamps designed by the likes of Adolf Loos, Kolo Moser and Josef Hoffmann.

UNGER UND KLEIN Map pp56-7 Wine

☎ 532 13 23; www.ungerundklein.at; 01, Gölsdorfgasse 2; 3pm-midnight Mon-Fri, 5pm-midnight Sat; 1, 2 2A, 3A

Unger und Klein's small but knowledgeable wine collection spans the globe, but the majority of its labels come from Europe. The best of Austrian wines – expensive boutique varieties to bargain-bin bottles –

MARKETS

With globalisation storming the world, multinational chain stores gobbling up local shops and independent retailers being forced into early retirement, it's refreshing to know that in Vienna the traditional market is still alive and kicking. Almost every district has at least one market selling fresh produce from Monday to Saturday, many reflecting the ethnic diversity of their neighbourhood. Some host *Bauernmärkte* (farmers markets) on Saturday mornings, where growers from the surrounding countryside travel to the big city to sell their wares: fresh vegetables, tree-ripened fruit, cured hams, free-range eggs, homemade schnapps and cut flowers. See also the Eating chapter, p149.

The best of the bunch:

Naschmarkt (Map pp84-5; 06, Linke Wienzeile & Rechte Wienzeile; 6am-6.30pm Mon-Fri, 6am-5pm Sat; U1, U2, U4 Karlsplatz, U4 Kettenbrückengasse) *The* market in Vienna. This massive market extends for more than 500m along Linke Wienzeile between the U4 stops of Kettenbrückengasse and Karlsplatz. The western end near Kettengasse is more fun, with all sorts of meats, fruit and vegetables (this is the place for that hard-to-find exotic variety), spices, wines, cheeses and olives, Indian and Middle Eastern specialities and fabulous kebab and felafel stands. (Check out the vinegar and oil place, with 24 varieties of fruit- and veg-flavoured vinegar, 11 balsamics and over 20 types of flavoured oil.) The market peters out at the eastern end to stalls selling Indian fabrics and jewellery and trashy trinkets – suddenly you'll feel like you're in a Nepali tourist town.

Brunnenmarkt (Map pp120-1; 16, Brunnengasse; 6am-6.30pm Mon-Fri, 6am-2pm Sat; U6 Josefstädter Strasse 2, 44) Brunnenmarkt is the largest street-market in Vienna and reflects the neighbourhood's ethnic make-up – most stallholders are of Turkish or Balkan descent. The majority of produce sold is vegetables and fruit, but there are a few places selling unbelievably tacky clothes – this is the place to pick up that Hulk Hogan T-shirt you've always wanted. The kebab houses here are truly superb (see Kent, p170). On Saturday nearby Yppenplatz features the best *Bauernmarkt* in the city.

Flohmarkt (Map pp84-5; 05, Kettenbrückengasse; dawn-4pm Sat; U4 Kettenbrückengasse) One of the best flea markets in Europe, this Vienna institution should not be missed. It's tacked onto the southwestern end of the Naschmarkt on Saturdays, and half of Vienna seems to converge here, either flogging or pawing through tonnes of antiques, *Altwaren* (old wares) and just plain junk. It stretches for several blocks of stands hawking books, clothes, records, ancient electrical goods, old postcards, ornaments, carpets...you name it. It's very atmospheric – more like the markets of Eastern Europe – with goods piled up in apparent chaos on the walkway. Try to get there early, as it gets more and more crammed as the morning wears on. Stallholders know the value of their goods (and the fact that this is a tourist attraction), so they'll quote high. Haggle!

Karmelitermarkt (Map pp112-13; 02, Im Werd; 6am-6.30pm Mon-Fri, 6am-2pm Sat; U2 Taborstrasse 2 5A) A market with a long tradition, the Karmelitermarkt reflects the ethnic diversity of its neighbourhood; you're sure to see Hasidic Jews on bikes shopping for kosher goods here. Set in a square with architecturally picturesque surrounds, the market is quiet during weekdays but has a good range of authentic ethnic places to eat; fruit and vegetable stalls share the marketplace with butchers selling kosher and halal meats. On Saturday the square features a Bauernmarkt.

Markt Freyung (Map pp56-7; 01, Freyung; 8am-7.30pm Fri & Sat; U2 Schottentor 1A) The Freyung market exclusively sells organic produce from farmers. The atmosphere here is quite sedate compared with the markets mentioned above.

are available. It's also a small, laid-back wine bar, with a reasonable selection of wines by the glass, which gets crowded on Friday and Saturday evenings.

WEIN & CO Map pp56-7 Wine

☎ 535 09 16; www.weinco.at, in German; 01, Jasomirgottstrasse 3-5; ⌚ 10am-2am Mon-Sat, 11am-midnight Sun; Ⓤ U1, U3 Stephansplatz

With a wide selection of quality European and New World wines, and a huge variety of local bottles, Wein & Co is probably your best bet for wine shopping – you should be able to pick up a bargain, as the specials here are always great. You can also buy cigars, and the wine bar has a terrace with a view of Stephansdom (try 'Happy Sunday', when all glasses are half-price from 11am to 4pm). Seven other Wein & Co shops are scattered around town.

VORSTADT SOUTHWEST

SOUTH OF MARIAHILFER STRASSE

THALIA Map pp84-5 Books

☎ 595 45 50; www.thalia.at; 06, Mariahilfer Strasse 99; ⌚ 9.30am-7pm Mon-Wed, 9.30am-8pm Thu-Fri, 9.30am-6pm Sat; Ⓤ U3 Zieglergasse

Vienna's biggest bookshop, spread over four floors including a cafe, Thalia has an 'International Bookshop' at the back of the ground floor, with lots of bestsellers in English and a small selection of books in Spanish, French, Italian and Russian.

FAIR KLEIDUNG Map pp84-5 Clothing

☎ 599 35 27; 05, Kettenbrückegasse 3; ⌚ 2-6pm Wed-Fri, 10am-4pm Sat; 🚌 59A

Handmade babies', children's and women's clothing in exquisite patterns dominate here – no two items are alike. All materials and workmanship are fair trade – most pieces are made by small, local designers, many from Vienna.

GÖTTIN DES GLÜCKS Map pp84-5 Clothing

☎ 358 74 15; 04, Operngasse 32; www.goettindesgluecks.com; ⌚ noon-7pm Tue-Fri, 11am-6pm Sat; 🚌 59A

Austrian's first fair fashion label conforms to the fair trade model throughout the production process through relationships with sustainable producers in India, Mauritius and beyond. For you, this equals supple, delicious cotton jerseys, skirts, skirts and shorts for men and women that manage the comfort of sleepwear in stylish, casual daywear. And yes, it also sells dreamy pyjamas (they'll make you want to indulge in a nap, pronto).

FLO VINTAGE MODE

Map pp84-5 Fashion & Accessories

☎ 586 07 73; www.vintageflo.com; 04, Schleifmühlgasse 15a; ⌚ 10am-6.30pm Mon-Fri, 10am-3.30pm Sat; 🚌 59A

In a city this enamoured with the glamorous past, it's no less than shocking that there are few true vintage clothing stores in town. The clothes here are fastidiously and beautifully displayed, from pearl-embroidered art nouveau masterpieces to 1950s and '60s New Look pieces and designer wear of the '70s and '80s (alphabetised Armani–Zegna). Prices (and quality) are high.

CLOTHING SIZES

Women's clothing

Aus/UK	8	10	12	14	16	18
Europe	36	38	40	42	44	46
Japan	5	7	9	11	13	15
USA	6	8	10	12	14	16

Women's shoes

Aus/USA	5	6	7	8	9	10
Europe	35	36	37	38	39	40
France only	35	36	38	39	40	42
Japan	22	23	24	25	26	27
UK	3½	4½	5½	6½	7½	8½

Men's clothing

Aus	92	96	100	104	108	112
Europe	46	48	50	52	54	56
Japan	S		M	M		L
UK/USA	35	36	37	38	39	40

Men's shirts (collar sizes)

Aus/Japan	38	39	40	41	42	43
Europe	38	39	40	41	42	43
UK/USA	15	15½	16	16½	17	17½

Men's shoes

Aus/UK	7	8	9	10	11	12
Europe	41	42	43	44½	46	47
Japan	26	27	27½	28	29	30
USA	7½	8½	9½	10½	11½	12½

Measurements approximate only; try before you buy

PHILI'S – WITH LOVE

Map pp84-5 Fashion & Accessories

☎ 504 50 16-00; www.phili-s.com; 06, Gumpendorfer Strasse 71; 10am-7pm Mon-Fri, 9am-4pm Sat; U4 Pilgramgasse 57A

A shop for girlie girls – think frilly pink umbrellas, glam-and-glitter jewellery, flowery hoodies, trainers and boots. Even tomboys might be swayed by the super-cute novelty totes and handbags from cult Danish label Apfelsina, and a range of other carefully chosen bits and bobs by hip labels from around the world.

WIE WIEN

Map pp84-5 Fashion & Accessories, Gifts

☎ 0699-113 49 33 8; www.wiewien.at; 05, Kettenbrückegasse 5; 2-7pm Mon-Fri, 11am-6pm Sat; 59A

A Vienna concept store like no other – each piece in the shop represents the city in some way, from delicate ceramics with a Riesenrad (giant Ferris wheel) stencilled upon them, to colouring books filled with Vienna scenes, to whimsical buttons and T-shirts depicting the Naschmarkt, the Stephansdom, and other landmarks.

PICCINI PICCOLO GOURMET

Map pp84-5 Food, Wine

☎ 587 52 54; 06, Linke Wienzeile 4; 9am-6.30pm Mon-Fri, 8.30am-2pm Sat; U1, U2, U4 Karlsplatz

Piccini stocks only the finest and freshest goods from Italy, all of which are handled with love and care – wines, multitudes of varieties of dried pasta, 20-odd different types of salami, olives and oil. It's also a superb restaurant (see p159).

top picks

MADE IN VIENNA

- **Art Up** (p132) The best in local fashion and design.
- **Vienna Bag** (p132) For chic and durable carry-alls.
- **Perzy Snow Globes** (p146) The original and the best.
- **Augarten Wien** (p141) Traditional porcelain designs and super-high quality (beware of the miniature poodles though).
- **Wie Wien** (above) Handcrafted souvenirs minus any tat.

GABARAGE UPCYCLING DESIGN

Map pp84-5 Furniture & Accessories

☎ 585 76 32 20; www.gabarage.at; 04, Schleifmühlgasse 6; 10am-6pm Mon-Fri, 10am-3pm Sat; 59A

Recycled design, ecology and social responsibility are the mottoes at gabarage upcycling design. Old sealing rings become earrings, former outdoor rubbish bins get a new life as tables and chairs, advertising tarpaulins morph into carrying bags, and fused ring binders reappear as recliners. Humans also receive a second shot at a new life: after completing therapy for substance abuse, former addicts receive jobs plus one year's training in various skills through gabarage's own occupational therapy program.

LICHTERLOH

Map pp84-5 Furniture & Accessories

☎ 581 83 06; www.lichterloh.com; 06, Gumpendorfer Strasse 15-17; 11am-6.30pm Mon-Fri, 11am-4pm Sat; 57A

This massive, ultracool space is filled with iconic furniture from the 1900s to 1970s, by names such as Eames, Thonet and Mies Van Der Rohe. Even if you're not planning to lug home a slick Danish sideboard, it's worth a look at this veritable gallery of modern furniture design.

RAVE UP

Map pp84-5 Music

☎ 596 96 50; www.rave-up.at; 06, Hofmühlgasse 1; U4 Pilgramgasse 13A

Friendly staff, loads of new vinyl and a massive collection make a trip to Rave Up a real pleasure. The store specialises in indie and alternative imports from the UK and US, but you'll find plenty of electronica, hip-hop and retro tunes, and you can listen before you buy, too.

TEUCHTLER

Map pp84-5 Music

☎ 586 21 33; 08, Windmühlgasse 10; 1-6pm Mon-Fri, 10am-1pm Sat; 57A

This is where you might just find that LP you've been searching the world for. Founded in 1948 and now run by the third generation of the family, this truly amazing record shop is a Vienna institution. The walls are lined with shelves of tightly packed vinyl – around 500,000 according to the owners' best guess. They buy and exchange records and CDs, including rare and deleted titles.

SHOPPING WITH LUCIE

'Three things are universal and defy language barriers: love, music and shopping.' Lucie's life philosophy has paid off: inspired by locals making their own wares, focusing on sustainability and creating something you can't find elsewhere (or a combination of all three), the former New York fashion stylist has been busy running specialty shopping tours in Vienna since 2008. Before each tour you receive a care package: a custom map with all the shops you visit (so you can return at your leisure), a pre-packed cluster of business cards and a coupon (valid for two weeks) for 10–20% off all the shops you hit (www.shoppingwithlucie.com; around €25 for a three-hour tour).

What's the difference between the two tours you offer? One covers the inner city (the 1st district) and includes avant-garde jewellery designers, top fashion and accessories and treats to satisfy your palate – most focus on Austrian designers and confectioners. The other, usually in and around Neubau (the 7th) covers a cross-section of creative designer shops including made-on-the-premises fashion and accessories, plus designers using ecofriendly and fair trade materials – so you can buy something exceptional *and* sustainable.

What's the best area to wander if you want to stumble upon unusual boutiques? Definitely the 7th district (Neubau) – every time I go something new has opened up, and it's relaxing to wander around the atmospheric lanes. For example, on a Saturday you can barely move on busy Mariahilfer Strasse (where all the big-name shops are), but Lindengasse, which runs parallel to it one block away, is quiet and mellow, yet chock full of fascinating small shops.

What do you love most about Vienna, besides the shopping scene? The fact that most things are high-quality and often have a personal touch – I also love that people are generally conscious consumers and concerned about sustainable living, which is reflected in the many ecofriendly businesses.

What's next for you? I'm thinking about adding two other tours: eight great skate shops and a Home Decor tour. There are so many more surprising elements to Vienna's shopping scene and it is fun to show everything we have to offer.

An interview with Lucie Lamster-Thury

MUSEUMSQUARTIER & AROUND

BUCHHANDLUNG WALTHER KÖNIG

Map pp84-5 Books

☎ 512 85 88 0; 07, Museumsplatz 1; 10am-7pm Mon-Sat, noon-7pm Sun; U2, U3 Volkstheater 48A

A must for coffee-table connoisseurs, this lofty 250-sq-metre space, with zinc shelves (to reflect light) and baroque touches, hosts a serious collection of books on art, photography, fashion and design theory, including a great range on the history of Austrian and Viennese art and design.

MOT MOT

Map pp84-5 Clothing, Fashion & Accessories

☎ 924 27 19; www.motmotshop.com; 07, Kirchengasse 36; noon-7pm Tue-Fri, noon-5pm Sat; 49 13A

This husband-and-wife team (both former graphic designers) creates custom clothes with fun flair – each piece is screenprinted by hand on American Apparel T-shirts and sweatshirts; choose from the 20-plus designs (imagine a comic book come to life) and colours. They also sell mugs, buttons, posters and art books. Their creations have caught the eyes of celebrities: recent projects include printing posters for The Kills and the Black Eyed Peas.

LOLLIPOP Map pp84-5 Confectionery

☎ 526 33 38; 07, Burggasse 57; 7.30am-8pm Mon-Fri, 8am-8pm Sat, 10am-8pm Sun; 13A, 48A

An old-fashioned neighbourhood confectioner with a selection of traditional and newfangled sweets, Lollipop is sure to have something to please even the fussiest sweet-tooth.

DAS STUDIO Map pp84-5 Fashion & Accessories

☎ 941 11 41; www.das-studio.at; 07, Kirchengasse 17; noon-7pm Tue-Fri, 11am-5pm Sat; 49 13A

This hub for the young Viennese fashion community in the dynamic Kirchengasse includes collections by Igor Zeus, Monikova, Milch, Shinyblink and the fair trade label Göttin des Glücks (p143), including the label's creative sock dress and shirt (created with repurposed socks sewn together to form remarkably stylish attire).

HOT DOGS Map pp84-5 Fashion & Accessories

☎ 236 88 14; www.thehotdogs.org; 07, Zollergasse 12; ⏲ 1-7pm Tue-Fri, 11am-5pm Sat; Ⓤ U3 Neubaugasse 🚌 13A

The Hot Dogs showcases individually tailored, figure-hugging clothing for women; smooth lines and quality fabrics (raw silk, delicate wool, flowing-yet-structured cotton) dominate, yet most items sell for less than €200. Mandarina, designer and owner, is nearly always at the tiny table in the centre of the tiny space, sewing her latest creation.

PARK Map pp84-5 Fashion & Accessories

☎ 526 44 14; www.park.co.at; 07, Mondscheingasse 20; ⏲ 10am-7pm Mon-Fri, 10am-6pm Sat; 🚋 49 🚌 13A

A serious designer store in a stark all-white 480-sq-metre space, Park stocks fashion books and magazines as well as cutting-edge fashion from designers such as Hussein Chalayan and Raf Simons. It also sells the fantastic artist-designed 2k tees (www.2ktshirts.com) from Japan.

DAS MÖBEL Map pp84-5 Furniture & Accessories

☎ 524 94 97; www.dasmoebel.at, in German; 07, Burggasse 10; ⏲ 10am-1am; Ⓤ U2, U3 Volkstheater 🚌 48A

Das Möbel is more of a bar than a shop (see p180), but it showcases some of the funkiest and most original furniture in Vienna. Local artists and designers fill the place with their latest creations, and it's all for sale. The bags hanging just inside the door, also locally designed and produced, are truly special creations.

top picks

WINDOW-SHOPPING

Vienna is a browser's dream; a city full of precious items in lavish outlets, and with a real respect for the art of browsing – you'll never be hurried along or frowned upon for just looking.

- J & L Lobmeyr (p141) A glittering palace of exquisite goods.
- Dorotheum (p141) Auction house and secondhand antiques and treasures.
- Lichterloh (p144) Put-me-in-your-swanky-loft, retro furniture classics at equally lofty prices – how appropriate.
- Freyung Passage Marvel in this sumptuous shopping arcade to buy chocolates from Xocolat (p131), and gape at the art-nouveau carved friezes, marble statuary and fountain.
- Buchhandlung Walther König (p145) Austrian and Viennese art and architecture books in the MuseumsQuartier, in a shop that feels more library than bookstore.

HOLZER GALERIE

Map pp84-5 Furniture & Accessories, Jewellery

☎ 412 64 17; www.galerieholzer.at; 07, Siebensterngasse 32; ⏲ 10am-noon & 2-6pm Mon-Fri, 10am-5pm Sat; 🚋 49

This is the place for high-quality, highly polished furniture, ornaments, lighting and art mainly from the art deco and Bauhaus periods. If you simply must have that Josef Hoffman sideboard, shipping can be arranged. You'll also find some easier-to-transport art-deco-inspired jewellery here.

SNOW GLOBES

There are many impersonators but only one true snow-globe original – the Perzy Snow Globe. Back in 1900 in his workshop in Vienna, Erwin Perzy I had the idea of designing a globe containing a church and filled with liquid and rice, which, when shaken, produced the effect of snow falling. It became an instant hit, even with Emperor Franz Josef.

More than a hundred years on the company is still going strong, and is still in family hands; Erwin Perzy III, the grandson of the snow-globe creator, is the current head of the company. Its products have travelled the globe, and have landed in some illustrious paws – a Perzy snow globe was produced for Bill Clinton's inauguration and contains the actual confetti from the event. One-off pieces have also been produced for the films *Citizen Kane, Heidi* and *True Lies*.

In a world of cheap-and-cheerful products, churned out in their thousands by automated production lines, its surprising, and refreshing, to learn that every snow globe is still handmade. The company's factory contains the small Perzy Snow Globe Museum (Map pp50-1; ☎ 486 43 41; www.viennasnowglobe.at; 17, Schumanngasse 87; ⏲ 9am-3pm Mon-Thu; 🚋 9, 42), which stocks its snow globes and can be visited by appointment.

CHRISTMAS MARKETS

From around the middle of November, *Christkindlmärkte* (Christmas markets) start to pop up all over Vienna. Ranging from kitsch to quaint in style and atmosphere, they all have a few things in common: plenty of people, loads of Christmas gifts to purchase, mugs of gluhwein (mulled wine) and hotplates loaded with *Kartoffelpuffer* (hot potato patties) and *Maroni* (roasted chestnuts). Most close a day or two before Christmas day.

Some of the best:

Altes AKH (Map pp94-5; tram 43, 44) A favourite of students, this small market occupies a corner of the Altes AKH's largest courtyard. There are farm animals and a horse-drawn sleigh for the kids.

Freyung (Map pp56-7; U-Bahn U2 Schottentor bus 1A) Freyung's stalls devote themselves to Austrian arts and crafts, and the entire market attempts, with some success, to emit an old-worldy feel.

Heiligenkreuzerhof (Map pp56-7; U-Bahn U1, U4 Schwedenplatz tram Schwedenplatz trams) This often-forgotten market is arguably the most authentic and quaint of all the *Christkindlmärkte*. It's off Schönlaterngasse, hidden within a residential courtyard.

Karlsplatz (Map pp84-5; U-Bahn U1, U2 U4 Karlsplatz) The Karlsplatz market mainly has stalls selling arty gifts and is situated close to the Karlskirche. People flock here to crowd around flaming metal barrels, clutching their cup of gluhwein.

Rathausplatz (Map pp56-7; tram 1, 2) This is easily the biggest and most touristy Christmas market in Vienna, held on the square in front of the *Rathaus* (town hall). Most of the Christmas gifts on sale are kitschy beyond belief, but the atmosphere is lively and the gluhwein just keeps on flowing.

Schönbrunn (Map pp120-1; U-Bahn U4 Schönbrunn bus 10A) Directly in front of the palace, the circle of stalls are generally quite upmarket, but there's loads of events for the kids, and daily classical concerts at 6pm (more on weekends).

Spittelberg (Map pp84-5; U-Bahn U2, U3 Volkstheater tram 49 bus 48A) Occupying the charming cobblestoned streets of the Spittelberg quarter, this market is traditionally the most beloved of the Viennese. Stalls sell quality arts and crafts, but not at the cheapest prices. No matter what the temperature, you'll find people crowded around gluhwein stalls, especially outside Lux and Plutzerbräu.

LOMOSHOP Map pp84-5 — Photography

☎ 523 70 16; 07, Museumsplatz 1; 11am-7pm Mon-Sun; U-Bahn U2, U3 Volkstheater bus 48A

The Lomographic Society's (www.lomography.com) first ever Lomography shop is in MuseumsQuartier. Lomo is a worldwide cult and the Lomoshop is considered its heart. There's all manner of Lomo cameras, gadgets and accessories for sale; an original Russian-made Lomo will set you back around €160, and you can get single-use disposable Lomo camera for €14. There's also a wall full of Lomo photos on display, for inspiration.

SHU! Map pp84-5 — Shoes

☎ 523 14 49; 07, Neubaugasse 34; noon-6pm Tue-Fri, noon-5pm Sat; tram 49 bus 13A

Shoe fanatics flock to this store in droves, for the latest styles by Camper, Vic Matie, Gidigio and more at easy-on-the-wallet prices. In this spot for over a decade, Shu! stocks men's and women's shoes.

VORSTADT NORTHWEST

K&K SCHMUCKHANDELS

Map pp94-5 — Jewellery

☎ 408 99 53; 08, Josefstädter Strasse 5; 10am-6pm Mon-Fri, 10am-2pm Sat; tram 2 bus 13A

This is one giant treasure chest, with strings of semiprecious stones heaped over every surface, as well as Chinoiserie, polished coral, shell and wooden beads. Bangles, bracelets, necklaces and earrings are on display, or you can get the trinket of your dreams custom-made from the gems of your choice.

EAST OF THE DANUBE CANAL

GUTER STOFF

Map pp112-13 — Fashion & Accessories

☎ 338 43 57; http://guterstoff.com, in German; 02, Glockengasse 8a; 11am-1pm & 2-6pm Tue-Fri, 11am-1pm Sat; U-Bahn U2 Taborstrasse

The name means Good Stuff, which it is: fair trade clothing from a handful of labels including Move At (handmade-in-Vienna leather wallets and bags), Earth Positive and Continental Clothing (both casual street garb). Or give your favourite T-with-a-tear a rebirth: it sells its own 'hole pimps' (patches) in a variety of styles, colours and shapes.

NAGY STRICKDESIGN

Map pp112-13 Fashion & Accessories

☎ 925 13 74; 02, Krummbaumgasse 2-4; 2-7pm Tue, Wed & Fri, 2-8pm Thu & Sat; 5A

The stripy cotton and viscose knitwear here is both classic and up-to-the-minute, with flattering shapes and vivid colours, and designs for hot and cold weather. There are also linen pants and skirts in a refreshing range of bright colours and casual styles.

SOUTHWEST & THE GÜRTEL

STAUD'S Map pp120-1 Food

☎ 406 88 05-21; http://stauds.com; 16, Yppenplatz; 8am-12.30pm Tue-Sat, plus 3.30-6pm Fri only; U6 Josefstädter Strasse 2, 44

This family business has been making jams and pickled vegetables and fruit for more than 30 years. Prices are more than you'd pay in supermarkets for other brands, but the quality is by far the best in Vienna. Saturday morning is a great time to visit, when the nearby Brunnenmarkt (see the boxed text, p142) is in full swing.

GOLD N' GUITARS

Map pp120-1 Musical Instruments

☎ 877 49 80; www.gitarrenwerkstatt.at; 13, Maxingstrasse 2; 10am-12.30pm & 2-6pm Mon-Fri, 9am-12.30pm Sat; U4 Hietzing 10, 58

This is one of a kind in Vienna: owner and guitar craftsman Michael Eipeldauer restores and sells contraguitars, also known as a Schrammelguitar, used for folk music, jazz and other styles – they have a standard neck and a second fretless one for bass notes. A prize piece is a Biedermeier model from the 1840s. Expect to pay from €1600 (used) to €3500 (new). Stylish secondhand East German guitars such as models from Musima, as well as Arthur Lang jazz guitar classics, glisten on stands around the store.

EATING

top picks

What's your recommendation? www.lonelyplanet.com/vienna

EATING

One of the most exciting aspects of visiting Vienna is indulging in the local cuisine, which is currently experiencing a renaissance driven by a new wave of talented Viennese chefs, such as Heinz Reitbauer from Steirereck im Stadtpark (p154), Tommy Möbius from Restaurant Bauer (p155), Markus Mraz from Restaurant Mraz & Sohn in Brigittenau (p168) and Thomas Dorfer from Landhaus Bacher in Mautern (across the Danube from Krems in Lower Austria; see p223). This revival is also driven by a movement back to the roots of Viennese cuisine – best typified by the *Beisln* (a word of Yiddish origin meaning 'little houses'), the traditional taverns where enjoying good, homemade-style food is just as important as sipping a fine wine or beer.

The summer surge of visitors to Vienna has also helped boost the number and variety of places to eat. Choosing what kind of food you want to eat on a given morning, day or night will be one aspect of your eating experience in Vienna – the choices are many. Another key factor will be the type of place you choose to eat in – a fully fledged restaurant or a *Beisl,* for instance (see opposite). Another factor will be the time of day – whether you choose a lunch menu or go all out for an evening splash. And despite the modern age of the jet-setting winter tomato, season still plays a crucial role in good Viennese dining.

HISTORY

As a wit once noted, the good thing about history is that it's so old. Historically, classic Viennese cuisine has always thrived on foreign influences and change. Wiener Schnitzel (a true Wiener Schnitzel is made with veal) is rumoured – though hotly disputed today – to have originated from the recipe for Milanese crumbed veal cutlet brought back by Field Marshal Radtetzky in 1857. *Gulasch* (goulash) comes from Hungary, but the dumplings served with it come from Czech regions. Interestingly, *Tafelspitz* (prime boiled beef, served with radish) was the favourite dish of Kaiser Franz Josef, but when foreign guests visited Schönbrunn Palace, he fed them French delights. Once they had left, he ate his Wiener Schnitzel and *Tafelspitz* again.

The fastidious Viennese approach to coffee and the tradition of the *Kaffeehaus* (coffee house, where you can also eat a light meal) owes much to Ottoman Turks who brought their exotic elixir into Vienna's Vorstadt in 1683. This approach captures the essence of *die klassische Wiener Küche* (classic Viennese cuisine): pilfered by the Habsburgs wherever they reigned, localised at home, shoehorned into the imperial tradition, and given new blood by the great culinary capitals abroad, like Paris – in this case, one of the relatively few places where the Habsburgs didn't actually rule – before being stylised in all its rich features for the contemporary table.

top picks

VIENNA'S BEST SCHNITZELS

- **Figlmüller** (p156)
- **Gasthaus Wickerl** (p165)
- **Schloss Concordia** (p170)
- **Zu den Zwei Liesln** (p163)
- **Zum Alten Fassl** (p162)

SPECIALITIES

Classic Cuisine

Undoubtedly the best-known classic Viennese dish is Wiener Schnitzel. Goulash, another dish familiar to almost everyone, arguably attains its highest form as the *Rindsgulasch* (beef goulash), which excels at Meierei im Stadtpark (see the boxed text, p154). *Tafelspitz* has conquered if not the world, then at least the German-speaking countries, and often swims in the juices of the locally produced *Suppengrün* (fresh soup vegetables) that it's stewed in, before being served with *Kren* sauce (horseradish sauce). Try it in *neo-Beisln* (see p152) to get some new angles on this dish.

Beuschel (offal, usually sliced lung and heart with a slightly creamy sauce) is another *Beisln*-type dish, but at Aubergine (p155) it has been elevated to new culinary heights by chef Florian Hrachowina, who adds locally produced snails, topped off by snail caviar.

GUMMY BEAR GOULASH

Heinz Reitbauer, the *chef de cuisine* at Steirereck im Stadtpark (p154), has a philosophy of 'deceleration' (ie slow cooking) when it comes to goulash. He probably wouldn't think much of some of the other approaches to the dish outlined in an article a while back in the German *Stern* magazine, dedicated to the noble art of whipping up a goulash. Neogoulash faddists are adding papaya juice (the Asian food fans) and olive oil (the 'everything-Tuscany' brigade), but some are even using gummy bears to get the right consistency (the...um, well, it's hard to say who is so perverse as to do this). Others use osso bucco – aka a good old shank – because the marrow thickens the sauce well if cooked slowly. All of which is to say, there's more to a good goulash than meets the eye.

In Meierei im Stadtpark it's served with chive-laced dumplings *(Schnittlauchknödel)*.

Simpler classics cropping up are *Backhendl* (fried breaded chicken; Halle generally offers one or the other version of this – see p163), *Zwiebelrostbraten* (slices of roast beef smothered in gravy and fried onions) and *Schinkenfleckerln* (oven-baked ham and noodle casserole) or a *Bauernschmaus* (platter of cold meats).

The undeniable monarchs of all desserts are *Kaiserschmarrn* (sweet pancake with raisins) and *Apfelstrudel* (apple strudel), but also look out for *Marillenknödel* (apricot dumplings) in summer.

Seasonal & Local Food

The trend in recent years has been towards seasonal and local food, which usually go hand in hand, including growing support for the *locavore* ('local eater') and Slow Food movements. Several years ago Andreas Gugumuck revived a Viennese tradition of snail farming and today the top restaurants serve his produce (see the boxed text, p152) at their tables. Meanwhile, out in the lush and often overlooked Kamptal (Kamp Valley, a side valley of the Danube), Robert Paget supplies Viennese tables with exquisite, organically produced goat's cheeses and buffalo mozzarella (see p222). Vienna is famous for its vegetables, and Gugumuck perhaps illustrates this best, integrating the tradition of Viennese *Suppengrün* into his farming cycle.

Capital cities live from their backyards – the rural regions on their doorstep – and Vienna is no exception. Mangalitza ham (see Urbanek, p162 and Thum Schinkenmanufaktur, p82) comes from Burgenland, Styria and elsewhere. The best apricots *(Marillen)* come from the Wachau in the Danube Valley, where about 180 producers harvest around mid-July and throw Viennese gourmands into a state of *Marille* madness (also a good time to visit the Wachau). Marchfeld asparagus from the southern Weinvertal reaches Viennese tables from late April, and beef from the Waldviertel (hung for at least 10 days) is served in *Beisln* such as Silberwirt (p160) year-round.

Restaurants such as Die Burgermacher (p164) and Hollmann Salon (p156) – the former an organic burger place, the latter an organic upmarket restaurant – source their meats locally, in the case of Hollmann Salon especially from the Waldviertel. Toni Mörwald's Restaurant zur Traube in Feuersbrunn (see the boxed text, p223) illustrates well the seasonal variety on local tables. It starts the year serving fish such as locally produced trout, then skips to spring lamb in April, asparagus from late May and completes a culinary cycle via *Schwammerln* (chanterelle forest mushrooms) in August to duck and game in September and October respectively, before reaching the culinary highlight of Austria's festive season – goose in November and December.

WHERE TO EAT

Vienna's neighbourhoods offer a wide choice of places to eat. Central Vienna is packed with options, especially around Stephansplatz and the streets leading down towards the Danube Canal. A sprinkling of excellent choices is also situated near Börsenplatz and the streets around it, catering mainly to the lunchtime stock exchange crowd.

The Vorstadt Southwest neighbourhood has the greatest variety, with food stalls that are fully fledged restaurants on Naschmarkt and the streets around it, but not to be forgotten are the great choices in the MuseumsQuartier and around. In Vorstadt Northwest, Servitengasse has a small cluster in an attractive street; the Altes-AKH university campus and the eateries on and around Währinger Strasse cater to a university crowd. The Gürtel offers few places of real quality until you reach Yppenplatz, which more than makes up for the dearth elsewhere. East of the Danube Canal boasts a decent number of places in Leopoldstadt west of Taborstrasse, and Landstrasse has a fair sprinkling, especially around Rochusmarkt. Bearing this in

REVIVING A VIENNESE TRADITION OF SLOW FOOD

Andreas Gugumuck is a man who knows his snails. Several years ago the former IT professional began raising them in Vienna, reviving a long tradition of Viennese snail production. Today Gugumuck supplies Vienna's finest restaurants with snails as well as locally produced snail caviar – the surprisingly delicious white eggs laid by snails. A couple of hundred years ago, he explained, there was a snail market on Graben where the produce was sold. Snails used to be a food for poor people and were valued for their healthy, protein-rich flesh.

We stood on the edge of an open-air snail yard, about the size of a basketball court, where snails reposed in the shadows among new grass, herbs and soup vegetables. It was mid-April and not all inhabitants had woken up from winter hibernation in the ground.

Two different varieties of Viennese snails are raised on the property: *Helix pomatia,* a variety common in Central Europe that has something of a gamy taste, and *Helix aspersa,* the variety most often found in France. Young *aspersa* are bought in from France for their Viennese upbringing.

'The *pomatia* start emerging out of the earth in late March and April and begin mating right away', says Gugumuck, casting a knowledgeable eye around the compound to find a couple in the act. In a stroke of luck, we discover a threesome. 'Most of the mating is done in May. The act usually lasts about 12 hours. They fertilise each other and lay in the earth about 40 or 50 eggs over about 20 days, and out of the earth emerge about 30 baby snails. They're experts in the art of survival.'

He picks up another snail and it emerges gradually from its shell. Behind the snail on Andreas Gugumuck's hand, the wide green fields spill into Vienna's Rothneusiedl countryside on the southern fringe of the capital. This was slow food in its most literal sense.

Check out Andreas' farm, capped off by a snail kebab and glass of wine, on a one-hour tour (office@wienerschnecke.at; 10, Rosiwalgasse 44; €10; 2.30pm Sun May-Oct, reservation required).

mind, good food is never far away, no matter where you are.

The choice of where you eat is not only going to influence the type of meal you enjoy, but obviously its price. Traditional coffee houses, where waiters not only rule the tables but also the spaces between them (which is to say, the world at large) generally serve traditional fare of average quality (see p172).

Beisln

This venue unique to Vienna is usually a simple beer house featuring wood- panelling, ceramic ovens, plain tables and hearty Viennese cuisine such as schnitzel and *Tafelspitz,* topped off by *Kaiserschmarrn*. Fairly recently, marginally more expensive *neo-Beisln* have emerged – eateries that have added a few new touches to old recipes; see the boxed text, opposite, for our favourites.) Vienna is full of *Beisln* and most these days have gone back to the roots of seasonal, regional cooking. By and large, they are inexpensive midrange options (about €15 to €25 for two courses, sometimes with a drink thrown in).

Heurigen

Heurigen, informal wine taverns mostly on the outskirts of the city, sport overflowing buffets of salads and pork, plus an endless supply of new wine. Standout examples include Zawodsky (p186) and Göbel (p184). For more about *Heurigen,* see p173.

Restaurants

Vienna is a fine place for formal or informal restaurant dining. In keeping with the Habsburg tradition, if a restaurant has a French influence, it will invariably be more expensive. For the price, however, you can eat snails bred and lovingly raised for your plate in Vienna, and in some cases (as in Aubergine, p155) even snail caviar (yes, the eggs). At the other end of the scale, informal or alternative and offbeat places like The Point of Sale (p161) and Kantine (p164) offer budget food and the chance to use free WLAN. Ethnic (non-Austrian) restaurants and takeaway joints also abound for those looking for a shot of sushi or Punjab pickle.

VEGETARIANS & VEGANS

Vegans are less well catered for in Vienna's restaurants, and the few places that serve vegan food are low-budget alternative-style eateries. Vegetarians, however, will have no problem finding dishes based on pulses and beans, fruit and dairy products. Some of them, such as the low-budget burger eat-in and takeaway Die Burgermacher (p164) and the midrange Hollmann Salon (p156), use organic ingredients. Naschmarkt (p161) and other farmers markets offer lots of choices for vegetarian picnics, takeaway or sit-down meals, and Biomarkt Maran stores (see the Farmers Markets & Supermarkets boxes in each neighbourhood throughout this chapter) have good vegetarian and organic selections of produce and packaged foodstuffs.

COOKING COURSES

Like something you've tried and want to whip it up at home? Here's where you can get a few cooking tips from old hands and rising stars:

Babettes (Map pp84-5; ☎ 585 51 65; www.babettes.at, in German; 04, Schleifmühlgasse 17; 🕑 10am-7pm Mon-Fri, 10am-5pm Sat) Offers evening courses (€110–120) for a variety of cuisines including Viennese and vegetarian; the result is a gourmet meal!

Gesundes (Map pp112-13; ☎ 219 53 22; www.gesundess.at; 02, Lilienbrunngasse 3; courses €77; U1, U4 Schwedenplatz N) Evening courses cover vegetarian/vegan/microbiotic cuisine and all-round healthy cooking.

Noi (☎ 403 13 47; www.restaurantnoi.net; 16, Yppenplatz; courses €100-120; U6 Josefstädter Strasse 2) Afternoon courses on a theme or seasonal dishes, usually using organic ingredients. See also p169.

Wrenkh (☎ 533 15 26; 01, Bauernmarkt 10; courses from €48; U1, U3 Stephansplatz) Learn from one of Vienna's most respected vegetarian chefs, including tips on breakfasts. See also p156.

PRACTICALITIES

Opening Hours

You can eat at any time of day or night in Vienna. Cafes are generally open from 8am to midnight; restaurants from 11am to 3pm, and 6pm to 11pm or midnight. Breakfast is usually served between 7am and 10am, but some places extend this to noon or late afternoon. As a rule, lunch is served between 11am and 3pm (the kitchen may take last orders at 2.30pm) and evening meals between 6pm and 11pm. Opening hours that vary from these are given in reviews for each restaurant. Often a restaurant will be closed for one day a week, usually Sunday or Monday. Outside those hours, you can gravitate towards pizza joints, sausage stands (a couple are almost 24-hour) and mostly Turkish takeaway or eat-in places.

top picks

BEST BEISLN

Traditional *Beisln:*

- **Beim Czaak** (p157)
- **Gasthaus Wickerl** (p165)
- **Figlmüller** (p156)
- **Griechenbeisl** (p156)

Neo-Beisln:

- **Silberwirt** (p160)
- **Glacis Beisl** (p163)
- **Hollmann Salon** (p156)

How Much?

That's up to you. Obviously, how much you want to pay for a meal is also going to influence the *type* of eating experience you have; but thanks to the trend towards fresh, locally produced ingredients, a meal even in a budget place can be of a very high standard. Eat at Gary Cooper time – ie high noon – and you can take advantage of lunch menus, usually less than €15 for two courses. With a glass of wine, most midrange dining will cost between €20 and €30 for two courses.

Reviews in this chapter are grouped by neighbourhood, and ordered by budget, from most expensive to least expensive for a two-course meal (excluding drinks).

Booking Tables

If you have your heart set on a particular restaurant, make a reservation. We've noted in reviews when it's highly advisable. The alternative is to eat at the fringe times – early or late during the opening hours.

Tipping

When tipping, it is usual to round up the bill about 10% in most places (unless, as in rare instances, the service is poor). Do this by

PRICE GUIDE

The price guide we use is for a two-course meal, excluding drinks.

€€€	over €30
€€	€15-30
€	under €15

stating the total amount you want to pay. In the classier establishments, leave the tip inside the bill folder. Sometimes restaurants charge extra for the bread and sundries, about €2 and known as *Gedeck*.

Self-Catering

As well as supermarkets such as the local giant Billa, Vienna has farmers markets in many of its districts. We've included the best of these in boxed texts in each neighbourhood section. The largest of the markets is the Naschmarkt in the Vorstadt Southwest neighbourhood, which attracts foodies from all over the capital.

Smoking

Some travellers will find cigarette smoke in Viennese restaurants occasionally bothersome. In theory, larger places in Austria that serve food have to provide separate smoking and nonsmoking rooms unless it's impractical to do so. In reality, enforcement has been patchy and instead you often find smoking and nonsmoking 'areas' – different areas of the restaurant but not separated by a wall. In some places this is effective, in others it's absolutely useless. A crackdown in recent times is likely to improve the situation for nonsmokers. In this book, we use the nonsmoking symbol to indicate that a place either has separate rooms or is completely nonsmoking.

CENTRAL VIENNA

With its high density of restaurants, the Innere Stadt offers something for the hungry of all persuasions. Although a number of restaurants here do aim squarely at a tourist trade, this is by no means a bad thing, as the best of them recreate a typically Viennese eating experience at affordable prices. At the other end of the scale, some of Vienna's most genuinely modern and innovative eating experiences are also to be had in the centre.

MEINL'S RESTAURANT

Map pp56-7 International €€€

☎ 532 33 34; www.meinlamgraben.at; 01, Graben 19; mains from €30, 3-course menus €35; 🕑 8am-8pm Mon-Fri, 9am-8pm Sat; Ⓤ U1, U3 Stephansplatz 🚌 1A, 2A, 3A; Ⓥ

Meinl's combines cuisine of superlative quality with an unrivalled wine list and views of Graben. Head chef Joachim Gradwohl uses the freshest of ingredients to create inviting dishes, often integrating delicate Mediterranean sauces and sweet aromas. The waiters are professional to a fault, the atmosphere is surprisingly easygoing and you can even chill out on sofas and admire the Pestsäule. Meinl's Weinbar, in the cellar, is open until midnight, and there is also a quality providore, Meinl am Graben (p132), onsite.

GOULASH, CHEESES & BREAKFAST

Attached to Steirereck im Stadtpark (below), Meierei im Stadtpark (☎ 713 31 68; http://steirereck.at; Am Heumarkt 2a; 🕑 8am-11pm Mon-Fri, 9am-7pm Sat & Sun; Ⓥ) serves a bountiful breakfast until noon, with set breakfasts costing from €18.50 to €22.50. Between 11.30am and 4.30pm from Monday to Friday only, it does a selection of Viennese classic fare (mains €9.50 to €14.50) with unusual twists, some based around fresh vegetables. It's most famous, though, for its goulash (weekdays only) and selection of 120 types of cheese. A four-course menu (€39) is served from 5pm weekdays and from 11.30am on weekends.

STEIRERECK IM STADTPARK

Map pp56-7 Austrian €€€

☎ 713 31 68; http://steirereck.at; 03, Steirereck im Stadtpark; mains €24-44, 5-/6-course menus €95/105; 🕑 noon-2.30pm & 6.30pm-midnight Mon-Fri; Ⓤ U3 Stubentor 🚋 1, 2

A long-established name on the scene, Steirereck im Stadtpark took the leap a while back by moving into an early-20th-century former dairy building set in the pretty Stadtpark. Here Otto Wagner's embankments along the Vienna River create an unusually attractive backdrop for exquisite dining. Lunch and dinner are a five- or six-course affair (usually with two choices per course), with seasonal Austrian flavours. An accompanying course of wine is an additional €53/63 (five/six courses).

DO & CO STEPHANSPLATZ

Map pp56-7 International €€€

☎ 535 39 69; 01, Stephansplatz 12, Haas-Haus; mains €19-28.50; 🕑 noon-3pm & 6pm-midnight; Ⓤ U1, U3 Stephansplatz; Ⓥ

DO & CO is the favourite hang-out of Vienna's politicians and business elite.

With subtle lighting, pseudo lounge chairs and light-brown shades, it assumes a vaguely retro look, while the silver service and views of Stephansdom are bonuses. The international menu features Austrian favourites, its highlight is the exceptional pan-Asian cuisine, and between these culinary poles you find Uruguay beef with potato and shallot puree, served with a caramelised sauce (€26).

AUBERGINE Map pp56-7 French, Austrian €€€

☎ 968 31 83; 01, Gonzagagasse 14; mains €21-24, 3-course business lunches €21.50, 3–5-course evening menus €42-62; 11.30am-2.30pm & 6pm-midnight Mon-Fri Jan-Nov, plus 6pm-midnight Sat Dec; U2 Schottentor 1

Aubergine greets you with its namesake, a delicate slither of salted, marinated eggplant to whet the appetite. After that it leads you into a culinary wonderland that might include *Kalbsbeuschel,* thin slices of offal accompanied by snails and garnished with snail caviar for €16.80 (snail caviar is less salty than sturgeon caviar and doesn't explode as easily when you bite on it). Plenty of delicate meats and accompaniments also feature on the menu. The wine list is mammoth – about 800 bottled Austrian wines. Reserve for an evening table.

RESTAURANT BAUER Map pp56-7 French €€€

☎ 512 98 71; 01, Sonnenfelsgasse 17; mains €26-34; 6pm-midnight Mon, noon-3pm & 6pm-midnight Tue-Fri; U1, U3 Stephansplatz

This intimate, exquisite French restaurant serves from a small, seasonal menu and has the relaxed style of a French noble bistro. The patron, Walter Bauer, and the *chef de cuisine,* Tommy Möbius – both celebrated figures on the Austrian restaurant scene – complement French styles with broader influences from Mediterranean countries such as Spain. Delicious pigeon breast can feature on the menu here.

AURELIUS Map pp56-7 Italian, Croatian €€€

☎ 535 55 24; 01, Marc-Aurel-Strasse 8; antipasti €8.50-10.50, mains €19.90-23.90; 11.30am-2.30pm & 6-11pm Mon-Sat; U1, U3 Stephansplatz; V

This stylish Italian and Croatian restaurant has a large, loyal following for its fantastic range of antipasti and main-course seafood and beef. The roasted calamari on a base of rucola (rocket) and tomato salad (€9) is one of the antipasti served here, or consider the Charolais beef with chanterelle mushrooms (€21.90). There's a small garden for outdoor dining in summer. The bar stays open until 1am.

top picks

UPMARKET EXPERIENCES

- **Steirereck im Stadtpark** (opposite) Modern and eclectic, impressive flashes of New World with terrace and garden.
- **Aubergine** (left) Chic Viennese styling meets Mediterranean noble bistro – woods and blackboard set tone.
- **Restaurant Bauer** (below) Intimate, good for seductions of all kinds.
- **Meinl's Restaurant** (opposite) Bastion of upmarket traditional.
- **Hollmann Salon** (p156) Mostly large shared tables (discuss secrets elsewhere), upmarket alternative, superlative courtyard seating.

VESTIBÜL Map pp56-7 International €€€

☎ 532 49 99; 01, Dr-Karl-Lueger-Ring 2; mains €16-24, evening menus from €39; 11am-midnight Mon-Fri, 6pm-midnight Sat; D, 1, 2; V

The interior of Vestibül, which takes pride of place in the southern wing of the Burgtheater, is a heady mix of marble columns and chandeliers topped off with a glorious sparkling mirrored bar. The menu has a strong focus on regional, seasonal produce, such as organic Waldviertel beef or a snack of *Presswurst* (head cheese) from Mangalitza ham. Reservations are recommended.

ZUM SCHWARZEN KAMEEL Map pp56-7 International €€

☎ 533 81 25; 01, Bognergasse 5; sandwiches around €3, soups €6, mains €21-33, 3-course menus €33; 8.30am-midnight Mon-Sat; 1A, 2A

Zum Schwarzen Kameel is an eclectic cross between a deli/sandwich shop and highbrow wine bar. The mostly well-heeled folks who frequent it nibble on sandwiches at the bar while facing the difficult choice of which *Achterl* (serving of wine; glass holding 0.125L) to select from the lengthy list. Soups are available to go, while more-substantial dishes are served in the wood-panelled dining area upstairs.

YOHM Map pp56-7 Asian €€

☎ 533 29 00; 01, Petersplatz 3; mains €13.50-28, 3-course menus €19.90-35; noon-3pm & 6pm-midnight; U1, U3 Stephansplatz 2A; V

A typical scene in Yohm is of black-clad waiters gliding between tables to refill glasses with celebrated Austrian wines as diners revel in views of Peterskirche while enjoying contemporary Asian cuisine. Sushi looms large on the menu, but consider ordering one of the kitchen's more unusual offerings – udon noodles with Scottish salmon or fried duck roll with fresh mint and plum sauce. Set menus are cheaper on weekdays.

EXPEDIT Map pp56-7 Italian €€

☎ 512 33 13 23; 01, Wiesingerstrasse 6; mains €8-25; 10am-1am Mon-Sat, 10am-10pm Sun; 1, 2

Expedit has successfully moulded itself on a Ligurian *osteria* and become one of the most popular Italian restaurants in town. Its warehouse decor, with shelves stocked full of oil, pesto, olives and wine from Liguria, helps to create a busy yet informal atmosphere and a clean, smart look. Every day brings new, seasonal dishes to the menu, but count on a few divine vegetarian, meat and fish specialities. Reservations are recommended. The affiliated Expedit Lager in the same building does takeaway.

GRIECHENBEISL Map pp56-7 Beisl €€

☎ 533 19 77; 01, Fleischmarkt 11; mains €11-24; 11am-1am; U1, U4 Schwedenplatz 1, 2, 21

As the oldest guesthouse in Vienna (dating from 1447), and once frequented by the likes of Ludwig van Beethoven, Franz Schubert and Johannes Brahms, Griechenbeisl quite rightly aims at the tourist trade. It is a lovely haunt, with vaulted rooms, age-old wood panelling and a figure of Augustin trapped at the bottom of a well just inside the front door. Every classic Viennese dish is on the menu, and in summer the plant-fringed front garden is pole position.

FIGLMÜLLER Map pp56-7 Beisl €€

☎ 512 61 77; 01, Wollzeile 5; mains €7-15; 11am-10.30pm, closed Aug; 1A

Vienna, and the Viennese, would simply be at a loss without Figlmüller. This famous *Beisl* has some of the biggest – and best – schnitzels in the business. Sure, the rural decor is contrived for its inner-city location, and beer isn't served (only wine from the owner's own vineyard), but it's a fun Viennese eating experience and one you won't find anywhere else in the world.

WRENKH Map pp56-7 Vegetarian €€

☎ 533 15 26; 01, Bauernmarkt 10; mains €8.50-19.50, midday menus €9.50-10.50; noon-4pm & 6-10pm Mon-Fri, 6-10pm Sat; U1, U3 Stephansplatz; V

Wrenkh was long the cutting edge of vegetarian cuisine, and today is still the serrated edge – owner Christian Wrenkh has more recently introduced a handful of meat and fish dishes. The quality and presentation can be exquisite and everything is prepared with organic produce. Choose from the vibrant front section with its glass walls and chatty customers, or the quieter back room with its intimate booths.

HOLLMANN SALON Map pp56-7 Neo-Beisl €€

☎ 961 19 60 40; www.hollmann-salon.at; 01, Grashofgasse 3; mains €14-19, 3–4-course menus €29-39; noon-3pm & 6-10pm Mon-Sat, from 10am Sat; U1, U3 Stephansplatz, U3 Stubentor 71; V

Situated inside the extraordinarily beautiful Heiligenkreuzerhof, Hollmann Salon combines the rural flavour of a country homestead with urban chic. Its succulent organic meats come from the Waldviertel north of the Danube and its menu changes every month, ensuring the very best of seasonal produce from local producers. A four-course menu might begin with filet of hare or offer the alternative of hare as a main dish. Seating is mostly at communal tables, and last orders are at 9pm. Book ahead in the evening. Cakes and breads are homemade and there's outstanding outdoor eating in summer.

ÖSTERREICHER IM MAK Map pp56-7 Austrian €€

☎ 714 01 21; 01, Stubenring 5; lunch specials €6.40, mains €14.50-20.80; 8.30-1am; U3 Stubentor 1, 2

Located in the Museum für angewandte Kunst (Museum of Applied Arts; see p60), Österreicher im MAK is the brainchild of Helmut Österreicher, one of the country's leading chefs and a force behind the movement towards back-to-the-roots Austrian flavours. He goes beyond strictly classical Viennese dishes such as *Tafelspitz* by complementing

A SLICE OF ITALY IN THE INNERE STADT

One of the most useful places to know about in the Innere Stadt is Zanoni & Zanoni (Map pp56-7; ☎ 512 79 79; 01, Lugeck 7; ice creams from €2; 7am-midnight; 1A, 2A, 3A). This Italian *gelateria* and *pasticceria* has some of the most civilised opening times around (365 days a year) and is just right when you realise you'd like a late-night dessert (about 35 varieties of gelati, with more cream than usual). It does breakfast and some great cakes with cream, but best of all, it's a buzzing place on a Sunday where you can mull over a coffee and plan your moves for the day.

them with exotic or non-regional ingredients. These are served in two sections of the restaurant – a lounge and bar area up front where you can also get breakfast from 8.30am until 11am, and the more formal restaurant out back. Inside sleek architectural lines create a modern flourish.

LIMES Map pp56-7 International €€

☎ 905 800; 01, Hoher Markt 10; light dishes €5.50-12, mains €12-22.50; 11am-midnight Mon-Fri, 10am-midnight Sat; U1, U3 Stephansplatz 1A, 2A, 3A

Limes is one of Vienna's most popular places for crossover eating and drinking experiences. The drinks list offers a reasonable selection of bottled wines and a few by the glass, and about a dozen cocktails are mixed here too. Expect a broad, culinary spread – salads with anchovies, buffalo mozzarella, prosciutto, pastas, lamb and the Angus steak (€22.50). The interior has a chilled-out feel. The kitchen is open from 11.30am to 10.30pm.

EN Map pp56-7 Japanese €€

☎ 532 44 90; 01, Werdertorgasse 8; midday menus €8.20-9.70, mains €9-23; 11.30am-2.30pm & 5.30-10.30pm Mon-Sat; 3A; V

A Tokyo chef and Hokkaido staff banded together to create this exceptionally relaxed Japanese restaurant in a quiet corner of the Innere Stadt. The many different varieties of sushi (including octopus and sweet shrimp) are among the best in Vienna. The *gyoza* is delightful and warm sake or *genmaicha* (green tea with roasted rice) makes a perfect accompaniment. It's completely nonsmoking during the day.

BODEGA MARQUÉS Map pp56-7 Spanish €€

☎ 533 91 70; 01, Parisergasse 1; tapas €2.80-14.50; 5pm-1am Mon-Sat; 2A, 3A

Calamari specialities, *Gambas* (shrimps) and over 30 different tapas imported from Spain help make Bodega Marqués an excellent Mediterranean choice in the Innere Stadt. Throw in 120 varieties of wine, vaulted ceilings and subdued lighting and you've got the makings of a romantic atmosphere. Friday and Saturday nights are the exception, when live flamenco music is featured. Steaks and mixed tapas as mains cost €16.50 to €35.

BEIM CZAAK Map pp56-7 Beisl €

☎ 513 72 15; 01, Postgasse 15; midday menus €6.90-7.90, mains €8-16.50; 11am-midnight Mon-Sat; U1, U4 Schwedenplatz 1, 2

In contrast to more-heavily touristed *Beisln* in the Innere Stadt, Beim Czaak has a genuine and relatively simple interior. As you would expect, meat dishes dominate the menu, with choices like *Waldvierteler Schnitzel* (with fried bacon, onions and mushrooms) and the *Haus Schnitzel* (weighted down with ham, cheese, mushrooms and onions – yum). Standard Viennese vegetarian, such as *Eiernockerl* (egg pasta) and *Spinatknödel* (spinach dumplings), are also options. In summer, take advantage of the umbrella-shaded tables on the tiny square out front.

KIANG Map pp56-7 Asian €

☎ 533 08 56; 01, Fleischmarkt 6; light mains €2-3.90; 11.30am-11.15pm Mon-Sat; U1, U3 Stephansplatz; V

There are three Kiangs in Vienna (for the Landstrasse branch, see p167), but this one conveniently close to Stephansplatz is your best option for a snack on the run. Quality stand-up light sushi, meat or vegetarian curries and noodles (even wraps if they're not sold out) are surprisingly inexpensive. For sit-down sushi and sashimis, though, head out to the Landstrasse Kiang as the designer tones there create a more relaxed setting. Prices for mains (€11.80 to €19.50) in all branches are the same.

MASCHU MASCHU Map pp56-7 Middle Eastern, Israeli €

☎ 533 29 04; 01, Rabensteig 8; mains €3.50-8; 9.30am-midnight; U1, U4 Schwedenplatz 1, 2, 21; V

Zippy service, a relaxed atmosphere, and delicious felafels, hummus and salads are the keys to Maschu Maschu's success. This branch on Rabensteig, with its meagre number of tables, is better used as a take-away joint, while another branch in Neubau is best for sit-down meals (see p163).

SOUPKULTUR Map pp56-7 Soups & Salads €

☎ 532 46 28; 01, Wipplingerstrasse 32; soups €3.90-4.50, salads €5.80-7.20; 11.30am-3.30pm Mon-Thu, 11.30am-3pm Fri; 1A, 3A;

Soupkultur is popular among office workers seeking a healthy bite on the hop. Organic produce and aromatic spices are used to create eight different soups and eight varieties of salads each week, which can range from red-lentil soup or a traditional Hungarian goulash to Caesar salad or chicken and orange salad. There's token seating, but count on taking it away (a leafy park is just around the corner).

BITZINGER WÜRSTELSTAND AM ALBERTINAPLATZ Map pp56-7 Sausage Stand €

01, Albertinaplatz; sausages €2.80-3.50; 10am-4am Nov-Mar, 24hr Apr-Oct; U1, U2, U4 Karlsplatz D, 1, 2, 62

Vienna has very many sausage stands but this one located behind the Staatsoper offers the contrasting spectacle of ladies and gents dressed to the nines, sipping wine while enjoying sausage at outdoor tables after performances. It's no coincidence that here you find Moët & Chandon (€19.90 for 0.2L); for the less well-heeled, there's house wine (€2.80) and Stiegl Goldbräu beer (€2.90). Prime winter position is at the heated counter.

FARMERS MARKETS & SUPERMARKETS

Markt Freyung (Map pp56-7; 01, Freyung; 10am-6.30pm Tue, Wed & Thu May–mid-Nov; 1A) A produce market.

Bio-Markt Freyung (Map pp56-7; 8am-7.30pm Fri & Sat odd-numbered weeks of the year; 1A) Has organic produce.

Billa supermarkets At Biberstrasse (Map pp56-7; Biberstrasse 15; 2), Kärntner Ring (Map pp56-7; Kärntner Ring 9-13; 1, 2, D) and Singerstrasse (Map pp56-7; Singerstrasse 6; U3, U1 Stephansplatz).

TRZESNIEWSKI Map pp56-7 Sandwiches €

☎ 512 32 91; 01, Dorotheergasse 1; bread with spread per 100g from €2.80; 8.30am-7.30pm Mon-Fri, 9am-5pm Sat; U1, U3 Stephansplatz

Possibly the finest sandwich shop in Austria, Trzesniewski has been serving spreads and breads to the entire spectrum of munchers (Kafka was a regular here) for over 100 years. Choose from 21 delectably thick spreads – paprika, tuna with egg, salmon and Swedish herring are but a few examples – for your choice of bread, or simply pick a selection from those waiting ready-made. Plan on sampling a few; two bites and they're gone. This branch is one of seven in Vienna (see p167).

VORSTADT SOUTHWEST

The four inner-city districts of Wieden, Margareten, Mariahilf and Neubau are so densely packed with fantastic eating options that you could spend two gastronomic lifetimes exploring and enjoying them. Naschmarkt, the bustling city market, has food from all parts of the world and is perfect for grabbing picnic supplies or a sit-down meal in elaborate market stands. Elsewhere south of the Vienna River you find great options in Wieden and Margareten – often with an alternative edge or in a Vorstadt atmosphere. Mariahilf around Gumpendorfer Strasse and especially Neubau in and around the MuseumsQuartier and Spittelberg have some good places for all budgets and styles. You definitely won't go hungry in this neighbourhood.

SOUTH OF MARIAHILFER STRASSE

The vicinity south of Mariahilfer Strasse is truly the mother lode for gourmands, taking in Naschmarkt but also a string of great places south of the Vienna River in Margareten and Wieden.

RESTAURANT COLLIO Map pp84-5 Italian €€€

☎ 589 18 82; 04, Wiedner Hauptstrasse 12; mains €11.90-24.90, 2-course lunch menus €15, 5-course menus €48.90; noon-2.30pm & 6.30-10pm Mon-Fri, 6.30-10pm Sat; U4 Kettenbrückengasse, Karlsplatz 1, 62;

Inside the Hotel Stadt Triest in Wieden, this fine Italian restaurant has a lounge atmosphere, mellow sounds trickling out of the speakers and parquet floor offset by the browns of padded benches – an interior from British designer Sir Terence Conran, who also did Café Drechsler (p179). The food lives up to the top-class design and is exceptionally well priced. Like the best of Vienna's eating establishments, Collio changes its menu regularly and by season, and in a cold February you might find duck with a fig mustard and served with fried polenta (€17.90) to warm the soul. It has a Venetian focus but wades across a broad and interesting culinary lagoon.

GERGELY'S Map pp84-5 — Steaks €€

☎ 544 07 67; 05, Schlossgasse 21; mains €15-30; 6pm-1am Tue-Sat; U4 Pilgramgasse

The flagship of the four eateries around Schlossplatz (don't miss the garden, replete with a tractor and lovely trees and seating), Gergely's is inside a 14th-century vaulted cellar and focuses exclusively on steaks made from quality beef sourced locally and internationally. Top of the range is a 500g T-bone from US-bred Hereford (€30), but there's almost a steak with a provenance and size for everyone, which you can enjoy with a strong selection of sauces and accompaniments.

MOTTO Map pp84-5 — International €€

☎ 587 06 72; 05, Schönbrunner Strasse 30; mains €10-23; 6pm-2am Mon-Thu & Sun, 6pm-4am Fri & Sat; U4 Pilgramgasse 59A

A fusion of Asian, Austrian and Italian influences is the secret behind Motto's long-running success, with the likes of chicken satay with peanut sauce and coriander rice or expertly prepared Styrian baked chicken among the mouth-watering choices. One of the most fascinating is fillet steak with chocolate-chilli sauce. Motto is very popular, particularly with the gay crowd, so reservations are recommended. Entrance is through the forbidding chrome door on Rüdigergasse.

BEOGRAD Map pp84-5 — Serbian €€

☎ 587 74 44; 04, Schikanedergasse 7; mains €8.90-19.10; 11.30am-2am Thu-Tue; U4 Kettenbrückengasse 1, 62

Half of the pictures adorning the walls here are crooked, but that's the charm of this eccentric restaurant in Wieden. What you get is an atmospheric and sometimes wild Balkan experience that includes red roses on the table, a piano on one side of the main room, a violinist scratching away at his instrument and a wiry fellow who glides about squeezing out sensational sounds from his harmonium. He also croons very decently while appreciative guests press banknotes into his instrument. Servings are very generous and the ingredients fresh and of exceptional quality. Beograd does a good *ćevapčići*, or skinless sausages.

> ## top picks
> ### BEST NEIGHBOURHOOD EATS
> - **Restaurant Collio** (opposite) The high end with lounge style.
> - **Haas Beisl** (p160) The real McCoy.
> - **Silberwirt** (p160) The neo-real McCoy.
> - **Neni** (p160) The Naschmarkt ethno-experience.
> - **Die Burgermacher** (p164) Homemade burgers, organic to boot.
> - **Point of Sale** (p161) or **Kantine** (p164) Alternative, snacky, wi-fi while grazing.
> - **ON** (p162) Asian fusion, relaxed – especially good if you're alone.

UMAR Map pp84-5 — Fish €€

☎ 587 04 56; 04, Naschmarkt 76; midday menus €12-13, mains €13-30; 11am-midnight Mon-Sat; U1, U2, U4 Karlsplatz

Umar is one of the best fish restaurants in Vienna, serving fresh seafood imported from Italy and Turkey at its large Naschmarkt stall. Choose between whole fish, mussels in white-wine sauce and giant shrimps fried in herb butter. Seriously good wines from the Wachau (p218) round off a delicious eating experience.

PICCINI PICCOLO GOURMET
Map pp84-5 — Italian €€

☎ 587 52 54; 06, Linke Wienzeile 4; mains €8-19; 11am-7.30pm Mon-Fri, 10.30am-3.30pm Sat; U1, U2, U4 Karlsplatz; V

'Gourmet' is a term all too frequently bantered around these days – gourmet pizzas, gourmet burgers, gourmet sandwiches, you name it – but here it's taken very seriously. 'Piccini' has the finest antipasti restaurant in town, with around 40 different antipasti rolls, fish treats and stuffed vegetables. It also knows its *Brunello* from its *Vino Nobile*, which, with 60 varieties of wine available, is a good thing. Its shop next door has been selling imported Italian foods since 1856.

TANCREDI Map pp84-5 Neo-Beisl €€

☎ 941 00 48; 04, Grosse Neugasse 5; lunch menus €7.50-15, mains €7.80-19.80; 11.30am-2.30pm Mon, 11.30am-2.30pm & 6pm-midnight Tue-Sat; 1, 62; V

This former *Beisl* serves lovingly prepared regional and fish specialities, seasonal fare, organic dishes and an extensive range of Austrian wines. The harmonious surroundings are the icing on the cake: warm, pastel-yellow walls, stripped-back wooden floors, fittings from yesteryear and a tree-shaded garden that fills up quickly in summer. The entrance is on Rubengasse.

HAAS BEISL Map pp84-5 Beisl €€

☎ 586 25 52; 05, Margaretenstrasse 74; mains €6.80-14.90; 11am-midnight Mon-Fri; U4 Kettenbrückengasse 1, 62

This small, very traditional Margareten *Beisl* doesn't have the revamped, streamlined culinary edges of a *neo-Beisl*, but Haas is absolutely genuine and a place where you can enjoy decent food and soak up a very local atmosphere. Classics like offal and sweetmeats are prepared the way your grandmother might have done them, but local pundits often head straight for the celery soup. Above the bar are football (soccer) trophies won by the gentlemen players at Haas who have exceeded their own football prime (but not by much, as the trophies testify). The toilets have an 'art' touch.

SILBERWIRT Map pp84-5 Neo-Beisl €€

☎ 544 4907; 05, Schlossgasse 21; mains €7.40-14.50; noon-midnight; U4 Pilgramgasse; V

This atmospheric *neo-Beisl*, another in the four eateries on Schlossplatz, offers traditional Viennese cuisine, mostly using organic and/or local produce. Tuscan cordon bleu (with prosciutto, mozzarella and basil; €10.40), Wiener Schnitzel (€13.40), local trout with pumpkin-seed butter and fresh herbs (€12.80) and Styrian corn-fed chicken drumstick (€8.40) are complemented by some liver, vegetarian and Austrian noodle dishes. Don't miss the garden area out back – it's one of the best in Vienna! Alongside Silberwirt is a pizza restaurant (open from noon to midnight).

NENI Map pp84-5 Middle Eastern, Israeli €€

☎ 585 20 20; 06, Naschmarkt 510; breakfasts €4-8.50, salads & snacks €4-11, mains €9-15; 8am-midnight Mon-Sat; U4 Kettenbrückengasse 57A; V

Some of Naschmarkt's 'stands' take on the proportions of the Belvedere. Neni is no exception. The area downstairs is mostly used as a cafe and bar, and upstairs is a main eating area where tasty delights mostly have a Middle Eastern focus. Dishes such as caramelised aubergine with ginger and chilli (€9) are served alongside expertly prepared lamb chops with truffle-laced polenta (€14) or a pulse ragout with cranberries and rice (€9.50). Tables can be at a premium most nights, so reserve ahead or drop by outside prime time. Breakast is served until 2pm.

SAIGON Map pp84-5 Vietnamese, Asian €€

☎ 585 63 95; 06, Getreidemarkt 7; lunch menus €7, mains €8.20-16.90; 11.30am-11pm Tue-Sun; U1, U2, U4 Karlsplatz

Saigon was one of the first Asian restaurants in Vienna and remains one of the best. Expect to find a large selection of rice and noodle dishes, including a delicious *Pho Tai Bo* (beef noodle soup). A second Saigon is conveniently located in Ottakring (see p170) not far from the Brunnenmarkt.

RA'MIEN Map pp84-5 Asian €€

☎ 585 47 98; 06, Gumpendorfer Strasse 9; mains €7-16; 11am-midnight Tue-Sun, closed Aug; U2 Museumsquartier 57A; V

Picture a grey-white room in minimalist look and lots of bright, young hip things bent over piping-hot noodles and you have Ra'mien. The menu covers a good swath of Asia, with a choice of Thai, Japanese, Chinese and Vietnamese noodle soups and rice dishes. Ra'mien fills up quickly at night, so it's best to book to avoid having to wait for a table; the lounge bar downstairs has regular DJs and stays open until at least 2am. Next door, the affiliated Shanghai Tan (Map pp84-5; ☎ 585 49 88; 06, Gumpendorfer Strasse 9; dim sum €3.50-4.50, lunch specials €6.90-9.50, mains €9.50-13.80; 11.30am-3pm & 6pm-2am Mon-Sat) does sushi/sashimi, noodle soups and fried noodles, satay and other excellent pan-Asian dishes. Downstairs is an opium den minus the opium – a chilled-out area with hidden corners and pillows for reclining.

FARMERS MARKETS & SUPERMARKETS

Naschmarkt (Map pp84-5; 6am-7.30pm Mon-Fri, 6am-6pm Sat; U4 Kettenbrückengasse) Situated between Getreidemarkt and Kettenbrückengasse; Vienna's largest produce and food market.

Biomarkt Maran (Map pp84-5; 526 58 86 18; 07, Kaiserstrasse 57-59; 8am-7pm Mon-Thu, 8am-7.30pm Fri, 8am-6pm Sat; 5) Excellent for organic foods and produce.

Billa supermarket Has branches at Rechte Wienzeile (Map pp84-5; Rechte Wienzeile 39; U4 Kettenbrückengasse), Mariahilfer Strasse (Map pp84-5; Mariahilfer Strasse 35; 49 13A), Schottenfeldgasse (Map pp84-5; Schottenfeldgasse 87; 48A) and Neubaugasse (Map pp84-5; Neubaugasse 56; 48A).

VAPIANO Map pp84-5 Italian €€

581 12 12; 01, Theobaldgasse 19; mains €6.50-9.50; 11am-midnight Mon-Sat, noon-11pm Sun; U2 Museumsquartier; V

This eat-in Italian cafeteria-style chain offers pizza, homemade pasta and salads in several different categories. You collect a card at the door and make your choice at one of the counters, where dashing young lads and lasses will whip up the dish before your very eyes. Hold onto your card and pay at the door when you leave. Bonuses are a nappy-changing room and long opening hours. The downside is that the eating is often shoulder-to-shoulder and the noise level can make spaghetti of your nerve endings.

CHANG ASIAN NOODLES Map pp84-5 Asian €

961 92 12; 04, Waaggasse 1; midday menus €6.90-7.10, mains €7.20-10; 11.30am-3pm & 5.30-11pm Mon-Sat; 1, 62; V

Chang is a small, well-established Asian diner a short walk from the Innere Stadt. The venue is bright, open, uncomplicated and highly relaxed, while the service is quick and attentive. Noodles (either fried or in a soup) are the mainstay of a menu spanning the Asian continent (at least from China to Singapore) – expect plenty of chicken, prawns (both baby and tiger) and vegetable choices. Everything is available for takeaway. The affiliated duck restaurant next door (mains €13 to €16) has the same hours.

NASCHMARKT DELI Map pp84-5 American €

585 08 23; 04, Naschmarkt 421; sandwiches €4-7, mains €6-12; 7am-midnight Mon-Sat; U4 Kettenbrückengasse

Among the many enticing stands along the Vienna River, Naschmarkt Deli has an edge on the others for its delicious snacks. Sandwiches, felafel wraps, big baguettes and quick soups (lentil soup is a good bet) fill the menu, but much space is dedicated to a heady array of breakfasts. Come Saturday morning this glass box overflows with punters waiting in anticipation for the continental or English breakfast.

UBL Map pp84-5 Beisl €

587 64 37; 04, Pressgasse 26; mains €9-15; noon-2pm, 6pm-midnight Wed-Sun; 59A;

This much-loved *Beisl* is a favourite of the Wieden crowd. Its menu is heavily loaded with Viennese classics, such as *Schinkenfleckerl, Schweinsbraten* (roast pork) and four types of schnitzel, and is enhanced with seasonal cuisine throughout the year. You could do worse than finish the hefty meal off with a stomach-settling plum schnapps. The quiet, tree-shaded garden is wonderful in summer.

POINT OF SALE Map pp84-5 Fast Food €

941 63 97; 04, Schleifmühlgasse 12; light mains €6.90-11.90; 7am-1am; U4 Kettenbrückengasse, 1, 62; V

Situated in the alternative strip of Wieden on the cusp of Margareten, the Point of Sale draws a colourful crowd for light dishes, ranging from chicken satay through pasta to burgers. There's lounge-type seating in a front mezzanine level, benches along the side and regular seating out back. You can do a lot here: eat very decently, surf to find your next port of call or simply hang out over a drink. Vegetarians and vegans are well catered for, as are those looking for a good breakfast, which is served until 3pm.

AROMAT Map pp84-5 International €€

913 24 53; 04, Margaretenstrasse 52; menus €7.90, mains €10-15; 5-11pm Tue-Sun, closed mid-Jul–Aug; 59A

The mainstay of this funky little eatery is fusion cooking with a strong emphasis on Upper Austrian and Vietnamese cuisine, but you'll mostly find a menu that changes daily with the whims of the chef. It has an open kitchen and often caters for those with an intolerance to wheat and gluten. The charming surroundings feature simple Formica tables, 1950s fixtures, a blackboard menu, and one huge glass frontage. Personable staff help to create a convivial, barlike atmosphere.

ON Map pp84-5 Asian €€

☎ 585 49 00; 05, Wehrgasse 8; lunch menus €7.50-8.50, mains €9-16.30; noon-midnight Mon-Sat, noon-10.30pm Sun; 59A

ON is quite rightly seen as the best Austro-Asian fusion restaurant in the southern Vorstadt. The ambience is relaxed and friendly, and the young staff are likely to kick off the meal with a complimentary appetiser of bread in cold-pressed olive oil and a few prawn chips. After that, order from a menu that spans *neo-Beisl* fare such as chicken liver with chilli, *gan-bien* (fried) beef strips or trout with ginger. The menu changes according to season and the whim of the chef. The small, private garden is lovely in summer; reserve in the evening.

ZUM ALTEN FASSL Map pp84-5 Beisl €€

☎ 544 42 98; 05, Ziegelofengasse 37; midday menus €5.70-6.80, mains €7.50-13.90; 11.30am-3pm & 5pm-1am Mon-Fri, 5pm-1am Sat, noon-3pm & 5pm-midnight Sun; 13A

With its private garden amid residential houses, and a polished wooden interior (typical of a well-kept *Beisl*), Zum Alten Fassl is worth the trip just for a drink. But while here sample the Viennese favourites and regional specialities, like *Eierschwammerl* (chanterelle mushrooms) and *Blunzengröstl* (blood sausage with fried potato). When it's in season, *Zanderfilet* (fillet of zander) is the chef's favourite. Between 1974 and 1982 the singer Falco lived upstairs in this building – a plaque marks the spot.

AMACORD Map pp84-5 Austrian, International €

☎ 587 47 09; 05, Rechte Wienzeile 15; breakfasts €5.10-12.80, mains €8.90-14.90; 10am-2am; U1, U2, U4 Karlsplatz, 59A; V

The popularity of this small eatery stems from its convivial vibe, friendly staff, lovely vaulted ceilings, comfy surroundings and good, affordable food. Viennese classics are mixed in with a healthy range of Italian pastas, the odd curry and ragout, and an extensive salad selection. However, some will find the smoke overpowering as the evening rolls on, and trying to find a seat on a Saturday morning is a fruitless enterprise. Eat off-peak here.

CUADRO Map pp84-5 International €

☎ 544 75 50; 05, Margaretenstrasse 77; snacks & mains €4.20-9.20; 8am-midnight Mon-Sat, 9am-11pm Sun; U4 Pilgramgasse; V

Cuadro is a stylish cafe and eatery that uses organic ingredients for many of its offerings and has risen to fame for its trademark Cuadro burger (€4.20) made from local beef. There are also vegetarian and pan-Asian variations on burgers, but the menu is by no means limited to these – it spans light Viennese favourites, grilled prawn on skewers, salads, pasta and sandwiches.

DO-AN Map pp84-5 Cafe €

☎ 585 82 53; 06, Naschmarkt 412; breakfasts €5-7, salads €4.80-6.60; 7am-midnight Mon-Sat; U4 Kettenbrückengasse; V

Located in the heart of Naschmarkt, Do-An does an eclectic mix of sandwiches, rice and noodle dishes, delicious salads and meats as well as some Turkish staples at affordable prices. Many of its diners head straight for the breakfasts from around the globe; the American reads more like a traditional English fry-up and the continental is a nice, light starter of bread and spreads. Like Naschmarkt Deli (p161), Do-An is a rectangular aquarium with huge glass walls and a steadfast following who enjoy the relaxed vibe and sunny corners.

URBANEK Map pp84-5 Austrian €

☎ 5872 080; 04, Naschmarkt 46; ham with bread €3.60; 9am-6.30pm Mon-Thu, from 8am Fri, 7.30am-4pm Sat; U1, U2, U4 Karlsplatz; ⊠

Stepping inside Urbanek is to enter a world of cured meats in all their different varieties – smoked, salted, cooked or raw. The atmosphere is rarefied but relaxed as you squeeze into a corner and enjoy a glass of wine (about €5) and perhaps delicately cut slices of Mangalitza pig – a woolly variety prized for its delicious ham. The roast beef is organic, as are many other offerings here, and the selection of cheeses is just as good. Although there's scarcely enough room to swing a cat inside, it's well worth finding an empty few square inches to enjoy some of the finest cuts around.

MUSEUMSQUARTIER & AROUND

The vicinities north of the Vienna River are also packed with restaurants of all descriptions, including some good choices right inside the MuseumsQuartier.

SCHON SCHÖN Map pp84-5 International €€

☎ 0699-15 37 77 01; 07, Lindengasse 53; 3–6-course menus €36-46; 🕑 11am-11pm Tue-Sat; Ⓤ U3 Zieglergasse

Dining is a unique social experience at this eatery in Neubau. With only one table (seating about 20) you'll certainly get to know your immediate fellow diners, if not the whole table. The imaginative cuisine changes daily but includes a handful of vegetarian and meat or fish dishes. It's gay-run but attracts all genders; a groovy lounge area downstairs is open from 7pm to 2am Thursday to Saturday.

GAUMENSPIEL Map pp84-5 International €€

☎ 526 11 08; 07, Zieglergasse 54; mains €17.50-21.50, menus €32-40; 🕑 6pm-midnight Mon-Sat; 🚋 49 🚌 48A; ⊠ Ⓥ

Gaumenspiel is an immaculate, modern *Beisl* with a menu that changes every three weeks. The food is international with a heavy Mediterranean influence, but here you might also find braised veal cheeks with polenta, potato dumplings and artichokes. The decor is light in detail and the handful of streetside tables are popular in summer. Reservations are recommended.

GLACIS BEISL Map pp84-5 Neo-Beisl €€

☎ 526 56 60; 07, Museumsplatz; mains €8.90-17.60; 🕑 11am-2am; Ⓤ U2, U3 Volkstheater, U2 Museumsquartier; Ⓥ

Hidden downstairs behind the buildings along Breite Strasse (follow the signs from MUMOK) in the MuseumsQuartier, Glacis Beisl does an authentic goulash, an accomplished Wiener Schnitzel and some very decent other Austrian classics, which you can wash down with excellent Austrian reds and whites. If you're staying immediately in the area, the chances are high this one will evolve into your regular *Beisl*.

HALLE Map pp84-5 International €€

☎ 523 70 01; 07, Museumsplatz 1; midday menus €6.80-8.50, mains €6.90-16.50; 🕑 10am-2am; Ⓤ U2, U3 Volkstheater, U2 Museumsquartier; 📶 Ⓥ

Managed by the owners of Motto (p159), Halle is the versatile resident eatery of the Kunsthalle with little kitchen downtime – the pots and pans are hung up at midnight. The interior has plenty of optical tricks, like cylindrical lamps and low tables, and the chefs churn out antipastos, pastas, salads, several Austrian all-rounders (breaded chicken, but not a Wiener Schnitzel) and pan-Asian dishes. On steamy summer days it's usually a fight for an outside table between the Kunsthalle and MUMOK. It sells Noan olive oil (€9.90), with proceeds flowing into children's projects.

PODIUM Map pp84-5 International €€

☎ 522 15 87; 07, Westbahnstrasse 33; 2-course lunch menus €8.50, mains €9-12; 🕑 11am-1am Mon-Fri, 6pm-1am Sat; 🚋 49; 📶 Ⓥ

This designer restaurant and bar in the fashionable Neubau district has lollipop chairs near the floor-to-ceiling windows and big, comfy couches to the rear. Podium offers a small but imaginative menu that on some days ranges from hamburgers to pumpkin curry with basmati rice. The menu changes every couple of months – the lunch menu each day – and the crowd, which often just drops in for a drink and a chat, is arty and relaxed.

MASCHU MASCHU II

Map pp84-5 Middle Eastern, Israeli €€

☎ 990 47 13; 07, Neubaugasse 20; mains €7.20-16.50; 🕑 10.30am-midnight; Ⓤ U3 Neubaugasse; Ⓥ

This second branch of the Maschu Maschu takeaway in the Innere Stadt is a fully fledged restaurant with sunny streetside seating – when the weather's playing along – and a menu loaded with lamb dishes. Punters looking out for Vienna's best felafel should drop by here first for some of the best around.

ZU DEN ZWEI LIESLN Map pp84-5 Beisl €

☎ 523 32 82; 07, Burggasse 63; lunch menus €4.90-5.30, mains €6-11.90; 🕑 11am-11pm; 🚌 48A

A classic, budget *Beisl* of legendary status, Zu den Zwei Liesln has been serving celebrities, politicians, office workers and students for decades. Six varieties of schnitzel crowd the menu (the *Haus Schnitzel*, filled with Gorgonzola, ham and pepperoni, is killer bee), but there are other Viennese options, and even two vegetarian choices. The wood panelling, simple wooden chairs and chequered tablecloths create a quaint and cosy interior, complemented by a tree-shaded inner courtyard.

BANKOK Map pp84-5 Thai €

☎ 526 52 01; 07, Neustiftgasse 15; curries €8.60-10.50; 5.30-10.30pm Mon-Sat; U2, U3 Volkstheater 46; V

The pink curtains may not be to everyone's taste, and in summer the woods dominate and lack a lightness in tone, but the Thai curries here, served in vegetarian varieties with tofu or traditionally with meats, are among the best in town. The Thai noodle dishes are also popular, and its location (close to the MuseumsQuartier) means you can easily head here for post-dinner drinks. Takeaway is also available.

AMERLINGBEISL Map pp84-5 Beisl €

☎ 526 16 60; 07, Stiftgasse 8; midday menus €5, mains €7-10; 9am-2am; U2, U3 Volkstheater 48A

Serving solid Austrian fare (and a sprinkling of Italian pasta dishes), Amerlingbeisl is a lovely place situated in the pedestrian quarter of Spittelberg, an old-worldly spot of tight cobblestone streets and quirky shops. The inner courtyard of this *Beisl* is a lush oasis, and on balmy summer nights the roof slides back to create a lovely outdoor feel.

DIE BURGERMACHER Map pp84-5 Burgers €

☎ 0699-11 58 95 99; 07, Burggasse 12; burgers €5.80-8.80; 11.30am-10.30pm Tue-Sat; U2, U3 Volkstheater 46; V

The interior of this small, alternative burger joint is simple, well-styled and comfortable. The burgers here are made using organic ingredients and served in meat and vegetarian varieties, and if you can't get a table – which can happen because it's popular – grab a spot at the side bench or get takeaway…and in summer eat it in the MuseumsQuartier a few hops away.

ST JOSEF Map pp84-5 Vegetarian €

☎ 526 68 18; 07, Mondscheingasse 10; small/large plates €6.80/8.20; 8am-5pm Mon-Fri, 8am-4pm Sat; 49 13A; V

You'll find lots of places with vegetarian offerings in this neighbourhood, but St Josef is a canteenlike vegetarian place that cooks to a theme each day (Indian, for instance) and gives you the choice of a small or large plate filled with the various delights. It has a sparse, industrial character, which is part of its charm, and super-friendly staff who will point you in the right direction if you don't quite know where to start.

KANTINE Map pp84-5 Cafe €

☎ 523 82 39; 07, Museumsplatz 1; soups €2.90-5.90, wraps €5.10-6.40, light mains €7.20-8.90; 9am-2am Mon-Thu, 9am-4am Fri-Sat, 9am-midnight Sun; U2 Museumsquartier, U2, U3 Volkstheater; V

This upbeat cafe-bar housed in the former stables of the emperor's personal steeds is the most laid-back spot to eat in the MuseumsQuartier. It has a couple of old sofas down the back where you can lounge about and surf in comfort, and you can grab a cocktail from the extensive list and make good use of the outdoor patio on MuseumsQuartier's main square. It's a versatile place, like most in the MuseumsQuartier, and a good place to meet up before moving on.

VORSTADT NORTHWEST

The Vorstadt Northwest neighbourhood has a good spread of eating options for all budgets, some of these in and around the Altes AKH university campus. Hof 1 (enter via Alser Strasse; see p92) is the main courtyard for eating and drinking, and it has the advantage of a large children's playground. Servitengasse has a few elegant, midrange cafes and restaurants and in summer lends itself to strolling or contemplating the world from a street bench.

KIM KOCHT Map pp94-5 Asian €€€

☎ 319 02 42; 09, Lustkandlgasse 4; lunch mains €8, business lunch menus €39, evening menus €42-62; noon-3pm & 6pm-midnight Tue-Fri; U6 Währinger Strasse-Volksoper 40, 41, 42

The Korean and Japanese cuisine of Kim Kocht is highly sought after in Vienna's culinary circles for its originality, quality and the creativity shown in presentation. The three- to five-course menus are constantly changing but often feature fish as the main, and organic produce is always used. Although the restaurant has more recently moved into larger premises, reservations of about one month ahead are still advisable. Kim Kocht also offers cooking courses.

WEINKELLEREI ENRICO PANIGL
Map pp94-5 Italian €€€

☎ 406 52 18; 08, Josefstädter Strasse 91; mains €19-25; 🕑 6pm-1am; Ⓤ U6 Josefstädter Strasse 🚋 2 🚌 13A

Although the menu is small, this wine restaurant serves delicious dishes such as tuna with a truffle and porcini sauce accompanied by grilled polenta (€19.90). The atmosphere is genuinely rustic right down to the wooden floors, offset by art from Vienna's postmodernist guru Hermann Nitsch. The choice of 150 wines from Italy and Austria means that the pleasure of being here is as much about the wines as is it about good food and contemporary art.

SCHNATTL Map pp94-5 International €€€

☎ 405 34 00; 08, Lange Gasse 40; mains €18-23, veg menus €33, 3-course menus €38; 🕑 6pm-midnight Mon-Fri; 🚋 2 🚌 13A; Ⓥ

Despite its weekday-only operning hours, Schnattl is a culinary institution in Josefstadt, especially among artists from the nearby Theater in der Josefstadt (see p197). Idyllic outdoor seating in a courtyard is perfect for summer dining, whereas the simple wooden panels inside create a light mood. Seasonally changing dishes such as a roulade of beef loin with prosciutto, or lamb filet with polenta spiced with wild garlic (each €22), are served here.

KONOBA Map pp94-5 Dalmatian €€

☎ 929 41 11; 08, Lerchenfelder Strasse 66-68; mains €11-19; 🕑 11am-2pm & 6pm-midnight Sun-Fri, 6pm-midnight Sat; 🚋 46

Few restaurants in the city come close to Konoba's expertise with fish. The Dalmatian chefs know their product inside out and serve some of the freshest catch in town. Zander and *Goldbrasse* (sea bream) are often on the menu, but expect to find a healthy array of seasonal dishes too. The open-plan interior creates a convivial atmosphere.

STOMACH Map pp94-5 Austrian €€

☎ 310 20 99; 09, Seegasse 26; mains €10-18; 🕑 4pm-midnight Wed-Sat, 10am-10pm Sun; Ⓤ U4 Rossauer Lände

Stomach has been serving seriously good food for years. The menu brims with meat and vegetarian delights, such as Styrian roast beef, cream-of-pumpkin soup, and, when in season, wild boar and venison. The interior is authentically rural Austrian, and the overgrown garden creates a picturesque backdrop. The name 'Stomach' comes from the rearrangement of the word Tomaschek, the butcher's shop originally located here. Reservations are highly recommended.

GASTHAUS WICKERL Map pp94-5 Beisl €€

☎ 317 74 89; 09, Porzellangasse 24a; midday menus €6.20, mains €7.90-16; 🕑 9am-midnight Mon-Fri, 10am-midnight Sat, 10am-4pm Sun; 🚋 D

Wickerl is a beautiful *Beisl* with an all-wood finish and a warm, welcoming mood. Seasonal fare, such as *Kürbiscremesuppe* (cream-of-pumpkin soup) and *Kürbisgulasch* (pumpkin goulash) in autumn, *Marillenknödel* in summer and *Spargel* (asparagus) in spring are mixed in with the usual Viennese offerings of *Tafelspitz, Zwiebelrostbraten* (steak with onions) and veal and pork schnitzel.

SCALA Map pp94-5 Italian €€

☎ 310 20 79; 09, Servitengasse 4; pastas & meat mains €8.20-16.90; 🕑 11am-midnight; 🚋 D

Scala is an unpretentious Italian restaurant where on a rainy day you can find refuge behind a plate of pasta, a pizza or a more substantial dish while warming up over a glass of wine. In summer there's outdoor seating and alongside or further along Servitengasse you'll find a sprinkling of cafes and bars. Xocolat (Servitengasse 5; 🕑 10am-6pm Mon-Fri, 9am-1pm Sat) is where some of Vienna's finest local chocolate is manufactured and sold (see also p131).

FLEIN Map pp94-5 Austrian €€

☎ 319 76 89; 09, Boltzmanngasse 2; mains €7-18; 🕑 11.30am-3pm & 5.30-11.30pm; 🚋 37, 38, 40, 41, 42

SUMMER STAGE

One of the interesting options to check out during the warmer months between May and September is the Summer Stage (Map pp94-5), a culinary and entertainment conurbation of restaurants and stages that each summer is set up on the banks of the Danube Canal. It has a lively, festive atmosphere, and there are regular jazz and classical concerts here too. It's located on Rossauer Lände and opens in the evening between 5pm and 1am from May to September (take the U4 to Rossauer Lände).

Every day brings a new, creative menu to Flein. Zucchini quiche and *Eierschwammerl* risotto may, for instance, be served up for vegetarians, while grilled calamari and herbed lamb *Stelze* (hocks) will please the meat eaters. The small garden, backing onto the French Cultural Institute, is peaceful and secluded despite busy Währinger Strasse. In summer, book ahead.

PARS Map pp94-5 Persian €€

☎ 405 82 45; 08, Lerchenfelder Strasse 148; midday menus €7.90-9.90, mains €10.50-17.80; 11am-midnight Mon-Sat; 46

Favoured by Vienna's Iranian community, Pars serves authentic Persian cuisine, such as *Schekampareh* (eggplant filled with meat), *Lubiapolo* (beans, lamb and rice) and a good selection of kebabs (shish, *Adana, Kubideh*), complemented by over 30 varieties of quality Austrian wine.

GU Map pp94-5 Asian €€

☎ 402 63 33; 08, Lederergasse 16; mains lunch €4.90-7.50, dinner €8.90-14.80; 11.30am-3pm & 5.30-11pm Mon-Fri, noon-11pm Sat; U6 Josefstädter Strasse 2 13A; V

If you choose carefully in the evening or take advantage of the lunch dishes, Gu can be a very inexpensive way to fill up on noodles, rice and pan-Asian curries between forays into Alsergrund and Josefstadt. A chicken curry with coconut milk costs about €9, and whatever hasn't been sold out from the lunchtime blackboard can be ordered at the day price in the evening. Gu doesn't aspire to culinary sensation, but it does honest, satisfying dishes.

FARMERS MARKETS & SUPERMARKETS

Brunnenmarkt (p170) The closest large farmers market to Josefstadt and Alsergrund; in Ottakring.

Billa supermarkets At Alser Strasse (Map pp94-5; Alser Strasse 4; 5), in the university courtyard, and nearby at Alser Strasse 23 (Map pp94-5; 5); at Josefstädter Strasse (Map pp94-5; Josefstädter Strasse 78; U6 Josefstädter Strasse), Währinger Gürtel (Map pp94-5; Währinger Gürtel 104; U6 Währinger Strasse-Volksoper) and Berggasse (Map pp94-5; Berggasse 26-28; D).

CURRYINSEL Map pp94-5 Sri Lankan €€

☎ 406 92 33; 08, Lenaugasse 4; curry portions €3.20-4.40, mains €6.90-13.50; 5pm-midnight Tue-Fri, 11am-midnight Sat & Sun; U2 Rathaus 2; V

Hoppers (made from baked rice) and string hoppers (steamed noodles made of rice and wheat) form the mainstays of the Sri Lankan curries at Curryinsel. You can pick and combine the different types of curry from a wide selection on the menu, and staff will help if you start combining curries that clash. The menu also has some more-expensive meat main dishes and for €13.50 a mixed curry plate with five vegetable and two meat curries served with accompaniments.

SUPPENWIRTSCHAFT
Map pp94-5 Soups & Salads €

☎ 317 67 45; 09, Servitengasse 6; soups €4.50-5.80; 11.30am-6pm Mon-Fri; D; V

This chic little soup eat-in and takeaway kitchen focuses mainly on soups and a few curries and salads from a weekly menu. Russian borscht (beetroot) may be served alongside pear soup one week, and all are made fresh each day using ingredients sourced at the Naschmarkt. It fits in well with the genteel style and flair of Servitengasse – while here, drop by the Servitenkirche (p98) and stroll around in the cloisters.

BAGEL STATION Map pp94-5 Fast Food €

☎ 276 30 88; 09, Währinger Strasse 2-4; bagels €1.70-4.20; 8am-7pm Mon-Fri, 10am-5pm Sat & Sun; U2 Schottentor 37, 38, 40, 41, 42, 43, 44; V

This local chain serves good New York-style bagels to students from the nearby uni, who hang out with their laptops talking, surfing and even studying (or so it seems). You can linger over coffee, muffins and bagels here while planning your next moves in the neighbourhood, catching up on emails from home or using it as your mobile office for a while.

SIDE STEP Map pp94-5 Spanish €

☎ 0676-782 02 30; 08, Lange Gasse 52; tapas €3-11.60; 6pm-2am Mon-Sat, 6pm-1am Sun; U2 Rathaus, 13A

Forty tapas (both hot and cold) and 20 wines by the glass make this slice of Spain in the heart of Josefstadt a treat. The wine is an obvious enough attraction, but you can also enjoy the likes of rissoles of lamb in tomato sauce, shrimp with garlic sauce, or goat's cheese with homemade olive spread. The brick surroundings, easygoing air and excellent grappa are but icing on the cake.

WIENER DEEWAN Map pp94-5 Pakistani €

☎ 925 11 85; 09, Liechtensteinstrasse 10; 11am-11pm; U2 Schottentor 37, 38, 40, 41, 42, 43, 44

Pakistani cuisine, cooked under the maxim 'good food, good mood', is one speciality of Wiener Deewan. The other is 'eat what you like, pay as you wish'. Three vegetarian and three meat dishes, accompanied by one dessert, are prepared daily and served in a buffet-style set-up; prices aren't set, and you can eat all five if you like. Most people are generous with payment, as the likes of the *lamb karah* (diced-lamb curry), *tinda* (pumpkin curry) and dhal *masur* (red lentil dhal) are excellent and full of subtle flavours. The atmosphere, like the staff, is very relaxed.

VORSTADT LANDSTRASSE

GASTHAUS WILD Map pp104-5 Neo-Beisl €€

☎ 920 94 77; 03, Radetzkyplatz 1; midday menus €7.50, mains €8.80-17.50; 9am-1am; 1, 0; V

Gasthaus Wild, formerly a dive of a *Beisl*, has in recent years morphed into a great *neo-Beisl*. Its dark, wood-panelled interior retains a traditional look, and the menu includes favourites like goulash and *Schnitzel mit Erdäpfelsalat* (schnitzel with potato salad), but also veal filet with dumplings spiced with blood sausage. The menu changes regularly, the ambience is relaxed, the staff welcoming and the wine selection good.

KIANG Map pp104-5 Asian €€

☎ 715 34 70; 03, Landstrasser Hauptstrasse 50; light mains €5.40-7.80, mains €11.20-17.80, sushi & sashimi €11.80-19.50; 11.30am-3pm & 6.30-11.30pm; U3 Rochusgasse; V

This ultra-modern pan-Asian restaurant near Rochusplatz is a relaxed and spacious experience where you can enjoy good sushi and sashimi. *Sha cha* noodle soup

> **FARMERS MARKETS & SUPERMARKETS**
>
> **Rochusmarkt** (Map pp104-5; 03, Landstrasser Hauptstrasse 37; 6am-7.30pm Mon-Fri, 6am-5pm Sat; U3 Rochusgasse) The main market in Landstrasse; has mostly produce and food stands.
>
> **Biomarkt Maran** (Map pp104-5; ☎ 710 98 84 28; 03; Landstrasser Hauptstrasse 37; 8am-7pm Mon-Thu, 8am-7.30pm Fri, 8am-6pm Sat; U3 Rochusgasse) Has organic produce, food products and cosmetics.
>
> **Billa supermarkets** At Untere Viaduktgasse (Map pp104-5; Untere Viaduktgasse 4; U3, U4 Wien-Mitte), Landstrasser Hauptstrasse (Map pp104-5; Landstrasser Hauptstrasse 32; 74A) and at Rennweg (Map pp104-5; Rennweg 9; 71) near the Belvedere.

with beef costs €10.80 and in summer there's outdoor seating. As well as a Mongolian lamb dish (served with pitta bread), Chinese, Thai and Japanese dishes figure on the menu. Kiang also has branches in the Innere Stadt (see p157).

RESTAURANT INDUS Map pp104-5 Indian, Pakistani €€

☎ 713 43 44; 03, Radetzkystrasse 20; mains €11.50-15; 11.30am-2.30pm & 6-11pm Mon-Fri & Sun, 6-11pm Sat; 1, 0; V

Although Indus could probably do with the decorative touch of a woman – a few flowers and a couple of knick-knacks on the shelves would round off the designer interior from Martin Hess well – the food and atmosphere is excellent. A *saag gosht* (lamb and spinach curry) costs €11.90; you can enjoy it in the garden out the back if the sloped, jagged ceiling and light interior doesn't keep you inside.

TRZESNIEWSKI Map pp104-5 Sandwiches €

☎ 715 28 19; 03, Rochusmarkt 8-9; bread with spread from €2.80 per 100 gram; 8.30am-7pm Mon-Fri, 8.30am-5pm Sat; U3 Rochusgasse; V

This branch of Vienna's famous open-sandwich shop in the Rochusmarkt is one of many stands where you can buy eat-in and takeaway on the hop. The quality and prices are the same as those of the Innere Stadt branch (see p158).

EAST OF THE DANUBE CANAL

The neighbourhood east of the Danube Canal received something of a boost after the metro line was extended a few years back. Two interesting parts of the neighbourhood to check out for eating are the Karmelitermarkt (Map pp112-13) and Volkertplatz, just west of Nordbahnstrasse.

RESTAURANT MRAZ & SOHN

Map pp112-13 Austrian, International €€€

☎ 0664-419 64 47; www.mraz-sohn.at; 20, Wallenstein Strasse 59; mains €28-30, 3–9-course menus €38-89; 11am-3pm & 7pm-midnight Mon-Fri; 33, 5

Mraz & Sohn is not only a snappy name, it really is a family-owned-and-run restaurant. The *chef de cuisine,* Markus Mraz, is the creative force behind the stars, chef hats and other accolades awarded for innovative dishes. The menu changes every couple of months, but in spring you might find expertly prepared venison with sesame cream, sweetheart cabbage and wakame salad. There's outdoor seating in summer, and a nonsmoking area. Book ahead – it's one of Vienna's best.

FARMERS MARKETS & SUPERMARKETS

The first four are the main produce markets in the area.

Karmelitermarkt (Map pp112-13; 02, Karmelitermarkt; 6am-7.30pm Mon-Fri, 6am-5pm Sat)

Volkertmarkt (Map pp112-13; 02, Volkertplatz; 6am-7.30pm Mon-Fri, 6am-5pm Sat; 2)

Vorgartenmarkt (Map pp112-13; 02, Ennsgasse; 6am-7.30pm Mon-Fri, 6am-5pm Sat; 5, 0) Between the Danube Canal and the Danube River.

Hannovermarkt (Map pp112-13; 20, Hannovergasse; 6am-7.30pm Mon-Fri, 6am-5pm Sat; 33) In Brigittenau.

Biomarkt Maran (Map pp112-13; ☎ 212 58 10; 02, Taborstrasse 10; 8am-7pm Mon-Fri, 8am-6pm Sat; 2) A convenient branch of this organic food and produce chain.

Billa supermarkets At Praterstern Bahnhof/Wien Nord (Map pp112-13; U1 Praterstern), Taborstrasse (Map pp112-13; Taborstrasse 8A; 2) and Obere Augartenstrasse (Map pp112-13; Obere Augartenstrasse 50; 5A).

RESTAURANT VINCENT

Map pp112-13 International €€€

☎ 214 15 16; 02, Grosse Pfarrgasse 7; mains €20-30, 10-course menus €98; 6pm-midnight Mon-Sat; U2 Taborstrasse 2 5A;

Vincent began life as a student place and over the years evolved into its higher calling – providing the Viennese with fine food. Today it sports a Michelin star and serves an interesting range of dishes à la carte or from menus that can be put together by the diner in flexible courses based on seasonal produce. The focus tends to be on classic produce such as lamb, beef, poultry and pheasant prepared expertly, but locally produced snails also feature. The ambience up front is historic and traditional, the back room is slightly bland, and beyond that is an atrium section.

SPEZEREI Map pp112-13 Tapas, Mediterranean €€

☎ 218 47 18; 02, Karmeliterplatz 2; tapas €6.90-10.90; 11.30am-11pm Mon-Sat; U2 Taborstrasse 2 5A; V

This small *Vinothek* (wine bar) and Mediterranean tapas place specialises in Spanish fish tapas (€6.90 to €9.90), focaccia and panini (from €4.70) and quality wines to wash them down with. And what a selection of wines it is too! About a dozen can be drunk by the glass and several hundred by the bottle, including four house varieties. The wall is full of them, mostly from Austria, and in summer you can enjoy by the bottle or glass, sitting outdoors soaking up the sun. (Karmeliterplatz is on Taborstrasse – not to be confused with nearby Karmelitermarkt.)

MADIANI Map pp112-13 Georgian €

☎ 0664-456 12 17; 02, Karmelitermarkt 21-24; antipasti €3.90-8.50, menus €7.50-8.50; 8.30am-10pm Mon-Fri, 8am-2pm Sat; 2 5A; V

This unpretentious Georgian eat-in and takeaway restaurant has indoor and outdoor table seating and does a fantastic *Melanzanirolle* (aubergine roll) filled with cream cheese and accompanied by beetroot salad and a traditional bean salad with fresh herbs, topped with pomegranate. Madiani has a simple cafe-style atmosphere, offering a great retreat

CLASSIC FARE EAST OF THE CANAL

While the food scene is on the move east of the canal, not to be forgotten is the classic fare for hearty appetites. All are midrange options.

Strandgasthaus Birner (Map pp112-13; ☎ 271 53 63; 21, An der Oberen Alten Donau 47; mains €5.70-12; 9am-11pm summer, 9am-10pm winter; U6 Floridsdorf 26) Great eating overlooking the Alte Donau.

Karl Kolarik's Schweizer Haus (Map pp112-13; ☎ 728 01 52; 02, Prater 116; mains €6.40-15.80; 11am-11pm; U1, U2 Praterstern/Wien Nord 5, 0) Vienna's premiere address for pork hocks.

Lusthaus (Map pp112-13; ☎ 728 95 65; 02, Freudenau 254; mains €9-16; noon-11pm Mon, Tue, Thu & Fri, noon-6pm Sat & Sun May-Sep, noon-6pm Thu-Tue Oct-Apr; 77A;) A former Habsburg hunting lodge where you can combine a Prater walk with an elegant ambience.

if you're shopping on Karmelitermarkt. Fixed menus are available from 3pm.

DANMAYR Map pp112-13 Italian €

☎ 0664-345 71 13; 02, Karmelitermarkt 37-39; antipasti €5-7.50; 11am-10pm Tue-Fri, 9am-2pm Sat Jun-Sep, 11am-7pm Tue-Fri Oct-May; 2 5A; V

This small eat-in and takeaway stand on Karmelitermarkt offers a delicious range of mostly southern Italian antipasti such as roasted capsicum salad, as well as prosciutto, salamis and a mortadella made from wild boar. In summer, nibblers can sit at the tables outside on the market place and watch the action. Eager punters will be aghast at the comings and goings directly next door, where a stand does a strong trade in cured meats and sausages made from horse meat.

SCHÖNE PERLE Map pp112-13 Neo-Beisl €

☎ 243 35 93; 02, Grosse Pfarrgasse 2; midday menus €7, mains €4-16; noon-11pm Mon-Fri, 10am-11pm Sat & Sun; U2 Taborstrasse 2 5A; V

Schöne Perle (beautiful pearl) has a simple look and serves everything from lentil soups through *Tafelspitz* to vegetarian and fish mains, and all are created with organic produce. Wines are from Austria, as are the large array of juices. Unusually for a Viennese restaurant, dogs are forbidden and kids welcome.

PIZZA MARI' Map pp112-13 Pizza €

☎ 0676-687 49 94; 02, Leopoldgasse 23a; pizzas €5.90-8.50; noon-11pm Tue-Sat; U2 Taborstrasse 2 5A; V

The kitchen in this pizza restaurant closes between 2.30pm and 6pm, the choice of pizza isn't enormous and (oddly for a pizza restaurant) it *never* uses anchovies – they're the downsides. The rest is good: Pizza Mari' serves some of the best pizzas this side of the canal, the inexpensive salads as side dishes are fresh and Mari' has a friendly, comfortable feel that makes you feel at home.

SOUTHWEST, THE GÜRTEL & GREATER VIENNA

This part of Vienna, though taking in a very large north–south swath along the Gürtel, is low on interesting places until you reach vibrant Yppenplatz, which admirably makes up for the deficit further south. Out in the Greater Vienna neighbourhood you will find some excellent *Heurigen* where you can enjoy wine and a meal in a leafy setting. See p173 for suggestions.

NOI Map pp120-1 International €€

☎ 403 13 47; www.restaurantnoi.net; 16, Yppenplatz; lunch menus around €8, mains €13.50-19, evening menus €23-31; 11am-midnight Tue-Fri, 9am-midnight Sat, 10am-5pm Sun; U6 Josefstädter Strasse 2; V

The natural wood floors and furnishings, and the cruisy music create the perfect backdrop for gourmet dining based around organic ingredients at Noi. The menus change each week, such as a chicken terrine with pumpkin pesto, lardon (speck or a bacon cut) and radish salad, followed by leg of chicken in a light rosemary sauce with celery puree and fig biscuit – brought together under the motto 'In chicken we trust' (€27.50). This top-class act also does surprise menus in which staff decide who gets what, also taking vegetarian preferences into account. It's elegant, down to earth and delicious, but book in the evening to be sure of a table.

AN-DO Map pp120-1 Fish €€

☎ 308 75 76; 16, Yppenmarkt 11-15; mains €11-29, pasta with seafood €12-14.50; 8am-11pm; U6 Josefstädter Strasse, 2; V

Vienna held its breath for some time to see what the new An-Do fish restaurant would bring to the Brunnenmarkt vicinity. The pundits like it. Order the octopus with *peperonata* and polenta (€13.80) and a tentacled monster arrives out of the pages of a Jules Verne novel. Start with a fish soup (€8) and you'll feel like you're eating your way through the Atlantic. The quality is excellent, the staff relaxed and efficient, and Yppenmarkt and the viaduct of the U6 has such a good range of places to move on to afterwards that you can make a lively night of it out here.

SCHLOSS CONCORDIA (KLEINE OPER WIEN) Map pp120-1 Austrian €€

☎ 769 88 88; 11, Simmeringer Hauptstrasse 283; mains €6.50-14, midday menus €8.75; 10am-1am; 71, 72; V

The gigantic stone Jesus that greets diners to Schloss Concordia is a fitting welcome mat, given the Zentralfriedhof directly opposite. It also sets the scene for inside; the bare wooden floors, gargantuan mirrors and stained-glass roof are suitably dated, and when lit by candlelight in the evening it all creates a rather eerie picture. The overgrown garden at the rear adds to the effect. The menu, which is crowded with schnitzels, will suit meat lovers; for a memorable experience, try *Degustationsmenü*, a hefty plate of different kinds of schnitzel. Thankfully there's a smattering of vegetarian options, too.

SAIGON Map pp120-1 Asian €

☎ 408 74 36; 16, Neulerchenfelder Strasse 37; mains €6-16; 11.30am-10pm; U6 Josefstädter Strasse J

The second of the Saigon restaurants (the other is in Mariahilf, see p160), this branch has an enormous, kitsch mural on the wall and like its brethren offers some of the best Asian (mostly Vietnamese) dining in Vienna, based on homemade noodles. Spicy grilled beef, fried duck served in pineapple and a range of noodle soups are its hallmarks.

QUELL Map pp120-1 Beisl €

☎ 893 24 07; 15, Reindorfgasse 19; mains €6.90-13.90; 11am-midnight Mon-Fri; 12A, 57A; V

FARMERS MARKETS & SUPERMARKETS

Brunnenmarkt (Map pp120-1; 16, Brunnengasse; 6am-7.30pm Mon-Fri, 6am-5pm Sat; U6 Josefstädter Strasse 2) One of Vienna's best produce and food markets, with lots of Turkish stands and some organic produce stalls.

Meidlinger Markt (Map pp120-1; 12, Niederhofstrasse; 6am-7.30pm Mon-Fri, 6am-5pm Sat; U6 Niederhofstrasse 10A) In Meidling.

Billa supermarkets At Nisselgasse near Schönbrunn (Map pp120-1; Nisselgasse 4; U4 Hietzing), Anschützgasse (Map pp120-1; Anschützgasse 26; 57A) and Thaliastrasse (Map pp120-1; Thaliastrasse 85; 46).

Time stands still at Quell, a traditional *Beisl* in suburban Rudolfsheim-Fünfhaus. The panelled-wood interior looks untouched for years, the archaic wooden chandeliers and ceramic stoves wouldn't be out of place in the Museum für Volkskunde, and some guests look as though they've been frequenting the place for decades. The menu is thoroughly Viennese, with *Schweinskotelett* (pork cutlets) and schnitzel featuring heavily, but there's also a surprising number of fish and vegetarian options. Genial staff and quiet streetside seating add to the attractions.

KENT Map pp120-1 Turkish €

☎ 405 91 73; 16, Brunnengasse 67; mains €5-10; 6am-2am; U6 Josefstädter Strasse J; V

Kent means 'small town' in Turkish, an appropriate name considering the hordes that frequent this ever-expanding Turkish restaurant. In summer the tree-shaded garden is one of the prettiest in the city, and the food is consistently top-notch. The menu is extensive, but highlights include shish kebab, *Ispanakli Pide* (long Turkish pizza with sheep's cheese, egg and spinach) and *Büyük Meze Tabagi* (a starter plate as big as a main with baked aubergine, carrots, courgettes, rice-filled vine leaves, green beans, hummus and other delights). The vegetarian and breakfast selections will please most, and everything is available for takeaway. For late-night desserts, try the Turkish bakery next door, which keeps practical opening times: 24-hours a day, seven days a week.

DRINKING & NIGHTLIFE

top picks

- **Halbestadt Bar** (p182)
- **Loos American Bar** (p175)
- **Café Drechsler** (p179)
- **10er Marie** (p184)
- **Pratersauna** (p188)
- **Rote Bar** (p190)

What's your recommendation? www.lonelyplanet.com/vienna

DRINKING & NIGHTLIFE

Kicking back with a glass of wine or beer, turning back time with coffee in an ancient coffee house: imbibing any liquid – alcoholic or caffeinated – while engaging in a heated discussion or simply having a laugh has a special place in the hearts and minds of the Viennese, and exudes a strong influence on the cultural make-up of the city. Despite the Viennese love of heading out on the town for quality drinks, they never forget that they live in the coffee capital of the world. The city's *Kaffeehäuser* (coffee houses) are as famous as the city's classical-music heritage, and are an attraction in their own right. The sheer number of coffee houses is staggering, but each has its own flair and flavour.

Wine is most beloved by the Viennese and outweighs beer in the consumption stakes. Seven sq km of vineyards lie within Vienna's borders, making it the world's largest wine-growing city. *Heurigen,* the city's equivalent of wine taverns, are rustic establishments on the outskirts of the city where 'new' wine (normally only a year old) is served to eager patrons on warm summer evenings.

The bar scene, where much of the city's beer disappears down parched throats, is highly accommodating to all tastes, ages and moods: whether you're looking for a family-friendly microbrewery, a student hang-out or a sophisticated wine bar, Vienna can provide. The distinction between bar and restaurant, bar and club or bar and coffee house is often blurred. In short: anywhere is great for a drink – where you go really depends on the atmosphere you crave.

This chapter lists the iconic coffee houses and *Heurigen* that you'll encounter in the capital, as well as the rest of the drinking pack, which ranges from swanky cocktail bars to grungy drinking holes, and everything in between. Drinking reviews in this chapter are grouped by neighbourhood, and ordered by type of establishment.

The best of Vienna's nightlife scene can also be found in this chapter (these reviews are listed alphabetically). The city's clubbing scene offers something for all tastes and preferences, from grooving to electronica in a former sauna-turned-club, to shaking your hips to mainstream pop under a glittering chandelier, to moving to hard-core techno at an underground stalwart. If you prefer to rest your feet and take in some live music, the choices are just as diverse; a number of spots feature top-quality classic or modern jazz and it's easy to catch performances by local bands in one of the small, frill-free venues across town.

DRINKING

WHERE TO DRINK

Coffee Houses

Vienna's coffee houses are legendary. As much a part of Viennese life as football in Britain, baseball in the USA, and barbecues in Australia, they are places to halt a busy schedule, order a coffee, cake or full meal, and replenish the system.

Coffee houses have for centuries graced Vienna's alleyways. Legend has it that coffee beans were left behind by the fleeing Turks in 1683, and by 1685 the first house had opened – at 01, Rotenturmstrasse 14. However, their popularity didn't take hold until the end of the 19th century; by this time there were a reputed 600 cafes in business. The tradition has waned over the years, but only slightly; the Viennese still love their coffee rituals and their coffee houses.

The traditional coffee house comes in a number of guises; the grand affairs of the 19th-century – Café Central and Café Griensteidl – share the streets with *Jugendstil* (art nouveau) delights, like Café Sperl, and post-WWII establishments, such as Café Prückel and Café Bräunerhof. *Konditoreien,* cake shops with seating and invariably an older clientele, are also commonplace; Aida is a classic example. Starbucks exists, but locals still favour their favourite coffee houses, and frequent them regularly and religiously.

No matter the decor, the environment is the same – paused. Nothing moves fast in a coffee house, not even the clouds of smoke hanging in the air. Patrons are encouraged to devour newspapers and magazines, including international titles, at their leisure, and pressure to order a second cup is non-existent.

Waiters command their territory; arrogant and scolding one minute (especially if your mobile phone goes off), courteous the next, they are annoyingly charming in their peculiar way of going about their business.

Coffee is king here, but most coffee houses offer a full food menu and a decent wine and beer list, making them excellent options for a bite, a meal or an alcoholic beverage.

Heurigen

Like *Beisln* (small taverns or restaurants) and *Kaffeehäuser, Heurigen* are an integral part of Vienna's cultural and culinary scene. These simple establishments date back to the Middle Ages, but it was Joseph II in 1784 who first officially granted producers the right to sell their wine directly from their own premises. It proved to be one of his more enduring reforms and *Heurigen* have since become a permanent fixture in the city.

Heurigen can normally be identified by a *Busch'n* (green wreath or branch) hanging over the door. Decor is normally rustic, with basic wooden tables and benches, and a large garden or inner courtyard. Food is served buffet-style; roast pork, blood sausage, pickled vegetables, potato salad and strudel are the mainstay of *Heurigen* cuisine. Don't pass over the chance to try *Schwarz Wurzel Salat* (black root salad) and *Senf Gürke* (mustard gherkins), which taste spectacularly better than they sound. Wine, the most important feature of any *Heuriger,* is traditionally made by the owner and is usually only a year old, quite tart, and best when mixed with soda water. *Sturm* (literally 'storm' for its cloudy appearance and chaotic effects on drinkers), fermenting grape juice with a high alcohol content and deceptively sweet, nonlethal taste, is available from around early September to the middle of October. *Buschenschenken* are a variation on *Heurigen* and only exist in the countryside bordering the city; open a few weeks of the year (normally in September), they are family-run and offer a small selection of food and wine. *Stadtheurigen* reside in the city's urban confluence and are often very basic affairs with tiny inner courtyards or multilevel cellars.

Heurigen are concentrated in and around Vienna's wine-growing regions. In the north, Grinzing has the largest concentration, but most cater to tour groups with kitsch live music and pseudo folk art and are often beyond the pale. Nearby Neustift am Walde is slowly going the way of Grinzing, while Sievering, squeezed between the two, still retains an air of authenticity. Olde-worldy Nussdorf has a string of inviting *Heurigen* that cater to a healthy number of regulars, and elevated Kahlenberg is harder to get to but the views make it worth the effort.

Most *Heurigen* to the west in Ottakring are within the city's built-up area, but offer excellent views and peaceful gardens. Mauer, a small suburb in the southwest reaches of the city, contains a tiny pocket of traditional *Heurigen;* Maurer Lange Gasse is a good place to start hunting.

To the north across the Danube the neighbourhoods of Strebersdorf and Stammersdorf produce around 30% of the city's wine, making it Vienna's largest wine-growing district. The *Heurigen* here are far more traditional, and less frequented by tourists.

Many *Heurigen* are only open part of the year, or every other month, which makes it a tad confusing, so check out the www.heurigenkalender.at, an online *Heurigen* calendar telling you what's open and when.

Bars, Pubs & Beyond

Vienna has a kicking bar scene. Many locations feature DJs on a regular basis and begin to fill from around 9pm onwards; some go on until 4am or later depending on the day, while others start to peter out around 1am and are completely dead by 2am.

Concentrations of bars, pubs and clubs (for more details on dedicated clubs, see p186) are clustered throughout the city, and due to Vienna's compact size and its stellar public transport system, getting from one to the next takes little effort. While the Innere Stadt never seems to empty of people, its scene is small and limited to a few select bars. The Bermuda Dreieck (Bermuda Triangle) in the old Jewish quarter is rammed with places, but most are heavily touristy. East of the Danube Canal, Leopoldstadt is the new darling of Vienna's night owls; its bars and clubs ooze 'underground' and attract a motley crew of students, and artists. Collectively, the Naschmarkt and its close neighbours Wieden and Mariahilf (in Vorstadt Southwest) contain the largest consolidation of bars – Schleifmühlgasse and Gumpendorfer Strasse in particular have some good pickings, as does most of Neubau. Around Josefstädter and Nussdorfer Strasse U-Bahn station on the Gürtel is yet another area sporting a profusion of bars – many under the *Stadtbogen* (arched spaces below the U-Bahn line), and some of which are leaders in the electronica and live-music scene while others have gone glam (read: swanky cocktail and wine bars).

With the advent of summer, many revellers descend on outdoor venues. The bars and shady courtyard at Altes AKH (Map pp94-5) attract plenty, as does the urban market square Yppenplatz (Map pp120-1) in Ottakring. The reinvention of the Danube Canal as a bar strip has to date been a huge success; Summer Stage (p165) and Flex (p187) are long-established locations, but the likes of Strandbar Herrmann (p183) and Badeschiff (p204 – pool by day, bar by night and in winter; and where the cargo hold of a ship becomes *the* venue for soul, jazz and house) have added an entirely new dimension to the waterway.

PRACTICALITIES

Opening Hours

Opening hours across Vienna's drinking and nightlife establishments vary greatly. Coffee houses tend to open for breakfast and close anywhere between 7pm and midnight during the week; sometimes later on weekends. Many close earlier on Sundays. Bars and pubs generally open around 4pm or 5pm and close around 2am during the week and often 4am or later on the weekends, but there is a fairly large number of places that remain open throughout the day. Some smaller bars close a bit earlier – around midnight during the week and roughly 2am or so on the weekend. *Heurigen* often have erratic opening hours – some are only open in summer or every other month; when they are open they start serving around 2pm or 3pm until midnight; sometimes from noon on Saturdays and Sundays. Clubs tend to open around 7pm or 8pm and close roughly 3am or 4am; many are only open Wednesday or Thursday through to Saturday.

How Much?

The price for a standard beer ranges from €2 to €5, depending on the location and venue – expect to pay around €2.50 for a small beer (0.2L) at a trendy coffee house in the main town – prices rise in Central Vienna. Coffees range from about €2 for a single espresso to around €3 or €4 for a *Melange* or a latte. Local wine is quite reasonable – you can easily get a decent glass of Austrian wine starting at around €3, though prices rise at fancier wine bars. Spirits are rarely cheap; expect to pay at least €7 for a simple mixed drink and around €9 and up for a cocktail.

Tipping

Tipping is standard: for smaller bills (under €10) it is customary to round up and add another euro if need be; for larger tabs, 5% to 10% is customary – edge towards the higher percentage if you've lingered long or eaten something with your drink.

CENTRAL VIENNA

CLUB U Map pp56-7 — Bar, Club

☎ 505 99 04; 04, Künstlerhauspassage; 9pm-4am; U1, U2, U4 Karlsplatz D, 1, 2 59A, 62

Club U occupies one of Otto Wagner's Stadtbahn Pavillons (p81) on Karlsplatz. It's a small, student-infested bar/club with regular DJs and a wonderful outdoor seating area overlooking the pavilions and park.

PALMENHAUS Map p66 — Bar, Cafe

☎ 533 10 33; 01, Burggarten; 10am-2am daily Mar-Oct, closed Mon & Tue Jan & Feb, reduced hr Jan-Feb; U1, U2, U4 Karlsplatz D, 1, 2 59A, 62

Housed in a beautifully restored Victorian palm house, complete with high arched ceilings, glass walls and steel beams, Palmenhaus occupies one of the most attractive locations in Vienna. The crowd is generally well-to-do, but the ambience is relaxed and welcoming. The outdoor seating in summer is a must, and there are occasional club nights.

URANIA Map pp56-7 — Bar

☎ 713 30 66; 01, Uraniastrasse 1; 9am-2am Mon-Sat, 9am-midnight Sun; 1, 2

Another addition to the canal's ever-increasing stock of bars, Urania occupies the first floor of a rejuvenated cinema and observatory complex. Its slick, clean decor, elevated position overlooking the canal, and extensive cocktail selection are all big pluses.

VOLKSGARTEN PAVILLON Map p66 — Bar, Outdoor Bar

☎ 532 09 07; 01, Burgring 1; 11am-2am Apr–mid-Sep; U2, U3 Volkstheater 1, 2, 46, 49, D

Volksgarten's second venue (after the club Volksgarten, p188) is a lovely 1950s-style pavilion with views of Heldenplatz. On Tuesday nights its ever-popular garden is packed to the gunnels.

LOOS AMERICAN BAR

Map pp56-7 Cocktail Bar

☎ 512 32 83; 01, Kärntner Durchgang 10; ⏲ noon-4am Sun-Wed, noon-5am Thu-Sat; Ⓤ U1, U3 Stephansplatz

The spot for a classic cocktail in the Innere Stadt, expertly whipped up by talented mixologists. Designed by Adolf Loos in 1908, this tiny box (seating no more than about 20) is bedecked from head to toe in onyx and polished brass; mirrored walls trick the mind into thinking it's in a far bigger space. Beware: gawkers popping in for a mere glimpse of the interior will be swiftly ejected.

AIDA Map pp56-7

Cafe

☎ 512 29 77; 01, Stock-im-Eisen-Platz 2; ⏲ 7am-8pm Mon-Sat, 9am-8pm Sun; Ⓤ U1, U3 Stephansplatz

An icon of the *Konditorei* scene, Aida is a time warp for coffee lovers. Its pink-and-brown colour scheme – right down to the waiters' socks – matches the 1950s retro decor perfectly and most of the clientele are well into retirement. Order a *Melange* and a slice of cake (there are almost 30 to choose from) and head upstairs to spy on the activity on Kärntner Strasse. Twenty-nine such Aida gems are scattered throughout Vienna.

CAFÉ ALT WIEN Map pp56-7

Coffee House

☎ 512 52 22; 01, Bäckerstrasse 9; ⏲ 10am-2am Sun-Thu, 10am-3am Fri & Sat; Ⓤ U1, U3 Stephansplatz 🚌 1A, 2A; 📶

Dark, bohemian and full of character, Alt Wien is a classic dive attracting students and arty types. It's also a one-stop shop for a lowdown on events in the city – every available wall space is plastered with posters advertising shows, concerts and exhibitions. The goulash is legendary and perfectly complemented by dark bread and beer.

CAFÉ BRÄUNERHOF Map p66

Coffee House

☎ 512 38 93; 01, Stallburggasse 2; ⏲ 8am-9pm Mon-Fri, 8am-7pm Sat, 10am-7pm Sun; 🚌 2A, 3A

Bräunerhof is an authentic coffee house of some standing among *Kaffeehäuser* aficionados. It remains little changed from the days when Austria's seminal writer Thomas Bernhard frequented the premises: smoke-stained walls, tight tables, surly staff, and a huge newspaper selection. Classical music from the Bräunerhof features from 3pm to 6pm on weekends and holidays.

CAFÉ CENTRAL Map pp56-7

Coffee House

☎ 533 37 64 26; 01, Herrengasse 14; ⏲ 7.30am-10pm Mon-Sat, from 10am Sun; Ⓤ U3 Herrengasse

Grand Central has a rich history – Trotsky came here to play chess, and turn-of-the-century literary greats such as Karl Kraus and Hermann Bahr regularly met here for coffee. Its impressive interior of marble pillars, arched ceilings and glittering chandeliers now plays host to tourists rather than locals, but it's worth stopping in for a look. There's live piano music daily from 5pm to 10pm, and the plaster patron with the walrus moustache near the door is a model of the poet Peter Altenberg.

CAFÉ GRIENSTEIDL Map p66

Coffee House

☎ 535 26 92; 01, Michaelerplatz 2; ⏲ 8am-11.30pm; Ⓤ U3 Herrengasse 🚌 2A, 3A

Griensteidl holds a prestigious position between the Hofburg and the Loos Haus, and was once the *Stammlokal* (local haunt) for Vienna's late-19th-century literary set.

EUROPE'S LAST BASTION OF SMOKING

Vienna is smoky. Despite the strict smoking bans that have swept across Europe over the last decade, Austria agreed on a multi-option compromise in 2009: in any locale under 50 sq metres, the proprietor is free to choose whether the venue is smoking or nonsmoking. If it's larger than 80 sq metres, a nonsmoking space must be provided with a partition and appropriate ventilation. Between 50 and 80 sq metres, establishments exist in a funny loophole (most escape the law on a variety of grounds: architecture is often cited). In practice, this partial ban means little – effective partitions between smoking and nonsmoking areas rarely exist. Many Viennese smoke and don't bat an eyelid about health risks or the effect of secondhand smoke on nonsmokers. Rumours of change in the smoky air rise periodically, but for the moment, expect to encounter thick smoke in most bars, clubs and coffee houses (see also p154).

It now caters mainly to tourists, but it still attracts with its *Jugendstil* lamps, wooden chairs and tables, and huge windows overlooking the comings and goings on Michaelerplatz.

CAFÉ HAWELKA Map pp56-7 Coffee House

☎ 512 82 30; 01, Dorotheergasse 6; 8am-2am Mon & Wed-Sat, from 10am Sun; U1, U3 Stephansplatz

At first glance it's hard to see what all the fuss is about: dirty pictures, ripped posters, brown-stained walls, smoky air and cramped tables don't look too appealing. But a second glance explains it: the convivial vibe between friends and complete strangers. A traditional haunt for artists and writers, it attracts the gamut of Viennese society. You'll be constantly shunted up to accommodate new arrivals at the table. Be warned: the organising elderly *Frau* seizes any momentarily vacant chair (curtail your toilet visits!) to reassign elsewhere.

CAFÉ LANDTMANN Map pp56-7 Coffee House

☎ 241 00; 01, Dr-Karl-Lueger-Ring 4; 7.30am-midnight; U2 Schottentor 1, 37, 38, 40, 41, 42, 43, D;

Landtmann attracts both politicians and theatre-goers with its elegant interior and close proximity to the Burgtheater, Rathaus and Parlament. The list of coffee specialities is formidable and the dessert menu features classics like *Sacher Torte* (chocolate cake) and *Apfelstrudel* (apple strudel). There's a huge selection of Austrian and international newspapers, and live piano music from 8pm to 11pm on Sunday to Tuesday.

CAFÉ PRÜCKEL Map pp56-7 Coffee House

☎ 512 61 15; 01, Stubenring 24; 8.30am-10pm; U3 Stubentor 1, 2

Prückel's unique mould is a little different from other Viennese cafes: instead of a sumptuous interior, it features an intact 1950s design. Intimate booths, aloof waiters, strong coffee and diet-destroying cakes are all attractions, but the smoke can at times be bothersome; thankfully there's a nonsmoking room at the rear. Live piano music is offered 7pm to 10pm Monday, Wednesday and Friday.

CAFÉ SACHER Map pp56-7 Coffee House

☎ 541 56-0; 01, Philharmonikerstrasse 4; 8am-11.30pm; U1, U2, U4 Karlsplatz D, 1, 2 59A, 62

top picks

SAMPLING AUSTRIAN WINE

- vis-a-vis (opposite)
- Wein & Wasser (p182)
- Sekt Comptoir (p180)
- Joanelli (p178)

Sacher is the cafe every second tourist wants to visit. Why? Because of the celebrated *Sacher Torte* (€4), a rich chocolate cake with apricot jam once favoured by Emperor Franz Josef. Truth be told, as cafes go Sacher doesn't rate highly for authenticity, but it pleases the masses with its opulent furnishings, battalion of waiters, and air of nobility.

CAFÉ TIROLERHOF Map pp56-7 Coffee House

☎ 512 78 33; 01, Führichgasse 8; 7am-10pm Mon-Sat, 9.30am-8pm Sun; 3A

A lovingly renovated *Jugendstil* decor from the 1920s and homemade *Apfelstrudel* help to make Tirolerhof an inviting Innere Stadt choice. Service is less tart than at other traditional coffee houses, and the location directly opposite the Albertina (p70) is a bonus.

DEMEL Map pp56-7 Coffee House

☎ 535 17 17; 01, Kohlmarkt 14; 10am-7pm; 2A, 3A

An elegant and regal cafe within sight of the Hofburg, Demel was once the talk of the town but now mainly caters to tourists. The quality of the cakes hasn't dropped however, and it wins marks for the sheer creativity of its sweets – its window displays an ever-changing array of edible art pieces (ballerinas and manicured bonsai for example). Demel's speciality is the *Ana Demel Torte*, a calorie-bomb of chocolate and nougat which rivals Café Sacher's *Torte*.

DIGLAS Map pp56-7 Coffee House

☎ 512 57 65; 01, Wollzeile 10; 8am-10.30pm; U1, U3 Stephansplatz 1A

Diglas comes straight from the classic coffee house mould, with swanky red-velvet booths, sharp-tongued waiters, an extensive (and good) coffee range, and old dames dressed to the nines. The reputation of Diglas' cakes precedes; some argue they're the best in town and the *Apfelstrudel* is unrivalled. Meals are delicate and more like snacks, but they extend beyond the normal Viennese specialities to include a variety of Hungarian dishes. Live piano music fills Diglas from 7pm to 10pm Monday through Wednesday, Friday and Saturday.

HAAS & HAAS Map pp56-7 Coffee House, Tearoom

☎ 512 26 66; 01, Stephansplatz 4; 8am-8pm Mon-Fri, 8am-6.30pm Sat; U1, U3 Stephansplatz 1A

The fragrance of tea from around the world greets customers on entry to Haas & Hass, Vienna's prime tearoom. Green, herbal, aromatic, Assam, Ceylon, Darjeeling; the selection seems endless. The rear garden is a shaded retreat from the wind, rain, sun and tourist bustle, while the front parlour sports comfy cushioned booths and views of Stephansdom. If you are more of a coffee person, lattes and various other coffee drinks are also available here.

KLEINES CAFÉ Map pp56-7 Coffee House

01, Franziskanerplatz 3; 10am-2am; U1, U3 Stephansplatz

Designed by architect Hermann Czech in the 1970s, Kleines Café exudes a bohemian atmosphere reminiscent of Vienna's heady *Jugendstil* days. It's tiny inside, but the wonderful summer outdoor seating on Franziskanerplatz is arguably the best in the Innere Stadt.

ESTERHÁZYKELLER Map pp56-7 Stadtheuriger

☎ 533 34 82; 01, Haarhof 1; 11am-11pm Mon-Fri, 4-11pm Sat & Sun; U3 Herrengasse 1A

Esterházykeller is tucked away on a quiet courtyard just off Kohlmarkt. Its enormous cellar is a tad claustrophobic, but after a few glasses of excellent wine, direct from the Esterházy Palace cellar in Eisenstadt, no one seems to mind. The rustic decor, complete with medieval weaponry and farming tools, reeks of kitsch, but the individual wooden booths are its saving grace. Unlike most *Heurigen,* Esterházykeller offers beer.

ZWÖLF APOSTELKELLER

Map pp56-7 Stadtheuriger

☎ 512 67 77; 01, Sonnenfelsgasse 3; 11am-midnight; U1, U3 Stephansplatz 1A

Even though Zwölf Apostelkeller (Twelve Apostle Cellar) plays it up for the tourists, it still retains plenty of charm, dignity and authenticity. This is mostly due to the premises themselves: a vast, dimly lit multilevel cellar. The atmosphere is often lively and rowdy, helped along by traditional *Heuriger* music from 7pm daily.

VIS-A-VIS Map pp56-7 Wine Bar

☎ 512 93 50; 01, Wollzeile 5; 4.30-10.30pm Tue-Sat; 1A

Hidden down a narrow, atmospheric passage (and directly across from famed *Beisl* Figlmüller, p156) is this wee wine bar – it may only seat close to 10 but it makes up for it with over 350 wines on offer (with a strong emphasis on Austrian faves). A perfect spot

COFFEE CONUNDRUMS

Ordering 'a coffee, please' won't go down well in most coffee houses. A quick glance at a menu will uncover an unfathomable list of coffee choices, and a little time studying the options is advisable. A good coffee house will serve the cup of java on a silver platter accompanied by a glass of water and a small sweet.

Some of the general selection of coffee available:

Brauner – black but served with a tiny splash of milk; comes in *Gross* (large) or *Klein* (small)
Einspänner – with whipped cream, served in a glass
Fiaker – *Verlängerter* (see below) with rum and whipped cream
Kapuziner – with a little milk and perhaps a sprinkling of grated chocolate
Maria Theresia – with orange liqueur and whipped cream
Masagran (or *Mazagran*) – cold coffee with ice and maraschino liqueur
Melange – the Viennese classic; served with milk, and maybe whipped cream too, similar to the cappuccino
Mocca (sometimes spelled *Mokka*) or *Schwarzer* – black coffee
Pharisäer – strong *Mocca* topped with whipped cream, served with a glass of rum
Türkische – comes in a copper pot with coffee grounds and sugar
Verlängerter – *Brauner* weakened with hot water
Wiener Eiskaffee – cold coffee with vanilla ice cream and whipped cream

to escape after a packed day of sightseeing – tapas, antipasto and gourmet olives round out the selection.

VORSTADT SOUTHWEST

South of Mariahilfer Strasse

ELEKTRO GÖNNER Map pp84-5 Bar

☎ 208 66 79; 06, Mariahilfer Strasse 101; 7pm-2am Sun-Thu, 7pm-4am Fri & Sat; U3 Zieglergasse

Elektro Gönner is an unpretentious bar opened by architects (and attracting plenty from the profession). Much of the interior is uncomplicated and bare, aside from the occasional art installation in the back room, and the music diverse. The bar hides at the back of a courtyard off Mariahilfer Strasse.

FUTUREGARDEN BAR & ART CLUB Map pp84-5 Bar, Club

☎ 585 26 13; 06, Schadekgasse 6; 6pm-2am Mon-Sat, from 8pm Sun; U3 Neubaugasse, 13A

With white walls, an open bar and basic furniture, it's hard to find a simpler place in Vienna. Its one piece of decoration – apart from the occasional art exhibition by local artists – is its rectangular disco 'ball', which swings from the ceiling. Futuregarden attracts a late 20s and 30s crowd with a cool atmosphere and electric sounds.

JOANELLI Map pp84-5 Bar, Wine Bar

☎ 311 84 04; 06, Gumpendorfer Strasse 47; 6pm-2am; U3 Neubaugasse

Vienna's oldest *Eissalon* (ice-cream shop; the ancient sign still hangs above the entrance) has morphed into an arty hangout, with relaxed tunes playing, and colourful lighting (sometimes pink, sometimes yellow) casting shadows on the plain white Formica tables and empty walls. The drinks list contains more than 20 quality wines by the glass (most of them Austrian) – staff expertly guide you between the *Blauburgunders* and the *Veltiners*. A full cocktail and beer menu, plus nibbles, is on offer too.

KUNSTHALLENCAFÉ Map pp84-5 Bar, Cafe

☎ 587 00 73; 04, Treitlstrasse 2; 10am-2am; U1, U2, U4 Karlsplatz D, 1, 2 59A, 62

The Kunsthallencafé carries plenty of 'cool' clout and attracts a relaxed, arty crowd with its DJs and close proximity to the Kunsthalle Project Space (p81). The big sofas go quickly, but there's plenty of small tables perfect for an intimate evening, and in summer the terrace (with more couches) is one enormous outdoor lounge.

LUTZ Map pp84-5 Bar, Club

☎ 585 36 46; 06, Mariahilfer Strasse 3; from 8am Mon-Fri, from 9am Sat, from 10am Sun; U3 Neubaugasse 13A;

Technically open during the day as a cafe and restaurant, evening is when to hit this modern, open space – try to snag a seat at the floor-to-ceiling windows gazing down to busy Mariahilfer Strasse below. A bar for everybody and any age, it boasts a fab location in the heart of the shopping district, and on weekends a subterranean club opens from 9.30pm, playing anything from house to disco.

MON AMI Map pp84-5 Bar

☎ 585 01 34; 06, Theobaldgasse 9; 4pm-1am Mon-Sat; U4 Neubaugasse

Don't let the dog and cat grooming sign fool you: this former pet-grooming salon morphed into a lovely '60s-style bar, mixes excellent cocktails, serves a short but decent beer, wine and snacks list and attracts a laid-back and unpretentious crowd. The rear of the bar is a shop (open to 10pm) stocking young designer creations so you can pick up a groovy new top and knock a few back in fewer than 10 steps.

ORANGE ONE Map pp84-5 Bar

☎ 586 22 20; 04, Margaretenstrasse 26; from 4pm; 59A

Once the haunt of down-and-outs and alcoholics, this former *Gastehaus* (guesthouse) received a complete makeover and reinvented itself as Orange One, a modern bar with a distinct retro feel and grown-up attitude. DJs play most nights and offbeat films are intermittently projected on the back wall. If smoke is a problem, it's best not to spend too much time here on winter nights.

PHIL Map pp84-5 Bar, Cafe

☎ 581 04 89; 06, Gumpendorfer Strasse 10-12; 9am-1am Tue-Sun, 5pm-1am Mon; 57A

A retro bar reminiscent of an East Berlin *Lokal*, Phil attracts a bohemian crowd happy to squat on kitsch furniture your

top picks

COFFEE & CLASSICAL

A handful of Viennese coffee houses feature regular classical music performances. It's a distinctly Viennese way to while away an afternoon or evening, and only costs the price of a cup of coffee (though we dare you to resist a slice of something sweet from the cake counter case).

- **Café Bräunerhof** (p175)
- **Café Central** (p175)
- **Café Landtmann** (p176)
- **Café Prückel** (p176)
- **Diglas** (p176)

grandma used to own. Half the establishment is store rather than bar; TVs from the '70s, DVDs, records and books are for sale, as is all the furniture. Staff are super-friendly and the vibe is as relaxed as can be.

SCHIKANEDER Map pp84-5 Bar

☎ 585 58 88; 04, Margaretenstrasse 22-24; 6pm-4am; 59A

Most of the colour in Schikaneder comes from the regularly projected movies splayed across one of its white walls – the students and arty crowd who frequent this grungy bar dress predominantly in black. But that's not to detract from the bar's atmosphere, which exudes energy well into the wee small hours of the morning. Schikaneder also hosts movies most nights (p199).

TANZCAFÉ JENSEITS Map pp84-5 Bar, Club

☎ 587 12 33; 06, Nelkengasse 3; 9pm-4am Mon-Sat; U3 Neubaugasse 13A

The red-velvet interior that might be out of a '70s bordello is a soothing backdrop for a night out at Jenseits. The tiny dance floor fills to overflowing on Fridays and Saturdays with relaxed revellers slowing moving around each other to soul and funk.

TOP KINO BAR Map pp84-5 Bar

☎ 208 30 00; 06, Rahlgasse 1; 10am-2am; U2 Museumsquartier 57A

Occupying the foyer of the cinema Top Kino (p199), Top Kino Bar is a pleasantly relaxed place that attracts a fashionable alternative crowd. The decor is highly retro, and there are tunes to match the furniture. Kozel, one of the Czech Republic's better pilsners, is lined up against Austria's finest lagers.

EBERT'S COCKTAIL BAR

Map pp84-5 Cocktail Bar

☎ 586 54 65; 06, Gumpendorfer Strasse 101; 6pm-2am Sun-Thu, 7pm-4am Fri & Sat; U3 Neubaugasse

Expert bartenders shake it up: all the mixologists here double as instructors at the bartending academy next door. The cocktail list is novel-esque, the vibe stylish, modern minimalism, the tunes jazzy to electronic, and on weekends you'll barely squeeze in. Bring your English Cinema Haydn (p198) ticket in anytime and receive a cocktail for €5.50.

CAFÉ DRECHSLER Map pp84-5 Coffee House

☎ 587 85 80; 06, Linke Wienzeile 22; 8am-2am Mon, 3am-2am Tue-Sat, 3am-midnight Sun; U4 Kettenbrückengasse

One of the liveliest coffee houses in town, Drechsler reopened with a smash after extensive renovations (Sir Terence Conran worked his magic with polished marble bar and table tops, Bauhaus light fixtures and whitewashed timber panels – stylish yet still distinctly Viennese). As well as the usual coffee-house suspects, its *Gulasch* (goulash) is legendary, as are the tunes the DJ spins, which seemingly change every few hours and always keep the vibe upbeat and hip.

CAFÉ RÜDIGERHOF Map pp84-5 Coffee House

☎ 586 31 38; 05, Hamburgerstrasse 20; 9am-2am; U4 Kettenbrückengasse

Rüdigerhof's facade is a glorious example of *Jugendstil* architecture, and the furniture and fittings inside could be straight out of an *I Love Lucy* set. The atmosphere is homely and familiar and the terrace huge and shaded. On Saturday mornings it fills up quickly with Naschmarkt shoppers.

CAFÉ SAVOY Map pp84-5 Coffee House

☎ 586 73 48; 06, Linke Wienzeile 36; 8am-2am Mon-Fri, 9am-2am Sat; U4 Kettenbrückengasse;

Café Savoy is an established gay haunt that has a more traditional cafe feel to it. The clientele is generally very mixed on a Saturday – mainly due to the proximity of the Naschmarkt – but at other times it's filled with men of all ages.

CAFÉ SPERL Map pp84-5 Coffee House

☎ 586 41 58; 06, Gumpendorfer Strasse 11; 7am-11pm Mon-Sat year-round, 11am-8pm Sun Sep-Jun; 57A;

With its gorgeous *Jugendstil* fittings, grand dimensions, cosy booths and unhurried air, Sperl is one of the finest coffee houses in Vienna. And that's to say nothing of a menu that features *Sperl Tort*, a mouth-watering mix of almonds and chocolate cream. Grab a slice and a newspaper, order a strong coffee, and join the rest of the patrons people-watching and daydreaming.

CAFÉ WILLENDORF Map pp84-5 Gay Bar

☎ 587 17 89; 06, Linke Wienzeile 102; 6pm-2am Mon-Sat, 10am-3pm & 6pm-2am Sun; U4 Pilgramgasse 13A

This is one of Vienna's seminal gay and lesbian bars. Housed in the pink Rosa Lila Villa (p234), it's a very popular place to meet for a chat, a drink or a meal. The lovely inner courtyard garden opens for the summer months.

MANGO BAR Map pp84-5 Gay Bar

☎ 587 44 48; 06, Laimgrubengasse 3; 9pm-4am; U4 Kettenbrückengasse 57A

Mango attracts a young, often men-only gay crowd with good music, friendly staff and plenty of mirrors to check out yourself and others. It usually serves as a kick-start for a big night out on the town.

SEKT COMPTOIR Map pp84-5 Wine Bar

☎ 432 53 88; www.sektcomptoir.at; 04, Schleifmühlgasse 19; 4-10pm Mon-Fri, 10am-5pm Sat; 59A

Oooh, sparkly. Szigeti vineyard in Burgenland, which produces a leading Austrian *Sekt* (sparkling wine), serves its own brand only at this tiny, wood-panelled wine bar. As it's located just a few blocks from the Naschmarkt, shoppers with bulging grocery bags often spill onto the sidewalk enjoying a tipple or four. It rarely offers much elbow room but the, er, bubbly spirit is so intoxicating that most just chuckle and squish with a wide grin. Note the early closing times – and its shop selling bottles a few doors down (at Schleifmühlgasse 23; open from 10.30am to 6pm Monday to Friday, and 10am to 5pm Saturday).

MuseumsQuartier & Around

BLUE BOX Map pp84-5 Bar

☎ 523 26 82; 07, Richtergasse 8; 10am-2am Sun-Thu, 10am-4am Fri & Sat; U3 Neubaugasse 13A

Don't let the smoke and the run-down appearance of Blue Box put you off. These trademarks, which seem to have been around for generations, are an integral part of the Blue Box experience. It's too small to afford dance-floor space, and most guests groove to the regular DJ beats in their seats. Superb breakfasts are available from 10am to 5pm Tuesday to Sunday.

CAFÉ LEOPOLD Map pp84-5 Bar, Cafe

☎ 523 67 32; 07, Museumsplatz 1; 9am-2am Sun-Wed, to 4am Thu-Sat; U2 Museumsquartier, U2, U3 Volkstheater 2A, 48A;

The pick of the MuseumsQuartier bars, Café Leopold sits high at the top of the Leopold Museum (p86). Its design is sleek and smart – its conservatory overlooks the MuseumsQuartier's square – and the atmosphere is more club than bar (DJs feature Monday to Saturday).

DAS MÖBEL Map pp84-5 Bar, Cafe

☎ 524 94 97; 07, Burggasse 10; 10am-1am; U2, U3 Volkstheater 48A;

Das Möbel wins points for its furniture, consisting entirely of one-off pieces produced by local designers. Half the fun is choosing a spot that takes your fancy – whether it be a swinging chair or a surfboard bench. Light fittings, bags and various odds and ends complete the look, and everything is for sale (see p146).

EUROPA Map pp84-5 Bar, Cafe

☎ 526 33 83; 07, Zollergasse 8; 9am-5am; U3 Neubaugasse 13A;

A long-standing fixture of the 7th district, Europa is a chilled spot any time day or night. During the sunny hours, join the relaxed set at a window table for coffee and food, and in the evening take a pew at the bar and enjoy the DJ's tunes. Its breakfast, served between 9am and 3pm daily, caters to a hungover clientele; Sunday features a sumptuous breakfast buffet (€9.50).

> **top picks**
>
> **GAY & LESBIAN HANG-OUTS**
>
> - Café Berg (p182) Friendly, open and stocks gay books.
> - Café Savoy (p179) The atmosphere of a traditional Viennese cafe, plus a little pizzazz thrown into the mix.
> - Café Willendorf (opposite) Rosa Lila Villa's house bar; always convivial and welcoming.
> - Mango Bar (opposite) Ever-popular bar open every night of the week.

WIRR Map pp84-5 — Bar

☎ 929 40 50; www.wirr.at, in German; 07, Burggasse 70; 11am-2am Mon-Wed, 11am-4am Thu & Fri, 10am-late Sat & Sun; 48A

On weekends it's often hard to find a seat – particularly on the comfy sofas – at this colourful, alternative bar. Its rooms are spacious and open, the walls are covered in local artists' work, including a large (albeit bizarre) tie collection, and light snacks are available. Eclectic clubbings – which range from '60s pop to Balkan rhythms – are well attended in the downstairs club.

CANETTI Map pp84-5 — Coffee House

☎ 522 06 88; 07, Urban-Loritz-Platz 2a; 10am-9pm Mon-Sat; U6 Burggasse Stadthalle 6, 18, 49

Canetti is one of only a handful of eateries in Vienna with rooftop views. Perched on top of the Bücherei Wien (p89), its vantage point provides a sweeping vista of Vienna to the south. Food is hit-and-miss, so come for a quiet coffee or cocktail with a view.

VORSTADT NORTHWEST

B72 Map pp94-5 — Bar, Club

☎ 409 21 28; www.b72.at, in German; 08, Hernalser Gürtel 72; 8pm-4am Sun-Thu, 8pm-6am Fri & Sat; U6 Alser Strasse 43, 44

Fringe live acts, alternative beats and album launches are the mainstay of B72's entertainment line-up, which collectively attracts a predominantly youthful crowd. Its tall glass walls and arched brick interior are typical of most bars along the Gürtel, as is the thick, smoky air and grungy appearance. Its name comes from its address, *Bogen* (arch) 72.

CAFÉ STEIN Map pp94-5 — Bar, Cafe

☎ 319 72 41; 09, Währinger Strasse 6-8; 7am-1am Mon-Sat, from 9am Sun; U2 Schottentor 1, 37, 38, 40, 41, 42, 43, D;

During the day this three-level cafe is a popular haunt of students from the nearby university; come evening the clientele metamorphoses into city workers with a lot more money to spend. DJs control the decks in the evenings, and the all-day menu is extensive. During the summer there is outside seating, which enjoys superb views of the Votivkirche (p99).

CHELSEA Map pp94-5 — Bar, Club

☎ 407 93 09; www.chelsea.co.at, in German; 08, Lerchenfelder Gürtel 29-31; 6pm-4am Mon-Sat, from 4pm Sun; U6 Thaliastrasse 46

Chelsea is the old, ratty dog on the Gürtel and is very much a favourite of the student/alternative scene. Posters and underground paraphernalia adorn walls, and DJs spin loud sounds (usually indie, sometimes techno) when live acts aren't playing. British and Irish beers are on tap, quite the crowd-pleaser when English premier league and Champions league football games are broadcast.

MAS! Map pp94-5 — Bar

☎ 403 83 24; www.restaurante-mas.at, in German 08, Laudongasse 36; 6pm-2am Mon-Sat, 10am-midnight Sun; 5, 33

A designer bar specialising in cocktails and Mexican food, Mas! attracts an affluent and well-groomed set. Choose from a high, wobbly stool at the long, shimmering bar backed by an enormous light installation, or for a more intimate evening, a low, dimly lit table. Its 'Mexican Sunday brunch' (all-you-can-eat buffet €18) – a mix of Cajun, English and American breakfasts between 10am and 4pm – is legendary, and happy hour is from 6pm to 8pm and 11pm to midnight daily.

RHIZ Map pp94-5 — Bar, Club

☎ 409 25 05; 08, Lerchenfelder Gürtel 37-38; 6pm-4am Mon-Sat, 6pm-2am Sun; U6 Josefstädter Strasse 2, 33;

Rhiz's decor of brick arches and glass walls is reminiscent of so many bars beneath the U6 line, but its status as a stalwart of the city's electronica scene gives it the edge over much of the competition. Black-clad boozers and an alternative set cram the interior during winter to hear DJs and live acts, while in summer the large outdoor seating area fills to overflowing.

HALBESTADT BAR Map pp94-5 Cocktail Bar

☎ 319 47 35; 09, Stadtbogen 155; 🕐 6pm-2am Mon-Thu, 7pm-2am Fri, to 4am Sat &Sun; U6 Nussdorferstrasse

It starts when you can't open the glass door. The host swings it forth, escorts you in, takes your coat and offers to advise you on what to order – impeccable hospitality, with no trace of snobbery. More than 500 bottles grace the walls of the tiny space under the *Boden* and mixologists hold court creating tongue-enticing works of art, shaken and poured into exquisite receptacles. South Pacific–inspired drinks arrive in a ceramic, Polynesian goblet, and *Sekt* comes in a shallow, retro champagne glass.

SHIRAZ Map pp94-5 Cocktail Bar, Hookah Bar

☎ 335 55 55; 09, Stadtbogen 185; 🕐 6pm-2am; U6 Nussdorferstrasse

Step into 1001 nights at this shisha bar/club/cocktail bar. Puff on hookahs, lounge in plush, velvety sofas and contemplate the oriental red-and-gold wallpaper butting up against the brick arches of the *Stadtbogen*. Exotic mixed drinks and a long list of (mainly Austrian and New World) wines lubricate while DJs spin international tunes and bodies boogie into the starry night.

CAFÉ FLORIANIHOF Map pp94-5 Coffee House

☎ 402 48 42; 08, Florianigasse 45; 🕐 8am-midnight Mon-Fri, 10am-8pm Sat & Sun; 5, 33;

This child-friendly cafe in Josefstadt serves food heavily laden with organic produce and a remarkable array of fruit juices. Paintings by local artists add a splash of colour to the clean white walls, and in summer the streetside seating fills quickly.

CAFÉ HUMMEL Map pp94-5 Coffee House

☎ 405 53 14; 08, Josefstädter Strasse 66; 🕐 7am-midnight Mon-Sat, from 8am Sun; 5, 33;

Unpretentious and classic, Hummel is a large *Kaffeehaus* catering to a regular Josefstadt crowd. The coffee is rich, the cakes baked on the premises, and the waiters typically snobbish. In summer, it's easy to spend a few hours at Hummel's outdoor seating area, mulling over the international papers and watching the human traffic on Josefstädter Strasse.

CAFÉ BERG Map pp94-5 Gay Bar

☎ 319 57 20; 09, Berggasse 8; 🕐 10am-1am daily, 10am-midnight Jul-Sep; U2 Schottentor, 37, 38, 40, 41, 42, 43, 44 40A;

Café Berg is Vienna's leading gay bar, although it's welcoming to all walks of life. Its staff are some of the nicest in town, the layout sleek and smart and the vibe chilled. Its bookshop, Löwenherz (🕐 10am-7pm Mon-Fri, 10am-5pm Sat), stocks a grand collection of gay magazines and books.

FRAUENCAFÉ Map pp94-5 Gay Bar

☎ 406 37 54; 08, Lange Gasse 8; 🕐 6pm-midnight Thu & Fri, also open for special events; 46

A strictly women-, lesbian- and transgendered-only cafe/bar, Frauencafé has long been a favourite of Vienna's lesbian scene. It has a homely, relaxed feel and is located away from the hub of gay and lesbian bars around the Rosa Lila Villa.

WEINSTUBE JOSEFSTADT
Map pp94-5 Stadtheuriger

☎ 406 46 28; 08, Piaristengasse 27; 🕐 4pm-midnight, closed Jan-Mar; 2 13A

Weinstube Josefstadt is one of the loveliest *Stadtheurigen* in the city. Its garden is a barely controlled green oasis among concrete residential blocks, and tables are squeezed in between the trees and shrubs. Food is typical, with a buffet-style selection and plenty of cheap meats (chicken wings go for only €1). The friendly, well-liquored locals come free of charge. The location is not well signposted; the only sign of its existence is a metal *Busch'n* hanging from a doorway.

WEIN & WASSER Map pp94-5 Wine Bar

☎ 403 53 45; 08, Laudongasse 57; 🕐 6pm-1am Mon-Sat; U6 Josefstrasse 5

The best place in Vienna to sample Austrian wine outside a *Heuriger*. Its name means 'Wine & Water' and the philosophy is to teach customers what it knows about wine. The staff warmly guide you through the lengthy list and more than 20 Austrian wines are served by the glass. If you prefer to stick to what you know, check out the 'The Foreigners' section for the usual suspects. Kick it all back in the subterranean space, with arched bricks flanked by lights oozing pale yellow and flickering candles. Nibbles and tapas round out the menu.

BLAUBURGUNDER & BOCKBIER BEFUDDLEMENT

Austrian Wine

Austrian wine is slowly gaining popularity and appearing on wine lists outside of Austria, particularly in the UK, but in Vienna you'll encounter some exceptional varietals on restaurant and bar menus.

Main wine varieties in Austria:
Blauer Burgunder Austria's version of Pinot noir; a complex and fruity red found near the Neusiedler See.
Blaufränkisch Dry, light-bodied red rich in tannin; grows best in middle and southern Burgenland.
Grüner Veltliner Austria's largest grape variety; a strong, fresh white with hints of citrus and pear.
Müller-Thurgau Mild and often flowery white found in Lower Austria and Burgenland.
Riesling Fruity white with strong acidity; predominantly produced in the Danube Valley.
St Laurent Dark, velvety red originating in the Bordeaux village of the same name.
Weissburgunder Mainly grown in Burgenland, this rich white has a slight almond taste and piquant acidity.
Welshriesling Fresh, fruity white with a touch of spice; planted mainly in Burgenland and Lower Austria.
Zweigelt Full-bodied red with intense cherry fruit aromas, found throughout Austria's wine-growing regions.

Austrian Beer

While wine is the chosen drink of the Viennese, beer features heavily in the city's cultural make-up. Gösser, Ottakring, Puntigamer, Stiegl, Wieselburger and Zipfer are typical labels. Mix it up: if you can't decide, order a glass of *G'mischt*, that is, half *Helles* (light) and half *Dunkel* (dark).

Main beer types:
Bockbier Knock-you-off-your-chair strong lager beer (sometimes as high as 12% alcohol volume) available around Christmas and Easter. A potentially dangerous potion.
Dunkel Thick dark beer with a very rich flavour.
Helles Clear beer; light hops taste and very common; think lager with a bite.
Märzen Red-coloured beer with a strong malt taste.
Pils Pilsner beer; very crisp and strong, and often bitter.
Weizen or Weissbier Full-bodied wheat beer, slightly sweet in taste. Can be light or dark, clear or cloudy; sometimes served with a lemon slice.
Zwickel Unfiltered beer with a cloudy complexion; should always be drunk fresh.

VORSTADT LANDSTRASSE

STRANDBAR HERRMANN

Map pp104-5 — Beach Bar

03, Herrmannpark; 10am-2am Apr–early Oct; 0, 1, 2;

You'd swear you're by the sea at this hopping canalside beach bar, with beach chairs, sand and hordes of Viennese livin' it up on hot summer evenings. Films occasionally feature, blankets are available and if you get bored of lounging, have a go at a game of boules. Cool trivia: it's located on Herrmannpark, named after picture postcard inventor Emanuel Herrmann (1839–1902).

EAST OF THE DANUBE CANAL

FLUC Map pp112-13

Bar, Live-Music Venue

www.fluc.at, in German; 02, Praterstern 5; 6pm-4am; U1, U2 Praterstern 0, 5

Located on the wrong side of the tracks (Praterstern can be uncomfortable at times) and looking for all the world like a prefab schoolroom, Fluc is the closest that Vienna's nightlife scene comes to anarchy – without the fear of physical violence. Black-clad students, smashed alcoholics, 30-something freelancers and the occasional TV celebrity all share the stripped-back venue without any hassle, and DJs or live acts play every night (electronica features heavily).

TACHLES Map pp112-13

Bar, Cafe

212 03 58; 02, Karmeliterplatz 1; 5pm-2am; U2 Taborstrasse 2;

Smack on the main square in up-and-coming Leopoldstadt, this bohemian cafe-bar attracts an intellectual and laid-back crowd of locals in relaxed, wood-panelled surrounds. Small bites with a Slavic slant

HEURIGER GÖBEL *Neal Bedford*

One of the few highly original *Heurigen* in Vienna is Göbel (off Map pp50-1; ☎ 294 84 20; www.weinbaugoebel.at; 21, Stammersdorfer Kellergasse 151; ⏲ from 4pm Mon & Wed-Sat, from 11am Sun, opening months vary, check website; 🚌 228, 233), the creation of owner Peter Göbel. Combining his significant talent at both winemaking and architectural design, Peter has fashioned a *Heuriger* that not only delivers quality produce (80% of his wine is red, some of which is among the best in Vienna) but provides a traditional atmosphere among stylishly clean lines and a strong natural-wood finish. Peter has been responsible for the family's winemaking since 1991 and Göbel since 1996, but the business is in his blood – three generations of it, in fact. We asked him for his learned opinion on Vienna's *Heuriger* scene.

'Viennese people like *Heurigen* because not much changes. The attraction will always be a garden, a courtyard, a food buffet, and wine from a local vineyard. *Heurigen* to the Viennese means spare time, weekends, recreation, a family outing – or sometimes simply a quick stop for a glass of wine.

'With an increase in restaurant choice and open-air events in the city, the attraction of a traditional *Heuriger* has waned. Accordingly, the *Heuriger* culture has begun to adapt and now tries to go with the flow – food specials are offered, and information is available on the internet. Nevertheless, traditional establishments still exist, and variations on the old *Heuriger* theme continue to open.

'When you go to a *Heuriger*, my advice is to drink everything, particularly the mixed varieties. Vienna has the advantage of diverse soils and a microclimate, which means a lot of varieties coexist, and every winemaker has special rarities, so it's best to ask. Eat anything that looks great – that's the advantage of a buffet – and what you're not familiar with. This is half the adventure.

'My favourite wine from my own production is the Alte Reben Zweigelt. It corresponds with my idea of a Viennese wine – not international, very autonomous, at the beginning quite distant and complicated, but with time and understanding for its qualities, a very personal wine. I also enjoy Grüner Veltiner from the Wachau and Kamptal (the Danube Valley).

'To experience traditional *Heurigen*, either visit places recommended here or drive to one of the wine areas on the city border and drop into every place that has a *Busch'n* hanging from its door. At the latter you should have no expectations of quality, just take it as it comes.'

(such as pierogi, borscht) are on offer and it hosts occasional live music and readings – the last Thursday of each month features young musicians in its vast cellar space.

SOUTHWEST & THE GÜRTEL

CAFÉ GLORIETTE Map pp120-1 Coffee House

☎ 879 13 11; 13, Gloriette; ⏲ 9am-1am; Ⓤ U4 Schönbrunn, Hietzing

Café Gloriette occupies the Gloriette, a neoclassical construction high on a hill behind Schloss Schönbrunn (p119), built for the pleasure of Maria Theresia in 1775. With sweeping views of the Schloss, its magnificent gardens and the districts to the north, Gloriette has arguably one of the best vistas in all of Vienna. And it's a welcome pit stop after the short but sharp climb up the hill.

LO:SCH Map pp120-1 Gay Bar

☎ 895 99 79; www.club-losch.at, in German; 15, Fünfhausgasse 1; ⏲ 10pm-2am Fri & Sat; Ⓤ U6 Gumpendorfer Strasse 🚌 57A

This leather-fetish bar is normally strictly men only, but occasionally it hosts unisex parties on Saturday nights. Lo:sch sometimes opens during the week for special events.

10ER MARIE Map pp120-1 Stadtheuriger

☎ 489 46 47; 16, Ottakringerstrasse 222-224; ⏲ 3pm-midnight Mon-Sat; Ⓤ U3 Ottakring 🚊 2, 10, 46

The oldest *Heuriger* in Vienna has been going strong since 1740 – back in the day Schubert, Strauss and Crown prince Rudolf all kicked back a glass or three here; today it welcomes a grand mix of visitors and locals. It's family run and operated, with the rustic ambience that a *Heuriger* ought to have, without the trek out to the far reaches of the city – the usual buffet is on offer, plus a handful of schnitzels.

BUSCHENSCHRANK STIPPERT

Map pp120-1 Stadtheuriger

☎ 486 89 17; 16, Ottakringerstrasse 225; ⏲ 3pm-midnight Wed-Sat, 10am-1pm Sun; Ⓤ U3 Ottakring 🚊 2, 10, 46

Blink and you'll think you've time travelled at this simple, basic *Heuriger* with sassy staff and traditional fare – come for the country chalet atmosphere and take a peek at the ancient green *Kachelofen* (ceramic-tiled wood-burning oven, used to heat kitchens back in the day) in the centre of the room.

GREATER VIENNA

ECKERT off Map pp50-1 Heuriger

☎ 292 25 96; 21, Strebersdorfer Strasse 158, Strebersdorf; ⏲ from 2pm Mon-Sat, from 10am Sun, every odd month & first half Dec, plus or minus a few days; 🚊 26

Located in the heart of Strebersdorf, a 10-minute walk from the tram 26 terminus (walk north on Russberg Strasse and right at Strebersdorfer Platz), Eckert is a cross between a traditional establishment and an arts centre. Paintings by local artists adorn walls, live music features once a month (anything from jazz to rock and roll) and readings are common. Tours of the wine cellars are offered, and kids generally get the run of the place.

EDLMOSER Map pp50-1 Heuriger

☎ 889 86 80; www.edlmoser.at, in German; 23, Maurer Lange Gasse, Mauer; ⏲ 2.30pm-midnight roughly the last half of each month Apr-Nov; 🚊 60

Edlmoser is run by dynamic young winemaker Michael Edlmoser, who apprenticed under California's highly respected Ridge Winery; his outward-looking attitude blends with a deep love of Austrian tradition to create what he calls cult wines. These are served in a four-centuries-old house with clean lines, modern wood furnishings and a superb swath of yellow fabric covering a vine-lined garden – a fusion of old and new, just like the wines.

HIRT Map pp50-1 Heuriger

☎ 318 96 41; 19, Eisernenhandgasse 165, Kahlenberg; ⏲ 2pm until late Wed-Sat, from 10am Sun every odd month & first half of Dec; 🚌 38A

Hidden among the vineyards on the eastern slopes of Kahlenberg, Hirt is a simple *Heuriger* with few frills. Basic wooden tables, a small buffet and marginal service all help to create a traditional atmosphere, while views of Kahlenbergerdorf and the 21st district across the Danube are a pleasure to enjoy over a few glasses of wine in the early evening. Hirt is best approached from the top of Kahlenberg on the Kahlenberg to Nussdorf walk; see p136.

MAYER AM PFARRPLATZ

Map pp50-1 Heuriger

☎ 370 12 87; 19, Pfarrplatz 2, Nussdorf; ⏲ 4pm-midnight Mon-Sat, from 11am Sun; 🚌 38A

Roughly 1.5km from U4 Heiligenstadt U-Bahn station, Mayer caters to tour groups but still manages to retain an air of authenticity, helped along by its peaceful ambience, vine-covered surrounds and history (Beethoven lived here in 1817). The huge shaded garden towards the rear includes a children's play area, and there's live music from 7pm to 11pm daily.

REINPRECHT Map pp50-1 Heuriger

☎ 320 14 71; 19, Cobenzlgasse 22, Grinzing; ⏲ 3.30pm-midnight mid-Feb–mid-Dec; 🚌 38A

Located in a former monastery in the heart of Grinzing, Reinprecht shines bright among the dull *Heurigen* in these parts. It still caters to the masses with its huge garden, enormous buffet and live music, but quality reigns throughout – it won numerous awards over the years and features some of the best wine in the city. Check out the cork collection; at 3500 pieces, it's the largest in Europe.

SCHMIDT off Map pp50-1 Heuriger

☎ 292 66 88; 21, Stammersdorfer Strasse 105, Stammersdorf; ⏲ 3pm-midnight Thu-Sat, from 2pm Sun, closed second week of May, last week of Jul & first week of Aug; 🚊 31 🚌 30A

A well-established Stammersdorf *Heuriger,* Schmidt stocks wonderful *Muskateller* and *Grüner Veltliner* and offers wine tastings of local vintages. In November, around the birthday of St Martin, you can also sample the traditional *Martinigansl* (goose). Schmidt is a few minutes' walk northwest of the tram 31 terminus, and the same distance southeast of the bus 30A terminus.

SIRBU Map pp50-1 Heuriger

☎ 320 59 28; 19, Kahlenberger Strasse 210, Kahlenberg; ⏲ 3pm-midnight Mon-Sat, mid-Apr–mid-Oct; 🚌 38A

Like Hirt (left), Sirbu has far-reaching views across Vienna's urban expanse from its quiet spot among the vineyards of Kahlenberg. Its wines have reached the pinnacle of Austrian success in recent years, and its garden is the perfect place to while away a sunny afternoon.

WEINGUT AM REISENBERG

Map pp50-1 Heuriger

☎ 320 93 93; 19, Oberer Reisenbergweg 15, Grinzing; 5pm-midnight Fri, 1pm-midnight Sat & Sun May-Sep, 6pm-midnight Wed-Sat Oct-Dec; 38A

A thoroughly modern premises with huge windows and a styled, brick interior, Weingut am Reisenberg is part of the new generation of *Heurigen*. Instead of the traditional Austrian buffet, it offers Italian cuisine and vegetarian dishes, which are best enjoyed in its green garden overlooking the expanse of Vienna. It's a good 10-minute walk up a steep hill just north of Grinzing village, first up Cobenzlgasse and then Oberer Reisenbergweg; another 20 minutes further up Obere Reisenbergweg is Cobenzl, where you'll find a cafe and even better views of Vienna.

WEINGUT SCHILLING

off Map pp50-1 Heuriger

☎ 292 41 89; 21, Langenzersdorferstrasse 54, Strebersdorf; 4pm-midnight Mon-Fri, from 3pm Sat & Sun even months; 26

With the spread of vineyards rising over Bisamberg hill in full view from its large garden, Schilling attracts many on warm evenings. Its reputation for quality wine also helps its popularity and tours of the wine cellar are available for those who ask nicely. Schilling is a 15-minute walk from the final destination of tram 26; walk north along Russbergstrasse to Langenzersdorferstrasse and then west for a short distance.

WIENINGER off Map pp50-1 Heuriger

☎ 292 41 06; 21, Stammersdorfer Strasse 78, Stammersdorf; 3pm-midnight Wed-Fri, from noon Sat & Sun Mar–late Jul & mid-Aug–Dec; 31 30A

Bus 30A stops a few minutes' walk east of Wieninger, a family-run *Heuriger* in central Stammersdorf. The food buffet, which features organic produce and a healthy smattering of vegetarian meal options, is extensive, the wine from its own vineyard fruity and light, and the atmosphere local and relaxed.

ZAHEL Map pp50-1 Heuriger

☎ 889 13 18; 23, Maurer Hauptplatz 9, Mauer; 11.30am-midnight first two weeks of each month; 60

One of the oldest *Heurigen* in Vienna, Zahel occupies a 250-year-old farmhouse on Maurer Hauptplatz. The buffet is laden with Viennese and seasonal cuisine and wine is for sale to take home. It sometimes closes for weeks at a time; if so, head two blocks south to Maurer Lange Gasse for some more options.

ZAWODSKY Map pp50-1 Heuriger

☎ 320 79 78; 19, Reinischgasse 3, Döbling; 5pm-midnight Mon & Wed-Fri, from 2pm Sat & Sun Mar-Nov; 38

Zawodsky is only a 1.5km walk from the touristy haunts of Grinzing, yet light years away in atmosphere. This stripped-back set-up features picnic tables surrounded by apple trees and vineyards, and a small selection of hot and cold meats complemented by various salads. From Grinzing, walk up Strassergasse, take tiny Rosenweg on your left past the Maria Schmerzen Kirche and Reinischgasse appears on your right.

BUSCHENSCHRANK HUBER

Map pp50-1 Stadtheuriger

☎ 485 81 80; 16, Roterdstrasse 5; 3pm-midnight Tue-Sat; 10, 44

At the foot of the Wilhelminenberg comes a *Heuriger* swathed in class: crisp white tablecloths lend an upmarket vibe to the otherwise traditional, wood-panelled space. The buffet is gargantuan, filling the mainly older crowd with a sensational selection of salads, meats and sweets.

NIGHTLIFE

CLUBBING

The Viennese aren't known for their tarantism ways, which means that the clubbing scene in Vienna is relatively small. Small doesn't mean dire though; clubs invariably feature excellent DJs and also a variety of music genres, which means that you'll always find something to fit your tastes. As most local folk detest queuing, crowded dance floors and hefty entry prices, clubs are generally quite intimate, and massive, bombastic venues are rare creatures. Entry prices can and do vary wildly – from nothing to €15 – and depend on who's on the decks.

The dividing line between a club and bar in Vienna is often quite blurred and hard to pick. Most contemporary bars tend to feature DJs on a regular basis and some, such as Europa (p180), Tanzcafé Jenseits (p179), Café Leopold (p180) and Wirr (p181) have small, but well-used dance floors.

The clubbing scene may be small, but quality over quantity, right? Home-grown DJs, such as Kruder & Dorfmeister and the Sofa Surfers, regularly perform alongside their international counterparts in clubs packed with revellers.

AUX GAZELLES Map pp84-5

☎ 585 66 45; www.auxgazelles.at; 06, Rahlgasse 5; 11pm-4am Thu-Sat; U2 Museumsquartier 57A

Aux Gazelles' club bar is beautifully Moorish and suitably filled with beautiful people. The music is an eclectic mix of smooth ethnic sounds, and there are plenty of dim corners and low, comfy couches to escape to if so desired. The rest of this gigantic club venue features a restaurant, bar and deli, and there's even a hammam (oriental steam bath; see p202). Aux Gazelles is one of the few clubs in town where a dress code is enforced.

BACH Map pp120-1

☎ 0676-844 260 214; www.bach.co.at, in German; 16, Bachgasse 21; 8pm-3am Wed-Sat; 9, 46

An underground club of sorts in the far-flung reaches of Ottakring, Bach features techno DJs and regular live acts from across Europe. The crowd leans towards the grungy side, and is genuine and relaxed, and the dance floor small and intimate.

BRICKS LAZY DANCEBAR Map pp112-13

☎ 216 37 01; www.bricks.co.at, in German; 02, Taborstrasse 38; 8pm-4am; U2 Taborstrasse 2

A cross between a bar and a dance spot, this retro, red-vinyl space attracts a mainly 20-something set. The dance floor is tiny but cosy, with DJs spinning anything from timeless dance classics from the last four decades to electric, indie and alternative beats. All cocktails are half-price before 10pm daily and all night on Monday.

FLEX Map pp50-1

☎ 533 75 25; www.flex.at, in German; 01, Donaukanal, Augartenbrücke; 6pm-4am, from 8pm Mon-Sat May-Sep; U2, U4 Schottenring 1, 2, 31

Flex has been attracting a more mainstream crowd than it did in its early days but it still manages to retain a semblance of its former edginess, and the title of best club in town. The sound system is without equal in Vienna (some would say Europe), entry price generally reasonable and dress code unheard of. The monthly DJ line-up features local legends and international names, and live acts are commonplace. 'Messed Up' on Monday (the night to catch serious techno) and 'London Calling' (alternative and indie) on Wednesday and Friday are among the most popular nights. In summer the picnic tables lining the canal overflow with happy partygoers.

GOODMANN Map pp84-5

☎ 967 44 15; www.goodmann.at; 04, Rechte Wienzeile 23; 3am-10am Mon-Fri, 3am-noon Sat & Sun; U4 Kettenbrückengasse 59A

A tiny club attracting clubbers who want to dance into the morning, Goodmann serves food upstairs (until 8am) and hides its night owls, who are an eclectic mix of old and young (but always in a merry state), downstairs.

PALAIS PALFFY Map p66

☎ 512 56 81; www.palais-palffy.at; 01, Josefsplatz 6; from 9pm Thu-Sat; U3 Herrengasse

This 550-sq-metre club occupies two floors of an illustrious old building used for live-music performances (see p195). The 1st-floor lounge bar – set with thousands of miniature glittering gemstones below a 12m chandelier with 80,000 Swarovski crystals – stocks more than 700 spirits. Less glittery is the luxurious upstairs dance floor. Thursday is mixed electronic and pop, Friday features house, and the Jetlag Club (oldies, current dance) comes to town on Saturday.

PASSAGE Map pp56-7

☎ 961 88 00; www.sunshie.at; 01, Babenberger Passage, Burgring 1; 8pm-4am Tue-Wed, from 9pm Thu, 10pm-6am Fri & Sat; D, 1, 2

Passage is the closest thing to a megaclub in Vienna. Its sleek interior, soothing colours and sweaty atmosphere attract the beautiful people of the city, their entourage and plenty of oglers and barflies. The music is loud (noise from the Ringstrasse traffic directly overhead is easily drowned out) and fairly mainstream, with R&B, hip-hop and house nights; 'Disco Fever Tuesday' draws some of the biggest crowds. Expect lines and black-clad, muscle-bound doormen after 10pm (11pm on Friday and Saturday).

PRATERSAUNA Map pp112-13

☎ 729 19 27; www.pratersauna.tv; 02, Waldsteingartenstrasse 135; 10pm-6pm Fri & Sat Jan-Apr, 9pm-6am Wed-Sun May-Sep; U1, U2 Praterstern

Pool, cafe, bistro and club converge in a former sauna – these days, you'll sweat it up on the dance floor any given night. Pratersauna hosts light installations and performance art to check out before or after you groove to electronica spinned by international DJs. On warm nights it all spills out onto the terrace, gardens and pool – if you need to cool down, nobody bats an eye if you take a quick dip.

ROXY Map pp84-5

☎ 961 88 00; www.roxyclub.at; 04, Operngasse 24; 11pm-4am Thu-Sat; U1, U2, U4 Karlsplatz 59A

A seminal club for years, Roxy still manages to run with the clubbing pack, and sometimes leads the way. DJs from Vienna's electronica scene regularly guest on the turntables and most nights it's hard to find a space on the small dance floor. Expect a crowded, but very good, night out here.

TITANIC Map pp84-5

☎ 587 47 58; www.titanicbar.at, in German; 06, Theobaldgasse 11; 11pm-6am Tue-Sat; U2 Museumsquartier 57A

This club is old school, with door check and bouncers (dress reasonably conservatively), but once you're past these party-poopers it's time to whoop it up. Two large dance floors soon fill with revellers either looking to pull or dance the night away to mainstream club sounds, R&B and '80s classics. Fun, but not to everyone's taste.

U4 Map pp120-1

☎ 817 11 92; www.u4club.at; 12, Schönbrunner Strasse 222; 8pm until late Mon, from 10pm Tue-Sun; U4 Meidling Hauptstrasse 10A

U4 was the birthplace of techno clubbing in Vienna way back when, and its longevity is a testament to its ability to roll with the times. A fairly young, studenty crowd are its current regulars, and while the music isn't as cutting edge as it used to be, it still manages to please the masses.

VOLKSGARTEN Map p66

☎ 532 42 41; www.volksgarten.at, in German; 01, Burgring 1; no set hr, Tue-Sat; U2, U3 Volkstheater 1, 2, 46, 49, D

A hugely popular club superbly located near the Hofburg, Volksgarten serves a clientele eager to see and be seen. The long cocktail bar is perfect for people-watching and the music is an ever-rotating mix of hip-hop, house, salsa and reggae, but is hardly ever challenging. Opening hours are not fixed. Dress well to glide past the bouncers.

WHY NOT? Map pp56-7

☎ 535 11 58; www.why-not.at; 01, Tiefer Graben 22; 10pm-4am Fri & Sat; U3 Herrengasse 1A, 2A

Why Not? is one of the few clubs focusing its attention solely on the gay scene. The small club quickly fills up with mainly young guys out for as much fun as possible.

LIVE MUSIC

Formerly the end of the line for bands touring Europe, Vienna is now a crossroads for those heading to Eastern Europe. Big-name and new bands regularly perform on the city's stages and the yearly repertoire is a healthy mix of jazz, rock (both alternative and mainstream) and world music. Posters and flyers advertising future concerts are plastered across the city, making lining up concerts a simple task. International names often sell out but touts are usually around.

Venues are invariably small and the crowds fairly subdued, making it easy to push your way to the front and not end the night bruised and winded. Concerts can cost as little as €5 for local performers (sometimes free) or €50 for an internationally acclaimed act. In general, however, most will set you back €15 to €25.

Bars and clubs, in particular Flex (p187), Rhiz (p181), Chelsea (p181) and B72 (p181), also regularly host touring bands. Festivals such as the Donauinselfest (see p17) and Jazz Fest Wien (see p17) are also excellent places to catch local and international talent.

ARENA Map pp104-5

☎ 798 85 95; www.arena.co.at, in German; 03, Baumgasse 80; U3 Erdberg

A former slaughterhouse turned music and film venue, Arena is one of the city's quirkier places to see live acts. Hard rock, rock, metal, reggae and soul (along with cinema) can be seen on its outdoor stage from May to September; over winter bands are presented in one of its two indoor halls. 'Iceberg', a particularly popular German-British 1970s new-wave bash, is held here once a month.

CAFÉ CARINA Map pp94-5

☎ 406 43 22; www.café-carina.at, in German; 08, Josefstädter Strasse 84; 6pm-2am Mon-Thu, 6pm-4am Fri & Sat; U6 Josefstädter Strasse 2, 33

Small, smoky, and pleasantly dingy, Carina is a muso's and drinker's bar. Local bands perform most nights, only a few feet from a normally enthusiastic audience, and the music is invariably folk, jazz or country.

CAFÉ CONCERTO Map pp94-5

☎ 406 47 95; www.cafeconcerto.at; 16, Lerchenfelder Gürtel 53; 7pm-4am Tue-Sat; U6 Josefstädter Strasse 2, 33

Concerto is another of the bars on the Gürtel that hosts local live acts. Jazz features heavily on the programme (which is also peppered with DJs) and both the cellar and ground-level bar are used for concerts, although the acoustics of the former may leave a little to be desired. Entry is often free.

JAZZLAND Map pp56-7

☎ 533 25 75; www.jazzland.at, in German; 01, Franz-Josefs-Kai 29; 7pm-2am Mon-Sat, from 7.30pm Jul & Aug; U1, U4 Schwedenplatz 1, 2

Jazzland has been an institution of Vienna's jazz scene for over 30 years. The music covers the whole jazz spectrum, and the brick venue features a grand mixture of both international and local acts.

METROPOL Map pp120-1

☎ 407 77 40; www.wiener-metropol.at, in German; 17, Hernalser Hauptstrasse 55; box office 10am-6pm Mon-Sat; 43

The Metropol is a bit of a musical chameleon: one week might see performances by international acts, the next kitsch musicals, cabaret and folk music. There's plenty of tables and bar stools so there should be no problem procuring a ticket.

MILES SMILES Map pp94-5

☎ 405 95 17; 08, Lange Gasse 51; 8pm-2am Sun-Thu, 8pm-4am Fri & Sat; 2 13A

One of two bars in town named after legend Miles Davis, Miles Smiles is for the discerning jazz fan who likes to see the whites of the artist's eyes.

VIENNA'S MICROBREWERIES

Venues where the beer is always fresh and the atmosphere boisterous, Vienna's microbreweries make for a hedonistic evening out. Most offer a healthy selection of beers brewed on the premises (and proudly display the shining, brass brewing equipment), complemented by filling Austrian staples.

1516 Brewing Company (Map pp56-7; ☎ 961 15 16; www.1516brewingcompany.com; 01, Schwarzenbergstrasse 2; 11am-2am; D, 1, 2 3A) Unfiltered beers and a few unusual varieties, such as Heidi's Blueberry Ale. Large choice of cigars and frequented by city workers and UN staff.

Fischer Bräu (Map pp50-1; ☎ 369 59 49; www.fischerbraeu.at, in German; 19, Billrothstrasse 17; 4pm-1am Mon-Sat, 11am-1am Sun; 38 35A) A new beer every four to six weeks, and a *Helles* (light) lager all year round. The large garden is a local fave and and its live jazz on Sundays is perennially packed.

Salm Bräu (Map pp104-5; ☎ 799 59 92; www.salmbraeu.com; 03, Rennweg 8; 11am-midnight; 71) Brews its own *Helles*, *Pils* (pilsner), *Märzen* (red-coloured beer with a strong malt taste), *G'mischt* (half *Helles* and half *Dunkel* (dark)), and *Weizen* (full-bodied wheat beer, slightly sweet in taste). Smack next to Schloss Belvedere and hugely popular, with a happy hour from 3pm to 5pm Monday to Friday and noon to 4pm Saturday.

Siebensternbräu (Map pp84-5; ☎ 523 86 97; www.7stern.at; 07, Siebensterngasse 19; 10am-midnight; 49) Large brewery with all the main varieties, plus a hemp beer, chilli beer and smoky beer (the malt is dried over an open fire); the hidden back garden is sublime in the warmer months.

Wieden Bräu (Map pp84-5; ☎ 586 03 00; www.wieden-braeu.at, in German; 04, Waaggasse 5; 11.30am-midnight Jul & Aug, from 4pm Sat & Sun; 1, 62;) *Helles*, *Märzen* and hemp beers all year round, plus a few seasonal choices, including a ginger beer. Happy hour from 5.30pm to 7.30pm.

Live acts are irregular but always enthralling, and the atmosphere enthusiastic and energetic.

PORGY & BESS Map pp56-7

☎ 512 88 11; www.porgy.at; 01, Riemergasse 11; from 7pm; U3 Stubentor 1A

Quality is the cornerstone of Porgy & Bess' continuing popularity. Its program is loaded with modern jazz acts from around the globe, including many from nearby Balkan countries, and DJs fill spots on weekends. The interior is dim and the vibe velvety and very grown-up.

REIGEN Map pp120-1

☎ 894 00 94; www.reigen.at, in German; 14, Hadikgasse 62; 6pm-4am Sep-Jun, 7pm-4am Jul & Aug; U4 Heitzing 60

Reigen's tiny stage is the setting for jazz, blues, Latin and world music in a simple space housing rotating art and photography exhibits, so you can groove while perusing art.

ROTE BAR Map pp84-5

☎ 521 11 2 18; www.rotebar.at; 07, Neustiftgasse 1; roughly 10pm-late; U2, U3 Volkstheater 1, 2, D, 49

This marble-, chandelier- and thick, red-velvet-curtain–bedecked space in the nether regions of the Volkstheater (p197) hosts Tuesday-night jazz sessions, Saturday dance nights with DJs, Wednesday readings and performance art, plus occasional one-offs like Milonga nights where you can try to tango.

STADTHALLE Map pp120-1

☎ 981 00-0; www.stadthalle.com, in German; 15, Vogelweidplatz 15; U6 Burggasse Stadthalle 6, 18, 49 48A

Stadthalle is the largest concert venue in the city and usually caters to large, mainstream rock bands and local heroes. Check the posters around town for upcoming shows or check the website.

SZENE WIEN Map pp104-5

☎ 749 33 41; www.szenewien.com; 11, Hauffgasse 26; U3 Zipperstrasse

Szene Wien tops the list of Vienna's small concert venues. Intimate and friendly, it's a superb place to catch international bands without fighting off the crowds. Concerts cover the music spectrum; rock, reggae, funk, jazz and world music have all been heard within these walls.

WUK Map pp94-5

☎ 40 121-0; www.wuk.at; 09, Währinger Strasse 59; U6 Währinger Strasse-Volksoper 40, 41, 41

WUK (Werkstätten und Kulturhaus; Workshop and Culture House) is many things to many people. Basically a space for art (government subsidised but free to pursue an independent course), it hosts a huge array of events in its concert hall. International and local rock acts vie with clubbing nights, classical concerts, film evenings, theatre and even children's shows. Women's groups, temporary exhibitions and practical skills workshops are also on site, along with a smoky cafe with a fabulous cobbled courtyard.

MUSIC & THE ARTS

top picks

- **Staatsoper** (p195)
- **Orangery** (p194)
- **Vienna's English Theatre** (p197)
- **Marionettentheater** (p197)
- **Breitenseer Lichtspiele** (p198)
- **Kino Unter Sternen** (p199)

What's your recommendation? www.lonelyplanet.com/vienna

MUSIC & THE ARTS

Vienna is the world capital of opera and classical music. Who else can claim Mozart, Beethoven, Strauss and Schubert among their historical repertoire? The rich musical legacy that flows through the city is evident everywhere: the plethora of monuments to its greatest composers and its princely music venues easily outnumber those of some countries, let alone other capital cities. A quick walk down Kärntner Strasse from the Staatsoper to Stephansplatz will turn up more Mozart lookalikes than you care to shake a baton at – they might not impress, but next thing you know a black-clad street performer sets up shop in a pedestrian zone and begins belting out opera, stopping shoppers dead in their tracks.

It doesn't end there. You can listen to Mozart in a space where he once practised; embrace decadence and operatic masterpieces at the Staatsoper (p195), one of the finest opera houses in Europe; be wowed by the sights and sounds of the world-renowned Vienna Philharmonic; or sway to the chorus of unceasing classical-music concerts at a whole array of venues.

Churches and coffee houses make fine venues to enjoy classical music. Augustinerkirche (p70), Minoritenkirche (p72) and Burgkapelle (p67) are just some of the city's churches complementing Mass on Sunday morning with a full choir and orchestra, and some have regular evening concerts.

Not a fan of classical music? Modern and alternative options abound too. Live-music venues such as Porgy & Bess (p190) attract superb, top-quality jazz acts year-round, while smaller locations cater to an array of local talent. Venues featuring live music are mentioned throughout the Drinking & Nightlife chapter (p171); otherwise, pick up the handy *Wiener Konzert Cafés (Vienna's Concert Cafés)* brochure from the tourist office.

Festivals such as the KlangBogen Festival (p17) and Wiener Festwochen (Vienna Festival; p17) are highlights on the music calendar, and the Rathausplatz plays host to the Musikfilm Festival (p18), a film festival screening opera and classical concerts, in July and August.

With such presence in the city, it should be no problem to catch a concert on your visit. The only stumbling block might be in obtaining tickets to the more salubrious venues, such as the Staatsoper and Musikverein (p194); with these, it's advisable to book well ahead. Otherwise just turn up and enjoy.

Ticket costs vary greatly. Standing-room tickets can go for as little as €2, whereas a prime spot at a gala performance in the Staatsoper will set you back €254. Most venues produce a handy map of the seating layout, which is invaluable in choosing the perfect seat to match your budget. For how to book and where to buy tickets, see p193.

And then there's the theatre, which started in the capital over 200 years ago with the creation of the Burgtheater (p196), the oldest theatre in the German-speaking world. Today some 50 theatres are thriving in this theatre-loving city, but invariably performances are in German.

Contemporary dance is centred at Tanzquartier Wien (p197), where it's going from strength to strength. ImPulsTanz (p17), a quality dance festival from mid-July to mid-August, is about the only other option for catching dance performances in Vienna. Traditional ballet also features at both the Staatsoper and the Volksoper (p196) during the opera season.

Vienna's weekly rag *Falter* (www.falter.at, in German) is the best source of entertainment information; it lists music concerts from every genre, cinema schedules, clubbing, theatre performances, children's events, and sporting fixtures. Both the paper and its virtual version are in German, but they shouldn't take much time to decipher. *City* (www.city-online.at, in German), another weekly German-language events paper, is thin on news and topical chat but has basic listings. Local radio station FM4 (103.8FM; fm4.orf.at, in German) provides the lowdown on events in English at various times throughout the day. The tourist office produces a monthly listing of events covering theatre, concerts, film festivals, exhibitions and more; also see its seasonal magazine, *Vienna Scene*.

Reviews in this chapter are grouped under the type of arts venue, and listed alphabetically by venue name.

OPERA, CLASSICAL MUSIC & BEYOND

Vienna inspires every walk of life to embrace culture with open arms; even visitors who haven't listened to Mozart in years flock to the opera or a classical-music performance. Luckily, most budgets and tastes will find something in the capital, but remember this: for the best selection of seats and options, book ahead and make sure you bring evening attire (dressing up is the norm for many upmarket venues). But even jean-lovers and nonplanners won't miss out: many coffee houses offer regular classical music performances.

ARNOLD SCHÖNBERG CENTER

Map pp104-5

☎ 718 18 88; www.schoenberg.at; 03, Schwarzenbergplatz 6, entrance at Zaunergasse 1; tickets free-€15; tram D

This brilliant repository of Arnold Schönberg's archival legacy is a cultural centre and celebration of the Viennese school of the early 20th century honouring Mr Schönberg, a Viennese-born composer, painter, teacher, theoretician and innovator known for his 'Method of composing with twelve tones which are related only with one another'. The exhibition hall regularly hosts intimate classical concerts, which people in the know flock to.

HOFBURG CONCERT HALLS Map p66

☎ 587 25 52; www.hofburgorchester.at; 01, Heldenplatz; tickets €39-52; U-Bahn U3 Herrengasse tram D, 1, 2

The Neue Hofburg's concert halls, the sumptuous Festsaal and Redoutensaal, are regularly used for Strauss and Mozart concerts, featuring the Hofburg Orchestra and soloists from the Staatsoper and Volksoper. Performances start at 8.30pm and tickets are available online and from travel agents and hotels. It's open-plan seating, so get in early to secure a good seat.

KAMMEROPER Map pp56-7

☎ 512 01 00 77; www.wienerkammeroper.at; 01, Fleischmarkt 24; tickets €5-69; box office noon-6pm Mon-Fri; U-Bahn U2, U4 Schwedenplatz tram 1, 2

The Kammeroper ranks as Vienna's third opera house after the Staatsoper and Volksoper. Its small venue is perfect for unusual and quirky opera productions and in summer the entire company is transported to the Schlosstheater Schönbrunn (Palace Theater; www.musik-theater-schoenbrunn.at)

TICKETS & RESERVATIONS

A number of local ticket offices and websites offer tickets to a number of venues throughout Vienna. Some charge commissions but each is a convenient one-stop-shop for visitors interested in obtaining tickets for set dates across multiple venues.

The state ticket office, Bundestheaterkassen (Map pp56-7; ☎ 514 44 78 80; www.bundestheater.at; 01, Operngasse 2; 8am-6pm Mon-Fri, 9am-noon Sat & Sun; U-Bahn U1, U2, U4 Karlsplatz tram D, 1, 2 bus 59A, 62), only sells tickets to federal venues: Akademietheater, Burgtheater, Staatsoper and Volksoper. The office charges no commission, and tickets for the Staatsoper and Volksoper are available here one month prior to the performance date. Credit cards are accepted and credit-card purchases can also be made by telephone. Alternatively, tickets for these federal venues can be booked over the internet.

Jirsa Theater Karten Büro (Map pp94-5; ☎ 400 600; viennaticket.at; 08, Lerchenfelder Strasse 12; 9.30am-5.30pm Mon-Fri Sep-Jun, 10am-1pm Jul & Aug; U-Bahn U2 Rathaus or Volkstheater, U3 Volkstheater tram 46 bus 13A) is one of the larger ticketing offices in the city. Tickets for a range of performances and venues are sold here, but you might be charged commission (some places add 20% to 30%).

Wien-Ticket Pavillon (Map pp56-7; ☎ 588 85; www.wien-ticket.at, in German; 01, Herbert-von-Karajan-Platz; 10am-7pm; U-Bahn U1, U2, U4 Karlsplatz tram D, 1, 2 bus 59A, 62), a ticket booth housed in the hut by the Staatsoper, is linked to the city government and charges anything from no commission up to a 6% levy. Tickets for all venues are sold here.

Online options:

Austria Ticket Online (www.austriaticket.at, in German) Extensive online ticketing agent, covering the whole entertainment spectrum.

ClubTicket (www.clubticket.at, in German) Another comprehensive online ticket agent, also with last-minute deals.

(closed for renovations at press time but due to reopen in 2011) to continue performances in more opulent surroundings. Students receive 30% discount, children under 14 receive 50% discount.

KONZERTHAUS Map pp104-5

☎ 242 002; www.konzerthaus.at; 03, Lothringerstrasse 20; tickets €12-120; box office 9am-7.45pm Mon-Fri, 9am-1pm Sat; U4 Stadtpark 4A

The Konzerthaus is a major venue in classical-music circles, but throughout the year ethnic music, rock, pop or jazz can also be heard in its hallowed halls. Up to three simultaneous performances, in the Grosser Saal, the Mozart Saal and the Schubert Saal, can be staged; this massive complex also features another four concert halls. Students can pick up €14 tickets 30 minutes before performances; children receive 50% discount.

KURSALON Map pp56-7

☎ 512 57 90; www.strauss-konzerte.at; 01, Johannesgasse 33; tickets €39-90, concert with 3-course dinner €66-117, with 4-course dinner €71-123; U4 Stadtpark 1, 2

Fans of Strauss and Mozart will love the performances at Kursalon, which holds daily evening concerts (8.15pm) devoted to the two masters of music in a splendid, refurbished Renaissance building. Also popular is the Concert & Dinner package (3- or 4-course meal – not including drinks – at 6pm, followed by the concert) in the equally palatial on-site restaurant.

MUSIKVEREIN Map pp56-7

☎ 505 81 90; www.musikverein.at; 01, Bösendorferstrasse 12; tours adult/child €5/3.50, tickets €4-90; box office 9am-8pm Mon-Fri, 9am-1pm Sat; U1, U2, U4 Karlsplatz D, 1, 2 59A, 62

The Musikverein holds the proud title of the best acoustics of any concert hall in Austria, which the Vienna Philharmonic Orchestra makes excellent use of. The interior is suitably lavish and can be visited on the occasional guided tour. Standing-room tickets in the main hall cost €4 to €6; there are no student tickets. Smaller-scale performances are held in the Brahms Saal.

ODEON Map pp112-13

☎ 216 51 27; www.odeon-theater.at; 02, Taborstrasse 10; tickets €20-45; box office 6pm–performance time; U1, U4 Schwedenplatz N, 1, 2

This oft-forgotten performance venue looks suitably grand from the outside but the interior doesn't impress as much – come for the performance versus a palatial theatre experience. Anything from classical concerts to raves are held within its walls.

ORANGERY Map pp120-1

☎ 812 50 04; www.imagevienna.com; 13, Schloss Schönbrunn; tickets €40-96; box office 8.30am-7pm; U4 Schönbrunn 10, 58 10A

Schönbrunn's lovely former imperial greenhouse is the location for year-round Mozart and Strauss concerts. Performances last around two hours and begin at 8.30pm daily.

VIENNA BOYS' CHOIR

As with Manner Schnitten (Manner's most popular hazelnut wafer cookies/biscuits; see p132), Stephansdom, Lipizzaner stallions and sausage stands, Vienna wouldn't be Vienna without the Vienna Boys' Choir (Wiener Sängerknaben; www.wsk.at). Founded more than five centuries ago by Maximilian I as the imperial choir, its members over the ages included famed composers Schubert and Gallus and conductors Richter and Krauss – Mozart composed for the choir in his day and Haydn was a member of another local choir but he occasionally stepped in to sing with this one. Today, it's the most famous boys' choir in the world, now consisting of four separate choirs – hand-selected each year and mainly Austrian – who share the demanding global tour schedule.

Catching the choir in concert takes some organisation. Tickets (€5 to €32) for Sunday performances at 9.15am (October to June) in the Burgkapelle (Royal Chapel; p67) in Hofburg should be booked around six weeks in advance (☎ 533 99 27; www.bmbwk.gv.at, in German). The choir also sings a mixed programme of music in the Musikverein (above; tickets €36 to €56) at 4pm on Friday in May, June, September and October. If you don't manage to obtain tickets, settle for a *Stehplatz* (standing-room space); simply show up by about 8.15pm for a spot (they give them out free – so if your legs get tired you can always leave early). In general, the only seats affording you an actual view of the choir are the most expensive ones – the boys are firmly esconced in the organ loft.

PALAIS PALFFY Map pp56-7

☎ 512 56 81; www.palais-palffy.at; 01, Josefsplatz 6; tickets €36-43; box office ⏲ 1hr before performances; Ⓤ U3 Herrengasse

Another Mozart and Strauss performance venue, this time in Palais Palffy's stunning baroque Figarosaal (Figaro Hall). Mozart himself performed here as a child in 1762, and although the music isn't of the same quality as that of the Philharmonic, it's lively and enthusiastic. Performances start at 8pm daily. It's also home to one of Vienna's most opulent clubs (see p187).

RAIMUND THEATER Map pp84-5

☎ 599 77; www.musicalvienna.at; 06, Wallgasse 18-20; tickets €10-109; box office ⏲ 10am-1pm & 2-6pm; Ⓤ U6 Gumpendorfer Strasse 🚋 6, 18

The Raimund Theater hosts big, Broadway-style musicals these days, but when it opened its doors in 1893 it produced only spoken dramas. With a seating capacity of more than 1000, obtaining a ticket won't be a problem. Standing-room tickets cost €5; students can pick up tickets for €11 30 minutes before performances.

RADIOKULTURHAUS Map pp84-5

☎ 501 70 377; www.radiokulturhaus.orf.at, in German; 04, Argentinierstrasse 30a; tickets €15-25; box office ⏲ 2pm until 30min before performances Mon-Fri, to 1hr before performances Sat & Sun; cafe ⏲ 9am-midnight Mon-Fri, per performance Sat & Sun; Ⓤ U1 Taubstummengasse 🚋 D

Expect anything from odes to Sinatra and R.E.M. or an evening dedicated to Beethoven and Mozart at the Radiokulturhaus. Housed in several performance venues including the Grosser Sendesaal – home to the Vienna Radio Symphony Orchestra (which hosts classical and modern music plus theatre productions) and the Klangtheater (used primarily for radio plays) – this is one of Vienna's cultural hot spots. The venue also presents dance, lectures, and literary readings as well as low-key performances in its cafe.

STAATSOPER Map pp56-7

☎ 514 44 22 50; www.wiener-staatsoper.at; 01, Opernring 2; tours adult/senior/child €5/4/2, tour plus Opera Museum Tue-Sun only €6.50/5.50/3.50, tickets €2-54; box office ⏲ 9am until 1hr before performances Mon-Fri, 9am-5pm Sat; Ⓤ U1, U2, U4 Karlsplatz 🚋 D, 1, 2 🚌 59A, 62

top picks

MOZART & STRAUSS

Mozart and Strauss may be long gone but they dominate the classical-music scene in Vienna. Absorb the timeless melodies at an unforgettable live performance – most venues are equally exquisite and only make the classics sound more extraordinary.

- **Wiener Residenzorchester** (p196)
- **Orangery** (opposite)
- **Kursalon** (opposite)
- **Hofburg Concert Halls** (p193)

The Staatsoper is *the* premiere opera and classical-music venue in Vienna. Built between 1861 and 1869 by August Siccardsburg and Eduard van der Nüll, it initially revolted the Viennese public and Habsburg royalty and quickly earned the nickname 'stone turtle'. Both architects took it the worst possible way: van der Nüll hanged himself and Siccardsburg died of a heart attack two months later. Neither saw the Staatsoper's first staged production. This shocked Franz Josef to such an extent that he kept his official comments from then on to: 'It was very nice. I enjoyed it very much.'

Despite the frosty reception, its opening concert was Mozart's *Don Giovanni* and it went on to house some of the most iconic directors in history, including Gustav Mahler (who later moved on to New York's Metropolitan Opera House), Richard Strauss and Herbert van Karajan.

Productions are lavish affairs; remember, the Viennese take their opera *very* seriously and dress up accordingly. In the interval, be sure to wander around the foyer and refreshment rooms to fully appreciate the gold and crystal interior. Opera is not performed here in July and August (tours, however, still take place), but its repertoire still includes more than 70 different productions.

Tickets can be purchased up to one month in advance. Standing-room tickets, which go for €3 to €4, can only be purchased 80 minutes before performances begin and any unsold tickets are available for €30 one day before a performance (call ☎ 514 44-2950 for more information). Tour information is available on ☎ 514 44-2606.

THEATER AN DER WIEN Map pp84-5

☎ 588 30 265; www.theater-wien.at; 06, Linke Wienzeile 6; tickets €12-160; box office 10am-7pm; U1, U2, U4 Karlsplatz D, 1, 2 59A, 62

The Theater an der Wien has hosted some monumental premiere performances, such as Beethoven's *Fidelo,* Mozart's *Die Zauberflöte* and Strauss Jnr's *Die Fledermaus*. These days the theatre is more attuned to popular culture and features musicals such as *Elisabeth* and *Mozart*. Discounts include €10 to €15 tickets for students on sale 30 minutes before shows, and €7 standing tickets available one hour before performances.

VOLKSOPER Map pp94-5

☎ 514 44 36 70; www.volksoper.at; 09, Währinger Strasse 78; tickets €5-80; box office 8am-6pm Mon-Fri, 9am-noon Sat & Sun; U6 Währinger Strasse-Volksoper 40, 41, 42

The Volksoper (People's Opera) specialises in operettas, dance performances, musicals and a handful of standard, heavier operas. Standing tickets go for €2 to €6 and, like many venues, there are a plethora of discounts and reduced tickets for sale 30 minutes before performances. It might come second place in comparison to the Staatsoper, but some feel the smaller space lends itself to a more intimate, and better, listening experience. The Volksoper closes for July and August.

WIENER RESIDENZORCHESTER Map pp94-5

☎ 817 21 78; www.wro.at; 08, Auerspergstrasse 1; tickets €39-54; performance 8.15pm daily Mar–early Jan, no box office – call or order tickets online; U2, U3 Volkstheater 1, 2, D, 49

The philosophy and mission of the Vienna Residence Orchestra – currently led by the esteemed pianist and conductor Paul Moser – is to present Viennese classics in their full glory and purest form. And its speciality? Wolfgang Amadeus Mozart and Johann Strauss, of course. Concerts are held at the opulent Auersperg palace, where between 15 and 30 musicians showcase their talents while dressed head to toe in rococo and Biedermeier costumes. The orchestra also occasionally plays at other venues in town, including the Börse Palais (see the boxed text, p75).

MOZART IN THE MAKING

Klangforum Wien (☎ 521 670; www.klangforum.at), an ensemble of 24 artists from nine countries, celebrates a unique collaboration between conductors, composers and interpreters who produce a wide range of musical styles, from improv to edgy jazz to classical notes. Many up-and-coming composers are represented here (more than 500 new pieces have premiered here since its opening in 1985), so don't be surprised if you are wowed with a sneak peak at the 'next best thing'. The Klangforum performs at various venues in the city – check the website for dates and details.

THEATRE & DANCE

The relationship between Vienna's theatre scene and that of other capitals is comparable to the independent film scene versus Hollywood blockbusters. That does not mean you won't find large, mainstream touring troupes in the city but, generally, the Viennese are far more interested in seeing smaller, one-of-a-kind productions. Sadly, options for non-German speakers are generally limited to two venues, International Theatre (opposite) and Vienna's English Theatre (opposite). While traditional dance is on offer at the city's large music and opera venues, contemporary dance dominates the scene – avant-garde performances and style are the norm.

BURGTHEATER Map pp56-7

☎ 514 44 41 40; www.burgtheater.at; 01, Dr-Karl-Lueger-Ring; tours adult/child €5.50/2, tickets €4-48; box office 8am-6pm Mon-Fri, 9am-noon Sat & Sun; D, 1, 2

The Burgtheater (National Theatre) is one of the prime theatre venues in the German-speaking world. Built in Renaissance style to designs by Gottfried Semper and Karl von Hasenauer, it had to be rebuilt after sustaining severe damage in WWII. The grand interior has stairway frescos painted by the Klimt brothers, Gustav and Ernst. Tours of the theatre are conducted daily at 3pm (September to June; English tours run Friday to Sunday only). The Burgtheater also runs the small theatre Kasino am Schwarzenbergplatz (Map pp56-7; 03, Schwarzenbergplatz 1; D, 1, 2 4a) theatre and the 500-seater Akademietheater (Map pp104-5; 03, Lisztstrasse 1; U4 Stadtpark 4A), which was built between 1911 and 1913.

Tickets at the Burgtheater and Akademietheater sell for 50% of their face-value an hour before performances, and students can purchase tickets for €7 half an hour before performances. Standing places are €1.50.

INTERNATIONAL THEATRE Map pp94-5

☎ 319 62 72; www.internationaltheatre.at; 09, Porzellangasse 8; tickets €20-25; box office ⏲ 11am-3pm Mon-Fri, 6-7.30pm on performance days; 🚊 D

The small International Theatre, with its entrance on Müllnergasse, has a mainly American company who live locally. Discounted tickets are available to students and senior citizens (€15). It closes around early July through to mid-September.

MARIONETTENTHEATER Map pp120-1

☎ 817 32 47; www.marionettentheater.at; 13, Schloss Schönbrunn; tickets full performances adult €10-33, child €7-22; box office ⏲ from 10am on performance days; Ⓤ U4 Schönbrunn 🚊 10, 58 🚌 10A

This small theatre in Schloss Schönbrunn puts on marionette performances of the much-loved productions *The Magic Flute* (2½ hours) and *Aladdin* (1¼ hours). They're a delight for kids young, old and in between; the puppet costumes are exceptionally ornate and eye-catching.

SCHAUSPIELHAUS Map pp94-5

☎ 317 01 01-18; www.schauspielhaus.at, in German; 09, Porzellangasse 19; tickets €18; box office ⏲ from 4pm Mon-Fri, from 6pm on performance days; 🚊 D

The Schauspielhaus pushes the boundaries of theatre in Vienna with unconventional productions. Whatever the theme, you can guarantee it will be contemporary and thought-provoking. The adjacent building also features readings by modern, cutting-edge writers (€6 to €9). Student tickets cost €9 and seniors' €12.

TANZQUARTIER WIEN Map pp84-5

☎ 581 35 91; www.tqw.at; 07, Museumsplatz 1; tickets €11-18; box office ⏲ 1hr before performances; Ⓤ U2 Museumsquartier, U2, U3 Volkstheater 🚌 2A

Tanzquartier Wien, located in the Museums-Quartier, is Vienna's first dance institution. It hosts an array of local and international performances with a strong experimental nature. Students receive advance tickets at 30% or €7 for unsold seats 15 minutes before showtime.

THEATER IN DER JOSEFSTADT Map pp94-5

☎ 427 00 300; www.josefstadt.org, in German; 08, Josefstädter Strasse 26; tickets €5-63; box office ⏲ 10am–performance time Mon-Fri, 1pm–performance time Sat & Sun; 🚊 2 🚌 13A

Theater in der Josefstadt is another theatre in the Volkstheater mould, with an ornate interior and traditional German productions. One hour before performances tickets are available to students and schoolchildren for €5; same-day standing-room tickets are available for €4 at 1pm for afternoon productions, and at 3pm for evening productions.

VIENNA'S ENGLISH THEATRE Map pp94-5

☎ 402 12 60-0; www.englishtheatre.at; 08, Josefsgasse 12; tickets €22-42; box office ⏲ 10am-7.30pm Mon-Fri, 5-7.30pm Sat when performances scheduled; Ⓤ U2 Rathaus 🚊 2 🚌 13A

Founded in 1963, Vienna's English Theatre is the oldest foreign-language theatre in Vienna (with the occasional show in French or Italian). Productions range from timeless pieces, such as Shakespeare, through to contemporary works. Students receive 20% discount on all tickets; standby tickets for €9 go on sale 15 minutes before showtime.

VOLKSTHEATER Map pp84-5

☎ 523 05 89-77; www.volkstheater.at, in German; 07, Neustiftgasse 1; tickets €8-45; box office ⏲ 10am–performance time Mon-Sat Sep-Jun, reduced hr late Jun–Aug; Ⓤ U2, U3 Volkstheater 🚊 1, 2, D, 49

With a seating capacity close to 1000, the Volkstheater is one of Vienna's largest theatres. Built in 1889, its interior is suitably grand. While most performances are translations (anything from Woody Allen to Ingmar Bergman to Molière), only German-language shows are produced. Unsold tickets go on sale one hour before performances start, for €3.60, but only to students. Be sure to grab a drink before or after the show at the Rote Bar (p190).

CINEMA

The Viennese love their *Kino* (cinema) and attend in droves. Both independent art-house films and Hollywood blockbusters are well patronised, and, unlike Austrian TV, where

THE VIENNALE

Vienna's annual international film festival, the Viennale, is the highlight of the city's celluloid calendar. By no means as prestigious as Cannes or Berlin, it still attracts top-quality films from all over the world and is geared to viewers rather than the filmmakers. For two weeks from mid-October city cinemas continuously play screenings that could broadly be described as fringe, ranging from documentaries to short and feature films. Tickets for the more popular screenings and most evening screenings can be hard to come by. Tickets can be bought two weeks before the festival starts from a number of stands around town. To get a jump on fellow festivalgoers, call ☎ 526 59 47 or check www.viennale.at.

99% of movies are dubbed in German, many cinema screenings are subtitled to retain as much of a film's original ambience as possible. The weekly *Falter* (www.falter.at, in German) and daily *Der Standard* (http://derstandard.at, in German) papers are the best sources for listings: *OF* or *OV* following a film title means it will screen in the original language; *OmU* indicates the film is in the original language with German subtitles; and *OmenglU* and *OmeU* signify that it's in the original language with English subtitles. Monday is known as *Kinomontag*, when all cinema seats go for around €7; a normal screening costs anything from €8 to €12.

ARTIS INTERNATIONAL Map pp56-7

☎ 535 65 70; www.cineplexx.at, in German; 01, Schultergasse 5; U1, U3 Stephansplatz; bus 1A, 2A, 3A

Artis has six small cinemas in the heart of the Innere Stadt. It only shows English-language films, of the Hollywood, blockbuster variety.

BREITENSEER LICHTSPIELE Map pp120-1

☎ 982 21 73; www.bsl.at.tf, in German; 14, Breitenseer Strasse 21; U3 Hütteldorfer Strasse; tram 10, 49

Pretend you've hopped back a century at this exceptional art nouveau cinema. Opened in 1909, it is the oldest cinema in Vienna and still retains its original wooden seats and the atmosphere of a bygone era. Films are usually in English with German subtitles; expect many alternative and independent films and occasional screenings of the classics.

BURG KINO Map pp56-7

☎ 587 84 06; www.burgkino.at; 01, Opernring 19; U1, U2, U4 Karlsplatz; tram D, 1, 2; bus 59A, 62

The Burg Kino is a central cinema that shows only English-language films. It has regular screenings of the *The Third Man* (see p140), Orson Welles' timeless classic set in post-WWII Vienna, at 10.55pm Friday, 4.30pm Sunday and 4.55pm Tuesday.

CINEMAGIC Map pp56-7

☎ 586 43 03; www.cinemagic.at, in German; 01, Friedrichstrasse 4; U1, U2, U4 Karlsplatz; tram D, 1, 2; bus 59A

An initiative of the City of Vienna aimed at entertainment for children, Cinemagic has an entire day programme totally devoted to the little 'uns. Films come from around the globe and screen Thursday through Sunday afternoons. In mid-November the cinema, along with three others, hosts a Children's Film Festival (www.kinderfilmfestival.at) showcasing international children's films. Evenings feature blockbusters and independent films geared to adults.

DE FRANCE Map pp56-7

☎ 317 52 36; www.defrance.at, in German; 01, Schottenring 5; U2 Schottentor; tram 37, 38, 40, 41, 42, 43, 44

De France screens films in their original language, with subtitles, in its two small cinemas. The schedule includes a healthy dose of English-language films. Every Saturday afternoon is 'Film & Wein' day, where you get a matinée and a quality glass of wine (usually an Austrian varietal) for €14.

ENGLISH CINEMA HAYDN Map pp84-5

☎ 587 22 62; www.haydnkino.at; 06, Mariahilfer Strasse 57; U3 Neubaugasse; bus 13A

The Haydn is a comfortable cinema screening mainly mainstream Hollywood-style films in their original language, in three separate screens.

FILMCASINO Map pp84-5

☎ 587 90 62; www.filmcasino.at, in German; 05, Margaretenstrasse 78; U4 Pilgramgasse; bus 13A, 59A

An art-house cinema of some distinction, Filmcasino screens an excellent mix of Asian and European docos and avant-garde

OPEN-AIR CINEMA

Open-air cinema is a growing phenomenon in Vienna. The city hosts at least seven such cinemas across town, the biggest of which is the Musikfilm Festival (p18), on Rathausplatz; Arena (p188) also hosts such a cinema in the summer months. Kino Unter Sternen (Cinema Under the Stars; Map pp112-13; ☎ 0800-664 040; www.kinountersternen.at, in German; 02, Augarten; 🚊 2 🚌 5A), a highly popular outdoor cinema (when the weather holds) in the shadow of one of Augarten's Flaktürme, shows films from mid-July to mid-August. The selection is an eclectic mix of classics, and films in English are often shown.

short films, along with independent feature-length films from around the world. Its '50s-style foyer is particularly impressive.

GARTENBAUKINO Map pp56-7

☎ 512 23 54; www.gartenbaukino.at, in German; 01, Parkring 12; Ⓤ U3 Stubentor, U4 Stadtpark 🚊 1, 2

Fortunately the interior of the Gartenbaukino has survived since the 1960s, making a trip to the flicks here all the more appealing. The actual cinema seats a whopping 750 people, and is often packed during Viennale screenings. Its regular screening schedule is full to overflowing with art-house films, normally with subtitles.

ÖSTERREICHISCHES FILMMUSEUM Map p66

☎ 533 70 54; www.filmmuseum.at; 01, Augustinerstrasse 1; 🕑 Sep-Jun; Ⓤ U1, U2, U4 Karlsplatz, U1, U3 Stephansplatz 🚊 D, 1, 2

After a much-needed overhaul that did away with the original arse-numbing seats, the Filmmuseum is now a pleasure to visit. The range of films on show is quite extensive; each month features a retrospective on a group of directors or a certain theme from around the world.

SCHIKANEDER Map pp84-5

☎ 585 28 67; www.schikaneder.at, in German; 04, Margaretenstrasse 24; 🚌 59A

Located next to the bar of the same name (see p179), Schikaneder is the darling of Vienna's alternative cinema scene. The film subject range is quite broad but also highly selective, and art-house through and through.

TOP KINO Map pp84-5

☎ 208 30 00; www.topkino.at, in German; 06, Rahlgasse 1; Ⓤ U2 Museumsquartier 🚌 57A

Part of the restaurant, club and bar arrangement Top Kino (p179), this cinema offers an ever-changing array of European films and documentaries, generally in their original language with German subtitles. Top Kino also holds a variety of themed film festivals throughout the year.

VOTIVKINO Map pp94-5

☎ 317 35 71; www.votivkino.at, in German; 09, Währinger Strasse 12; 🚊 37, 38, 40, 41, 42

Built in 1912, the Votiv is one of the oldest cinemas in Vienna. It's been extensively updated since then and is now among the best cinemas in the city. Its three screens feature a mix of Hollywood's more quirky ventures and art-house films in their original language. The 11am Tuesday screening is reserved for mothers, fathers and babies, and weekend afternoons feature special matinées for kids.

SPORTS & ACTIVITIES

top picks

What's your recommendation? www.lonelyplanet.com/vienna

SPORTS & ACTIVITIES

Being active and outdoors is in the Viennese blood, despite all the cigarettes they smoke. With much of the country given over to mountainous splendour, snow sports are hugely popular in Austria. Almost every Austrian has skied since they could be pushed down beginner slopes, and the average child will literally ski circles around most tourists. The best skiing is in the western reaches of the country, where most competitions are held, but Vienna has a couple of tiny slopes and a handful of mountains within a couple of hours' drive.

Those looking for fresh air and exercise won't come up short either. The old and new waterways of the Danube are literally made for swimming and boating, and the city is peppered with exceptional pools. Green parklands such as the Prater and the Donauinsel (Danube Island) and the Wienerwald (Vienna Woods) on the city's western fringes both provide plenty of space to stretch the legs, take a hike or walk and tool through on a city or mountain bike. After all that outdoor activity you might be tempted to hit a hammam – the city's best, Aux Gazelles (sessions from €28; open from noon to 10pm Monday to Saturday), has no fewer than three temperature zones and is located inside a space that doubles as a club (see p187).

Hiking in the immediate area around Vienna is a breeze – hop on a streetcar or a bus to an end stop, and start climbing up. The beauty of it all is that you'll probably stumble across a *Heuriger* (wine tavern) or three, a perfectly respectable end to a day of hiking and walking. Many of the routes are suited to casual hikers – and for those wishing to take it easy, you can always start at the top and make your way down.

While the Viennese aren't what you'd call sports-mad, the city does have its fair share of spectator-sports fanatics, particularly when it comes to football and skiing. Summer is pretty much a dead time for spectator sports, but with the arrival of autumn and winter, things heat up, so to speak. The Austrian National Football League, the Bundesliga, kicks off at the end of autumn and runs until the beginning of spring, with a break during the severe winter months. A local derby is quite an affair, and while the actual football isn't the most scintillating, the match certainly brings out the best and worst in fans.

Reviews in this chapter are grouped by type of sport or activity, and ordered alphabetically by business/venue name.

ACTIVITIES

Vienna is a superb city for outdoor activities. The Wienerwald to the west is criss-crossed with hiking and cycling trails, while the Donau, Alte Donau, Donauinsel and Lobau to the east provide ample opportunities for boating and swimming (plus cycling and in-line skating), and the city itself has hundreds of kilometres of designated cycle paths and is dotted with green parks, some big (the Prater), some small (Stadtpark).

The city's website, www.wien.gv.at, has a rundown of the main outdoor activities available in Vienna, as does *Sports & Nature in Vienna*, a brochure produced by the Vienna tourist board. It can also be downloaded from the website www.wien.info.

HIKING & WALKING

Hiking and walking are popular Viennese pastimes. The green belt of the Wienerwald (p126), on the western edge of Vienna, is particularly inviting for both walkers and cyclists, but the likes of the Prater (p110), with its small woods and lengthy trails, and the Lainzer Tiergarten animal reserve (p126), a wild park located in the west of Vienna, attract plenty of locals looking for fresh air and exercise. For a relaxed but invigorating walking tour see our Kahlenberg to Nussdorf walk (read: you start at the top and work your way downhill, see p136).

The Vienna Forestry Office maintains a number of local hiking paths, all of which are well signposted and accessible by public transport. Many include children's playgrounds, picnic tables and exceptional views en route, For a comprehensive list of more than 10 local hiking trails in and around the Greater Vienna area, including detailed route descriptions and printable maps, go to www.wien.gv.at/english and type 'hiking' in the search box.

ICE SKATING

Most Viennese have ice skates collecting dust at the back of the wardrobe that are dragged out at least once over winter. Along with specialised ice-skating rinks, a number of outdoor basketball courts are turned into rinks during winter. For as little as €1 you can spend the whole day gliding around one of these temporary rinks; 08, Buchfeldgasse 7a (Map pp94-5), 16, Gallitzinstrasse 4 (Map pp50-1) and 19, Osterleitengasse 14 (Map pp94-5). When it's cold enough, the Alte Donau is transformed into an ice-skater's paradise, with miles of natural ice.

WIENER EISLAUFVEREIN Map pp104-5

☎ 713 63 53; www.wev.or.at, in German; 03, Lothringerstrasse 22; adult/child €6.50/3, boot hire €5.50; 🕑 9am-8pm Sun-Mon, to 9pm Tue-Fri; U4 Stadtpark

At 6000 sq metres, the Wiener Eislaufverein is the world's largest open-air skating rink. It's close to the Ringstrasse and Stadtpark. Remember to bring mittens and a hat.

WIENER EISTRAUM Map pp56-7

☎ 409 00 40; www.wienereistraum.at; 01, Rathausplatz; adult/child from €4, boot hire €6.50/4; 🕑 9am-11pm daily late Jan–early Mar; U2 Rathaus D, 1

This is not your ordinary ice-skating rink: Rathausplatz is transformed into two connected ice rinks in the heart of winter. It's a bit of a mecca for the city's ice-skaters, and the rinks are complemented by food stands, special events and Glühwein (mulled wine) bars. The path zigzags through the nearby park and around the entire square and you boogie your way along to music from live DJs.

CYCLING

Vienna is easily handled by bicycle – over 800km of cycle tracks criss-cross the city, making it a breeze to avoid traffic, but not always pedestrians. Many one-way streets do not apply to cyclists; these are indicated by a bicycle sign with the word *ausgen* alongside it. The colour 'Capital Revealed' section in this book offers a cycle tour that takes you through Vienna's parklands and waterways (p138), while popular cycling areas include the 7km path around the Ringstrasse, the Donauinsel (Danube Island), the Prater and along the Donaukanal (Danube Canal).

All the bike-hire places listed here offer significant information and local tips about where to cycle, including maps.

COPA CAGRANA RAD UND SKATERVERLEIH Map pp112-13

☎ 263 52 42; www.fahrradverleih.at, in German; 22, Am Kaisermühlendamm 1; per hr/half-/full day from €5/15/25; 🕑 9am-6pm Mar & Oct, 9am-8pm Apr & Sep, 9am-9pm May-Aug; U1 Kaisermühlen

All manner of bikes are on offer here – city, mountain, trekking, tandem, kids, and more. Also has rollerblades for hire (from €6 per hour).

PEDAL POWER Map pp112-13

☎ 729 72 34; www.pedalpower.at; 02, Ausstellungsstrasse 3; per hr/half-/full day €5/24/32; 🕑 8am-7pm Apr-Oct; U1, U2 Praterstern

City and mountain bikes dominate here – you can pick them up at the office or, for an extra €4, arrange for the two wheels to be conveniently dropped off and picked up at your hotel. Pedal Power also offers 'City Segway' tours of the city; see p237 for more information. Child seats and helmets are €4 extra a piece.

VIENNA CITY BIKE

☎ 0810 500 500; www.citybikewien.at, in German; 1st/2nd/3rd hr free/€1/2, 4th hr & above €4

Everywhere you go in Vienna you'll encounter stands with bicycles provided by the City of Vienna to promote cycling in the city; currently more than 60 of these bike stands are scattered throughout the city. A credit card is required to hire bikes; just swipe your card in the machine and follow the instructions (in a number of languages). Keep in mind that these bikes are mainly for use as an alternative to transport (they can only be locked up at a bike station, unless you have your own bike chain, of course). A lost bike will set you back €600.

CLIMBING

In general, most quality outdoor climbing occurs outside the Vienna area in the famed Austrian Alps, but Vienna does have an unusual climbing tower (an old WWII relic) in the centre of the city – ideal for practising your technique.

KLETTERANLAGE FLAKTURM
Map pp84-5

☎ 585 47 48; 06, Esterházypark; climbing/bouldering per 2hr €9/5; 2pm-dusk Mon-Fri, 1pm-dusk Sat & Sun Apr-Oct; U3 Neubaugasse 13A, 14A

The stark outside walls of the *Flakturm* (flak tower) in Esterházypark are used for climbing exercises organised by the Österreichischer Alpenverein (Austrian Alpine Club). Twenty routes (gradients four to eight) climb to a maximum height of 34m.

SWIMMING

Swimming is easily the favoured summer pastime of the Viennese. The Donauinsel, Alte Donau and Lobau are often swamped with citizens eager to cool off on steamy hot summer days. Topless sunbathing is quite the norm, as is nude sunbathing, but only in designated areas; much of Lobau and both tips of the Donauinsel are FKK (*Freikörperkultur;* free body culture/naked) areas.

Alongside the natural swimming areas are a large number of swimming pools owned and run by the city which are open from early May to the beginning of September as follows: 9am to 9.30pm Monday and Friday, to 6pm Tuesday, 7am to 9.30pm Thursday, to 8pm Saturday, to 6pm Sunday. On Monday they are open from 12.30pm to 3pm for seniors and people with disabilities only. Entry, including locker rental, costs €4.70/2.60 per adult/child. Amalienbad, Krapfenwaldbad, Strandbad Alte Donau, and Strandbad Gänsehäufel all fall within this category. For a full list of pools, call ☎ 601 12 80 44 between 7.30am and 3.30pm Monday to Friday, or log on to www.wien.at/baeder.

AMALIENBAD Map pp50-1

☎ 607 47 47; 10, Reumannplatz 23; U1 Reumannplatz

This stunning *Jugendstil* (art nouveau) bath-house with stunning mosaics and columns has a range of facilities, including a solarium, steam room, massage, cosmetic treatments and a restaurant. There are separate saunas for men and women, and a unisex one.

BADESCHIFF Map pp56-7

☎ 513 07 49; www.badeschiff.at, in German; 01, Danube Canal; adult/child €5/2.50 10am-midnight May-Oct; U1, U4 Schwedenplatz

Swim on but not in the Danube. Floating smack on the bank of the Danube, between Schwedenplatz and Urania, this pool doubles as a bar at night (in winter the pool is enclosed and becomes a bar only). Multiple decks are covered with lounge chairs, cocktail and snack bars abound and the location is supreme for swimming, chillin' to tunes with an afternoon tipple and gazing out at the river.

KRAPFENWALDBAD Map pp50-1

☎ 320 15 01; 19, Krapfenwaldgasse 65-73; 38A

With its elevated position among vineyards on the edge of the Wienerwald, Krapfenwaldbad has the best views of the city. Many who frequent the baths aren't too interested in the cityscape (or the two small pools), however, but rather their fellow bathers. Even though there are plenty of grassy areas, it's often full to overflowing.

STRANDBAD ALTE DONAU Map pp112-13

☎ 263 65 38; 22, Arbeiterstrandbadstrasse 91; U1 Alte Donau 91A

This bathing area makes great use of the Alte Donau during the summer months. It's a favourite of the working class and gets extremely crowded at weekends during summer. Facilities include a restaurant, beach-volleyball court, playing field, slides and plenty of tree shade.

STRANDBAD GÄNSEHÄUFEL
Map pp112-13

☎ 269 90 16; 22, Moissigasse 21; 90A, 91A, 92A

Gänsehäufel occupies half an island in the Alte Donau. It does get crowded in summer, but there's normally enough space to escape the mob. There's a swimming pool and FKK (read: nudist) area.

THERMALBAD OBERLAA Map pp50-1

☎ 680 09 96 00; www.thermewienmed.at, in German; 10, Kurbadstrasse 14; 67

At press time, these thermal baths were closed, due to reopen in autumn 2010 as Europe's largest thermal spa resort in an urban area, featuring a 75,000-sq-metre resort and an expanded pool area (almost doubled, to 3800 sq metres).

BOATING

The Alte Donau is the main boating and sailing centre in Vienna, but the Neue Donau, a long stretch of water separated from the Danube by the Donauinsel, also provides opportunities for boating, windsurfing and waterskiing.

SAILING SCHOOL HOFBAUER

Map pp112-13

☎ 204 34 35; www.hofbauer.at, in German; 22, An der Obere Alte Donau 191; Apr-Oct; U1 Alte Donau

Hofbauer rents sailing boats (from €13.80 per hour) and row boats (€7.80 per hour) on the eastern bank of the Alte Donau and can provide lessons (in English) for those wishing to learn or brush up on their skills. Pedal boats (€11 per hour) are also available for hire.

INLINE SKATING

With wide, smooth tar-sealed paths, the Donauinsel and Prater are just made for inline skating. Skates can be hired from a number of places on the island, particularly around the Copa Cagrana area. If you'd like to hook up with like-minded skaters, roll along to Heldenplatz at 9pm on Friday from May to September and join the Friday Night Skating (wien .gruene.at/skater) team on a tour of the city. Participation is free.

SKIING

Yes, there is skiing in Vienna. Only a handful of places offer skiing within the city limits, but if you've come this far and want to go skiing you're much better off heading west and taking advantage of Austria's stunning Alps.

SKIANLAGE DOLLWIESE Map pp50-1

☎ 812 12 01; 13, Ghelengasse 44; 10 lift rides €4; noon-dusk Mon-Fri, 10am-dusk Sat & Sun Dec-Mar; 54B, 55B

Edging up to the Lainzer Tiergarten is Dollwiese, reputedly one of Austria's oldest ski slopes. At only 400m long, it's quite short but it is perfectly sufficient for beginners.

SKIANLAGE HOHE WAND Map pp50-1

☎ 979 10 57; 14, Mauerbachstrasse 172-174; day pass adult/child €13/6; 9am-9pm daily Dec-Mar; U4 Wien Hütteldorf 249, 250

The Hohe Wand ski slopes can be used only when there is enough natural snow on the ground to bond with daily layerings of artificial snow. It's in the Wienerwald and offers rides down the Rodelbahn (like a bobsled on wheels/on a track: adult/child €8/5 per ride).

SPECTATOR SPORTS

The only spectator sport of note to gain regular – albeit small – audiences is football (see below). The Stadthalle (p190) is a major player in hosting sporting events. Tennis tournaments (including the Austrian Open), horse shows and ice-hockey games are just some of the diverse events held here. The swimming pool is a major venue for aquatic events like races, water polo and synchronised swimming.

FOOTBALL

Vienna is home to two of the Bundesliga's bigger teams, Rapid Vienna and Austria Magma, whose rivalry is similar to England's Arsenal and Tottenham Hotspur. It may be hard to purchase a ticket for the local derby, but at any other time it won't be a problem.

ERNST-HAPPEL-STADION Map pp50-1

☎ 728 08 54; 02, Meiereistrasse 7; U2 Stadion

With a seating capacity nearing 50,000, the Ernst-Happel stadium near the Prater is the largest sporting venue in Vienna and is the preferred venue for international games.

HORR-STADION Map pp50-1

☎ 688 01 50; www.fk-austria.at; 10, Fischhofgasse 12; 67 15A

This stadium, seating nearly 12,000 fans, is the home ground of Austria Magma, arch rival of Rapid Vienna.

RAPID VIENNA GERHARD-HANAPPI-STADION Map pp50-1

☎ 914 55 19; www.skrapid.at; 14, Keisslergasse 6; U4 Wien Hütteldorf 49

Hanappi stadium is the home ground for Rapid Vienna, the city's team of the working class. Of Vienna's two national league teams, Rapid has been the more successful internationally, fighting its way through to the European Cup finals on two occasions.

HORSE RACING

Spend a few hours relaxing at the races with Viennese of all ages, backgrounds and walks of life.

FREUDENAU Map pp50-1

☎ 728 95 31; www.freudenau.at, in German; 02, Rennbahnstrasse 65; Mar-Nov; 77A

In the southern extremes of the Prater is Freudenau, Vienna's premier horse-racing track and one of Europe's oldest.

KRIEAU Map pp112-13

☎ 728 00 46; www.krieau.at, in German; 02, Nordportalstrasse 247; U4 Krieau 83B, 84B

Sidling up to the Ernst-Happel-Stadion in the Prater is Krieau, the track where Vienna's trotting meets (tickets from €5) are held. It's normally only open on Saturday afternoons from September to June; an open-air cinema operates here in July and August (see p199).

SLEEPING

top picks

- **Boutiquehotel Stadthalle** (p215)
- **Pension Hargita** (p213)
- **Belvedere Appartements** (p214)
- **Hotel Rathaus Wein & Design** (p213)
- **All You Need Vienna 2** (p215)
- **Landhaus Fuhrgassl-Huber** (boxed text, p216)
- **Hotel Kärntnerhof** (p210)

SLEEPING

From palatial abodes to swanky minimalism, from youth hostels to luxury establishments where chandeliers, antique furniture and original 19th-century oil paintings are the norm rather than the exception, Vienna's lodgings cover it all. In between are homely *Pensionen* (B&Bs) and less ostentatious hotels, plus a small but smart range of apartments, many of which can be rented for just a few nights.

Standards remain high, and generally so do prices; bargains are few and far between. As a rule, budget doubles are available for under €80 a night, midrange from €80 to €200, and top end anything above that (and the sky's the limit in this city). Breakfast – normally a continental buffet – is invariably included in the price, but parking isn't (you'll pay anything between €6 and €30 per 24 hours for parking).

Central Vienna is the priciest and most popular area to stay in but you can walk to many of the major attractions and the most popular (read: also the most touristy) restaurants and coffee houses; there's also a smattering of nightlife options here. While the convenience of central Vienna is undisputed, take note that in high summer season, this area is clogged with visitors, so unless you avoid the main arteries you'll frequently be wading through the masses. For those wishing to stay close to the main sights but seeking something a touch more affordable with plenty of nightlife, Vorstadt Southwest is your best bet: you'll never be far from bohemian and trendy bars and excellent restaurants (from casual to upmarket), plus it's home to the foodie destination of choice, the Naschmarkt. Another affordable option close to the centre is Vorstadt Northwest, a quiet area with a handful of mainly upmarket restaurants in its core, with many Gürtel bars in its western section.

Beyond the core lodging areas, Vorstadt Landstrasse offers little in the way of sights beyond the Belvedere but it's a quiet neighbourhood well connected by tram and subway to the nightlife action and major sights. East of the Danube Canal is an excellent choice – public transport swiftly whisks you to the main sights, you're close to some of the most up-and-coming alternative bars, restaurants and nightlife options, and in the summer you're only a hop from the Danube and its adjacent green spaces. Southwest and the Gürtel is residential and light on sights – you'll be close to Schönbrunn but little else, with the exception of the northwestern fringe (home to the multicultural Brunnenmarkt).

Central Vienna is first to fill up, so book well ahead if you're keen to be around the corner from many major sights. Rooms in districts one to nine are the next to go, with the outer districts (Greater Vienna) mopping up the leftovers. If you arrive without accommodation, head to Tourist Info Wien (p238), which books rooms for a small fee.

Accommodation listings in this chapter are grouped by neighbourhood, and ordered by budget (from most expensive to least expensive). The average price for a double room in the Innere Stadt is around €175, but there are cheaper rooms in the surrounding districts. Peak season is June to September, Christmas, New Year and Easter; expect high prices and a lack of availability at popular times. Over winter, rates can drop substantially and many places offer discounts and specials for longer stays. Some, especially the five-star hotels, offer special weekend rates, or 'two nights for the price of one' packages. It's definitely worth inquiring about cheaper rates before signing on the dotted line. Prices quoted in this chapter are high-season summer rates.

Note that reservations are binding; compensation may be claimed by the hotel if you do not take a reserved room, or by you if the room you booked is unavailable.

ACCOMMODATION STYLES

Hotels & Pensionen

As hotels and *Pensionen* make up the bulk of accommodation options in Vienna, huge variations in style and taste exist. Leaving aside the city's luxury hotels, which are in a league of their own, hotels tend to be larger than *Pensionen*, have more facilities (on-site parking, bars and restaurants) and come with more extras (room service, laundry service and the like). *Pensionen* are often located in apartment blocks, and can be far more personable and less standardised, with larger rooms. Prices start at around €60 to €70 for a basic double room with shared bathroom, and top out at approximately €250 to €350 for an upmarket en suite double in a four-star hotel. On average, expect to pay €120 to €160 for a decent double room in a hotel or *Pension*.

Note that many of the older hotels and *Pensionen* have a range of rooms and facilities, the cheapest of which share a toilet and shower with other guests.

Hostels & Student Residences

Vienna has a smattering of *Jugendherberge*, private hostels or hostels affiliated with Hostelling International (HI). In the former, no membership is required. Dorm beds, singles and doubles are generally available in both; expect to pay around €18 for a dorm bed and €25 to €35 for a double room in high season.

Austria has two HI-affiliated youth-hostel organisations: Österreichischer Jugendherbergsverband (ÖJHN; off Map pp56-7; ☎ 533 53 53; www.oejhv.or.at; 01, Schottenring 28; 11am-5pm Mon-Fri, 11am-3pm Sat Sep-Apr; U2, U4 Schottenring 1, 2) and Österreichischer Jugendherbergswerk (ÖJHW; off Map pp84-5; ☎ 533 51 37; www.jungehotels.at; 07, Mariahilfer Strasse 22-24; 9.30am-6pm Mon-Fri; U2 Museumsquartier). Either can provide information on all of Vienna's HI hostels.

Longer-Term Rentals

Viennese looking for apartments rely on word of mouth or turn to *Bazar* magazine (www.bazar.at). It's *the* magazine if you're looking to buy, sell or rent anything, including apartments or rooms. Students are also partial to the classified ad website www.jobwohnen.at, which lists many short-term sublets, particularly when students have school holidays (such as February and over the summer). The time scale of places on offer may range from indefinite rental to occupation of a flat for a month or so while the resident is on holiday. *Falter*, *Kurier* and *Standard* also carry accommodation ads.

A couple of short-term apartment rentals are listed in this chapter.

CENTRAL VIENNA

Central Vienna – or the Innere Stadt – is the capital's prime accommodation location, with an excellent selection of sights, restaurants, bars and music venues. Comparatively, prices here tend to outdo those in the rest of Vienna, and reservations are well advised. The upside is that you can walk to most of the major landmarks; in summer, the downside is that you'll be stumbling over all the other visitors doing the same. The Innere Stadt may have some beautiful hotels, but the Ringstrasse outguns it with the big boys in town – it's home to the Imperial and the Bristol. Luxury is the mainstay here, where 'If you have to ask, you can't afford it' truly applies.

PRICE GUIDE

Each sleeping option has been given a price ranking, indicating the room price at double occupancy.

€€€	over €200 a night
€€	€80-200 a night
€	under €80 a night

HOTEL SACHER Map pp56-7 Hotel €€€

☎ 514 56-0; www.sacher.com; 01, Philharmonikerstrasse 4; d from €375; U1, U2, U4 Karlsplatz D, 1, 2 59A, 62;

Walking into the Sacher is like turning back the clocks 100 years. The reception, with its dark-wood panelling, deep red shades and heavy gold chandelier, is reminiscent of an expensive fin de siècle bordello. The smallest rooms are surprisingly large, with beds the size of small ships; suites are truly palatial and everything has received a recent upgrade. All boast baroque furnishings and genuine 19th-century oil paintings (the hotel has the largest private oil painting collection in Austria) and your arrival is sweet: a tiny cube of the hotel's famous *Sacher Torte* in each room greets you upon arrival. The top floor is a hi-tech spa complex, with herbal sauna, ice fountain and fitness room.

HOTEL IMPERIAL Map pp56-7 Hotel €€€

☎ 501 10-333; www.luxurycollection.com/imperial; 01, Kärntner Ring 16; r from €350; U1, U2, U4 Karlsplatz D, 1, 2 59A, 62;

A mere mention of the Imperial makes most Viennese nod in awe and respect. This former palace, with all the glory and majesty of the Habsburg era, gives any respectable classical museum a run for its money. The Fürsten Stiege, cloaked in rich red carpet, is a flamboyant opening, leading from the reception to the Royal suite. Suites are filled with 19th-century paintings and genuine antique furniture (and come with butler service), while 4th- and 5th-floor rooms in Biedermeier style are far cosier and may come with balcony.

HOTEL AM STEPHANSPLATZ

Map pp56-7 Hotel €€€

☎ 534 05-0; www.hotelamstephansplatz.at; 01, Stephansplatz 9; s/d from €170/220; U1, U3 Stephansplatz;

You'd think you couldn't beat the view – it overlooks the Gothic spires of Stephansdom – yet its interior almost tops its location. Plus the entire structure is a model of ecofriendly design – all building materials used, right down to the glue, were subject to environmental restrictions. Even the breakfast is a compilation of organic produce. Rooms are filled with modern furniture and warmed with earthy colours, while the bedding is a treat – thick, snug and uber-skin-friendly. Room 702, a rooftop suite with balcony views across to the hallowed doors of Stephansdom, steals the show.

KÖNIG VON UNGARN

Map pp56-7 Hotel €€€

☎ 515 84-0; www.kvu.at; 01, Schulerstrasse 10; s/d €150/219; U1, U3 Stephansplatz;

The oldest hotel in Vienna (1746) balances class and informality with a wonderful inner courtyard (its pyramid skylight, wood panelling and leather furniture will easily impress) and excellent service. Little acts of decadence, such as gold-plated, free-standing ashtrays, are everywhere (even in the lift). Rooms are individually furnished with antiques and range in style from rather plain to downright extravagant: the best face Domgasse.

APPARTEMENTS RIEMERGASSE

Map pp56-7 Apartments €€

☎ 512 72 20; www.riemergasse.at; 01, Riemergasse 8; apt per night from €155; U3 Stubentor 1, 2;

Riemergasse is an excellent option for travellers requiring a few home comforts while they're away. Studios are a little poky but include a kitchenette, while larger apartments are quite sizeable and come with full cooking facilities; fittings in all apartments are more modern than most Viennese enjoy. Views from some of the top-floor apartments catch the spire of Stephansdom, and all rooms have a smooth, modern feel. Breakfast is available for an extra €8.

AVIANO

Map pp56-7 Pension €€

☎ 512 83 30; www.secrethomes.at; 01, Marco-d'Aviano-Gasse 1; s/d €104/148; U1, U3 Stephansplatz;

Aviano earns its points for a supremely central position, high standards and all-round value for money. Rooms are small without being claustrophobic and feature high ceilings, decorative moulding and whitewashed antique furnishings; corner rooms have a charming alcove overlooking Vienna's main pedestrian street. The breakfast room is sunny and bright, and in summer utilises a small balcony on the inner courtyard. Its sister hotel in Josefstadt, the Baronesse (Map pp56-7; ☎ 405 10 61; 08, Lange Gasse 61; 1, 2;), offers the same ambience at slightly lower prices.

HOTEL KÄRTNERHOF

Map pp56-7 Hotel €€

☎ 512 19 23; www.karntnerhof.com; 01, Grashofgasse 4; s/d from €95/140; U1, U3 Stephansplatz;

Tucked away from the bustle down a side street, this tall treasure fuses old Vienna charm with cosy ambience, from the period paintings lining the walls to the wood- and frosted glass–panelled lift to the surprising roof terrace. Rooms mix a few plain pieces with antiques, chandeliers and elegant curtains, but all exude warmth and charm. With Stephansplatz less than five minutes away, this place is a steal.

HOLMANN BELETAGE

Map pp56-7 Pension €€

☎ 961 19 60; www.hollmann-beletage.at; 01, Köllnerhofgasse 6; r from €140; U1, U4 Schwedenplatz 1, 2;

A minimalist establishment of sorts, Holmann Beletage is a *Pension* for guests with an eye for style and a penchant for clean lines. Rooms are slick units, with natural wood floors, bare walls, simple, classic furniture and designer lamps and door handles. Space is utilised to the max; bathrooms and cupboards are cleverly hidden behind tall double doors, creating a Tardis-like effect. Beyond is a garden terrace and a home cinema screening Vienna-focused films three times per day.

HOTEL AM SCHUBERTRING

Map pp56-7 Hotel €€

☎ 717 02-0; www.schubertring.at; 01, Schubertring 11; s/d from €99/128; Ⓤ U4 Stadtpark 🚊 1, 2; 📶

Of the highly sought-after hotels on the Ringstrasse, Hotel am Schubertring is the only option available to the average joe. Rooms are either Biedermeier or art nouveau; the former are characterised by floral designs and graceful lines and may look disturbingly similar to your granny's flat, while the latter are more dynamic, with flowing lines and little flourishes. All rooms are in very good condition. Staff are friendly while keeping a healthy professional distance and the hotel spreads itself across the upper floors of two buildings.

PENSION NOSSEK

Map pp56-7 Pension €€

☎ 533 70 41-0; www.pension-nossek.at, in German; 01, Graben 17; s/d from €65/120; Ⓤ U1, U3 Stephansplatz; 📶

When it comes to real estate, it's all about location, location, location. And with a front door facing the Graben, and Stephansdom within sight, Nossek has oodles of all three. Service is professional, polite, a little stiff but typically Viennese; rooms are spotless, highly adequate, generally spacious and enhanced with baroque-style furnishings; views are of either the pedestrian street below or the quiet inner courtyard. Note that the hotel does not accept credit cards.

PENSION PERTSCHY

Map pp56-7 Pension €€

☎ 534 49-0; www.pertschy.com; 01, Habsburgergasse 5; s/d from €79/119; Ⓤ U1, U3 Stephansplatz; 📶

It's hard to find fault with Pension Pertschy. Its quiet yet central location, just off the Graben, is hard to beat, staff are exceedingly able, willing and friendly, and children are welcomed with gusto (toys for toddlers and high chairs for tots are available). Rooms are not only spacious but filled with a potpourri of period pieces and a rainbow of colours; you'll find one bedecked in subtle hues of pink while its neighbour is awash in yellow. A little gem in the Innere Stadt.

BENEDIKTUSHAUS

Map pp56-7 Guesthouse €€

☎ 534 98 90 0; www.benediktushaus.at; 01, Freyung 6a; s/d €66/99; Ⓤ U2 Schottentor 🚊 1, D, 37, 38, 41, 42, 43, 44; 📶

Rest your weary head in a Benedictine monastery – you'd never guess you're in the heart of the action when you peer out your window into the tranquil, tree-filled courtyard. It's run by the Scottish Abbey next door and the tidy rooms are solid and frill-free, though a few period antiques line the halls. Note that there are no TVs in the rooms and internet is only available on the reception level.

top picks

LUXURY HOTELS

- **Radisson SAS Palais** (Map pp56-7; ☎ 515 17-0; www.radissonsas.com; 01, Parkring 16; r from €240) A combination of two former fin de siècle palaces.
- **Hotel Bristol** (Map pp56-7; ☎ 515 160; www.westin.com/bristol; 01, Kärtner Ring 1; r from €375) Old-world extravagance and state-of-the-art amenities.
- **Hotel Hilton** (Map pp104-5; ☎ 71 700-00; www.hilton.com; 03, Am Stadtpark 3; s/d €220/280) Top business hotel with luxury and flair.
- **Hotel Imperial** (see p209) When royalty visit Vienna, this is where they stay.
- **Hotel Sacher** (see p209) A baroque gem with modern conveniences.

PENSION RIEDL

Map pp56-7 Pension €€

☎ 512 77 79; www.pensionriedl.at; 01, Georg-Coch-Platz 3; s/d from €65/90; 🚊 1, 2; 📶

A traditional *Pension* on the fringes of the Innere Stadt, this warm and welcome stalwart consistently impresses. Rooms are generally large and bedecked with mismatched furniture (bathrooms are on the small side); Nos 6 and 7 have tiny balconies overlooking Georg-Coch-Platz (and Otto Wagner's celebrated Postsparkasse), while the balcony in No 8 enjoys the peace of the inner courtyard.

PENSION AM OPERNECK

Map pp56-7 Pension €€

☎ 512 93 10; 01 Kärntner Strasse 47; s/d €65/80; Ⓤ U1, U2, U4 Karlsplatz 🚊 D, 1, 2 🚌 59A, 62; 📶

It's hard to beat Pension am Operneck on two very important points: location and price. Directly across from the famous Hotel Sacher, its front doors open out onto Kärntner Strasse, the busiest street in the city. Its rooms are similar to its owner – fading after years of use but still going strong and easily making guests feel comfortable and at home. As there are only six rooms (all of which are quite large), it's essential to book well ahead.

SCHWEIZER PENSION Map pp56-7 Pension €

☎ 533 81 56; www.schweizerpension.com; 01, Heinrichsgasse 2; s/d from €48/65; 1, 2;

Rooms at this pleasant little *Pension* are super clean and, while not flushed with the most up-to-date amenities, everything you find inside – from big, comfy beds to ornamental ceramic stoves – has a cosy, homely feel to it. The feeling of wellbeing extends; Schweizer uses energy-saving light bulbs, equips rooms with wind-up clocks and serves bio-breakfasts. As it's one of the cheapest options in the city centre, the 11 rooms fill up quickly, so book ahead. Wi-fi is only available in the common areas.

VORSTADT SOUTHWEST

This is one of the best-value options in the capital; places in this neighbourhood are close enough to the city centre, yet prices here drop by an average of €20 to €30 simply because they aren't enclosed within the Ringstrasse. Transport is easy and nightlife and food options are plentiful – and less touristy – than those in Central Vienna.

DAS TRIEST Map pp84-5 Hotel €€€

☎ 589 18-0; www.dastriest.at; 04, Wiedner Hauptstrasse 12; s/d €224/289; 62, 65;

This Sir Terence Conran creation is a symbiosis of history and modern design. The 300-year-old building (former stables) is cutting-edge, with an overall nautical theme; portholes replace spyholes and windows, and stairwell railings would be just as at home on the *Queen Mary 2*. Rooms are stylish in their simplicity and bathed in pastel warmth, while little touches such as fresh flowers and folded toilet rolls polish the scene off. Staff are professional but informal.

ALTSTADT Map pp84-5 Pension €€€

☎ 522 66 66; www.altstadt.at; 07, Kirchengasse 41; s/d from €149/249; 13A, 48A;

Altstadt is arguably the finest *Pension* in Vienna. Each room is individually decorated, but all are charming, tasteful, quirky, arty and welcoming (without being overcooked), with the right consistency of art, practicality, comfort and, above all, warmth. Add to this brew high ceilings, plenty of space and natural light, and a cosy lounge with free afternoon tea and cakes. Staff are genuinely affable, artwork is from the owner's personal collection and at press time a hopping bar was being built on the ground floor below the Pension.

DAS TYROL Map pp84-5 Hotel €€

☎ 587 54 15; www.das-tyrol.at; 06, Mariahilfer Strasse 15; s/d from €109/149; U2 Museumsquartier;

Das Tyrol ranks among the top design hotels in the city. Each floor is devoted to a theme (one floor is humorously dedicated to Donald Duck and his love, Daisy; another gives an ode to modern art, with splashes of colour everywhere). The cosy rooms are a subdued mix of greens and yellows and spacious enough to fit a small couch and desk, while bathrooms are a spotless combination of white-and-black tiling. Try for one of the corner rooms, which enjoy a small balcony overlooking busy Mariahilfer Strasse. Breakfast, served with champagne, will keep you going for most of the day.

HOTEL FÜRSTENHOF Map pp84-5 Hotel €€

☎ 523 32 67; www.hotel-fuerstenhof.com; 07, Neubaugürtel 4; s/d from €70/120; U3, U6 Westbahnhof 5, 9, 52, 58;

This family-run affair overflowing with personality has been the choice of touring alternative bands (see the reception for proof) and knowledgeable visitors for years – don't be surprised if you encounter a burgeoning rock star in the reception-lounge, which doubles as a library (oodles of used books to peruse). Rooms are basic, with blood-red carpets, full-length curtains and deep colours creating a warm feel, and simple yet highly functional furniture. The house dates from 1906, so ceilings are higher than normal and the lift is a museum piece (thankfully, the motor isn't).

PENSION CARANTANIA Map pp84-5 Pension €€

☎ 526 73 40; www.carantania.at; 07, Kandlgasse 35; s/d €75/105; U6 Burggasse Stadthalle

Carantania, a tiny, family-run *Pension* of only six rooms, exudes warmth and cosiness in its sizeable rooms: all are flooded with natural light and filled with a hotchpotch of furniture – some of which looks antique, some of which could do with refurbishing – while bathrooms are the only modern corner of the *Pension*. The reception area is pleasantly cluttered with plants, brochures and books, and the breakfast room is big enough for a banquet.

HOTEL DREI KRONEN Map pp84-5 Pension €€

☎ 587 32 89; www.hotel3kronen.at; 04, Schleifmühlgasse 25; s/d €79/100; 59A;

Within stumbling distance of the Naschmarkt (some rooms overlook it), this family-owned abode is one of Vienna's best-kept secrets on the lodging scene. Tiny palatial touches (shiny marble, polished brass, white-and-gold wallpaper) are distinctly Viennese, but nonetheless a casual feel prevails. Rooms are fitted with *Jugendstil* (art nouveau) furniture and art (including many prints by Klimt). The breakfast buffet is gargantuan and includes free *Sekt* (sparkling wine), an unheard-of luxury in a three-star Pension.

PENSION KRAML Map pp84-5 Pension €

☎ 587 85 88; www.pensionkraml.at; 06, Brauergasse 5; s/d from €35/76, apt from €99; U4 Pilgramgasse 13A, 57A;

A cosy *Pension* in a quiet neighbourhood, Kraml is family-run and from the 'Old-Skool' of hospitality, where politeness is paramount and the comfort of guests a top priority. Rooms are surprisingly large, accommodating twin beds, bedside tables and a solid wardrobe, while leaving plenty of room for a close waltz. Furniture and fittings, including those in the bathroom, are a little dated but by no means past their use-by dates. Internet is only available in the common areas.

PENSION HARGITA Map pp84-5 Pension €

☎ 526 19 28; www.hargita.at; 07, Andreasgasse 1; s/d from €57/68; U3 Zieglergasse;

Ignore the bland exterior – one step into the wood-panelled lobby and you'll think you've entered a mountain chalet. Named after the Hargita region in the Carpathians, this (Hungarian-Austrian) family-operated space is tasteful simplicity: fresh, crisp blues and whites with tiny touches like delicate paper flowers placed in sweet, tiny vases make each room homely, and Hungarian plates hanging on walls in the breakfast room lend a slight country feel.

> **DESIGN HOTELS**
>
> In a city noted for its architecture, it's no surprise that Vienna boasts a fine collection of design hotels, the pick of which are listed here:
>
> Das Triest (p212) The hotel that planted the design hotel seed in Vienna.
>
> Das Tyrol (p212) A lovely combination of art, comfort and champagne.
>
> DO & CO (Map pp56-7; ☎ 241 88; www.doco.com; 01, Stephansplatz 12; r from €310) Swanky and sexy, with views of Stephansdom.
>
> Style Hotel (Map pp56-7; ☎ 122 780; www.stylehotel.at; 01, Herrengasse 12; r from €250) Top contender for the title 'most fashionable hotel address' in Vienna, with overtones of art nouveau and art deco.
>
> Roomz (p214) *The* design hotel for budget-conscious stylistas.

WESTEND CITY HOSTEL

Map pp84-5 Hostel €

☎ 597 67 29; www.westendhostel.at; 06, Fügergasse 3; dm from €20.50, s/d €52/62; U3, U6 Westbahnhof;

This independent hostel received a head-to-toe revamp in 2009 and the change is evident everywhere – bright walls, splashes of colour and comfy, Ikea-style furnishings. All dorm rooms have en suite, with wooden bunks, bright-red lockers and ample space for moving around, and the ivy-lined inner courtyard is superb.

VORSTADT NORTHWEST

Just north of Neubau, but just as relaxed and lively, lies this area covering Josefstadt and Alsergrund. On the southern boundaries you'll be hard-pressed not to stumble into a restaurant on each block. Further north into Alsergrund the streets quieten down a tad, though the university keeps the vibe young and hip. The entire area is criss-crossed with convenient tramlines for a pleasant hop to the centre.

HOTEL RATHAUS WEIN & DESIGN

Map pp94-5 Hotel €€

☎ 400 11 22; www.hotel-rathaus-wien.at; 08, Lange Gasse 13; s/d €138/198; 2, 46

Rathaus is a shrine to Austrian winemakers. Each stylish room in this boutique hotel is dedicated to a quality Austrian winemaker and the minibar is stocked with premium wines from the growers themselves. Interiors are an elegant mix of dark woods, pale yellows and personal touches (cut flowers, designer vases and the like), with rain showers in each room; some peer out onto their stylish inner courtyard space. The hotel offers wine tastings in its designer bar, and excursions to Austria's nearby winegrowing regions.

CORDIAL THEATERHOTEL

Map pp94-5 Hotel €€

☎ 405 36 48; http://cordial-theaterhotel-wien.h-rsv.com; 08, Josefstädter Strasse 22; s/d €184/196; 🚋 2; 📶

A hotel for theatre and music lovers. Theatre memorabilia lines the hallways, stairwells and rooms, and art nouveau touches hark back to the days when the stage was all the rage. Rooms (all with kitchenette) are filled with dark-wood furniture – each is inspired by a different composer (Mozart, Schubert etc), with elements like sketches of the master or a print of a famous composition's notes. Bonus: the hotel includes a sauna and solarium. Internet is only available in the bar and cafe-restaurant.

LEVANTE LAUDON Map pp94-5 Apartments €€

☎ 407 13 70; www.thelevante.com; 08, Laudongasse 8; apt per day/week from €165/945; 🚋 43, 44

Stay as long as a year or as little as a day at the Levante Laudon, an apartment building catering to short-term rentals. Apartments come in two varieties – Superior and Standard. Stylish touches such as freestanding sinks, make-up mirrors, space-age coat racks and flat-screen TVs make the Superior apartments truly inviting; Standards have less panache but are just as large. Personal touches, such as fresh flowers in rooms, daily housekeeping and a complimentary self-service continental breakfast, add to an already homely atmosphere.

PENSION WILD Map pp94-5 Pension €

☎ 406 51 74; www.pension-wild.com; 08, Lange Gasse 10; s/d from €41/43; 🚋 46

Wild is one of the very few openly gay-friendly *Pensionen* in Vienna, but the warm welcome extends to all walks of life. The top-floor Luxury rooms are simple yet appealing, with plenty of light-wood furniture and private bathrooms, the latter a big advantage over Wild's other two categories, Standard and Comfort. All, however, are spotlessly clean and kitchens are available for guests to use and abuse. Note that 'Wild' is the family name, not a description.

VORSTADT LANDSTRASSE

Hugging the Belvedere on one side and straddling the Danube on the other, this area is low on nightlife and slim on the restaurant front, but it's a prime choice for proximity to all the major sights and numerous tramlines, and a swift subway whisks you into the action in no time.

BELVEDERE APPARTEMENTS

Map pp104-5 Apartments €€

☎ 235 00 50; www.belv.at; 03, Fasangasse 18; apt from €85, reductions for stays over 1 week; 🚋 0, 71; 📶

Butting up against the grounds of the Belvedere (p102) are these exceptional apartments – modern furnishings and designs reign in the fully renovated *Altbau* (an old, traditional Viennese building). High ceilings and massive windows make all the spaces feel airy, from the 25-sq-metre studios to the 60-plus-sq-metre multibedroom units.

ROOMZ Map pp104-5 Hotel €€

☎ 743 17 77; www.roomz-vienna.at; 03, Paragonenstrasse 1; s/d from €70/82; Ⓤ U3 Gasometer; 📶

Its far-flung location is the only drawback, though you are smack around the corner from the eye-catching Gasometer (p107). This is prime stuff for design fanatics on a budget who want minimalism through and through. Rooms are white with a dominant second colour (some soothing greens, others vibrant lavender), and floor-to-ceiling windows make each small room feel far bigger.

EAST OF THE DANUBE CANAL

For a touch of the alternative scene in Leopoldstadt and the iconic Prater, home to a kicking nightlife scene and the famous Ferris wheel, this is an excellent location with affordable lodgings and quick connections to the centre. The waterways of the Danube River and Canal are at your doorstep, as are the hopping beach bars, making it a prime location during Vienna's balmy summers and for those wanting to embrace the waterways during their stay.

ALL YOU NEED VIENNA 2

Map pp112-13 Hotel €€

☎ 212 16 68; www.allyouneedhotels.at; 02, Grosse Schiffgasse 12; s/d from €69/89; U2, U4 Schottenring 1, 31;

This modern, multi-floor high-rise only a short walk from the Innere Stadt across the Danube Canal is sleek, modern and vibrant. Its youngish clientele lounges in the art-filled reception, and rooms (on the small side, though some include balconies) are fitted with light wood and large windows. On warm days, the expansive garden here is ideal for morning breakfast and plotting your day of sightseeing.

GAL APARTMENTS

Map pp112-13 Apartments €€

☎ 561 19 42; www.apartmentsvienna.net; 02, Grosse Mohrengasse 29; apt from €80; U2 Taborstrasse, U1 Nestroyplatz;

For a superb home away from home, check into these modern apartments smack in the action of up-and-coming Leopoldstadt. Spaces range from 30 to 60 sq metres – all apartments in the renovated Biedermeier structure feature modern furniture flanked by tasteful, *Jugendstil*-inspired paintings. It's a short walk to the Karmelitermarkt, the Prater Ferris wheel and the Augarten, and the subway whips you to the centre of town in less than 10 minutes.

SOUTHWEST & THE GÜRTEL

You won't be in the thick of things if you stay in these heavily residential outlying suburbs, but you will be among the Viennese, whether it is in the predominantly rich 13th district (Hietzing), the working-class neighbourhoods of the 14th and 15th (Penzing and Rudolfsheim-Fünfhaus) or the Turkish- and Balkan-influenced 16th (Ottakring). You'll also have the advantage of close proximity to some of Vienna's largest attractions, Schloss Schönnbrunn, as well as Ottakring's exceptional Brunnenmarkt, a colourful market with oodles of low-cost kebab haunts.

top picks

CLASSIC VIENNESE PENSIONEN

Sample traditional Viennese hospitality in comfort and style:

- **Pension am Operneck** (p211)
- **Pension Carantania** (p212)
- **Pension Kraml** (p213)
- **Pension Nossek** (p211)
- **Pension Riedl** (p211)

BOUTIQUEHOTEL STADTHALLE

Map pp120-1 Hotel €€

☎ 982 42 72; www.hotelstadthalle.at; 15, Hackengasse 20; s/d from €68/98; U6 Burggasse Stadthalle 6, 9, 18, 49

The most sustainable hotel in Vienna: solar panels heat all the hot water; cisterns collect rainwater from the roof (for flushing toilets and watering the hotel garden and lavender roof, Vienna's largest lavender plantation); the new wing has no traditional heat or air-con – special water pipes in the walls cool and heat the structure; and LED lights are used throughout. It also encourages green transport: anyone who arrives by bike or train receives a 10% discount. Rooms have a blend of modern and antique furnishings flanked by colourful walls, from lavender and purple to mauve and peach (a different palette reigns over each floor). The same operators also run a cheap *Pension* (singles/doubles from €39/49) down the street (Hackengasse 33; reception at the main hotel).

ALTWIENERHOF Map pp120-1 Hotel €€

☎ 892 60 00; www.altwienerhof.at; 15, Herklotzgasse 6; s/d €79/99; U6 Gumpendorfer Strasse 6, 18

Altwienerhof, a pseudo-plush family-run hotel just outside the Gürtel ring, offers ridiculously romantic abodes that hark back to a bygone era when the *Orient Express* was all the rage. Miniature chandeliers, antique pieces, floral bed covers and couches, and lace tablecloths all do a fine job of adding a touch of old-fashioned romance. Breakfast is taken either in the conservatory or in the large inner courtyard on sultry summer days.

WOMBAT'S Map pp120-1 Hostel €

☎ 897 36 23; www.wombats.at; 05, Mariahilfer Strasse 137; dm/r €20/56; U3, U6 Westbahnhof;

Offering up a bit of Australian hostel vibe in the Capital of Culture, Wombat's is the choice for the savvy backpacker. The interior is a rainbow of bright colours, common areas include a bar, pool tables, music and comfy leather sofas, and all dorms have en suite and are superbly outfitted with modern furnishings. Bike hire is available and staff are experienced and relaxed. A second Wombat's (☎ 897 23 36; 15, Grangasse 6; dm/r €20/56; 52, 58 12A;) is a prime choice if this one fills up, and a third location near the Naschmarkt is slated to open in late 2011 – check the website for updates.

DO STEP INN Map pp120-1 Hostel, Hotel €

☎ 982 33 14; www.dostepinn.at; 15, Felberstrasse 22/6; hostel s/d from €15/44, hotel s/d from €45/52; U3, U6 Westbahnhof

This small, clean hostel/hotel offers some of the cheapest rooms in town. None of the hostel rooms has more than four beds, but all share a bathroom down the hall. Rooms are generally bright, colourful and simple, and kitchens are available for use – in short, a superb choice for budget travellers. Ten per cent is added to the price if you're only staying one night.

GREATER VIENNA

The city it ain't, but the wine-tavern-filled outskirts of Vienna lend a country feel to this area while maintaining easy connections into town. With rolling hills all around, you can leave your home away from home and start a hike right outside your door.

HOTEL SCHLOSS WILHELMINENBERG Map pp56-7 Hotel €€€

☎ 485 85 03-0; www.austria-trend.at/wiw; 16, Savoyenstrasse 2; r from €250/260; 46B, 146B

COUNTRY SLEEPING

For a touch of the Tyrol a mere jaunt uphill from the city, look no further than the thick, whitewashed walls, rows of flowering pot plants and creeping vines of Landhaus Fuhrgassl-Huber (Map pp50-1; ☎ 440 30 33; www.fuhrgassl-huber.at; 19, Rathstrasse 24; s/d from €77/115; 35A). Set amid a slew of *Heurigen* (wine taverns), this country *Pension* features panelled-wood ceilings, folk art, ornamental carpets and warm tiled floors, and all staff don traditional garb. Flowery designs are the norm and the huge buffet breakfast (taken in the secluded garden on warm mornings) makes you feel far, far away from anything urban...but you're only a 30-minute bus ride from the city centre.

Schloss Wilhelminenberg is a fully fledged palace with unbridled views of the entire city, and a resort ambience. The reception and cafe are suitably palatial (featuring high ceilings, detailed wall- and ceiling-inlays, chandeliers), and while rooms are in contemporary style they complement rather than detract from the building's neo-imperial architecture. Standard rooms on the top floor are small but boast excellent views, and the more expensive maisonette variety are unusually narrow but they do have exceptionally high ceilings and loft beds.

SCHLOSSHERBERGE AM WILHELMINENBERG/PALACE HOSTEL Map pp56-7 Hostel €

☎ 481 03 00; www.hostel.at; 16, Savoyenstrasse 2; dm from €22.50, s/d from €50/31; 46B, 146B;

This HI hostel in the grounds of Schloss Wilhelminenberg may be a long hop from the centre, but the glorious views of the city and easy access to the Wienerwald make up for it. Like most of Vienna's hostels, the rooms are colourful and modern with solid wooden bunk beds, en suite bathrooms, and lockers. The grounds include a minigolf course, table tennis, a PlayStation and large meadows.

EXCURSIONS

EXCURSIONS

Vienna is blessed with a bountiful array of day trips and short-stay destinations. The Danube Valley (below), to the northwest of Vienna, is perfect for day trips and longer explorations. The region is also a paradise for hikers and cyclists. The stretch of the valley between Krems an der Donau (Krems) and Melk is known as the Wachau – it is easily the most spectacular section of the Danube in Austria.

South of Vienna in Burgenland, wine features, particularly in the lakeside town of Rust (p224), arguably the prettiest town in the region and certainly one of the most interesting when it comes to the nectar of the gods.

If medieval towns are your passion, don't miss Znojmo (p225) in the Czech Republic, where you can immerse yourself in one of the best-preserved historic towns in Central Europe, dip into some delicious Bohemian wines and enjoy some cycling or hiking in the Podyjí National Park.

In the east, Bratislava (p226), across the border in Slovakia, can be reached within an hour from the capital and offers a glimpse of the 'new Europe' within a stone's throw of Vienna.

THE DANUBE VALLEY

The Wachau, the section of the Danube Valley between Krems and Melk, is arguably the prettiest stretch along the entire course of the Danube, and is a Unesco World Heritage Site. Here the dustless highway bends and twists between high hills whose slopes are layered with vineyards, offset by peaks topped with castles.

Highlights are numerous, but rivalling the cultural offerings and architecture of Krems, Dürnstein and Melk is the region's wining and dining. Some of the country's finest wines are from the Wachau, and the seasonal fare, using the freshest ingredients from the valley, attracts gourmands from across Austria.

The best place to begin a tour is Krems, where you can hire bicycles for riding along the riverside path or organise other transport. For more information, see below and p221.

KREMS

Krems (population 24,000) is one of the larger towns in the Wachau region; with its historical core dating back over 1000 years, and excellent restaurants, it's a perfect starting point for exploring the culinary, vinicultural and historical sights of the Wachau. It's on the northern bank of the Danube, surrounded by terraced vineyards, and has been a centre of the wine trade for most of its history. Today it also has a small university.

The town is comprised of three parts: Krems to the east, the smaller settlement of Stein 2km to the west, and the connecting suburb of Und – an unusual name that inspires the joke: 'Krems and (*und* in German) Stein are three towns'.

The tourist office (see p220) has an excellent walk-by-numbers map that leads you past the sights. The walk begins at the imposing

TRANSPORT: THE DANUBE VALLEY

Direction 64km west of Vienna to Krems; 73km to Dürnstein; 83km to Melk

Travel time One hour

Bicycle A bicycle path runs along both sides of the Danube from Vienna to Melk, passing through Krems, Dürnstein, Weissenkirchen and Spitz (these are all on the northern bank)

Boat Sunday morning services run from Vienna between mid-May and mid-September

Car For Krems and Dürnstein take the A22 north out of Vienna towards Stockerau, then the S5 west to Krems; from Krems, the Bundesbahn 3 continues west and passes through Dürnstein, Weissenkirchen and Spitz. Melk is best reached by the A1 autobahn, which connects Vienna with Salzburg. See Cruising, Railing & Riding the Danube Valley, p221, for transport options in depth, and the detour to the Kamptal and Waldviertel (p222) for a road trip north

Train Frequent direct trains travel between Franz-Josefs-Bahnhof in Vienna and Krems (€13.90, one hour)

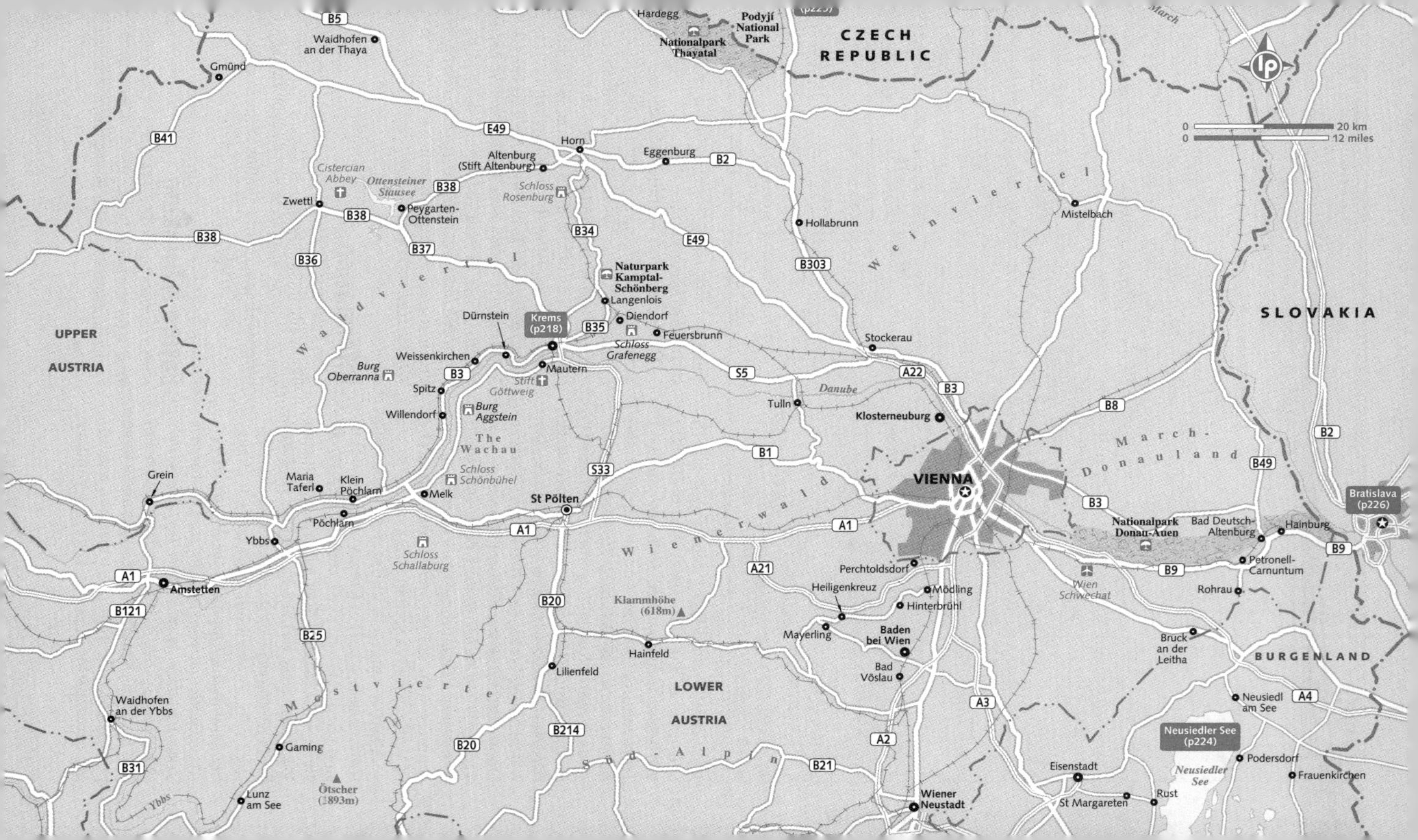

CZECH REPUBLIC
SLOVAKIA
UPPER AUSTRIA
LOWER AUSTRIA
BURGENLAND
VIENNA
Bratislava (p226)
Krems (p218)
Neusiedler See (p224)
0 20 km
0 12 miles
Hardegg
Nationalpark Thayatal
Podyjí National Park
Waidhofen an der Thaya
Gmünd
Horn
Eggenburg
Altenburg (Stift Altenburg)
Cistercian Abbey
Ottensteiner Stausee
Schloss Rosenburg
Zwettl
Peygarten-Ottenstein
Hollabrunn
Mistelbach
Weinviertel
Waldviertel
Naturpark Kamptal-Schönberg
Langenlois
Diendorf
Feuersbrunn
Schloss Grafenegg
Dürnstein
Weissenkirchen
Burg Oberranna
Mautern
Stift Göttweig
Spitz
Willendorf
Burg Aggstein
The Wachau
Stockerau
Danube
Tulln
Klosterneuburg
March-Donauland
Schloss Schönbühel
Grein
Maria Taferl
Klein Pöchlarn
Melk
St Pölten
Pöchlarn
Ybbs
Schloss Schallaburg
Amstetten
Wienerwald
Nationalpark Donau-Auen
Bad Deutsch-Altenburg
Hainburg
Petronell-Carnuntum
Rohrau
Wien Schwechat
Perchtoldsdorf
Mödling
Heiligenkreuz
Hinterbrühl
Mayerling
Baden bei Wien
Bad Vöslau
Klammhöhe (618m)
Hainfeld
Lilienfeld
Bruck an der Leitha
Mostviertel
Waidhofen an der Ybbs
Gaming
Ötscher (1893m)
Lunz am See
Ybbs
Süd-Alpin
Wiener Neustadt
Eisenstadt
St Margareten
Rust
Neusiedler See
Neusiedl am See
Podersdorf
Frauenkirchen
March
B5
B41
E49
B38
B36
B37
B34
B2
E49
B303
B35
B3
S5
A22
B8
B1
S33
A1
A21
B20
B25
B121
B214
B21
A2
A3
A4
B9
B49
B31

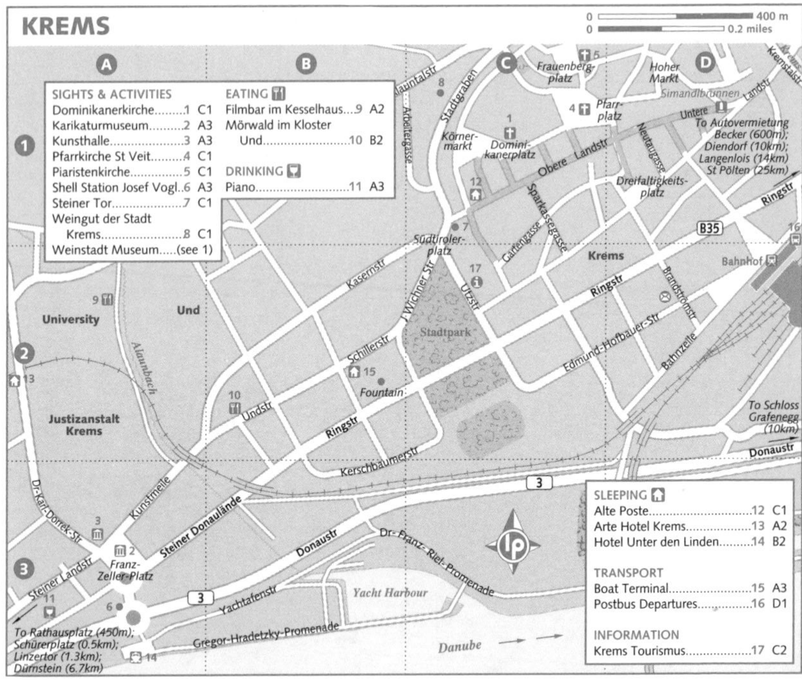

15th-century Steiner Tor (Stein Town Gate), and takes in the Pfarrkirche St Veit (☎ 02732-832 85; Pfarrplatz 5; ⌚ dawn-dusk) with its colourful 18th-century frescos, continues with the Piaristenkirche (☎ 02732-820 92; Frauenbergplatz; ⌚ dawn-dusk) before taking you to the Weinstadt Museum (☎ 02732-801 567; www.weinstadtmuseum.at; Körnermarkt 14; adult/child/student €4/2/3; ⌚ 10am-6pm Wed-Sat & 1-6pm Sun Mar-Nov), housed in a former Dominican monastery (Dominikanerkirche). This is home to collections of religious and modern art (including works by Kremser Schmidt, who did the frescos in Pfarrkirche St Veit), as well as winemaking artefacts.

Approaching Stein in the west, you reach the Kunstmeile, a part of Krems where you find some first-rate art. The Kunsthalle (☎ 02732-908 010-19; www.kunsthalle.at; Franz-Zeller-Platz 3; adult/under 19yr/student/family €9/3.50/8/18, combined ticket for 3 Kunstmeile museums €11; ⌚ 10am-6pm Apr-Oct, 10am-5pm Nov-Mar) is small but has excellent changing exhibitions. Opposite, the Karikaturmuseum (☎ 02732-908 020; www.karikaturmuseum.at, in German; Steiner Landstrasse 3a; adult/under 19yr/student/family €9/3.50/8/18; ⌚ 10am-6pm Apr-Oct, 10am-5pm Nov-Mar) also features changing exhibitions and a large permanent collection of caricatures, including cartoons by Manfred Deix, a legendary Austrian with an eye for the absurd coupled with sharp social commentary.

Make sure you continue to Schürerplatz and Rathausplatz in Stein, a magnificent part of Krems with the feel of an Adriatic village.

There are numerous *Heurigen* (wine taverns) just out of town. The tourist office has a calendar showing the weeks when each is open. Weingut der Stadt Krems (☎ 02732-801 441; Stadtgraben 11; ⌚ 9am-noon & 1-5pm Mon-Fri, 9am-1pm Sat) is the city-owned vineyard, yielding about 200,000 bottles per year (90% is Grüner Veltliner and Riesling), some of which you can sample free and buy.

Information

Krems Tourismus (☎ 02732-826 76; www.krems.info; Utzstrasse 1; ⌚ 9am-6pm Mon-Fri, 11am-5pm Sat, 11am-4pm Sun May-Oct, 9am-5pm Mon-Fri Nov-Apr) Helpful office with lots of information on the Wachau and Waldviertel.

Eating & Drinking

Filmbar im Kesselhaus (☎ 02732-893 35 99; www.filmbar.at, in German; Dr-Karl-Dorreck-Strasse 30; mains €5-10; ⌚ 10am-2.30pm Mon & Tue, 10am-midnight Wed-Sun)

CRUISING, RAILING & RIDING THE DANUBE VALLEY

A leisurely way to see the Danube Valley is by boat. Cruising down the Danube with a glass of Riesling in one hand and a camera in the other can be the highlight of a trip to Vienna. From the capital it is easily organised. DDSG Blue Danube (Map pp56-7; ☎ 01-588 800; www.ddsg-blue-danube.at; 02, Handelskai 265; 9am-6pm Mon-Fri, ticket sales desk 10am-5pm daily; U1 Vorgartenstrasse) runs a Sunday service (one-way/return €23/29.50, 6 hours upstream, 4¼ hours downstream, 8.30am from Vienna, 4.40pm from Dürnstein) between Vienna and Dürnstein, stopping at Krems at 2pm and returning from Krems at 5pm. Boats leave from near the DDSG office at Quay 5 (Handelskai 265) alongside the Wien/Reichsbrücke. Tickets can also be bought from the Twin City Liner sales office on Schwedenplatz in Vienna (see p228).

A number of boat companies, including DDSG Blue Danube, operate boats from Krems to Melk, stopping in at Dürnstein and Spitz, from April to October. DDSG boats leave Krems at 10.15am all season, and from late April to September two extra sailings depart at 1pm and 3.45pm. Return sailings are at 1.50pm all season, and 11am and 4.15pm from late April to September (one-way/return €20/25, 3 hours upstream, 1¾ hours downstream). Bikes can be taken on board all boats free of charge.

Direct trains from Franz-Josefs-Bahnhof in Vienna to Krems are the easiest way into the valley (see p218). For Dürnstein (the station is called Dürnstein-Oberloiben; €15.70, 1¼ hours) from Franz-Josefs-Bahnhof you need to change at Krems. Trains from Vienna's Westbahnhof (€15.70, 1¼ hours) direct to Melk go via St Pölton and *don't* follow the Danube Valley. From Krems to Melk (€3.60, one hour) a useful integrated rail connection with a change to bus in Spitz works best if you leave Krems in the morning.

Another option is to combine rail and boat. DDSG Blue Danube (p236) and the Österreiche Bundesbahn (ÖBB; Austrian Federal Railway; p231) offer a combined train/boat/train ticket (adult/6-14yr €46.60/23.30) for one-way train connections to Krems and Melk, and the boat trip in between the two. Tickets can be purchased at any train station or from the DDSG Blue Danube office.

A great way of cruising the valley is by bicycle. Many hotels and *Pensionen* (B&Bs) are geared towards cyclists, and most towns have at least one bike-hire shop. Pick up a copy of *Donauradweg – Von Passau bis Bratislava,* which provides details of distances, hotels and information offices along the route. Copies (and lists of bicycle-hire locations) are available in tourist offices in the Wachau and also in Tulln; the text is in German only. The 38km section of the route between Krems and Melk can be done easily one-way in a single day with lots of stops. Bicycles (day ticket €5) can be taken on trains to and from Vienna from there and elsewhere, but not on buses. In Krems, Shell Station Josef Vogl (☎ 02732-844 24; Steiner Donaulände 17; bicycle per day €24) is one convenient bicycle-hire location. Also in Krems, Autovermietung Becker (☎ 02732-824 33; www.rent.becker.at, in German; Wachauer Strasse 30) hires cars from €59 per day. See p236 for further information on transport.

This sleek student restaurant and bar is the hub of eating and drinking activity on the university campus. Beyond that, it also shows art-house films. Two-/three-course lunches cost €6.90/7.90.

Mörwald im Kloster Und (☎ 02732-704 930; Undstrasse 6; mains €20-33, 5-course menus €85, 3-course lunches €25; 11am-11pm Tue-Sat) Mörwald is the most central of a crop of restaurants run by Toni Mörwald outside Vienna; it offers exquisite delights ranging from roast pigeon breast to beef, poultry and fish dishes with French angles. A lovely yard and an impressive wine selection round off one of the best restaurants in the Wachau.

Piano (☎ 02732-858 09; Steiner Landstrasse 21; 5pm-2am Mon-Thu, 5pm-3am Fri & Sat, 5pm-midnight Sun) A crossover crowd of students, young workers and mellow jazz types gathers at this lively and offbeat pub. It does a couple of local sausage snacks to go with its great selection of beer; a few other decent bars and restaurants are on this street.

Sleeping

Alte Poste (☎ 02732-822 76; www.altepost-krems.at, in German; Obere Landstrasse 32; s €30-59, d €58-79) This guesthouse located in a historic 500-year-old house has an enchanting courtyard and 23 cosy rooms.

Hotel Unter den Linden (☎ 02732-821 15; www.udl.at; Schillerstrasse 5; s €50, d €74-98;) This big, yellow, family-run hotel has knowledgeable and helpful owners, bright, comfortable rooms and a convenient location in Krems itself. Book ahead, as it gets bus groups and is arguably the best deal in town.

Arte Hotel Krems (☎ 02732-711 23; www.arte-hotel.at, in German; Dr-Karl-Dorrek-Strasse 23; s €89-105, d €128-162;) This comfortable new art hotel close to the university has large, well-styled rooms in bright designs and a clever use of colour

DETOUR: KAMPTAL & WALDVIERTEL

The region immediately northeast of Krems on the Kamptal (Kamp Valley) around Langenlois is a major centre of winegrowing. Here the volcanic soil lends the Pinot blanc *(Weissburgunder)*, chardonnay, Grüner Veltliner, Riesling and red wines of the region a distinctive character. This route, which can be done by train between Krems or Hadersdorf train station and Schloss Rosenburg (€5.40, 40 minutes), or by bicycle if you use the Kamptalradweg (Kamp Valley Bicycle Path; 107km), combines traditional *Heurigen* (wine taverns) with a castle, top-class dining, wellness and wine.

From Krems the Weinstrasse Kremstal (Krems Valley Wine Rd; B35) takes you northeast. About 2km past Gedersdorf – just before Hadersdorf train station – veer off right under the railway line and immediately left to Diendorf, where you find Hofkäserei Robert Paget (☎ 0650-731 08 43; www.mozzaundjazz.at; Kirchenweg 2, Diendorf am Kamp; 🕑 10am-6pm Fri & Sat). Here Robert Paget produces Austria's finest mozzarella cheese from buffalo, as well as goat's cheese. You can buy from the shop and eat it outside where the buffalo roam.

From Hadersdorf train station, you can easily walk or cycle the 2km to Diendorf, and one good tip we got from Robert Paget was to continue by foot or bicycle along Diendorfer Weg about another 1.5km to Hadersdorf's Hauptplatz, the magnificent town central square with Renaissance and baroque buildings, some of them *Heurigen*.

About 6km south of Diendorf is Schloss Grafenegg (☎ 02735-220 522; www.grafenegg.com; Haitzendorf; adult/concession & child/family €5/3/7.50; 🕑 10am-5pm Tue-Sun mid-Apr–Oct), a castle with the look and feel of an ornate Tudor mansion set in English woods. The castle's manicured gardens are perfect for a picnic, but for fine dining don't pass up Restaurant & Hotel Schloss Grafenegg (☎ 02735-2616-0; www.moerwald.at; Grafenegg 12; 3-/4-course menus €29/37; 🕑 10am-10pm Wed-Sun Easter-Dec; V); it also has rooms (singles/doubles from €88.50/118).

The wine-focused Loisium Hotel (☎ 02734-771 00-0; www.loisiumhotel.at; Loisium Allee 2, Langenlois; mains €15-30, 4-course menus €47; 🕑 lunch & dinner) is a useful stopover, with single rooms starting at €134, and doubles from €188. Highlights are massages and wine treatments (some using sparkling wine or grapeseed oil), large spa facilities, and the 20m heated outdoor pool that's open all year. Alongside the hotel is the Loisium Weinwelt (☎ 02734-322 40-0; Loisium Allee 1; 90min audio tour adult/child/concession €11.50/6.30/9.20; 🕑 10am-7pm), an aluminium cube designed by New York architect Steven Holl that slopes to the south. Multilingual audio tours here set off every 30 minutes and lead you through a 1.5km network of ancient tunnels. Bring a pullover; it's chilly.

Continuing north from Langenlois, the B34 passes through the picturesque Naturpark Kamptal-Schönberg to Schloss Rosenburg (☎ 02982-2911; www.rosenburg.at, in German; Rosenburg am Kamp; tours & falconry adult/concession & child/family €10/8.50/24, extra €3 for falconry with pageantry; 🕑 9.30am-4.30pm Tue-Sun Mar, Apr & Oct, 9.30am-5pm May-Sep), a Renaissance castle 50km north of Krems where falconry shows take place at 11am and 3pm.

From here follow the L53 and B38 5km to the Benedictine Stift Altenburg (☎ 02982-3451; www.stift-altenburg.at, in German; Stift 1; adult/child/concession/family €9/4.50/7/18, audio guide €2; 🕑 10am-5pm Apr-Oct), which can trace its foundations back to 1144. The abbey library (which has ceiling frescos by Paul Troger) and the crypt (with frescos by Troger's pupils) are highlights.

By continuing along the B38 you pass Peygarten-Ottenstein on the Ottensteiner Stausee, one of several dams in the Waldviertel, and finish the tour near Zwettl at the baroque Cistercian Abbey (☎ 02822-202 02 17; www.stiftzwettl.at, in German; Stift Zwettl 1; admission & audio guide adult/child/concession/family €9/4/8/18; 🕑 10am-4pm Easter-Oct). The B36 leads you the 25km south back to the Danube Valley.

The Waldviertel's central tourist office (☎ 02822-541 09-0; www.waldviertel.at; Sparkasseplatz 4, Zwettl; 🕑 8am-4pm Mon-Fri) can help with tips and planning.

and natural lighting. The bathrooms (but not the toilets) are open plan. Rooms have LAN (bring your network cable), the lobby has wi-fi and the entire hotel is nonsmoking. There's a separately owned wellness studio in the building, and a decent grill restaurant in the same complex (mains €7.50 to €29).

FROM KREMS TO MELK

The section of the Wachau on the northern bank of the Danube between Krems and the bridge crossing to Melk takes you through Dürnstein, which achieved 12th-century notoriety for its imprisonment of King Richard the Lionheart of England. High on the hill, commanding a marvellous view of the curve of the Danube, stand the ruins of Kuenringerburg, where Richard was incarcerated from 1192 to 1193. His crime was insulting Leopold V; his misfortune was being recognised despite his disguise when journeying through Austria on his way home from the Crusades. His liberty was achieved only upon the payment of a huge ransom, which funded the building of Wiener Neustadt. The hike up to the ruins from the village takes 15 to 20 minutes.

Anyone wishing to hike further can take the Schlossbergweg (marked green) from here to Fesselhütte (☎ 02732-41277; www.fesslhuette.at, in German; Dürsteiner Waldhütten 23; goulash soup €2.30; ⌚ 9.30am-6pm Wed-Sun Easter-Oct), about one hour by foot from the castle, and enjoy sausage, soup or wine afterwards in this forest tavern; a road also leads up here from Weissenkirchen.

The dominating feature of Dürnstein is the blue spire of the Chorherrenstift (Abbey church; ☎ 02711-375; Stiftshof; adult/child/student €2.60/1.50/2; ⌚ 9am-6pm Apr-Oct). Inside, its baroque interior effectively combines white stucco and dark wood, and its balcony offers a grand view of the Danube.

Travelling west from Dürnstein alongside the Danube, you pass beneath steep hills densely covered with vineyards. Riesling and Grüner Veltliner are grown in these parts, and served in traditional *Heurigen*. Six kilometres on from Dürnstein is Weissenkirchen. Its centrepiece is a fortified parish church (☎ 02715-2203; Weissenkirchen 3; admission free; ⌚ 8am-7pm Easter-Oct, 8am-5pm Sat & Sun Nov-Easter) rising from a hill, with a labyrinth of covered pathways leading to its front doors. This Gothic church was built in the 15th century and has an impressive baroque altar. Directly below the church is the tiny Wachau Museum (☎ 02715-2268; Weissenkirchen 32; adult/child/concession €5/2.50/3.50; ⌚ 10am-5pm Tue-Sun Apr-Oct), which showcases artists of the Danube School.

A further 5km west you reach Spitz, a village surrounded by vineyards and lined with quiet, cobblestoned streets. If the Gothic parish church (☎ 02713-2231; Kirchenplatz 12; ⌚ 8am-6pm) in Spitz is one too many Danube churches, then pick up some maps from the tourist office (see right) and hike up to Burgruine Hinterhaus (Hinterhaus castle ruin) on the bluff for fantastic views of the valley; other trails run through the forests of Jauerling Naturpark (Jauerling Nature Reserve) behind the castle ruin.

Lying in the lee of its imposing monastery-fortress, Melk (35km from Krems) is home to one of the Danube's most popular attractions, Stift Melk (Benedictine Abbey of Melk; ☎ 02752-5550; www.stiftmelk.at; Abt Berthold Dietmayr Strasse 1; adult/student & child/family €7.70/4.50/15.40, with guided tour €9.50/6.30/19; ⌚ 9am-5.30pm May-Sep, 9am-4.30pm mid-Mar–Apr & Oct-Nov). This was once the residence of the Babenberg family. Benedictine monks transformed it into a monastery in 1089 and today its elegant rooms are complemented by a mineral collection in the museum.

Schloss Schallaburg (☎ 02754-6317; www.schallaburg.at; Anzendorf; adult/child/concession/family €9/3.50/8/18, combined ticket with Stift Melk €15; ⌚ 9am-5pm Mon-Fri, 9am-6pm Sat), 5km south of Melk, is a 16th-century Renaissance palace with magnificent terracotta arches and prestigious temporary exhibitions. There's also a permanent exhibition of toys through history.

Information

Dürnstein Information Office (☎ 02711-200; www.duernstein.at; Dürnstein Bahnhof; ⌚ 9am-2pm Apr–mid-May & early Oct, 9am-5pm mid-May-Sep) Located east of town near the train station.

Melk Tourist Office (☎ 02752-523 07-410; www.niederoesterreich.at/melk; Babenbergerstrasse 1; ⌚ 9am-noon & 2-6pm Mon-Fri, 10am-noon Sat & Sun May-Aug, 9am-noon & 2-5pm Mon-Fri, 10am-2pm Sat Apr, Sep & Oct) Useful for accommodation in town.

Spitz Tourist Office (☎ 02713-2363; www.spitz-wachau.at, in German; Mittergasse 3a; ⌚ 9am-noon & 1.30-7pm Mon-Sat, 2-6pm Sun May-Oct, 2-6pm Mon-Sat Apr, limited hrs Mon-Fri Nov-Mar) Helpful office with good hiking maps, but has unspecified and irregular hours in low season.

Eating & Sleeping

Restaurant Loibnerhof (☎ 02732-828 90-0; Unterloiben 7, Dürnstein-Unterloiben; mains €15-26, 3- & 4-course menus €26-52; ⌚ 11.30am-midnight Wed-Sun) Situated 1.5km east of Dürnstein's centre, this family-run

GOURMET TIPS

A day spent indulging in wine and food is a fine experience in the Danube Valley. Across the Danube from Krems, in Mautern, Landhaus Bacher (☎ 02732-829 37; www.landhaus-bacher.at; Südtiroler Platz 2; mains €26-40; ⌚ lunch & dinner Wed-Sun; Ⓥ) has won numerous awards (including two Michelin stars) for its creative take on Austrian specialities, and its summer garden, complete with walnut trees, is a joy in summer.

In Feuersbrunn, 2km from Schloss Grafenegg (see p222), Toni Mörwald's Hotel Villa Katharina (☎ 02738-229 80; www.moerwald.at; Kleine Zeile 10; s €111-125, d €147-167; ⊠), with its Restaurant zur Traube (☎ 02738-229 80; Kleine Zeile 13-17; mains €12.50-25; ⌚ 11.30am-10pm; Ⓥ), combines quality food and wine with accommodation.

Sweet tooths shouldn't miss Café Maria/Schaubackstube Krenn (☎ 02732-747 43; Rathausplatz 4, Mautern; ⌚ 7.30am-7pm Mon-Tue & Thu-Fri, 8am-6pm Sat, 9am-6pm Sun), a hot tip for Austria's best *Schaumrollen* (cream pastry).

restaurant inside a 400-year-old building has a lovely garden where you can enjoy delicious seasonal specialities.

Hotel Sänger Blondel (☎ 02711-253; www.saengerblondel.at; Klosterplatz/Dürnstein 64, Dürnstein; s €68, d €86-112) One of the nicest options in town, this hotel has good-sized rooms furnished in light woods, some with sofas. A couple have views to the Danube and others look out onto the castle or garden.

Hotel Schloss Dürnstein (☎ 02711-212; www.schloss.at; Dürnstein 2, Dürnstein; s €165, d €216-384;) This castle is the last word in luxury in town and has a high-end restaurant. Most rooms are furnished tastefully with antiques, a massage can be arranged for your arrival, and bonuses are a sauna and steam bath. Stay five nights and you will be treated to a free 'surprise menu' in the terrace restaurant (mains €15 to €32.50) with staggering views over the river. Stay 10 and you get a night on the house (which might be useful if you happen to be broke by that stage).

BURGENLAND – NEUSIEDLER SEE

Europe's second-largest steppe lake (after Balaton in Hungary), Neusiedler See is not only a popular summer holiday getaway and a top winegrowing region, it's also a favourite place for cycling and wellness offerings. The lake is shallow (1.8m at its deepest) and has no natural outlet, giving the water a slightly saline quality. It's ringed by a wetland area of reed beds, particularly thick on the western bank, which provides an ideal breeding ground for birds. Birdwatchers flock to the area to catch a glimpse of the multitude of species; the national park on the east shore is a grassland interspersed with a myriad smaller lakes and a popular spot for birds and bird-voyeurs.

From April to October – the only time worth visiting – the best way to enjoy the water, wine and wellness offerings of the region is by bicycle. Begin a tour at Neusiedl am See, where at the train station you can pick up a bicycle from Fahrräder Bucsis (☎ 02167-207 90; www.fahrraeder-bucsis.at, in German; train station, Neusiedl am See; per day €15; 8.30am-1.30pm & 4-7pm Mar–mid-Oct, 8.30am-7pm Sat & Sun). From here the 135km Neusiedler See bike trail leads south, crossing into Hungary (bring your passport!) for 38km before the path re-emerges in Austria just south of Mörbisch on the western side of the lake.

In Frauenkirchen, 8km inland from Podersdorf, you can take the cure at St Martins Therme & Lodge (☎ 02172-205 00; www.stmartins.at; Im Seewinkel 1, Frauenkirchen; d €128-226), a spa resort fed by hot springs (spa day ticket adult/under 15yr €20/14, or free with overnight stay; 9am-10pm). Book ahead at the hotel for free pick-up from Frauenkirchen train station if arriving by rail or bus.

At Podersdorf itself (about 10km from Neusiedl am See) you can grab a ferry to Rust (adult/child €6.40/4) across the lake. Another ferry leaves from Illmitz (about 25km from Neusiedl; adult/child €6.50/4) near the Neusiedler See-Seewinkel National Park (☎ 02175-344 20; www.nationalpark-neusiedlersee-seewinkel.at, in German; Illmitz; 8am-5pm Mon-Fri, 10am-5pm Sat & Sun Apr-Oct, 8am-4pm Mon-Fri Nov-Mar).

About 60 winegrowers are located around Rust, but don't miss rustic Weingut Gabriel (☎ 02685-236-0; www.weingut-gabriel.at; Hauptstrasse 25, Rust; cold platters about €12; from 4pm Thu & Fri, from 2pm Sat & Sun Apr-Oct). Not only is the pay-by-weight buffet brimming with delicious sausage and cold cuts, the wine is a treat, and in season the idyllic cobblestone courtyard is a wonderful vantage point to observe storks.

Before setting out, pick up a copy of *Radtouren*, a handy map of the lake with cycle paths and distances marked, from any tourist office on the lake. Neusiedler See Tourismus (☎ 02167-8600; www.neusiedlersee.com; Obere Hauptstrafe 24, Neusiedl am See; 8am-5pm Mon-Fri) is the

TRANSPORT: NEUSIEDLER SEE

Direction 53km southeast of Vienna

Travel time 45 minutes

Car The A4 leads to Neusiedl am See. For Neusiedl and Podersdorf, take the A4 southeast out of Vienna to the Neusiedl am See exit; signposts direct you from there. For Rust, head south out of Vienna on the A2 and exit onto the A3 at the Guntramsdorf junction. When the A3 ends, follow the signs to Eisenstadt (east), exit the road at Eisenstadt Süd and continue east, passing through Trausdorf and St Margareten before arriving in Rust

Ferries From late spring to early autumn ferries connect Illmitz with Möbisch, Rust and Fertörákos in Hungary; and Rust with Podersdorf, Breitenbrunn and Fertörákos. See www.neusiedler-see.au (under Reiseführer/Fahrradfähren) for current schedules

Train Frequent direct trains connect Vienna's Südbahnhof (Ostbahn) (the future Hauptbahnhof) with Neusiedl am See (€11, 38 minutes)

information centre for the lake region – for telephone, post and email enquiries. Neusiedl's city tourist office (☎ 2229; www.neusiedlamsee.at; Untere Hauptstrasse 7, Neusiedl am See; 🕑 8am-6pm Mon-Fri, 8am-noon & 2-6pm Sat, 9am-noon Sun Jul-Aug, 8am-noon & 1-5pm Mon-Fri May, Jun & Sep, 8am-noon & 1-4.30pm Mon-Thu, 8am-noon Fri Oct-Apr) has a map of the town and the lake, as well as information on other towns.

ZNOJMO

Perched high above the Dyje River on the border between southern Moravia in the Czech Republic and Austria, Znojmo (Znoymo) is a delightful city of 38,000 inhabitants with a hilltop castle and, directly across the river, access to hiking and cycling in the Podyjí National Park.

From the train station, walk up 17 listopadu and, at the roundabout (Mariánské náměstí), veer left onto Pontassievská, which leads to the main square, Masarykovo náměstí, and the South Moravian Museum (Jihomoravské muzeum; ☎ 00420-515 226 529; www.znojmuz.cz; Masarykovo náměstí 11; adult/concession & child 40/20Kč; 🕑 9am-5pm Tue-Sat). The collection here includes Czech religious icons, sculpture and temporary art exhibitions.

Go right (northwest) into Obroková, which takes you to the handsome and scalable Town Hall Tower (Radniční věž; ☎ 00420-773 475 612; Obroková; admission 30Kč; 🕑 9am-5pm), 66m tall and one of Moravia's best examples of late-Gothic architecture (c 1448). Continue along Obroková to the large square Horni náměstí and head south to the Znojmo Castle (☎ 00420-515 222 311; adult/concession & child 20/10Kč; 🕑 9am-5pm Tue-Sun May-Sep, Sat & Sun only Apr), housing a small museum about the castle but only partly accessible due to restorations, and the 11th-century Rotunda of Our Lady & St Catherine (rotunda Panny Marie a sv Kateřiny; ☎ 00420-515 222 311; admission 90Kč; 🕑 9.15am-4.15pm Tue-Sun May-Sep, Sat & Sun only Apr). This is one of the Czech Republic's oldest Romanesque structures and contains a beautiful series of 12th-century frescos showing the life of Christ. Forming part of the fortress complex, the lookout point (🕑 9am-9pm Mon-Thu & Sun, 9am-11pm Fri & Sat May-Sep, to 8pm Tue-Sun & to 5pm Mon Apr & Oct, closed Nov-Mar) offers wonderful views along the Dyje River valley.

Below the castle is the whacky Muzeum motorismu (Motoring Museum; ☎ 00420-603 443 053; Koželužská 44; adult/child 50/30Kč; 🕑 9am-5pm Tue-Sun), which has a large collection of Czech and Slovak cars dating mostly from the 1930s. You can reach it by backtracking along Hradní and descending to the river on the winding paths.

> **TRANSPORT: ZNOJMO**
>
> **Direction** 90km north of Vienna, in the Czech Republic
>
> **Travel time** 1½ hours
>
> **Car** Take the A22 north out of Vienna towards Prague, change to the B303 and (in the Czech Republic) follow the 38
>
> **Train** At least six direct trains daily from Wien-Praterstern (return EURegio ticket valid for three days €15, 1½ hours)

Cycle route 5000 into the national park begins across the bridge near the Muzeum motorismu. A 41km tour along this is described in detail in English on the city website (www.znojmocity.cz) under 'Tips on trips' (cycle tour outing no 2).

For detailed information on entry requirements for the Czech Republic, check www.czech.cz, or one of the Czech embassy websites – visa regulations change from time to time. Everyone requires a valid passport (or identity card for EU citizens) to enter the Czech Republic. Citizens of EU and EEA (European Economic Area) countries do not need a visa for any type of visit. Citizens of Australia, Canada, Israel, Japan, New Zealand, Switzerland and the USA can stay for up to 90 days without a visa. Visas are not available at border crossings; you'll be refused entry if you need one and arrive without one.

INFORMATION

Tourist information office (Turistické Informační Centrum; ☎ 00420-515 222 552; www.znojmocity.cz; Obroková 10; 🕑 8am-7pm Mon-Fri, 9am-7pm Sat, 10am-7pm Sun Jul & Aug, 8am-6pm Mon-Fri, 9am-5pm Sat, 10am-5pm Sun May-Jun & Sep-Oct, 8am-6pm Mon-Fri, 9am-1pm Sat Nov-Apr) Has maps of town, and an accommodation list.

EATING & SLEEPING

Althanský Palác Hotel (☎ 00420-731 441 090; info@althanskypalac.cz; Horní náměstí 3; s/d/tr 890/1590/2200Kč) This new hotel and restaurant offers a choice of historic- or modern-style rooms. Ask for a quiet one if you're sensitive to noise (it's popular for weddings). Staff can arrange bicycles and massages if you book ahead, and the restaurant (mains 109-250Kč; 🕑 10am-11pm Mon-

Thu, to 1am Fri & Sat, to 10pm Sun) is one of the best options in town.

Pension s vinotékou Jesuitská (☎ 00420-515 221 440; www.jesuitska.cz, in Czech; Jesuitská 5/183; r 1000-1200Kč;) This small, cyclist-friendly guesthouse has comfortable rooms and hires bicycles for 300Kč per day.

BRATISLAVA

Slovakia's capital is a vibrant, pulsating city just over an hour from Vienna by train. Its historical centre is small, easy to explore on foot and crammed with restored, historical buildings.

From Hlavná stanica, Bratislava's main train station, it's around a 20-minute walk to Hurbanovo námestie, the northern edge of the old town. Dominating the city from above is Bratislava Castle (Bratislavský hrad; grounds admission free; 9am-9.30pm Apr-Sep, to 6pm Oct-Mar), the city's reconstructed 15th-century castle with views from the ramparts. Inside the castle, the Historical Museum covers folk crafts, furniture, modern art and history. At the time of writing the museum was being renovated. On the ground floor, the Treasury of Slovakia (☎ 00421-2-2048 3111; adult/student/child €2.50/1/1.80; 10am-6pm Tue-Sun) has a small collection of archaeological finds.

Židovská, the most direct path from the castle to the old town, passes through what remains of the former Jewish quarter. What is reputedly the skinniest house in Central Europe contains a little Museum of Clocks (Múzeum hodín; ☎ 00421-2-5441 1940; Židovská 1; adult/student & child €2.30/1.30; 10am-5pm Tue-Fri, 11am-6pm Sat & Sun) and nearby, the Museum of Jewish Culture (Múzeum Židovskej kultúry; ☎ 00421-2-2049 0109; www.chatamsofer.com; Židovská 17; adult/student & child €7/2; 11am-5pm Sun-Fri) houses moving exhibits about Slovakia's Jewish community lost during the Holocaust and WWII.

Down in the old town, St Martin Cathedral (Dóm sv Martina; Rudnayovo námestie; admission €2; 9-11.30am & 1-5pm Mon-Sat, 1.30-4pm Sun), the city's finest Gothic structure, dominates. Of the museums here, the best is the Municipal Museum (☎ 00421-2-5920 5130; Hlavné nám; adult/student & child €2.50/1.50; 10am-5pm Tue-Fri, 11am-6pm Sat & Sun), located in the 14th-century town hall. It comes complete with Renaissance courtyard and green-roofed neo-Gothic annexe.

Next door to the Municipal Museum is the Primatial Palace (Primaciálny Palác; Primaciálne námestie 1; adult/student & child €2/free; 10am-5pm Tue-Sun), where Napoleon signed a peace treaty with Austria's Franz I in 1805. The town's only surviving tower gate, Michael Tower (Michalská veža; ☎ 00421-2-5443 3044; Michalská 24; adult/student & child €4.30/2.30; 10am-5pm Tue-Fri, 11am-6pm Sat & Sun), has a 14th-century base, a 16th-century top and an 18th-century steeple. Climb to the top for views across the rooftops, and a small display of antique swords, armour and guns.

For information on entry visa requirements for Slovakia, see www.mzv.sk (under Ministry and then Travel Advice). Citizens of EU countries, Australia, New Zealand, Canada, Japan and the USA can enter Slovakia visa-free for up to 90 days. South Africans do need a visa. If you require a visa it must be bought in advance – they are not issued on arrival at the border.

TRANSPORT: BRATISLAVA

Direction 65km east of Vienna

Travel time One hour

Boat For information on boats to Bratislava see p228

Bus For information on bus connections to Bratislava's airport see p228

Car Head east on the A4 from Vienna until the Fischamend junction, where you continue on Bundesbahn 9, which passes through Petronell and Hainburg and eventually ends at the Slovakia border, just south of Bratislava

Train From Südbahnhof (Ostbahn)/Hauptbahnhof, over a dozen trains daily (return EURegio ticket €14, 1¼ hours) travel to both Bratislava's main train station, 1km north of the old town, and Petržalka station, 3km south of the old town

INFORMATION

Bratislava Culture & Information Centre (BKIS; ☎ 00421-2-16186; www.bkis.sk; Klobučnícka 2; 9am-6pm Mon-Fri, 9am-3pm Sat, 10am-3pm Sun) The central tourist office, with printed visitor guides and English- and German-speaking staff.

Slowakische Zentrale für Tourismus (Map pp56-7; ☎ 0043-1-513 95 69; sacr-wien@aon.at; 01, Parkring 12, Vienna; 9am-12.30 & 1.30-5pm Mon-Fri) Slovak Tourist Board's representative in Vienna.

EATING

Prašná Bašta (☎ 00421-2-5443 4957; Zámočnicka 11; mains €6.60-14.50; 11am-11pm) This restaurant in the old town serves good Slovak food in a charm-

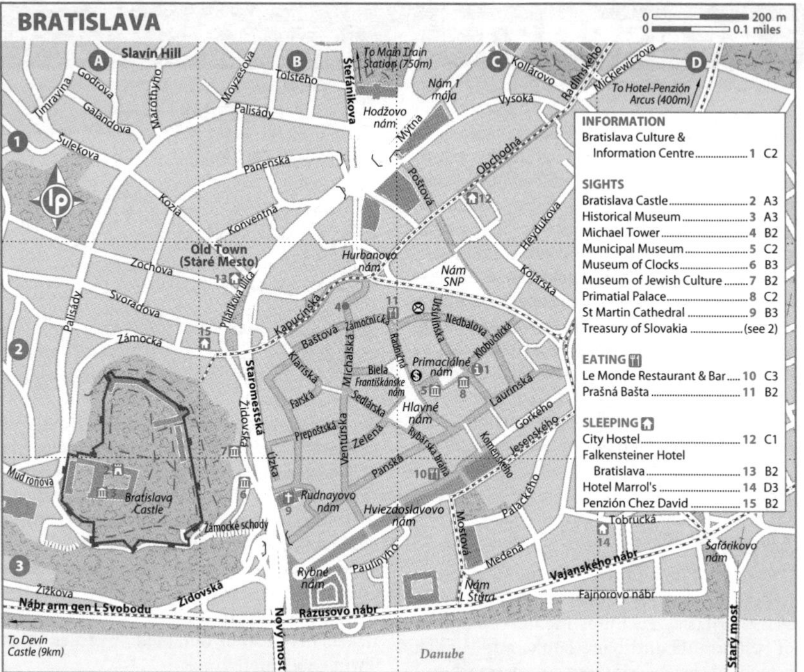

ing round vaulted interior and one of the most private inner courtyards in the city.

Le Monde Restaurant & Bar (☎ 00421-2-5441 5411; Rybárska brána 8; mains €15-27; 8am-midnight Mon-Fri, from 10am Sat;) Le Monde is one of Bratislava's class acts for international fare, serving dishes such as grilled octopus with a warm black lentil salad and basil sauce (€22.65) or sushi and sashimi with soya-citrus dressing and glass noodles – all in a formal lounge setting.

SLEEPING

City Hostel (☎ 00421-2-5263 6041; www.cityhostel.sk; Obchodná 38; s/d/tr/q €39/56/72/86;) Although breakfast is not served in this modern hostel, you can always grab a bite to eat at one of the eateries on Obchodná. Rooms are comfortable if a little sterile, but each has its own bathroom. It has small, modern singles and doubles that are more basic hotel than hostel. Internet downstairs is free.

Penzión Chez David (☎ 00421-2-5441 3824; www.chezdavid.sk; Zámocká 13; s/d €59/76; 11.30am-11pm) Small but comfortable rooms at this cool blue (and Jewish) pension. Kosher food is available from its attached restaurant (mains €6.50 to €15).

Falkensteiner Hotel Bratislava (☎ 00421-2-5923 6100; www.falkensteiner.com; Pilárikova ulica 5; r €167/149 with/without breakfast;) This modern business hotel is currently one of the best deals in town, offering great value if you're travelling as a couple. All rooms are either twins or doubles, decorated in stylish orange tones, complemented by a fitness area and a sauna with a chill-out zone offering a view over the rooftops. This is included in the price, but wi-fi costs €9 per 24 hours.

Hotel Marrol's (☎ 00421-2-5778 4600; www.hotelmarrols.sk; Tobrucká 4; s/d €179/189;) Retro refinement, black-and-white movie stills, sleek leather chairs, sumptuous fabrics: Hotel Marrol's is straight off the silver screen – c 1940. The Jasmine spa downstairs is welcome relief after a day of sightseeing, but most rooms also have a bathtub.

TRANSPORT

Situated in the centre of Europe, Austria is sandwiched between Eastern and Western Europe. Its train lines fan out in all directions, flight links are plentiful, if Europe-focused, and getting around is a breeze: the central city is easily walkable or bikeable, and swift, reliable subways, trains and those ubiquitous, slow-but-fun streetcars snake their way all over town and into the suburbs. Getting across the centre of town takes less than 10 minutes by subway; factor around 30 minutes by streetcar or bus.

Flights, tours and rail tickets can be booked online at www.lonelyplanet.com/bookings.

AIR

Airports

Located 20km southwest of the city centre is Vienna International Airport (☎ 700 72 22 33; www.viennaairport.com). Facilities include a handful of restaurants and bars, banks and ATMs, money-exchange counters, a supermarket, a post office, car-hire agencies and a 24-hour left-luggage counter.

Bratislava, Slovakia's capital, only 60km east of Vienna, is a highly feasible alternative to flying into Austria. Airport Letisko Bratislava (☎ 0421 2 4857 3353; www.airportbratislava.sk), serving Bratislava, is connected to Vienna International Airport by seven buses daily (www.terravision.eu; one-way/return €10/16).

BICYCLE

Vienna is a fabulous place to get around by bike: see p203 for more information about bicycle hire in the city. Bicycles can be carried on carriages marked with a bike symbol on the S-Bahn and U-Bahn from 9am to 3pm and after 6.30pm Monday to Friday, after 9am Saturday and all day Sunday for half the adult fare. It's not possible to take bikes on trams and buses. The city also runs a City Bike programme, with bike stands scattered throughout the city; see p203. For information on bike tours, see p237.

BOAT

The Danube is a traffic-free access route for arrivals and departures from Vienna. Eastern Europe is the main destination; Twin City Liner (Map pp56-7; ☎ 588 80; www.twincityliner.com; 01, Schwedenplatz; one-way adult/2-12yr from €17/8.50; 🕑 8am-4.30pm) connects Vienna with Bratislava in 1½ hours from March to October, while DDSG Blue Danube (Map pp56-7; ☎ 588 80; www.ddsg-blue-danube.at; 01, Handelskai 265; one-way/return €89/109, 2-14yr 50% off; 🕑 9am-6pm Mon-Fri) links Budapest with Vienna from May to October. DDSG tickets may also be obtained or picked up at Twin City Liner.

The Danube is connected to the Rhine by the River Main tributary and the Main-Danube Canal in southern Germany; imaginatively named ships like the MS *Sound of Music* and MS *River Empress* cruise along this route, from Amsterdam to Budapest, between May and November. Bookings can be made through Noble Caledonia (☎ 020-7752 0000; www.noble-caledonia.co.uk) in Britain and Uniworld (☎ 1-800-360 9550; www.uniworld.com) in the USA.

For boat trips through the Wachau region northwest of Vienna, see the Excursions chapter (p217).

> **THINGS CHANGE...**
>
> The information in this chapter is particularly vulnerable to change. Check directly with the airline or a travel agent to make sure you understand how a fare (and ticket you may buy) works and be aware of the security requirements for international travel. Shop carefully. The details given in this chapter should be regarded as pointers and are not a substitute for your own careful, up-to-date research.

BUS

Vienna has no central bus station; your arrival destination will depend on which company you're travelling with.

Eurolines (Map pp104-5; www.eurolines.com; ☎ 798 29 00; www.eurolines.at; 03, Erdbergstrasse 202; 🕑 6.30am-8.30pm Mon-Fri, 6.30-11am & 4.30-8.30pm Sat & Sun) has basically tied up the bus routes connecting Austria with the rest of Europe. Its main terminal is at the U3 U-Bahn station Erdberg but some buses stop at the U6 and U1 U-Bahn and train station Praterstern (Map pp112-13).

CAR & MOTORCYCLE

Driving

You may consider hiring a car to see the sights mentioned in the Excursions chapter (p217) but in Vienna itself it's best to stick with the excellent public transport system (see below).

Hire

Car-hire rates start at around €80 per day and all the big names in car hire are present in Vienna (and have desks at the airport). Here are the details for a couple of major companies in the city:

Europcar (Map pp56-7; ☎ 714 67 17; www.europcar.at; 01, Schubertring 9; 7.30am-6pm Mon-Fri, 8am-1pm Sat, 8am-noon Sun)

Hertz (Map pp56-7; ☎ 512 86 77; www.hertz.at; 01, Kärntner Ring 17; 7.30am-6pm Mon-Fri, 9am-3pm Sat & Sun)

PUBLIC TRANSPORT

Vienna has a comprehensive and unified public transport network that is one of the most efficient in Europe. Flat-fare tickets are valid for trains, trams, buses, the underground (U-Bahn) and the S-Bahn regional trains. Services are frequent and you rarely have to wait more than 10 minutes. From Sunday through Thursday, public transport starts at around 5am or 6am; buses (with the exception of night buses) and trams finish between 11pm and midnight and S-Bahn and U-Bahn services between 12.30am and 1am. On Friday and Saturday nights the U-Bahn runs through the following morning at a reduced schedule.

Transport maps are posted in all U-Bahn stations and at many bus and tram stops. Free maps and information pamphlets are available from Wiener Linien (☎ 7909-100 information line; www.wienerlinien.at, in German; 6am-10pm Mon-Fri, 8.30am-4.30pm Sat & Sun), located in nine U-Bahn stations. The Karlsplatz, Stephansplatz and Westbahnhof information offices are open 6.30am to 6.30pm Monday to Friday and 8.30am to 4pm Saturday and Sunday. Those at Schottentor, Praterstern, Floridsdorf, Philadelphiabrücke and Erdberg are closed at weekends.

Buses

Buses go everywhere, including within the Innere Stadt, and either have three digits or a number followed by an 'A' or 'B'. Very logically, buses connecting with a tram service often have the same number, eg bus 38A connects with tram 38, bus 72A with tram 72.

Night Buses

Vienna's comprehensive Nightline service takes over when trams, buses and the U-Bahn stop running. Routes cover much of the city and run every half-hour from 12.30am to 5am. Schwedenplatz, Schottentor and the Staatsoper are starting points for many

CLIMATE CHANGE & TRAVEL

Climate change is a serious threat to the ecosystems that humans rely upon, and air travel is the fastest-growing contributor to the problem. Lonely Planet regards travel, overall, as a global benefit, but believes we all have a responsibility to limit our personal impact on global warming.

Flying & Climate Change

Pretty much every form of motor transport generates carbon dioxide (the main cause of human-induced climate change) but planes are far and away the worst offenders, not just because of the sheer distances they allow us to travel, but because they release greenhouse gases high into the atmosphere. The statistics are frightening: two people taking a return flight between Europe and the USA will contribute as much to climate change as an average household's gas and electricity consumption over a whole year.

Carbon Offset Schemes

Climatecare.org and other websites use 'carbon calculators' that allow travellers to offset the greenhouse gases they are responsible for with contributions to energy-saving projects and other climate-friendly initiatives in the developing world – including projects in India, Honduras, Kazakhstan and Uganda.

Lonely Planet, together with Rough Guides and other concerned partners in the travel industry, supports the carbon offset scheme run by climatecare.org. Lonely Planet offsets all of its staff and author travel.

For more information check out our website: www.lonelyplanet.com.

GETTING INTO TOWN

Bus Link (☎ 05 17 17; www.postbus.at; adult one-way/return €6/11, under 6yr free, 6-15yr €3/5.50; ⏲ every 30min 5am-11pm from Westbahnhof, 5.15am-11.15pm from Meidling, 5am-11.30pm from Schwedenplatz, 6.38am-6.38pm from UNO City) The Westbahnhof service calls in at Wien Meidling station.

C&K Airport Service (☎ 444 44; www.ck-airportservice.at; one-way €33, up to 4 persons) C&K car service is a better, cheaper option than a taxi as its rates are fixed. On arrival at the airport, head to its stand to the left of the exit hall; when leaving Vienna, call ahead to make a reservation.

City Airport Train (CAT; Map p104-5; ☎ 252 50; www.cityairporttrain.com; return adult/under 15yr €18/free, booked online €16; ⏲ every 30min 5.38am-11.08pm) Departs from Wien-Mitte; has luggage check-in facilities and boarding-card-issuing service.

Schnellbahn 7 (☎ 05 17 17; www.oebb.at; one way €3.60, valid for 1hr & includes transfer to connecting city transport; ⏲ every 30min 4.32am-9.56pm Mon-Sat) Cheapest way to get to the airport; departs from Wien Nord and Floridsdorf and passes through Wien-Mitte.

Taxi A standard taxi to central Vienna costs roughly €35–37.

services; look for buses and bus stops marked with an 'N'. All transport tickets are valid for Nightline services.

S-Bahn

S-Bahn trains, designated by a number preceded by an 'S', operate from train stations and service the suburbs or satellite towns. If you're travelling outside of Vienna, and outside of the ticket zone, you'll probably have to purchase an extension; check on maps posted in train stations.

Tickets & Passes

Tickets and passes can be purchased at U-Bahn stations – from automatic machines (with English instructions and change) and occasionally staffed ticket offices – and in *Tabakladen* (tobacconists). Once bought, tickets need to be validated before starting your journey (except for weekly and monthly tickets); look for small blue boxes at the entrance to U-Bahn stations and on buses and trams. Just pop the end of the ticket in the slot and wait for the 'ding'. It's an honour system and ticket inspection is infrequent, but if you're caught without a ticket you'll be fined €62, no exceptions.

Tickets and passes are as follows:

Single Ticket *(Einzelfahrschein)* – €1.80; good for one journey, with line changes; costs €2.20 if purchased on trams and buses (correct change required)

Strip Ticket *(Streifenkarte)* – €7.20; four single tickets on one strip

24-Hour Ticket *(24 Stunden Wien-Karte)* – €5.70; 24 hours' unlimited travel from time of validation

48-Hour Ticket *(48 Stunden Wien-Karte)* – €10; 48 hours' unlimited travel from time of validation

72-Hour Ticket *(72 Stunden Wien-Karte)* – €13.60; 72 hours' unlimited travel from time of validation

Eight-day Ticket *(8-Tage-Karte)* – €28.80; valid for eight days, but not necessarily eight consecutive days; punch the card as and when you need it

Weekly Ticket *(Wochenkarte)* – €14; valid Monday to Sunday only

Monthly Ticket (*Monatskarte*) – €49.50; valid from the 1st of the month to the last day of the month

Vienna Shopping Card *(Wiener Einkaufskarte)* – €4.60; for use between 8am and 8pm Monday to Saturday; only good for one day after validation

The Vienna Card *(Die Wien-Karte)* – €18.50; 72 hours of unlimited travel from time of validation plus discounts; see p233 for more information on discount cards

Children aged six to 15 travel for half-price, or for free on Sunday, public holidays and during Vienna school holidays (photo ID necessary); younger children always travel free. Senior citizens (women over 60, men over 65) can buy a €2.30 ticket that is valid for two trips; inquire at transport information offices.

Trams

There's something romantic and just plain good about travelling by tram, even though they're slower than the U-Bahn. Vienna's tram network is extensive and it's the perfect way to view the city on the cheap (see p133 for suggestions for touring the city by tram). Trams are either numbered or lettered (eg 1,

44, D) and services cover the city centre and some suburbs.

U-Bahn

The U-Bahn is a quick and efficient way of getting around the city. There are five lines: U1 to U4 and U6 (there is no U5). Platforms have timetable information and signs showing the exits and nearby facilities.

TAXI

Taxis are reliable and relatively cheap by Western European standards. City journeys are metered; the minimum charge is roughly €2.60 from 6am to 11pm Monday to Saturday and €2.70 any other time, plus a small per-km fee. A small tip is expected; add about 10% to the fare. Taxis are easily found at train stations and taxi stands all over the city, or just flag them down in the street. To order one, call ☎ 31 300, ☎ 60 160 or ☎ 40 100. Few taxis accept credit cards.

TRAIN

Austria's train network is a dense web reaching the country's far-flung corners. The system is fast, efficient, frequent and well used. **Österreiche Bundesbahn** (ÖBB; Austrian Federal Railway; 24hr information ☎ 05 17 17; www.oebb.at) is the main operator, and has information offices at all of Vienna's main train stations. Tickets can be purchased at ticket offices or on the train, but the latter will normally cost a little extra.

At press time, a massive construction project is in progress at Vienna's former Südbahnhof: essentially the station is shut but an eastern section, called the Südbahnhof (Ostbahn), has been set up as a temporary station, serving some regional trains to/from the east, including Bratislava. The entire complex is due to reopen as the main rail hub in late 2012/early 2013; it'll be called the Hauptbahnhof Wien (Vienna Central Station) and will again receive international trains. As a result, all long-distance trains are being rerouted among the rest of Vienna's train stations. Additionally, **Westbahnhof** (Map pp84-5) is undergoing major renovation; at press time, the entire ticket hall and Europaplatz in front of it has been shut. A provisional station has been created to the left of the main hall so that the station may remain in operation – it is slated to reopen in late 2011; after the new Hauptbahnhof opens, the Westbahnhof will only handle regional trains. Further train stations include **Franz-Josefs-Bahnhof** (Map pp94-5) **Wien Mitte** (Map pp104-5), **Wien Nord** (Map pp112-13) and **Meidling** (Map pp120-1).

DIRECTORY

BUSINESS HOURS

Banks 8am or 9am to 3pm Monday to Friday, with extended hours until 5.30pm on Thursday. Many smaller branches close from 12.30pm to 1.30pm for lunch.

Cafes 7am to midnight.

Post offices 8am to noon and 2pm to 6pm Monday to Friday; some also open 8am to noon Saturday. The **main post office** (Map pp56-7; 01, Fleischmarkt 19) is open 24 hours, and the branch at Franz-Josefs-Bahnhof has extended hours.

Pubs and clubs Opening times vary; closing is normally between midnight and 4am throughout the week.

Restaurants Generally 11am to 3pm and 6pm to 11pm or midnight.

General office hours 8am to 5pm Monday to Friday.

Shops Normally open 9am to 6.30pm Monday to Friday and until 5pm Saturday. Some have extended hours until 9pm on Thursday or Friday.

Supermarkets 7.30am or 8am to 6pm or 7pm Monday to Friday, to 5pm Saturday; closed Sunday.

CHILDREN

For more years than anyone would care to remember, the Viennese had the reputation of loving their dogs more than their children. Thankfully, this attitude has changed, and now children are given more reign to just be kids. Facilities have also improved, with new trams easily accessible for buggies or prams (the older ones, however, are a nightmare); the U-Bahn and buses are also parent friendly. Children receive discounts on public transport (see p230), some restaurants have children's menus, and often children under 12 can stay in their parents' hotel room free of charge. Breastfeeding in public is a common sight and nappy-changing ruffles few feathers. There's even an information centre, the **WienXtra-Kinderinfo** (p238), for parents and their offspring. However, babysitters for visitors are hard to arrange; the best idea is to check with the hotel you're staying at.

The Neighbourhoods chapter (p47) features more options, and we've included 'Top Picks for Children' in that chapter.

For helpful travelling tips, pick up a copy of Lonely Planet's *Travel with Children* by Cathy Lanigan.

CLIMATE

Austria falls within the Central European climatic zone, though the eastern part of the country (where Vienna is situated) has a Continental Pannonian climate, characterised by a mean temperature in July that hovers around 20°C and annual rainfall usually under 800mm.

The differences in temperature between day and night and summer and winter are greater here than in the west of the country. July and August can be very hot, and a hotel with air-conditioning would be an asset at this time. Winter is surprisingly cold, especially in January, and you would need to bring plenty of warm clothing then. Damp maritime winds sometimes sweep in from the west, and the *Föhn*, a warm wind from the south, is not an uncommon occurrence throughout the entire year. The average rainfall is 710mm per year, with most falling between May and August, causing the Danube to flood in recent years.

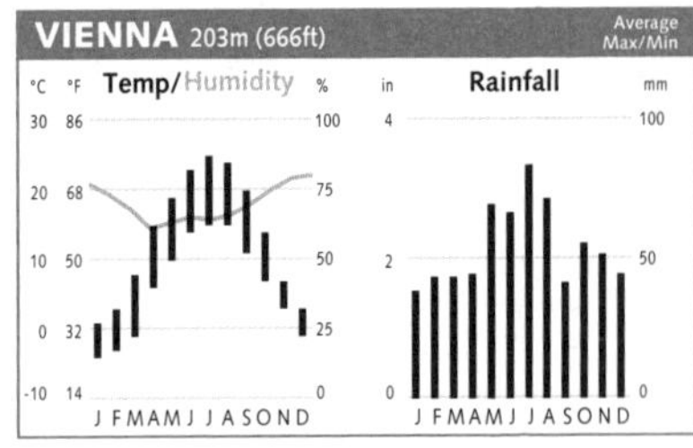

COURSES

Many places offer German language courses, and they can usually offer the option of accommodation for the duration of the course. Two of the better-known course providers are:

Berlitz (Map pp56-7; ☎ 0820-820 082; www.berlitz.at; 01, Graben 13; 8am-8pm Mon-Fri) Offers a range of private, intensive and evening courses and has four offices in Vienna.

Inlingua Sprachschule (Map pp56-7; ☎ 512 22 25; www.inlingua.at; 01, Neuer Markt 1; 9am-6pm Mon-Fri) Courses run for a minimum of two weeks, and can either be taken during the day or at night. Classes are limited to eight students; individual tuition is also available.

See the Eating chapter for cooking courses (p153).

CUSTOMS REGULATIONS

Theoretically there is no restriction on how much you can bring into Austria from other EU states. However, to ensure that these goods remain for personal use, guideline limits are 800 cigarettes (25 cigarettes if entering by car or ship), 200 cigars, 1kg tobacco, 10L of spirits, 90L of wine, 110L of beer and 20L of other alcoholic beverages. The same quantity can be taken out of Austria, as long as you are travelling to another EU country.

For duty-free purchases made outside the EU, you may bring 200 cigarettes or 50 cigars or 250g tobacco, plus 2L of wine and 1L of spirits into Austria. Items such as weapons, drugs (both legal and illegal), meat, animal products and certain plant material are subject to stricter customs control.

DISCOUNT CARDS

The Vienna Card (*Die Wien-Karte;* €18.50) allows three days' unlimited travel on the public transport system (including night buses) and provides discounts at selected museums, cafes, *Heurigen* (wine taverns), restaurants and shops across the city, and on guided tours and the City Airport Train (CAT; p230). The discount usually amounts to 5% to 10% off the normal price, or a free gift. It can be purchased at Tourist Info Wien (p238) and many concierge desks at the top hotels.

ELECTRICITY

The voltage used in Vienna and throughout Austria is 220V. Sockets are the round two-pin type, which are standard throughout most of Continental Europe. North American 110V appliances will need a transformer if they don't have built-in voltage adjustment.

EMBASSIES

The Austrian Foreign Ministry website (www.bmaa.gv.at, in German) has a complete list of embassies and consulates.

Australia (Map pp56-7; ☎ 506 740; www.australian-embassy.at; 04, Mattiellistrasse 2)

Canada (Map pp56-7; ☎ 531 38 3000; www.kanada.at; 01, Laurenzerberg 2)

Czech Republic (Map pp120-1; ☎ 899 581 11; www.mzv.cz/vienna; 14, Penzingerstrasse 11-13)

France (Map pp56-7; ☎ 502 75 200; www.consulfrance-vienne.org; 01, Wipplingerstrasse 24-26)

Hungary (Map pp56-7; ☎ 537 80 300; kom@huembvie.at; 01, Bankgasse 4-6)

Italy (Map pp104-5; ☎ 713 56 71; www.ambvienna.esteri.it; 03, Ungargasse 43)

Slovakia (Map pp50-1; ☎ 318 90 55; www.vienna.mfa.sk; 19, Armbrustergasse 24)

Slovenia (Map pp56-7; ☎ 585 22 40; vdu@gov.si; 01, Nibelungengasse 13)

Switzerland (Map pp104-5; ☎ 795 05-0; www.eda.admin.ch/wien; 03, Prinz-Eugen-Strasse 7)

UK (Map pp104-5; ☎ 716 130; www.britishembassy.at; 03, Jauresgasse 12)

USA (Map pp56-7; ☎ 319 39; www.usembassy.at; 4th fl, Hotel Marriott, 01, Gartenbaupromenade 2-4)

EMERGENCY

In case of emergency, dial the following:

Ambulance *(Rettung)* ☎ 144

Fire *(Feuerwehr)* ☎ 122

Police *(Polizei)* ☎ 133

GAY & LESBIAN TRAVELLERS

Vienna is a city that is reasonably tolerant towards gays and lesbians, more so than the rest of Austria, and gay bashing is virtually unknown here (in contrast to the situation in ostensibly more gay-tolerant cities such as Amsterdam or Berlin). The situation is improving all the time; the restricting federal statute 209, which set the consenting age for sex between men at 18 (it is 14 for heterosexuals), was repealed in 2003. There is no set age of consent for lesbian sex, apparently because the legislators decided there was no discernible difference between mutual washing of bodily parts and intimate sexual contact. While lesbians welcome the lack of legislation, they see this as a typical (male) denial of female sexuality.

Information on the *Schwullesbische Szene* (gay and lesbian scene) is quite comprehensive. The Vienna Tourist Board produces the handy *Queer Guide,* a booklet listing gay bars, restaurants, hotels and festivals, and the *Gay Guide,* a city map with gay locations marked. Both are freely available at the Tourist Info Wien office (p238), from the organisations listed on p234 and at many gay and lesbian *Lokale* (bars). *Xtra* (www.xtra-news.at, in German), a free monthly publication, is an additional supplement packed with news, views and listings. For online resources, try www.gayboy.at, www.rainbow.or.at and www.gaynet.at, which can provide further information and up-to-date news on events.

Events to look out for on the gay and lesbian calendar include the Regenbogen Parade (Rainbow Parade), the Life Ball, and Identities (Vienna's Queer Film Festival); see p16 for more details. Bars, venues and clubs are listed throughout the Drinking & Nightlife chapter (see p171).

Organisations

Homosexuelle Initiative Wien (HOSI; Map pp112-13; ☎ 216 66 04; www.hosiwien.at, in German; 02, Novaragasse 40; from 7pm Tue & Wed, from 5.30pm Thu, from 9pm Fri; closed Jul & Aug) HOSI is a politically minded gay and lesbian centre with regular events.

Rosa Lila Villa (Map pp84-5; www.villa.at, in German; 06, Linke Wienzeile 102) Probably the best organisation in Vienna for information, the Rosa Lila Villa has telephone counselling, a small library with books in English, and advice and information on what's on offer in the city. There is a separate lesbian centre (☎ 586 81 50; 5-8pm Mon, Wed & Fri) and a gay men's centre (☎ 585 43 43; 5-8pm Mon & Fri, 1-8pm Wed).

HOLIDAYS

The Viennese take their holiday time seriously; and the entire city basically shuts down on public holidays. The only establishments remaining open are bars, cafes and restaurants, and even some of these refuse to open their doors. Museums like to confuse things – some stay closed while others are free. The big school break is July and August; most families go away during this time, so you'll find the city is a little quieter, but the downside is that a high percentage of restaurants and entertainment venues close. Consult When to Go (p16) for details of festivals and events.

Public holidays:

New Year's Day *(Neujahr)* 1 January

Epiphany *(Heilige Drei Könige)* 6 January

Easter Monday *(Ostermontag)* March or April

Labour Day *(Tag der Arbeit)* 1 May

Ascension Day *(Christi Himmelfahrt)* Sixth Thursday after Easter

Whit Monday *(Pfingstmontag)* Sixth Monday after Easter

Corpus Christi *(Fronleichnam)* Second Thursday after Pentecost

Assumption *(Maria Himmelfahrt)* 15 August

National Day *(Nationalfeiertag)* 26 October

All Saints' Day *(Allerheiligen)* 1 November

Immaculate Conception *(Mariä Empfängnis)* 8 December

Christmas Day *(Christfest)* 25 December

St Stephen's Day *(Stephanitag)* 26 December

INTERNET ACCESS

Vienna is well geared to travellers wishing to stay in touch via email while on holiday. Many of the main streets leading away from the city centre outside the Gürtel are lined with cheap, albeit slightly grungy, call centres doubling as internet cafes. Additionally, a large number of coffee houses, cafes and also some bars have free or low-cost internet. Look for the wireless connection sign – called WLAN hot spots.

Most hotels have wireless or wired internet, but as yet it's not possible to organise an ISP in Austria for a short period (minimum contracts run for 12 months). For a relatively up-to-date list of venues offering free wi-fi, see www.freewave.at/en/hotspots; you can use the handy drop-down menu to search by district (1010 for the first, 1110 for the 10th, etc).

MAPS

For most purposes, the free *Stadtplan* (city map) provided by the tourist office will be sufficient. It shows bus, tram and U-Bahn routes, has a separate U-Bahn plan and lists major city-wide sights. It also has a blow-up of the Innere Stadt. For a street index, you'll need to buy a map. Freytag & Berndt's 1:25,000 fold-out map, available at most bookshops, is very comprehensive, but its *Buchplan Wien* (scale 1:20,000) is the Rolls-Royce of city maps and is used by locals.

MEDICAL SERVICES

EU, EEA (European Economic Area) and Swiss nationals receive free emergency medical treatment, although payment may have to be made for medication, private consultations and non-urgent treatment. To receive treatment, you'll need to present a European Health Insurance Card (called the *e*card in Austria) to take advantage of reciprocal health agreements in Europe; arrange one before leaving home. Nothing, however, beats having full health insurance.

If you're staying a long time in Vienna it would facilitate matters if you got a certificate from the health insurance office, the Gebietskrankenkasse (Map pp50-1; ☎ 601 22-0; www.wgkk.at, in German; 10, Wienerbergstrasse 15-19; ⏰ 7.30am-2pm Mon-Wed & Fri, 7.30am-4pm Thu). This office can also tell you the countries that have reciprocal agreements with Austria (the USA, Canada, Australia and New Zealand don't).

Emergency Rooms

The following hospitals *(Krankenhäuser)* have emergency rooms open 24 hours a day, seven days a week:

Allgemeines Krankenhaus (Map pp94-5; ☎ 404 00; www.akhwien.at; 09, Währinger Gürtel 18-20; Ⓤ U6 Michelbeuern-AKH 🚊 5, 33)

Lorenz Böhler Unfallkrankenhaus (Map pp112-13; ☎ 331 10; www.ukhboehler.at, in German; 20, Donaueschingenstrasse 13; Ⓤ U6 Dresdener Strasse 🚌 5A, 37A)

Unfallkrankenhaus Meidling (Map pp50-1; ☎ 601 50-0; 12, Kundratstrasse 37)

If you require a pharmacy *(Apotheke)* after hours, dial ☎ 1550 (German-speaking).

MONEY

Austria's currency is the euro, which is divided into 100 cents. There are coins for one, two, five, 10, 20 and 50 cents, and €1 and €2. Notes come in denominations of €5, €10, €20, €50, €100, €200 and €500.

See the Quick Reference (inside front cover) for exchange rates at the time of going to press. For the latest rates, check out www.oanda.com.

ATMs

Bankomats (ATMs), which accept credit, debit and Eurocheque cards, are never very far away in Vienna – just look for a neon sign with two green and blue stripes sticking out from a bank facade. *Bankomats* can also be found in the main train stations and at the airport.

Check with your home bank before travelling to see how much the charge is for using a *Bankomat* in Vienna; normally there's no commission to pay at the Austrian end.

Changing Money

Banks are the best places to exchange cash, but it pays to shop around as exchange rates and commission charges can vary a little between them. Normally there is a minimum commission charge of €2 to €3.50, so try to exchange your money in large amounts to save on multiple charges.

There are plenty of exchange offices in the Innere Stadt, particularly around Stephansplatz and on Kärntner Strasse. Commission charges are around the same here as at banks, but quite often their exchange rates are uncompetitive.

American Express (Map pp56-7; ☎ 515 400-40; www.americanexpress.com, in German; 01, Kärntner Strasse 21-23; ⏰ 9am-5.30pm Mon-Fri, 10am-3pm Sat) exchanges cash as well as travellers cheques (Amex travellers cheques for free, cheques of other institutions incur a small charge). It also has a travel section and financial services, and will hold mail (not parcels) free of charge for up to one month for customers who have an American Express card.

Credit Cards

Visa, EuroCard and MasterCard are accepted a little more widely than American Express and Diners Club, although a surprising number of shops and restaurants refuse to accept any credit cards at all. Plush shops and restaurants will usually accept cards, though, and the same applies for hotels. Train tickets can be bought by credit card in main stations.

To report lost or stolen credit cards, call the following:

American Express ☎ 0800 900 940

Diners Club ☎ 501 35 14

MasterCard ☎ 0800 218 235

Visa ☎ 0800 200 288

NEWSPAPERS & MAGAZINES

English-language newspapers are widely available in Vienna, usually late in the afternoon of the day on which they're published. The first to hit the stands are the *Financial Times* and the *International Herald Tribune. USA Today, Time, Newsweek, The Economist* and most British newspapers are also easy to find. You'll find most titles sold at newsstands and by pavement sellers, particularly around the main train stations and at U-Bahn stations on the Ringstrasse.

Of the several German-language daily newspapers available, the magazine-size *Neue Kronen Zeitung* has the largest circulation by a long shot, despite its sensationalist slant and lack of hard news. Serious papers include *Der Standard* and *Die Presse;* the former usually takes a stance on the left-hand side of the fence, the latter on the right. For entertainment listings and on-the-button political and social commentary, the winner hands down is Vienna's own *Der Falter*. This weekly publication comes out on Wednesday and is only in German, but the listings are quite easy to decipher. *City* is a cheaper, slimmed-down *Der Falter*, with none of the politics and less listings coverage. *Augustin*, Vienna's version of the *Big Issue*, is partially produced and sold by the homeless, who receive a portion of the sales. Vienna's home-grown paper in English, *Austria Today* (www.austriatoday.at), is only available online and the *Vienna Review* (www.austriantimes.at) is a decent opinion and newspaper produced by a mixture of students and graduates from Vienna's English-language Webster University.

ORGANISED TOURS

Vienna is a city easily attacked on your own, but if you'd prefer the hassle taken out of touring, or if time is of the essence, the city has a tour to suit; choose from bus, boat, bicycle, horse-drawn carriage or the traditional walking tour.

It's also possible to organise your own tram tour; trams 1 and 2, which circle the Innere Stadt along the Ringstrasse, are perfect self-guided tours of the Ringstrasse's architectural delights, and our Do-it-Yourself Ringstrasse Tram Tour (p134) provides an option for exploring on your own. For suggestions of walking and cycling tours of the city, see p77, p89, p100, p108, p116 and p123.

Bus Tours

Bus tours are good for covering a lot of ground and taking in the further-flung sights.

Cityrama (Map pp56-7; ☎ 534 13; www.cityrama.at; 01, Börsegasse 1; various city tours adult €39-47, child €15-30, excursions beyond Vienna adult/child from €69/30; 10am-5pm; U1, U2, U4 Karlsplatz D, 1, 2 59A, 62) Cityrama offers tours lasting from an hour to a day, taking in not only Vienna (bus times are the same as on the Hop On Hop Off Vienna Line) but attractions within a day's striking distance of the city, including Salzburg, Budapest and Prague. Some tours require an extra fee for admission into sights, such as training at the Spanish Riding School. All details are on the website.

Hop On Hop Off Vienna Line (Map pp56-7; ☎ 712 46 83; www.viennasightseeingtours.com; 04, Graf Starhemberggasse 25; 1hr/2hr/all-day/2-day ticket €13/16/20/25, child €7 for all tours; 10am-5pm; U1, U2, U4 Karlsplatz D, 1, 2 59A, 62) Like Cityrama, Vienna Line buses stop at 14 sights in Vienna. Tickets range from one hour to all day, and you can hop on and off the buses as many times as you wish. Buses circle the Innere Stadt, with a detour to Stephansplatz, departing every half-hour, Monday to Thursday, and every half-hour (every 15 minutes July and August) Friday to Sunday, from outside Staatsoper. Buses taking in the sights east of the Innere Stadt, such as UNO city and Prater, depart every half-hour between 11am and 6pm, and tours taking in Schönbrunn and Schloss Belvedere run at 10am, 2pm and 4pm (plus 1pm and 3pm in July and August).

Oldtimer Bus Tours (Map p66; ☎ 503 74 43 12; www.oldtimertours.at; 07, Seidengasse 32; tours adult/child €18/10; May–early Oct; 1, 2) Vintage open-top (closed if rainy) oldtimer coaches trundle around the city centre and occasionally up to the Wienerwald (Vienna Woods). Tours last an hour and leave from in front of the Hofburg at Heldenplatz daily at 11am, 12.30pm, 2pm and 4pm.

Redbus City Tours (Map p66; ☎ 512 48 63; www.redbuscitytours.at; 01, Führichgasse 12; tours adult/child from €14/7; 10am-7pm; U1, U2, U4 Karlsplatz D, 1, 2 59A, 62) Vienna's Redbus offers 1½-hour tours of the main sights in and around the Innere Stadt and a day tour of the city's big sights, including stops at Schönbrunn and Grinzing. Buses leave from outside the Albertina (p70).

Boat Tours

DDSG Blue Danube (Map pp56-7; ☎ 588 80; www.ddsg-blue-danube.at; 01, Schwedenbrücke; adult/child from €15/7.50, under 10yr free; tours 11am & 3pm Apr-Oct; U1, U4 Schwedenplatz 1, 2) DDSG Blue Danube's boats cover a variety of tour routes; some of the most popular include circumnavigating Leopoldstadt and Brigittenau districts using the Danube Canal and the Danube as their thoroughfare. It's more of a relaxing break than a huge sightseeing tour. Select tours include passing through the Nussdorf locks (built by Otto Wagner around 1900); the company offers tours starting at 1½ hours and longer, including sunset tours.

Guided Walking Tours

Verliebt in Wien (☎ 889 28 06; www.verliebtinwien.at; adult/child €12/6; Jun-Oct; U1, U2, U4 Karlsplatz D, 1, 2 59A, 62) Margarete Kirschner offers various themed walks covering such topics as medieval Vienna, art nouveau and Hundertwasser and modern architecture. Tours take around 1½ to two hours, leaving from outside the Tourist Info Wien office (p238). Book direct or try through your hotel.

Vienna Tour Guides (☎ 876 71 11; www.wienguide.at; adult/child €14/7) Vienna Tour Guides is a collection of highly knowledgeable guides who conduct over 60 different guided walking tours, some of which are in English. Everything from art nouveau architecture to Jewish traditions in Vienna is covered. The monthly *Wiener Spaziergänge* (Vienna's Walking Tours) leaflet from tourist offices (see p238) details all of these, gives the various departure points and also indicates those tours conducted in English. Tours last roughly 1½ hours; some require a valid public transport pass and extra euros for entrance fees into sights.

Other Tours

Fiaker (20min/40min/1-hr tour roughly €40/65/95) More of a tourist novelty than anything else, a *Fiaker* is a traditional-style open carriage drawn by a pair of horses. Drivers generally speak English and point out places of interest en route. Lines of horses, carriages and bowler-hatted drivers can be found at Stephansplatz, Albertinaplatz and Heldenplatz at the Hofburg.

Ring Tram (Map pp56-7 ☎ 790 91 00; www.wienerlinien.at; adult/child €6/4; 10am-6pm, to 7pm Jul & Aug; U1, U4 Schwedenplatz 1, 2) This ring tram runs the length of the Ringstrasse and is essentially a hop-on, hop-off service with video screens and guided commentary along the way. Tickets can also be combined to include 24 hours of public transport and other variations. Schwedenplatz is the start/end of the tour (arrives at 15 and 45 minutes past each hour; the entire ring tour is 24 minutes without disembarking); the first tour of the day starts at the Staatsoper station, however. For those who are keen to experience the same at lower prices without video commentary, check out our Do-It-Yourself Ringstrasse Tram Tour (p134).

City Segway Tours (Map pp56-7; ☎ 729 72 34; www.citysegwaytours.com/vienna; www.pedalpower.at; tour adult €70; Apr-Oct; U1, U2, U4 Karlsplatz D, 1, 2 59A, 62) Run by Pedal Power (which conducts bicycle tours in and around Vienna; see detail in the Sports & Activities chapter, p203), these Segway tours meet in front of the Staatsoper and cover the main city highlights including the Ringstrasse and the Rathaus, Hofburg and more. They look funny but function without a hitch, and they make certain you're comfortable on the apparatus before you head off.

POST

Austria's postal service (www.post.at) is reliable and easy to use. Post offices are commonplace, as are bright-yellow postboxes. Stamps can also be bought at *Tabakladen* (tobacconists). Sending letters (up to 20g) within Austsria or Europe costs €0.55 and worldwide €1.30. The normal weight limit for letter post *(Briefsendung)* is 2kg; anything over this limit will be sent as a package (from €4 within Austria, from €11.80 anywhere else). Up to 20kg can be sent via surface mail *(Erdwegpakete)*.

Poste restante is *Postlagernde Briefe* in German; address letters *Postlagernde Sendungen* rather than post restante. Mail can be sent care of any post office and is held for a month; a passport must be shown on collection.

The following post offices have longer hours:

Franz-Josefs-Bahnhof Post Office (Map pp94-5; 09, Althanstrasse 10; 7am-8pm Mon-Fri, 9am-2pm Sat & Sun)

Main Post Office (Map pp56-7; ☎ 0577 677 1010; 01, Fleischmarkt 19; 7am-10pm Mon-Fri, 9am-10pm Sat & Sun)

RADIO

State-run stations include Ö1 (87.8 and 92FM), which provides a diet of high-brow music, literature and science, and Ö3 (99.9FM), a commercial outfit with pop music. Radio Wien (89.9 and 95.3FM) is another state-run station, as is FM4 (103.8FM). FM4 is the pick of the crop for alternative music and topical current affairs; it broadcasts in English from 1am to 2pm and has news in English on the hour from 6am to 7pm.

SAFETY

You'd be hard-pressed to find a safer capital city in Europe than Vienna. At night it's not uncommon to see women walking home alone or elderly people walking dogs or using public transport. Tourists normally only experience petty crime, such as pickpocketing (especially at the Naschmarkt, on Mariahilfer Strasse or on crowded public transport).

There are, however, a few places to be extra alert, especially at night. Karlsplatz station and U6 Gumpendorfer Strasse are well-known spots for people to loiter and stagger about with a bottle in hand, and there are often clumps of people passed out or shouting incomprehensibly into the air. The Prater and Praterstern can still feel a bit dicey at night, though that is swiftly changing. Südtirolerplatz and the S-Bahn and tram stations along Margareten and Wiedner Gürtel can be quite unnerving after dark. Indeed, much of the Gürtel around the inner suburbs of Vienna is dotted with red-light clubs, but north of Westbahnhof, the Gürtel contains a higher proportion of them. Women may not always feel comfortable along the Neubaugürtel section, but generally it's OK, particularly as you edge further north past Thaliastrasse, where the nightlife really starts hopping.

TELEPHONE

Austria's country code is ☎0043, Vienna's code is ☎01. Freephone numbers start with ☎0800 or 0810, while numbers starting with ☎0900 are pay-per-minute. When calling from overseas drop the zero in the Vienna code; eg the number for Vienna's main tourist office is ☎0043 1 211 14 555. When calling a Vienna number from within Vienna, the Vienna code is not required; however, when calling Vienna from elsewhere in Austria (or from a mobile) the code needs to be used. Directory assistance is available on ☎11 88 77 and international assistance on ☎0900 11 88 77.

Telekom Austria (☎0800 100 100; www.telekom.at, in German) is Austria's main telecommunications provider and maintains a variety of public telephones throughout Vienna. These take either coins or phonecards and a minimum of €0.20 is required to make a local call. Many post offices have phone booths where both international and national calls can be made; rates are cheaper from 6pm to 8am Monday to Friday, and at weekends. Another option is call centres; they're generally found in the outlying districts and offer very competitive phone-call rates.

To reverse the charges (ie call collect), you have to call a freephone number to place the call. Some of the numbers are listed below (ask directory assistance for others):

Australia ☎0800 200 202

Ireland ☎0800 200 213

New Zealand ☎0800 200 222

South Africa ☎0800 200 230

UK ☎0800 200 209

USA (AT&T) ☎0800 200 288

TIME

Austrian time is on Central European time, one hour ahead of GMT/UTC. If it's noon in Vienna it is 6am in New York and Toronto, 3am in San Francisco, 9pm in Sydney and 11pm in Auckland. Clocks go forward one hour on the last Saturday night in March and back again on the last Saturday night in October.

Note that in German *halb* is used to indicate the half-hour before the hour, hence *halb acht* (half-eight) means 7.30, not 8.30.

TIPPING

Tipping is part of everyday life in Vienna; tips are generally expected at restaurants, bars (even ordering a beer at the bar normally incurs a tip), cafes and in taxis. In service establishments, it's customary to round up smaller bills (to the nearest 50 cents or euro) when buying coffee or beer, and to add 10% to the bill for full meals; taxi drivers will expect around 10% extra. Tips are handed over at the time of payment: add the bill and tip together and pass it over in one lump sum. It doesn't hurt to tip workers, hairdressers, hotel porters, cloakroom attendants, cleaning staff and tour guides a euro or two.

If you think the service stinks, voice your disapproval by not tipping.

TOURIST INFORMATION

Airport Information Office (🕑6am-11pm) Located in the arrivals hall.

Jugendinfo (Map pp56-7; ☎1799; www.jugendinfowien.at, in German; 01, Babenbergerstrasse 1; 🕑noon-7pm Mon-Sat) Jugendinfo is tailored to those aged between 14 and 26, and has tickets for a variety of events at reduced rates for this age group. Staff can tell you about events around town, and places to log onto the internet.

Niederösterreich Werbung (Map pp56-7; ☎536 100; www.niederoesterreich.at; 01, Fischhof 3/3; 🕑8.30am-5pm Mon-Fri) Provides information on Niederösterreich (Lower Austria), the province surrounding Vienna.

Rathaus Information Office (Map pp56-7; ☎525 50; www.wien.gv.at; 01, Rathaus; 🕑8am-6pm Mon-Fri) City Hall provides information on social, cultural and practical matters, and is geared as much to residents as to tourists. There's an info-screen with useful information.

Tourist Info Wien (Map pp56-7; ☎211 14; www.wien.info; 01, Albertinaplatz; 🕑9am-7pm) Vienna's main tourist office, with a ticket agency, hotel booking service, free maps and every brochure under the sun.

WienXtra-Kinderinfo (Map pp84-5; ☎4000 84 400; www.kinderinfowien.at; 07, Museumsplatz 1; 🕑2-7pm Tue-Thu, 10am-5pm Fri-Sun) Marketed firstly at children (check out the knee-high display cases), *then* their parents, this child-friendly tourist office has loads of information on kids activities and a small indoor playground.

TRAVELLERS WITH DISABILITIES

Vienna is fairly well geared for people with disabilities *(Behinderte)*, but not exceptionally so. Ramps are common but by no means ubiquitous; most U-Bahn stations have wheelchair lifts but trams and buses don't (though buses can lower themselves for easier access and the newer trams have doors at ground level); many, but once again not all, traffic lights 'bleep' to indicate when pedestrians can safely cross the road.

The tourist office can give advice and information. Its detailed booklet *Vienna for Visitors with Disabilities,* in German or English, provides information on hotels and restaurants with disabled access, plus addresses of hospitals, medical equipment shops, parking places, toilets and much more. Send an email (info@wien.info) for more details.

Organisations

Bizeps (Map pp84-5; ☎ 523 89 21; www.bizeps.at, in German; 07, Kaiserstrasse 55/3/4a; ⏲ appointments only 10am-4pm Mon-Thu, 10am-1pm Fri) A centre providing support and self-help for people with disabilities.

Faktor i (Map pp84-5; ☎ 274 92 74; www.faktori.wuk.at, in German; 05, Rechte Wienzeile 81; ⏲ 1-5pm Mon & Tue, 9am-7pm Thu, information line ⏲ 9am-5pm Mon & Tue, 9am-1pm Wed, 9am-7pm Thu) Faktor i is aimed at offering information to young people with disabilities.

VISAS

Visas for stays of up to 90 days are not required for citizens of the EU, the EEA (European Economic Area) and Switzerland, much of Eastern Europe, Israel, USA, Canada, the majority of Central and South American nations, Japan, Korea, Malaysia, Singapore, Australia or New Zealand. All other nationalities require a visa. The Ministry of Foreign Affairs website, www.bmaa.gv.at, has a list of Austrian embassies where you can apply.

If you wish to stay longer you should simply leave the country and re-enter. EU nationals can stay indefinitely, but are required by law to register with the local magistrate's office *(Magistratisches Bezirksamt)* if the stay exceeds 60 days.

Austria is part of the Schengen Agreement, which includes all EU states (minus Britain and Ireland) and Switzerland. In practical terms this means a visa issued by one Schengen country is good for all the other member countries and a passport is not required to move from one to the other.

WOMEN TRAVELLERS

Overall, Vienna is a very safe city and women travellers should experience no special problems. Attacks and verbal harassment are less common here than in many countries. However, normal caution should be exercised in unfamiliar situations.

The **Frauen Büro** (Map pp94-5; ☎ 4000 83 515; 08, Friedrich-Schmidt-Platz 3; ⏲ 8am-4pm Mon-Fri) has loads of pamphlets and brochures (mostly in German) on women's issues and can help with many problems you may have. A 24-hour hotline for women is the *Frauennotruf* (Women's Emergency Line; ☎ 71 719).

WORK

EU, EEA (European Economic Area) and Swiss nationals can work in Austria without a work permit or residency permit, though as intending residents they need to register with the police.

Non-EU nationals need both a work permit and a residency permit, and will find it pretty hard to get either. Inquire (in German) about job possibilities via local Labour Offices; look under '*Arbeitsmarktservice*' in the White Pages for the closest office. The work permit needs to be applied for by your employer in Austria. Applications for residency permits must be applied for via the Austrian embassy in your home country.

Teaching is a favourite of expats; look under '*Sprachschulen*' in the *Gelbe Seiten* for a list of schools. Outside that profession (and barkeeping), you'll struggle to find employment if you don't speak German. Some useful job websites:

www.ams.or.at (in German) Austria's Labour Office

www.stepstone.at (in German) Directed towards professionals

www.jobpilot.at (in German) Another for professionals

www.virtualvienna.net Aimed at expats, with a variety of jobs, including UN listings

LANGUAGE

German is the official language of Austria, but the German spoken in each region has its own distinct features. Viennese German has many similarities to High German (considered the standard German), but is more relaxed and is peppered with lively local words and expressions. It's also sprinkled with French words, a hangover from the days when Maria Theresia encouraged her court to throw a bit of French into the conversation. Within Vienna there is also a further dialect, Tiefwienerisch, which oozes out between the lips, weighed down with expressive sayings that would make your mother blush. This is traditionally the language of the working class, but the nonworking-class folk of the city also love it and use it at every opportunity.

Despite these local characteristics, speakers of standard German (given in this chapter) will be well understood. If you don't speak much German, or none at all, don't worry – English is taught from kindergarten level and a high percentage of the younger population speaks English quite well.

If you want to learn more German than we've included here, pick up a copy of Lonely Planet's *German* phrasebook. Lonely Planet iPhone phrasebooks are available through the Apple App store.

SOCIAL

Meeting People

Hello.
Guten Tag.
Goodbye.
Auf Wiedersehen.
Please.
Bitte.
Thank you (very much).
Danke (schön).
Yes./No.
Ja./Nein.
Do you speak English?
Sprechen Sie Englisch?
Do you understand (me)?
Verstehen Sie (mich)?
Yes, I understand (you).
Ja, ich verstehe (Sie).
No, I don't understand (you).
Nein, ich verstehe (Sie) nicht.

Could you please ...?
Könnten Sie ...?
repeat that
das bitte wiederholen
speak more slowly
bitte langsamer sprechen
write it down
das bitte aufschreiben

Going Out

Is there a local entertainment guide?
Gibt es einen Veranstaltungskalender?

What's on ...?
Was ist ... los?
locally
hier
this weekend
dieses Wochenende
today
heute
tonight
heute Abend

Where are the ...?
Wo sind die ...?
clubs
Klubs
gay venues
Schwulen- und Lesbenkneipen
restaurants
Restaurants
pubs
Kneipen

PRACTICAL

Numbers & Amounts

1 eins
2 zwei
3 drei
4 vier
5 fünf
6 sechs
7 sieben
8 acht
9 neun
10 zehn

11	elf
12	zwölf
13	dreizehn
14	vierzehn
15	fünfzehn
16	sechzehn
17	siebzehn
18	achtzehn
19	neunzehn
20	zwanzig
21	einundzwanzig
22	zweiundzwanzig
30	dreizig
40	vierzig
50	fünfzig
60	sechzig
70	siebzig
80	achtzig
90	neunzig
100	hundert
1000	tausend

Days

Monday	Montag
Tuesday	Dienstag
Wednesday	Mittwoch
Thursday	Donnerstag
Friday	Freitag
Saturday	Samstag
Sunday	Sonntag

Banking

I'd like to …
Ich möchte …
- cash a cheque
  einen Scheck einlösen
- change money
  Geld umtauschen
- change some travellers cheques
  Reiseschecks einlösen

Where's the nearest …?
Wo ist der/die nächste …? m/f
- ATM
  Geldautomat
- foreign-exchange office
  Geldwechselstube

Post

I want to buy a/an …
Ich möchte … kaufen.

aerogram	ein Aerogramm
envelope	einen Umschlag
stamp	eine Briefmarke

I want to send a …
Ich möchte … senden.

parcel	ein Paket
postcard	eine Postkarte

Phones & Mobiles

I want to make a …
Ich möchte …
- call (to Singapore)
  (nach Singapur) telefonieren
- reverse-charge/collect call (to Singapore)
  ein R-Gespräch (nach Singapur) führen

I want to buy a phonecard.
Ich möchte eine Telefonkarte kaufen.

I'd like a/an …
Ich hätte gern …
- adaptor plug
  einen Adapter für die steckdose
- charger for my phone
  ein Ladegerät für mein Handy
- mobile/cell phone for hire
  ein Miethandy
- prepaid mobile/cell phone
  ein Handy mit Prepaidkarte
- SIM card for your network
  eine SIM-Karte für Ihr Netz

Internet

Where's the local internet cafe?
Wo ist hier ein Internet-Café?

I'd like to …
Ich möchte …
- check my email
  meine E-Mails checken
- get internet access
  Internetzugang haben

Transport

What time does the … leave?
Wann fährt … ab?

boat	das Boot
bus	der Bus
train	der Zug

What time does the plane leave?
Wann fliegt das Flugzeug ab?

What time's the … bus?
Wann fährt der … Bus?

first	erste
last	letzte
next	nächste

Where's the nearest metro station?
Wo ist der nächste U-Bahnhof?
Are you available? (taxi)
Sind Sie frei?
How much is it to ...?
Was kostet es bis ...?
Please take me to (this address).
Bitte bringen Sie mich zu (dieser Adresse).

FOOD

breakfast	Frühstück
lunch	Mittagessen
dinner	Abendessen
eat	essen
drink	trinken

Can you recommend a ...?
Können Sie ... empfehlen?

bar/pub	eine Kneipe
cafe	ein Café
coffee bar	eine Espressobar
restaurant	ein Restaurant
local speciality	eine örtliche Spezialität

I'd like to reserve a table for ...
Ich möchte einen Tisch für ... reservieren.

(two) people	(zwei) Personen
(eight) o'clock	(acht) Uhr

I'm vegetarian.
Ich bin Vegetarier/Vegetarierin. m/f
Enjoy your meal.
Güten Appetit.
Cheers!
Prost!

Please bring the bill.
Bitte bringen Sie die Rechnung.

EMERGENCIES

It's an emergency!
Es ist ein Notfall!
Call the police!
Rufen Sie die Polizei!
Call a doctor/an ambulance!
Rufen Sie einen Artzt/Krankenwagen!
Could you please help me/us?
Könnten Sie mir/uns bitte helfen?
Where's the police station?
Wo ist das Polizeirevier?

HEALTH

Where's the nearest ...?
Wo ist der/die/das nächste ...?

(night) chemist	(Nacht) Apotheke
dentist	Zahnarzt
doctor	Arzt
hospital	Krankenhaus

I need a doctor.
Ich brauche einen Arzt.

Symptoms

I have (a) ...
Ich habe ...

diarrhoea	Durchfall
fever	Fieber
headache	Kopfschmerzen
pain	Schmerzen

GLOSSARY

Abfahrt – departure (trains)
Achterl – 125mL glass of wine
Ankunft – arrival (trains)
Apotheke, Apotheken (pl) – pharmacy
Ausgang – exit
Autobahn – motorway

Bahnhof – train station
Bankomat – ATM
Bauernmarkt, Bauernmärkte (pl) – farmers market
Besetzt – occupied, full (ie no vacancy)
Bezirk, Bezirke (pl) – (town or city) district
Beisl, Beisln (pl) – Viennese term for beer house
Biedermeier – 19th-century art movement in Germany and Austria; decorative style of furniture from this period
Briefsendung – letter; item sent by letter post
Briefmarken – stamps
Buschenshank – family-run wine taverns located in semirural areas on the city outskirts
Busch'n – green wreath or branch, hung over the door of wine taverns
BZÖ – Alliance for the Future of Austria (political party)

Christkindlmarkt – Christmas market

Dag – abbreviation for 10g
Damen – women
Denkmal – memorial

Einbahnstrasse – one-way street
Eingang, Eintritt – entry

Fahrplan – timetable
Fahrrad – bicycle
Feiertag – public holiday

Fiaker – horse and carriage
Flakturm, Flaktürme (pl) – flak tower
Flohmarkt – flea market
Flugpost – air mail
Föhn – hot, dry wind that sweeps down from the mountains, mainly in early spring and autumn
FPÖ – Freedom Party (political party)
FKK (Freikörperkultur) – free body culture, naturism

Gästehaus – guesthouse, perhaps with a restaurant
Gasthaus, Gasthäuser (pl) – inn or restaurant, without accommodation
Gasthof – inn or restaurant, usually with accommodation
Gelbe Seiten – Yellow Pages
Glühwein – mulled wine

Haltestelle – bus or tram stop
Hauptbahnhof – main train station
Hauptpost – main post office
Herren – men
Heuriger, Heurigen (pl) – wine tavern

Jugendherberge – youth hostel
Jugendstil – art nouveau

Kellner/Kellnerin – male/female waiter
Konsulat – consulate
Krankenhaus, Krankenhäuser (pl) – hospital
Krügerl – 500mL glass of beer
Kunst – art
Kurzparkzone – short-term parking zone

Lokal, Lokale (pl) – bar or pub

Maut – toll (or indicating a toll booth); also Viennese dialect for a tip (gratuity)
Melange – Viennese version of cappuccino
Menü – meal of the day; the menu (ie food list) is called the *Speisekarte*
Mehrwertsteuer – MWST, value-added tax
Münze – coins

ÖAMTC – national motoring organisation
ÖAV – Austrian Alpine Club
ÖBB – Austrian Federal Railway
ÖVP – Austrian People's Party (political party)

Parkschein – parking voucher
Pension, Pensionen (pl) – B&B guesthouse
Pfarrkirche – parish church
Polizei – police
Postamt – post office
Prolos – Viennese word for working class

Radverleih – bicycle hire
Rathaus – town hall
Ruhetag – 'rest day', on which a restaurant is closed

Saal, Säle (pl) – hall or large room
Sacher Torte – rich chocolate cake with layers of apricot jam
Sammlung – collection
Säule – column, pillar
Schiff – ship
Schloss – palace or stately home
Schrammelmusik – popular Viennese music for violins, guitar and accordion
Schwullesbische Szene – gay and lesbian scene
Selbstbedienung (SB) – self-service (restaurants, laundries etc)
SPÖ – Social Democrats (political party)
Sprachschulen – language schools
Stadtheurigen – basic wine taverns or multilevel cellars
Stammlocal – regular watering hole
Studentenheime – student residences
Szene – scene (ie where the action is)

Tabak/Tabakladen – tobacconist(s)
Tagesteller/Tagesmenü – the set meal or menu of the day in a restaurant
Telefon-Wertkarte – phonecard
Tierpark/Tiergarten – animal park/zoo
Tor – gate

Urlaub – holiday
U-Bahn – underground rail network

Viertel – 250mL glass (drinks); also a geographical district (quarter)
Vignitte – motorway tax
Vorstadt/Vorstädte (pl) – inner-city suburb
Vorort – suburb

Wandern – hiking
Wien – Vienna
Wiener Schmäh – the dark, self-deprecating Viennese sense of humour, with sarcasm and irony
Wiener Werkstätte – workshop established in 1903 by Secession artists
Wäscherei – laundry
Würstelstand – sausage stand

Zahnarzt, Zahnärte (pl) – dentist
Zimmer frei/Privat Zimmer – private rooms (accommodation)
Zeitung – newspaper

BEHIND THE SCENES

THIS BOOK

This 6th edition of *Vienna* was researched and written by Anthony Haywood and Caroline Sieg. Neal Bedford wrote the previous edition with assistance from Janine Eberle. This guidebook was commissioned in Lonely Planet's London office, laid out by Cambridge Publishing Management Ltd, UK, and produced by the following:

Commissioning Editor Paula Hardy

Coordinating Editors Karen Beaulah, Kirsten Rawlings

Coordinating Cartographer David Kemp

Coordinating Layout Designer Julie Crane

Managing Editors Bruce Evans, Laura Stansfeld

Managing Cartographers Corey Hutchison, Herman So

Managing Layout Designer Celia Wood

Assisting Editors Kim Hutchins, Scarlett O'Hara, Ceinwen Sinclair, Angela Tinson, Saralinda Turner, Kelly Walker

Assisting Cartographers Csanad Csutoros

Cover Pepi Bluck, lonelyplanetimages.com

Internal Image Research Aude Vauconsant, lonelyplanetimages.com

Colour Designer Julie Crane

Indexer Marie Lorimer

Project Manager Imogen Bannister

Language Content Laura Crawford

Thanks to Helen Christinis, Melanie Dankel, Michelle Glynn, Michala Green, Carol Jackson, Lisa Knights, Katie Lynch, Jo Potts, Averil Robertson

Cover photographs Yellow restaurant in Grinzing, David Ryan (top); Horse-drawn carriage in front of Charlemagne relief at Peterskirche, Witold Skrypczak (bottom)

Internal photographs

All images are copyright of the photographer unless otherwise indicated. Many of the images in this guide are available for licensing from Lonely Planet Images: www.lonelyplanetimages.com.

Thanks to Hundertwasser Archive, Vienna (2010) for permission to reproduce Friedensreich Hundertwasser's artwork.

THANKS

ANTHONY HAYWOOD

Researching and writing about Vienna is always an enjoyable experience. For the professional advice or assistance in one way or the other I'd like to thank Michaela Egger (and the three cats) in Penzing, Frau Nina Kallina at the Liechtenstein Museum for some fact corrections, Neal Bedford for his excellent previous edition and some good tips on this book, and Mark Honan for the early editions, Frau Edith Kneifl for agreeing to be interviewed and showing me Margareten, Frau Scholz-Strasser and Herr Nömaier at the Sigmund Freud Museum, Andreas Gugumuck from Wiener Schnecke for the interview, Robert Paget and

THE LONELY PLANET STORY

Fresh from an epic journey across Europe, Asia and Australia in 1972, Tony and Maureen Wheeler sat at their kitchen table stapling together notes. The first Lonely Planet guidebook, *Across Asia on the Cheap*, was born.

Travellers snapped up the guides. Inspired by their success, the Wheelers began publishing books to Southeast Asia, India and beyond. Demand was prodigious, and the Wheelers expanded the business rapidly to keep up. Over the years, Lonely Planet extended its coverage to every country and into the virtual world via lonelyplanet.com and the Thorn Tree message board.

As Lonely Planet became a globally loved brand, Tony and Maureen received several offers for the company. But it wasn't until 2007 that they found a partner whom they trusted to remain true to the company's principles of travelling widely, treading lightly and giving sustainably. In October of that year, BBC Worldwide acquired a 75% share in the company, pledging to uphold Lonely Planet's commitment to independent travel, trustworthy advice and editorial independence.

Today, Lonely Planet has offices in Melbourne, London and Oakland, with over 500 staff members and 300 authors. Tony and Maureen are still actively involved with Lonely Planet. They're travelling more often than ever, and they're devoting their spare time to charitable projects. And the company is still driven by the philosophy of *Across Asia on the Cheap*: 'All you've got to do is decide to go and the hardest part is over. So go!'

family in Diendorf for tips and background information, and the folks at the various tourist offices (especially Marta Zeplaki in Krems) who provided valuable assistance throughout. At Lonely Planet I'd like to thank my fellow author Caroline Sieg; commissioning editor Paula Hardy; Craig Kilburn and Imogen Bannister; Herman So and Owen Eszeki in cartography; Sally Schafer; and Laura Stansfeld in-house in Melbourne. Thanks also go to Sylvia for holding the fort and Freddie for the fine, feline company during write-up.

CAROLINE SIEG

Thanks to my parents for instilling in me a lifelong zest for travel. Thanks mucho to Paula Hardy for giving me this gig and to Anthony Haywood for always maintaining a sense of humour. Thanks to Rafed & Company for a few truly excellent nights on the town and showing me how proper Viennese party it up, and to Neal Bedford for the valuable insights and recommendations. Last, this one's dedicated to you, Jules – the biggest Vienna fan I know and one of the best friends I could ever wish for.

OUR READERS

Many thanks to the travellers who used the last edition and wrote to us with helpful hints, useful advice and interesting anecdotes:

Yoram Adriaanse, Graham Anderson, Sara Atwater, Benjamin Blaise, Ryan Bushek, Jessica Carino, Marie Cochrane, Derek Cross, Nick Dorra, Michael Fischer, Asmaa Ghonedale, Adam Goss, Dominique Goubau, Judy Gourley, Anna-Clara Holmberg, Lukas Kaelin, Halley Ketchum, Vasilis Kyriazopoulos, Theresa Lingg, Uwe Meggers, Brian Morgan, Gunnar Narvehed, Brankica Opsenica, Shyam Parameswaran, Mike Piechura, Michael Raffaele, Loredana Rossi, Sally Rowell, Liz Smeeton, Peter Strowi, Engin Tanis, Ines Wagner, Dieter Zakel

SEND US YOUR FEEDBACK

We love to hear from travellers – your comments keep us on our toes and help make our books better. Our well-travelled team reads every word on what you loved or loathed about this book. Although we cannot reply individually to postal submissions, we always guarantee that your feedback goes straight to the appropriate authors, in time for the next edition. Each person who sends us information is thanked in the next edition and the most useful submissions are rewarded with a free book.

To send us your updates – and find out about Lonely Planet events, newsletters and travel news – visit our award-winning website: lonelyplanet.com/contact.

Note: We may edit, reproduce and incorporate your comments in Lonely Planet products such as guidebooks, websites and digital products, so let us know if you don't want your comments reproduced or your name acknowledged. For a copy of our privacy policy visit lonelyplanet.com/privacy.

ACKNOWLEDGMENTS

Thanks to Hundertwasser Archive, Vienna (2010) for permission to reproduce Friedensreich Hundertwasser's artwork.

Notes

Notes

Notes

Notes

Notes

Notes

INDEX

See also separate indexes for:
Arts p255
Drinking p255
Eating p256
Nightlife p256
Shopping p256
Sights p257
Sleeping p258
Top Picks p258
GreenDex p259

000 map pages
000 photographs

WINE TAVERNS

EATING
ASIAN

AUSTRIAN

000 map pages
000 photographs

BEISL

EAST EUROPEAN

FAST FOOD

FISH

FRENCH

INTERNATIONAL

ITALIAN

MARKETS

MIDDLE EASTERN

SOUPS & SANDWICHES

SOUTH ASIAN

SPANISH

STEAKHOUSES

VEGETARIAN

NIGHTLIFE
CLUBS

LIVE MUSIC

SHOPPING
BOOKS

CLOTHING

CONFECTIONERY

FASHION & ACCESSORIES

FOOD

HOMEWARES

JEWELLERY

MUSIC

PHOTOGRAPHY

WINE

SIGHTS

AMUSEMENT PARKS

ANIMAL ATTRACTIONS

ART GALLERIES

BUILDINGS & STRUCTURES

CEMETERIES & VAULTS

CHILDREN'S ATTRACTIONS

CHURCHES & CATHEDRALS

JEWISH HERITAGE

MONASTERIES

MONUMENTS & MEMORIALS

MUSEUMS

000 map pages
000 photographs

GREENDEX

GOING GREEN

The following sights, attractions, accommodation, eating places and transport options have been selected by the authors because they demonstrate a commitment to sustainability. Restaurants and cafes get the nod because of their use of seasonal, organic and locally sourced produce or they are formally accredited with an environmental badge *(Umweltzeichen)* for best environmental practices. We've also highlighted farmers markets and local producers in each neighbourhood in the Eating chapter. In addition, we've covered accommodation that we deem to be environmentally friendly, for example, either because they have the environmental seal or because they are committed to recycling or energy conservation. For more tips about travelling sustainably in Vienna, turn to p19. Also see the various parks and green spaces in the Neighbourhoods chapter (p47). If you would like to comment on our selection or think we've omitted someone who should be listed here, email us at www.lonelyplanet.com/contact. For more information about sustainable tourism and Lonely Planet see www.lonelyplanet.com/responsibletravel.

ACCOMMODATION

ATTRACTIONS

FOOD

SHOPPING

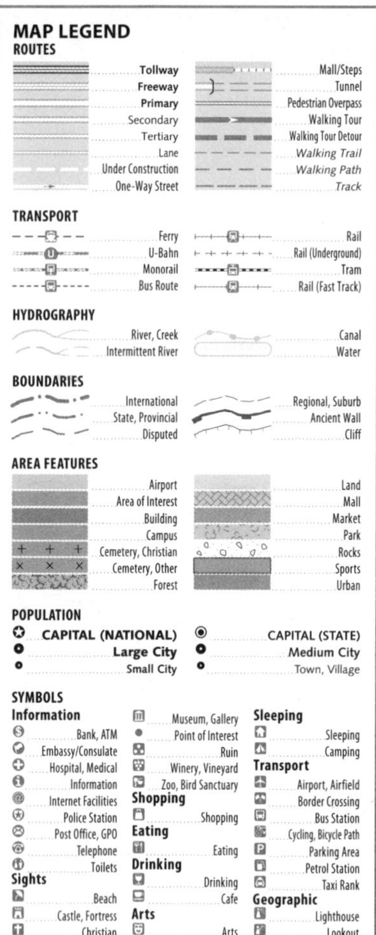

Published by Lonely Planet Publications Pty Ltd
ABN 36 005 607 983

Australia (Head Office)
Locked Bag 1, Footscray, Victoria 3011,
☎03 8379 8000, fax 03 8379 8111,
talk2us@lonelyplanet.com.au

USA 150 Linden St, Oakland, CA 94607,
☎510 250 6400, toll free 800 275 8555,
fax 510 893 8572, info@lonelyplanet.com

UK 2nd fl, 186 City Rd, London, EC1V 2NT,
☎020 7106 2100, fax 020 7106 2101,
go@lonelyplanet.co.uk

Printed by Colorcraft Ltd
Printed in China